THE BARRYMORES

by Hollis Alpert

THE
BARRYMORES

by Hollis Alpert

New York 1964 THE DIAL PRESS

For Herb and Nel Jaffe

"We who play, who entertain for a few years, what can we leave that will last."
—Ethel Barrymore

table of contents

Table of Contents

Part Five

PROLOGUE

GUSTS OF WIND rattled windows and signs of the Broadway theater district the evening of March 6, 1920, and buffeted the striped awning stretched in front of the Plymouth Theatre on West Forty-fifth Street. The awning had been put up for the benefit of celebrities arriving to attend the opening of the Arthur Hopkins production of *Richard III,* in which John Barrymore, youngest of three famous Barrymores, was making his debut as a Shakespearian actor. Among the opening-night guests was Michael Strange, known as "the society poetess" and as one of America's most beautiful women. Rumors were current that she was the beloved of John Barrymore, and that she had had much to do with encouraging the handsome and popular actor to play the evil, hunchbacked prince. The crowd of onlookers gathered around the theater entrance craned to view her as she stepped out of a limousine; her shining black coiffure, high satin pumps, the rich sables around her shoulders, drew excited murmurs. With seeming modesty she did not take a seat down front in the orchestra, but sat in the balcony from where she watched the minutest movement of her lover, the star. When the crooked-back king came forward to acknowledge the applause and cheers, she settled back into her furs and smiled as though she was the one who had triumphed.

A triumph for John Barrymore it was. Critics generally agreed that the American theater had reached one of its high points that evening and that no finer production of *Richard III* had ever been given in the country. But John was not the only Barrymore to dominate a stage on March 6. "The Barrymore family," remarked the *New York Times*, "is singularly well represented this week on the American stage." Singular, indeed, this family. Two brothers and a sister, all born during a period of four years, had become great stars of the stage and at this midpoint of their careers typified the highest standards of acting in America. Ethel Barrymore, assured and handsome at the age of forty, was established at the Empire in her long-running smash hit, *Déclassée*. Lionel Barrymore, her elder by a year and a half, starred in *The Letter of the Law* at the Criterion. The hopes of many devotees of American theatrical culture were bound up with the Barrymores, for it was thought their combination of popularity and talent might provide the key to the establishment of an American repertory theater which would present the best of modern and classic plays. John Barrymore's *Richard III* was regarded as an important step in that direction.

It was at just about this time that newspaper columnists and drama critics began referring to the Barrymores as "the royal family of the theater." How the appellation came about—perhaps a press agent dreamed it up—is not known, but it caught on, and they were referred to as the royal family of the theater for the rest of their lives. So familiar was this title, and so completely were they identified with it, that when Edna Ferber and George S. Kaufman wrote a play called *The Royal Family* and turned it into a Broadway hit, no one was in doubt that the temperamental and flamboyant principals who were called the Cavendishes were only thinly disguised Barrymores.

Let it be said at once that they were not of royal blood. The only hint of genuine nobility in their family tree came from a claim made by John Barrymore that his father, Maurice, was descended on the maternal side from "a seventh Earl of Barrymore." The more realistic Ethel never claimed any such thing, nor did Lionel. They knew well enough that their father was born to an upper-middle-class English family as Herbert Blythe, that he had invented Barrymore as a stage name (he might have remembered that a Barrymore once acted on the stage in England, but the fellow was no relation to the Blythes), and that he was not even of a mind to pass it on to his offspring, for each originally had the surname of Blythe.

But the names of all three *looked* royal enough when seen in glittering lights on the marquees of theaters, and theater chroniclers and their fellow players were well aware of the dynastic nature of their descendancy. If the name of Barrymore went back only as far as 1873 in stage history, the name of Drew (which had belonged to their actress mother) went back farther, and before that there were Lanes and Kinlocks, who were the acting ancestors of the Barrymores on the maternal side.

To the public of that time the Barrymores represented all that was glamorous and traditional in the theater. They were worthy of notice for their performances alone, but each (and Ethel and John especially) seemed to have the facility for attracting attention to their private lives, in which magazines and newspapers always found delectable copy. If Lionel was the quietest of the three, in the sense that he succeeded most in keeping to himself the details of his personal life, he could on the stage rouse an audience to the peak of enthusiasm, and by 1920 was regarded as the most important American character actor of the period. Ethel, by this time, was already impatient at being continually referred to as our "first lady of the theater." As for John, he was being called "the greatest of our younger actors," and there were thought to be no limits to the heights to which he someday might vault.

The careers of Ethel and Lionel began in the Mauve Decade, when they were hardly more than adolescents, for reasons of economic necessity. They simply followed the family profession. Ethel buckled down to her responsibilities and achieved her stardom, but Lionel bucked and kicked against the traces, and even after he had made a name for himself was seldom eager to follow his family's traditional way of life. He tried painting, he tried composing, he went off into vaudeville, he was one of the first stage actors to work in that inelegant medium, the movies, and eventually it took considerable persuasion to bring him back to the stage.

John, who on the night of March 6, 1920, made one of his most brilliant and profound impressions on the stage, still spoke wistfully of the career of drawing and illustrating he had begun and abandoned. To have to take to the stage had been something of a defeat for him and represented a relatively easy way of making a living. He was first thought to have possibilities as a comedian, that is, if he would ever learn to take the work seriously. It was with great trepidation that he turned to the portrayal of tragic roles. Broadway by this time knew him as the electrifying star of *The Jest* and *Redemption,* but the ordinary people of the hinterlands were more familiar with him as a farce comedian of the movies. He was simultaneously able to shatter the emotions of those who saw him on the stage in Galsworthy's *Justice* and to delight the movie public with his acrobatic pratfalls. His comic gift, some said, was second only to Chaplin's.

In his later life John Barrymore traded fame for notoriety. But for one glorious decade he was America's pre-eminent actor, setting standards of performance (particularly in *Hamlet*) that some long-memoried individuals say have never been equaled. His chiseled profile, according to Heywood Broun, "slid into a scene like an exquisite paper knife." When he went to Hollywood he became one of the screen's great lovers (although he termed himself in these roles "a silly, scented jackass"), and if he did not inflame females to quite the degree that Valentino did it may have been because he played many of his love scenes with a degree of mockery. In real life he managed to outshine Valentino as a lover.

All three Barrymores maintained their ascendancy on the stage for a full five years after that night of March 6, 1920, and then, at almost the same moment, John and Lionel decamped to Hollywood, where both became important stars. The doughty Ethel kept to the stage for another twenty years, and when she finally went to Hollywood it was more for the climate than for professional reasons. Yet Hollywood took her to its bosom enough to award her an Oscar for acting. In her long life there was no other American actress so deservedly revered.

John's Hollywood career began in a blaze of glory (partly of the synthetic kind ignited by studio publicists), was a long and sometimes rich one, but eventually turned into his playing roles that were like parodies of his former greatness. There was good and dramatic reason for his strange twilight, as we shall see. Lionel, on the other hand, did journeyman film acting for many years, and then developed into one of Hollywood's most famous stars. So familiar was his drawling voice that an imitation of it turned up every other week on the Major Bowes Amateur Hour. This did not prevent him from winning an Academy Award. Then, crippled by accidents and a rheumatic knee, he gave a rare demonstration of courage as he continued his career in a wheelchair.

The Barrymores among them earned during their careers, at a conservative estimate, well in excess of ten million dollars. Ethel and John, when they were at their peaks, could command the highest of stage salaries. For a time John was one of the best-paid stars of the movies. Yet none of this money was left at the time of their deaths, and the effects of John and Lionel had to be sold at auction to satisfy their posthumous obligations. They lived well, the Barrymores, and sometimes lavishly, and this accounts for their failure to hold on to their earnings. But they also took a rather cavalier attitude toward taxes for a while, and for this habit all three paid dearly. Economic necessity brought them to the stage, and the same necessity kept them working; but if each in the moment of death had been granted a day of further activity you may be sure it would have been spent acting. They may not have wanted to go on the stage, but once there they became and remained the most seasoned of professionals.

"We who play, who entertain for a few years," Ethel Barrymore once cried plaintively, "what can we leave that will last?" She attempted to leave in her *Memories* some notion of what she had done, what it had all been like. Lionel, too, recorded his life and times in his autobiography, *We Barrymores*, written with the aid of that fine journalist, the late Cameron Shipp. And Gene Fowler helped give some immortality to John with his deservedly popular and colorful biography, *Good Night, Sweet Prince*. But their story, oddly, has never been told as a unity, and, in fact, their lives diverged so greatly at times that when they met there was an odd formality between them, especially when, for the only time in their careers, they came together, all three, to act in a film called *Rasputin and the Empress*.

This chronicle of the Barrymore dynasty attempts to fill in the gaps, to pierce behind the curtain of their habitual reserve, and to provide a record of who the Barrymores were and what they did. If their voices on our stages have long died away, if some of the theaters in which they performed have collapsed under the wrecker's ball, their importance in our stage history has never dimmed. We see them now and again on television, in old and often-replayed movies, such as *Twentieth Century, Down to the Sea in Ships, None but the Lonely Heart,* and luckily some demonstration of their acting art has in this way been preserved. But the Barrymores amounted to more, much, much more, than anything that can be seen on television.

In searching out the nature of their lives and careers help was given the author by many people who contributed their knowledge and advice to the writing of this book. George Freedley, curator of the Theatre Collection of the New York Public Library, helped start things off by insisting that such a book ought to be done, then made available enormous amounts of research material, including an invaluable source, the Robinson Locke Collection of Dramatic Scrapbooks. The facilities of the Frederick Lewis Allen Room of the New York Public Library were provided the author by Gilbert A. Cam, Associate Librarian. In Hollywood, Betty Franklin, Librarian for the Academy of Motion Picture Arts and Sciences, was equally helpful.

Of immense help to the author was Spencer Berger, of Hamden, Connecticut, who not only allowed but insisted on full use of his fascinating collection of Barrymore documents, films, and memorabilia. Unstintingly generous with their time and help were Ethel Colt Miglietta, George Cukor, Maynard Smith, Gene Fowler, Jr., and Gerold Frank, experts all on the Barrymores. May Davenport Seymour and her daughter, Anne Seymour, provided much family background hitherto unrecorded, as did the grandson of John Drew, John Drew Devereaux. Dolores Costello Barrymore and Mrs. Jacques Gordon helped light the way with their vivid memories. Thanks are due Charles Brackett, Cary Grant, Elia Kazan, and Cornelia Otis Skinner for the many anecdotes they provided. The author wishes to thank, too, the following for their assistance: Richard Maney,

Fredric March, Otto Preminger, Stanley Kauffman, Arthur Knight, Harold Clurman, Mrs. Julia Warwick, Dr. Harold Hyman, Stan Musgrove, Elaine Barrymore, Bosley Crowther, James Silke and Rory Guy of *Cinema* magazine, Day Tuttle, Jean Muir, James Silberman, Henry Robbins, Carole Lewis, Max Wilk, Johnson Briscoe, Robert Downing and the Players, Sam Pearce, Acting Curator of the theater and music collection, Museum of the City of New York, and again Mrs. May Davenport Seymour, for allowing the author to use the museum's Theatre Collection, one rich in Barrymore material. To my wife, Joan Alpert, a special posy for her help and patience.

Sources consulted in addition to the books mentioned earlier include many of the thousands of newspaper magazines and articles written about the Barrymores over a period of several decades, and the following volumes:

Some Players, by Amy Leslie, Herbert Stone & Co., 1899

Autobiographical Sketch of Mrs. John Drew, Scribner's, 1899

My Years on the Stage, by John Drew, Dutton, 1922

The Print of My Remembrance, by Augustus Thomas, Scribner's, 1922

Famous Actor-Families in America, by Montrose J. Moses, Crowell, 1906

Charles Frohman, by Isaac F. Marcosson and Daniel Frohman, Harper, 1916

The Man Who Lived Twice, by Eric Wollencott Barnes, Scribner's, 1956

Who Tells Me True, by Michael Strange, Scribner's, 1940

John Barrymore, the Legend and the Man, by Alma Power-Waters, Messner, 1941

Roses and Buckshot, by James Montgomery Flagg, Putnam, 1946

Too Much, Too Soon, by Diana Barrymore and Gerold Frank, Holt, 1957

The Young Man from Denver, by Will Fowler, Doubleday, 1962

All My Sins Remembered, by Elaine Barrymore and Sandford Doty, Appleton, 1964

Curtain Time, by Lloyd Morris, Random House, 1953

The Passionate Playgoer, edited by George Oppenheimer, Viking, 1958

The Lion's Share, by Bosley Crowther, Dutton, 1957

Confessions of an Actor, by John Barrymore, Bobbs-Merrill, 1926

Fanfare, by Richard Maney, Harper, 1957

Tallulah, by Tallulah Bankhead, Harper, 1952

Letters to a Lonely Boy, by Arthur Hopkins, Doubleday, 1937

Reference Point, by Arthur Hopkins, Samuel French, 1948

Minutes of the Last Meeting, Gene Fowler, Viking, 1954

A Child of the Century, Ben Hecht, Simon and Schuster, 1954

Matinee Tomorrow, Ward Morehouse Whittlesey House, 1949

The Great White Way, Allen Churchill, Dutton, 1962

A Pictorial History of the American Theatre, Daniel Blum, Chilton & Co., 1960

Revolt of the Actors, Alfred Harding, William Morrow & Co., 1929

Footlights and Spotlights, Otis Skinner, Bobbs-Merrill, 1924

My Story, Mary Astor, Doubleday, 1959.

part **ONE**

THE AWESOME
MRS. DREW

chapter 1

WHEN ETHEL, Lionel, and John Barrymore were small children in the 1880s they were sometimes allowed to sit in a special box at the Arch Street Theatre in Philadelphia and watch plays performed by such renowned actors as Edwin Booth, Fanny Davenport, and Helena Modjeska. The key to the box was held by their grandmother, Mrs. John Drew, who, as manageress of the Arch Street, was the first woman in America to run an important theater. A small woman with oddly bulging large blue eyes, an imposing bosom, and a queenly carriage, Mrs. Drew was an illustrious actress in her own right, and during the days before "the combination house" came into fashion she was a leading light in her own stock company, known for its brilliant performances. By the time the little Barrymores came on the living scene Mrs. Drew had been forced to give way to changing times in the theater. She booked into the Arch Street stars such as Rose Eytinge and John McCullough, who usually traveled with their own road companies. Famous people of the theater were entertained in her Philadelphia house and the young Barrymores listened in tongue-tied silence to their talk—talk of other days, of changing times in the theater. Growing up in so heavy a theatrical atmosphere, as well as being the children themselves of well-known acting parents, it might be assumed that the Barrymores took naturally to their stage careers.

Not at all. None of them while growing up gave serious thought

3

to the possibility that they might become actors. Ethel's childhood and adolescent yearnings were directed toward becoming a concert pianist, although she sometimes thought of herself as a novelist, too. Lionel harbored a wish to become a great painter, and John doodled and drew through most of his youth, hoping someday to become an illustrator. Destiny, largely in the form and shape of Mrs. Drew, determined otherwise. Her bosomy shadow was cast over them the moment they were born, and while it was not in her mind to turn her grandchildren into actors, circumstances were such that eventually this became necessary. Before she died at the age of seventy-seven she had put Lionel and Ethel on the stage, and John was not long in following his brother and sister.

The children called her "Mum Mum," a name bestowed on her by Lionel as soon as he was able to gurgle. The lady's fierce visage could strike terror into the heart of an inept actor, but to the children she represented sternness tempered by kindness, and she gave them the motherly care and protection denied them by the frequent absences of their parents who toured much of the time in acting companies. The Barrymores (née Blythe) were born in one or another of Mrs. Drew's Philadelphia houses (she changed them according to the size of the flock she took it upon herself to tend); they were christened in the Episcopalian religion of Mrs. Drew (but were later rechristened in the adopted Catholic faith of their mother); they were watched over by nurses provided by Mrs. Drew; the home to which they always felt most attached was the home of Mrs. Drew.

Mum Mum in her childhood years had been an infant prodigy of the stage. She was born Louisa Lane in 1820 at Lambeth Parish, London, England, to Eliza Trentner and William Haycraft Lane, both members of acting families. Efforts made to trace back the Lane lineage in English stage history reveal that the Lanes were known in 1752 as a family of strolling players. No acting family still extant can claim that much of a tradition. Louisa Lane made her first appearance on the stage when she was only a year old, the occasion calling for a bawling baby. Eliza and William had assumed that any normal infant would at once break into screams of fear at

4

the sight of the crowded pit and the flaring lights, but Louisa was so delighted by what she saw that she cooed happily and ruined the scene. Four years later she was brought back to the stage by her mother as a professional, her father having meanwhile died. At age seven she was taken to America by her widowed mother, who made the crossing with an English stock company. Eliza was a pretty little woman who could sing ballads as well as act, and she soon caught the eye of a Philadelphia stage manager, John Kinlock. So did Louisa. After marrying Eliza, Kinlock decided to turn Louisa into a profitable family asset.

There was a rage in America at that time for "infant prodigies" of the stage, and several youngsters with the ability to mimic adult roles had brought small fortunes to their sponsors. One little girl, Clara Fisher, had made a truly phenomenal success, and attracted large crowds wherever she performed. "Father determined," Louisa recalled later, "that I should be a second Clara."

Kinlock took her first to Baltimore, where she appeared in *William Tell* as Albert, the boy who bravely allowed an apple to be shot from his head. Her co-star was the arrogant Edwin Forrest, acknowledged as the greatest actor of the period. Louisa's performance pleased Forrest so much that he presented her with an engraved medal.

It may be hard to imagine, but she also played the elderly Dr. Pangloss in a dramatized version of *Candide*.

For further proof of her extraordinary versatility, there is preserved the following extract from a Philadelphia newspaper, dated January 5, 1829.

CHESTNUT STREET THEATRE—Miss Lane. This astonishing little creature appeared at the Chestnut Street Theatre last evening. She is not more than ten years of age, and evinces a talent for and knowledge of the stage beyond what we find in many experienced performers of merit. *Twelve Precisely* is well adapted to the display of the versatility of her powers; and in *The Irish Girl* she may, with truth, be pronounced inimitably comic. Her brogue and manner are excellent. *The Young Soldier* was also admirably assumed; his coxcombial airs were natural, evinced astonishing observation in a child so young, and literally convulsed the house with laughter. Those who have a taste for the wonderful should not miss the present opportunity of gratifying it.

A rave review, certainly. But in spite of such encouragement the small girl occasionally balked and had to be promised rewards of candy to insure that she would do a full evening's work. Her formal education was neglected, amounting to little more than a bit of tutoring now and then. Her childhood was spent either rehearsing or performing on the stage—and the stage in those days meant continual and rigorous touring. On one of these tours, to the West Indies, her stepfather, Mr. Kinlock, was carried away by yellow fever. He was buried in Kingston, Jamaica, when Louisa was twelve, and on returning home her mother found an engagement for both of them in Boston, where their combined salaries amounted to sixteen dollars a week.

This amount was sufficient to provide them with comforts and well-being. Louisa remembered later that in Mrs. Lenthe's boarding-house in Bowdoin Square "there was a large closet in which we kept a barrel of ale and all our dresses, and passed a very happy season in the enjoyment of that large salary."

The first of Louisa's three marriages was at the age of sixteen to Henry Blaine Hunt, twenty-four years her senior. He was "a very good singer, a nice actor, and a very handsome man of forty." The marriage lasted ten years, during which they toured and traveled, sometimes together, sometimes separately. At eighteen Louisa was given the title of "leading lady" for one of the companies that employed her. A year later the Walnut Street Theatre in Philadelphia paid her the highest salary yet paid to an actress—twenty dollars a week. She appeared there in a series of roles, then toured as Lady Macbeth to Edwin Forrest's Macbeth.

In Albany, New York, after her divorce from Hunt, she married an Irish comedian and singer by the name of George Mossop. Mossop was a notorious drinker who was famous for a stutter which disappeared as soon as he came out on a stage.

One evening in Buffalo Mossop consumed several onions along with his usual ration of spirits. Between scenes Louisa overheard an actor saying, "Poor Mrs. Mossop. He's drunk again."

"Yes," Louisa broke in, "and tonight with *onions!*"

The marriage lasted only a few months. Mossop suddenly took ill and died, and Louisa left him, with few regrets, in an Albany graveyard. John Drew, her third husband, first fell in love with Louisa's half sister, Georgia, a frail girl twelve years her junior. John had an audience with Louisa during which he told her that he loved Georgia and wanted to marry the teen-age girl. "But my more forceful grandmother," Ethel related, "said 'nonsense,' and married him herself."

Daguerreotypes of that period reveal Louisa as possessing a bold nose and eyes of the type that present-day members of the family still term "the Drew pop-eyes." She was not a beauty. John Drew's photographs show him to have been a handsome man, on the short side, with a jovial expression. He had a quick sense of humor and was noted for his ability to play Irish characters. His family were Northern Irish of English descent, and his father, after a spell in Dublin, settled in Buffalo, New York, where he constructed pianos.

Between 1852 and 1856 Louisa and John had three children. The first, Louisa, was delicate, too frail to do much acting. John came next, and Georgiana (but always called Georgie) was the youngest, and became the mother, eventually, of the three Barrymores. The elder John Drew took on the management of the Arch Street Theatre for a short period, but then went traveling, while his wife managed the theater.

On a lengthy tour John Drew took to Australia, his original love, Georgia, went with him, and when they returned they had a baby girl with them. It seems that the child was promptly adopted by Mrs. Drew and given the name Adine Stevens. She lived long enough to be remembered as their Aunt Tibby by the Barrymore children. Mrs. Drew had a surprise of her own for her husband. While he was away she had adopted a little boy whose name, she said, was Sidney White. She raised him as her own, and he became Sidney Drew; the Barrymore children called him Uncle Googan. "I am proud to claim kin to him," Lionel stated, "although Louisa Lane Drew states that she had adopted Sidney. Mrs. Drew, of course, may say what she wishes in the matter, but Uncle Googan certainly *looked* like her."

After the Australian tour, the grandfather of the Barrymores took time out to help the sagging Arch Street Theatre, and, playing his public's favorite roles for one hundred nights, brought the theater out of its doldrums. But he fell ill suddenly, and died on May 21, 1862, at the age of thirty-five. Rumor had it that overconsumption of spirits had something to do with it.

"Had he lived to be forty-five he would have been a great actor," Mrs. Drew—who thereafter kept his name—wrote of her late husband. "But too early a success was his ruin. Why should he study when he was assured on all sides (except my own) that he was as near perfection as it was possible for a man to be?"

Mrs. Drew concentrated on running the Arch Street Theatre prudently, wisely, and strictly. She drilled the resident company herself, brought in stars to head the casts, and became a member of the solid citizenry of Philadelphia. She was at first against her children carrying on the acting traditions of the family, and would have vastly preferred that they avoid the hardships and uncertainties of the stage life. But Georgie, who as a child was allowed backstage on Friday nights, became irrevocably stage-struck. She begged her mother for a chance to act, and in 1872, when she was fifteen, was allowed to take part in *The Ladies' Battle,* in which her own mother appeared as her rival in love. Her talent was unmistakable, and she was permitted to give up her education and to join the resident company of the Arch Street Theatre.

Mrs. Drew possessed a chill austerity of manner with which she imbued wholesome respect in her actors. She kept a watchful eye on her daughter, but showed no partiality toward her. "I can distinctly remember the icy politeness of her tone," Georgie once said, "as she would turn to me at rehearsal, when I was gossiping away in a corner, instead of attending to my cue, and remark: 'Now, Miss Drew, if you are quite ready, we will resume.'"

Georgie was a tall, slender girl with fair hair and large blue eyes. Her temperament was bright and humorous, her wit was keen, and she possessed an immaculate sense of comic timing. She was to become what was known as "the leading lady to the feminine star"—this meant important secondary roles—and was to be well remembered by such as Otis Skinner, who recalled her as "the most accomplished comedienne of her time. On her the family gift was bestowed and shone with unabated brilliance."

Georgie's older brother, John, followed her into the company a year later. He had embarked upon the business life his mother foresaw for him by becoming a clock salesman at Wanamaker's Department Store, but clock-selling not proving stimulating enough, he decided he preferred acting. Mrs. Drew grudgingly allowed him a small role in W. Blanchard Jerrold's comedy, *Cool as a Cucumber.*

He was so entirely cool and self-possessed on his first appearance that his mother felt it necessary to interpolate a line for his benefit. "What a dreadful young man," she boomed out as she waved a fan. "I wonder if he will ever amount to anything? He has too much confidence." The knowledgeable Philadelphia audience showed its appreciation with loud laughter.

John Drew was to amount to a great deal as an actor, but not until he had participated in Georgie's mischievousness. He once packed face powder into the speaking tube that ran from the prompter's box to the orchestra leader. Just as the orchestra was about to begin the overture, John lured the prompter away, gave the signal to the orchestra leader, and blew through the tube. The orchestra men howled when they saw their leader suddenly turn white as a ghost. Mrs. Drew was forced to put on her shawl and take corrective action. John received a dressing-down that he never forgot. Mrs. Drew could, on occasion, be a terror.

And yet she could show uncommon understanding. John McCullough, a handsome, powerful actor who had supported Forrest, once went through a performance at the Arch Street in which he showed unmistakable signs of over-imbibing. Mrs. Drew summoned him to her presence and berated him; after the lecture she searched his dressing room and found the offending bottles, a distinctly inferior brand of rye. She confiscated these, but to McCullough's surprise replaced them with choicer liquors. "If you're to get drunk," she told him, "you might as well do it in style."

Mrs. Drew insisted on strict chaperonage while her daughters were being courted. Georgie was never allowed to see a man alone. Anyone who called on her had to bear up under the chill presence of Mrs. Drew at the other end of the parlor. "Mother snowed on us," was the way Georgie put it. Georgie's sister, Louisa, was the first to marry. Mrs. Drew had hired a young actor, Charles Mendum, who was also the scion of a Boston banking family, to manage the Arch Street in her behalf, but Mendum failed to live up to her exacting standards and was soon fired. He retaliated by asking Louisa to marry him, and took her off to Boston, where his father took the couple under his supervisory eye. They had two children, Edmund and Georgiana Drew Mendum. The latter turned to acting and became Ethel Barrymore's constant companion after she gained fame.

Sidney Drew was not chaperoned by his mother, who adopted a different policy toward this "adopted" son. Sidney showed aptitudes for billiards, comic acting, and falling in love. Each time he fell in love, which was frequent, he announced to his mother that he was engaged. Mrs. Drew would then hold a party for his beloved, a party to which she invited her acquaintances among the more august Philadelphia society. Sidney's fiancées were usually chosen from among less refined groups, and they invariably failed when put to the social test. Eventually Sidney married a daughter of Kitty and McKee Rankin, a famous acting family, and Mrs. Drew gave the union her blessing.

John Drew caused his mother less alarm by showing little desire for marriage during his first years on the stage. And his acting improved enough to win her cautious approval. Augustin Daly, the prominent theatrical manager in New York who ran Daly's Fifth Avenue Theater (one of the best of its day) scouted the Arch Street, noticed young John Drew, and with appropriate protocol requested permission from Mrs. Drew for his services. With his mother's consent, John went to New York to play relatively unimportant parts in Daly's repertory. More importantly, he met there the man who was to become the father of the Barrymores.

Mrs. Drew ran her theater as strictly and traditionally as she did her home. She would drive in a glass-windowed brougham to her office at the Arch Street. There she would go over the books, sign necessary bills and documents, and inspect the house front and back to see that it was run according to her impeccable standards. She was a staunch member of St. Stephen's Episcopal Church, maintained her own pew, and insisted that Georgie teach Sunday school. Before her mother, Eliza, became infirm and bedridden, the two ladies would inhabit their pew together on Sundays, all starched and ruffled and wearing black bonnets. So much a matriarch was she that it was never questioned that it should be her house in which the Barrymore-Blythes should be born. As long as she was able, she maintained the upkeep of the house, provided shelter for all the members of her family, hired and paid servants—usually three or four in number.

At Daly's Fifth Avenue in 1874 John Drew met a young English actor who called himself Maurice Barrymore. Both supported Edwin Booth's *Hamlet*, John Drew as Rosencrantz and Barrymore as Laertes. Barrymore escaped comment and criticism, but of John a critic wrote: "The gentleman who played Rosencrantz evidently had an engagement with a friend after the performance, so hurried was his speech and so evident his desire to get through with his part."

At the finish of the Booth engagement John suggested to Maurice that they fill an empty weekend by visiting his home in Philadelphia. Maurice accepted the invitation, and there on North Ninth Street he was introduced to Mrs. Drew, and also to the delightful young Georgie. For so strict a household it was amazing how passion could manifest itself. Maurice was immediately attracted by Georgie, and she by him. Mrs. Drew sniffed. This young Englishman was obviously an amateur at acting, his manners a pose. But the more her gaze upon Maurice Barrymore hardened, the more tender became Georgie's. Mrs. Drew snowed upon them, but it was to no avail.

THE MAN WHO
KNEW HOW
TO SWAGGER

chapter II

IT WAS SAID of the English father of Ethel, Lionel, and John Barrymore that his arrival in America came at a time when the native actors simply did not know how to swagger properly on the stage, especially if called upon to play gentlemen. These actors, a contemporary of Maurice Barrymore wrote, often "suggested the counter-jumper suddenly confronted with the exactions of evening dress." On his very first jaunt up Broadway Maurice somehow knew enough to head unerringly for that gathering place of sophisticated gentlemen, the Hoffman House bar. He wore a monocle and a top hat, and managed to give the appearance of "a man who had lived."

When he arrived in this country in 1874 he was slightly more than twenty-seven years old, and was not yet certain about whether or not to devote his energies to the pursuit of an acting career, and this hesitancy was apparent in the name he used: Maurice Blythe Barrymore. He had been born Herbert Blythe; his upper-middle-class family included in their lineage important civil servants and clergymen. His father had been a surveyor for the East India Company, and remaining in India, had become Judge Blythe of Madras. Herbert's birth and the Indian Mutiny of 1847 took place almost simultaneously, and his delivery, which took place of necessity in Fort Agra, was accompanied by the rattle of gunfire from within and without the fort. When Herbert was sent to England for his education, it was with the expectation that his studies would prepare him for the Indian Civil Service.

He attended the best schools: Blackheath, Harrow, and Oxford. He studied Greek, Latin, Hebrew, Persian, and Hindustani, which were all required in the Indian Service examination. But just before the examination Herbert was felled by a virulent attack of scarlet fever. Because an interim of a full year was necessary before he could take the examination again, it was arranged for him by his uncle, Henry Wace (who later became the Dean of Canterbury), to study law with a prominent barrister in the Temple. Herbert qualified for the bar, but the legal profession bored him, and there is no record that he ever actually practiced law.

Meanwhile, under another name, he had already acquired a certain amount of fame in England. While at Oxford he had become the lightweight boxing champion of the university, and in London he had continued boxing as an amateur middleweight, using the name Maurice Barrymore so as not to embarrass the proper Blythes. Although efforts were made to show that Barrymore was a name that belonged in the family, there is no evidence that Herbert chose it for much more reason than that it had a gentlemanly ring, suitable for both boxing and the stage. He was handsome, well-educated, muscular, wore a top hat and carried a cane and had all the necessary manners of a gentleman. In 1872 this dashing young gentleman was awarded the Marquis of Queensberry Cup as the outstanding amateur boxer of the year. Also in 1872 he made his first stage appearance at Windsor in Jerrold's *Cool as a Cucumber* to neither applause nor acclaim.

While strolling the boardwalk at Brighton one day in 1873 he rescued Charles Vandenhoff from two toughs who took offense at the fact that Vandenhoff, a veteran actor who also managed a touring stock company, had a girl on either arm. Barrymore dispatched the toughs with great ease and gained the friendship of Vandenhoff, who, upon hearing that his rescuer had acting ambitions, offered Maurice an engagement with his company. After touring provincial England for two years, Maurice was invited to accompany Vandenhoff and his company on a trip to America. The overseas engagements presumably never materialized, for Barrymore was left stranded in

New York, and Vandenhoff seems to have acted for a time in this country on his own rather than with his company. Maurice, undecided whether to return to England or try to make a go of it here, had the decision forced upon him when he quickly ate and drank himself out of funds.

The first engagement he could find was a benefit performance in Boston of a melodrama, *Under the Gaslight*. This play was the handiwork of Augustin Daly and became a favorite with audiences mainly because it was the first to employ that suspenseful device, a virginal heroine tied to the railroad tracks by a dastardly villain. Off-stage, the locomotive could be heard thundering in a baleful crescendo. Maurice was the handsome hero who saved the girl and foiled the villain in the nick of time. Daly was present at the performance and was impressed enough with the English actor to offer him a job with the touring company he sent on the rounds while his regular company in New York had its summer hiatus. When Barrymore finished this tour, he was invited by Daly to become a member of the permanent New York company. In New York he found himself rehearsing on the same stage with young John Drew.

Maurice, after meeting Georgie, wasted no time in falling in love with her, and she responded with equal alacrity. But the opposition of Mrs. Drew to her daughter's marriage, to a man she regarded as little more than an amateur actor, proved formidable and took a year to overcome. Maurice and Georgie were married on New Year's Eve, 1876. The bride withdrew from her mother's theater, went happily off to New York with Maurice, and acted in minor parts at Daly's for a year or so, until the theater was suddenly forced into bankruptcy.

But Maurice's popularity was on the rise, and offers of work were plentiful. One came from Fanny Davenport, an actress of power and eloquence, who headed her own company. She engaged Maurice to play opposite her in a season of Shakespeare; he cut as handsome a figure and looked as well in tights as did his son, John, many years later. Other great leading ladies were to vie with each other for Maurice as their leading man, and he achieved more renown as the stage consort of several of America's feminine stars than he did as a star in his own right.

The Barrymores' first child, Lionel, was born on April 28, 1878, in the house of Mrs. Drew, who then resided at 119 North Ninth Street in Philadelphia. The average weekly pay for a leading man at this time seldom amounted to more than forty dollars a week, hardly enough for a gentleman to sustain himself, a wife, and a son. Hoping for higher earnings, Maurice joined with another actor, Frederick Warde, and formed a road company to take a New York hit, Sardou's *Diplomacy,* on tour. Both he and Warde had acted in *Diplomacy* during its New York run. Georgie's brother, John Drew, was persuaded to join the tour, and Georgie participated in it for a short time, too, but had to withdraw and return to Philadelphia, for she was pregnant again. She was replaced by another young actress, Ellen Cummings.

The tour was to become part of our theatrical annals not because Maurice Barrymore was welcomed everywhere with acclaim, but because of an incident that occurred in the small, rough town of Marshall, Texas. Frederick Warde, after the first few months of touring, had taken part of the company off on a separate tour of the same play, figuring that two tours would bring in more receipts than one, and Maurice's contingent had gone on after recruiting extra actors to round out a company. They played the Opera House in Marshall, on March 19, 1879, and were waiting for a train to take them to the next stop, Texarkana. Barrymore, Miss Cummings, and another actor, Benjamin C. Porter, decided to have something to eat and went into the station lunchroom and bar, where they sat down.

James Currie, a deputy sheriff and an employee of the railroad, came into the bar. He was, as a newspaper account put it, "a notorious bully, known for his habit of carrying a gun." Currie noticed Ellen Cummings and made some coarse remarks to others at the bar about actresses and their morals. Maurice promptly told the loudmouth that he wouldn't be talking that way if he didn't happen to have a gun or a knife on him. Currie held up two big fists and said he thought they were enough to handle any trouble the actor might give him.

But when Maurice methodically removed his coat, Currie changed his mind, drew his gun, and fired. Somehow Maurice twisted enough to keep the bullet from going through his heart; it passed completely through his left arm and lodged in his shoulder.

When Barrymore staggered, Porter rushed to help him and was shot by Currie through the abdomen. He died within moments. John Drew, in the lobby of the nearby hotel, heard the shots and ran along the station platform into the lunchroom, where Currie was still brandishing his gun, but, for some reason, he didn't shoot Drew. He merely grabbed him and held him until the Marshall sheriff came along and told Currie to hand over the gun.

The shooting put an end to the tour of *Diplomacy*. Barrymore was taken to a house in the town, where he was kept in bed for a month before being allowed to leave. Upon returning home, he presented the bullet which had nearly killed him to Lionel as a toy. The profits the tour had made were more than lost by the two trips Maurice took at his own expense to testify in two trials against Currie. An account said that eleven known murderers sat on the jury in the first trial, which resulted in acquittal. He was acquitted again in the second trial, and it was understandable that a good many touring companies avoided Texas for several years thereafter. But justice eventually came to Currie. He was killed in a brawl in New Mexico.

Maurice was still convalescing in the Ninth Street home of Mrs. Drew when Ethel was born on August 15, 1879. Both Georgie and Mrs. Drew would have preferred naming the child Louisa, but Maurice suddenly became conscious of his English literary heritage and insisted that his daughter be named after his favorite character, Ethel, in Thackeray's *The Newcombes*. Ethel received her christening in St. Stephen's Church, but was not to remain a Protestant Episcopalian for very long.

The new father strengthened his stage reputation by playing George Hastings in *She Stoops to Conquer*. It was at about this time that income from the Arch Street Theatre began to lessen, and Mrs. Drew was forced to bow to the tide of change. She adopted that newfangled (but detested by her) custom of giving matinees, and she allowed other traveling companies to play in her theater, but receipts declined steadily. In 1880, while continuing to manage the Arch Street, she formed a company with Joseph Jefferson, and for eleven seasons thereafter they played *The Rivals* together. Her Mrs. Malaprop became known far and wide. Maurice, who had joined Lester Wallack's company in New York for a time, supported his mother-in-law and Jefferson in that first glittering production of *The Rivals,* doing his bit to strengthen family finances.

But his stage habits did not strengthen her regard for him. He made a dashing, handsome Captain Absolute, but unlike the Drews, who were invariably line perfect, Maurice often simply could not remember his lines, no matter how hard he studied. His solution to the perplexing difficulty was, when he forgot, to say whatever came into his head. When this happened while playing with Mrs. Drew, he blandly ignored her scorn and anger. The more Mrs. Drew switched her petticoats and glared at him, the more delightedly Maurice smiled and bowed at her. During one performance he was so hopelessly remiss that he sent Mrs. Drew a bag of peanuts as a token of apology. But even here his cocksure humor asserted itself, for he knew full well that his mother-in-law abhorred peanuts. In return she sent him a copy of *The Rivals,* with every part in it except his.

It was at this period that Maurice took up playwriting. His first effort was an adaptation of a French play, which he titled *Honor,* and which he took to London for presentation at the Haymarket on September 21, 1881. *Honor* ran for one hundred performances, which was in the nature of a considerable success for Maurice. Not long after his return from England, where he had made the name of Maurice Barrymore count for something, another son was born and named John Sidney Blythe Barrymore, in honor of every side of the family. John's birth took place on February 15, 1882, at 2008 Columbia Avenue. With so many to house, Mrs. Drew moved almost at once to a larger home at 140 North Twelfth Street in Philadelphia.

In this year Maurice began an association with the renowned actress, Helena Modjeska. Before coming to America, Madame Modjeska had been a star at the Imperial Theater in Warsaw, under the name of Helena Modrzejewska. Her husband, Count Charles Bozenta, had engaged in anti-Czarist activities; partly because of this, partly because of the strain of her nightly performing, the two had emigrated to the United States and become part of a utopian Polish émigré community in California which exemplified communal living and personal freedom. Madame Modjeska's personal freedom included a love affair with Henry Sienkiewicz, the Polish author of *Quo Vadis*. She had been lured back to the stage by a theatrical manager in San Francisco (who also shortened her name) and quickly gained great fame in spite of her limited English. She and her entourage always traveled by private railway car, which at that time was unheard-of luxury for actors. So great an actress was she that she once drew tears at a dinner party by a dramatic reading (so Otis Skinner reported) in Polish of what was revealed to be nothing more than the alphabet. She was a gifted exponent of what passed for realistic acting at the time, gave the first performance of Ibsen's *A Doll's House* in the United States, and when Maurice Barrymore joined her, was at the peak of her popularity.

This magnificent woman, then in her late thirties, was extremely fond of her "dandy leading man," as she called him, and insisted that he contract with her for a period of four years. Their success together in several plays led to stories of a more than professional attachment between them. Though Georgie, who was also engaged for the company, became jealous when she first heard the rumors, they later proved false, and eventually she became entirely devoted to Madame Modjeska.

About Barrymore, Modjeska recalled in her memoirs: "He was one of those handsome men who have the rare gift of winning all hearts. He was equally liked by men and women. Sentimental girls used to send him flowers, and to his great amusement."

The tender-hearted Madame Modjeska had an empathetic understanding of Maurice's difficulties in memorizing. The cast was amazed once to see Modjeska and Maurice in each other's arms weeping. He was in tears over his fluffs, and she consoled him by sharing his misery. A different reaction was called for from her when Maurice during a performance not only completely failed to remember the lines of his scene with her but made up for the fault by launching himself into the lines from another play. Her consternation lasted for only a moment. She did the scene from the *other* play with him. The audience applauded wildly, taking it as a demonstration of the great actress's artistry.

Ethel and Lionel were packed up one day and taken to a private car on a siding at Broad Street Station. Inside the car they were greeted by an entrancing woman. Ethel was only four, but she was always to remember Modjeska, and the performances she witnessed from backstage were more vivid to her than those of Duse, Bernhardt, and Ellen Terry, whom she saw when she was older.

The two children (John was at home with his grandmother) toured most of a season with Modjeska and their parents. "The boy," Madame Modjeska remembered, "was always busy painting ships and trains, and Ethel, at age four, was an actress. They composed impossible dialogues and played them together. Lionel was always Pap, and Ethel was Madame. She could not pronounce all the letters of the alphabet, but she acted with conviction. I often saw her eager eyes watching me from behind the scenes during matinees." This early foray into acting was not remembered by either Ethel or Lionel, however.

Modjeska was gracious to the two children. She would take them out to tea and buy them the rich cakes their eyes feasted upon. She would hold little parties for them in her hotel suite, serving the Polish sweets that were traditional in her former country. Ethel adored Modjeska, and one afternoon she put her adoration into tangible form. From a bunch of lilies left at the stage door by one of Maurice's many admirers she selected two beautiful white blooms and brought them to Modjeska in her dressing room. Ethel had no way of knowing that for the superstitious Polish actress lilies were a harbinger of catastrophe, a matter she had often told Maurice about. She swept past the dismayed child, entered Maurice's dressing room, and accused him of heartlessly using his own child to play a vile trick on her.

Maurice flared back with outrage and scorn.

"Kindly remember," Modjeska said, "that I am the one who made you what you are today."

"And kindly remember," Maurice answered, "that I was well

known here when Americans thought Modjeska was the name of a mouthwash." The remark hit home, for there was such a well-known mouthwash.

But for the most part Maurice, and Georgie too, were spellbound by her brilliant personality. If Modjeska was a Catholic, this automatically meant to Georgie that Catholicism could only be the one and true faith, and when she became a convert she insisted on rebaptizing her children as Catholics. Maurice was a nonpracticing Anglican and did not object very strenuously to these conversions, but Mrs. Drew was outraged. However, there was nothing she could do about it, for Georgie had taken advantage of her absence from Twelfth Street when she was away playing *The Rivals* to speed Lionel and Ethel to New York for the watery ceremony. John escaped temporarily, for he was still too young to be removed from his crib. Several years later Ethel took it upon herself to oversee John's change of religion.

Count Bozenta, Modjeska's husband and also her manager, regarded the years spent with Maurice as the most terrible of his life. The two were in constant argument. Arguing with Maurice was not easy, even for one of accomplished English vocabulary, for he possessed a formidable wit and could top any insult with a crackling remark. If Bozenta gave it as his opinion that so-and-so was an excellent actor, Maurice would immediately contradict him. Their wrangles were a daily affair. Bozenta became so frustrated by Maurice's retorts that he would steal up on the actor backstage, shout an opinion at him, and rush away before it could be countered. Sometimes the arguments ended either with Maurice offering his resignation from the company or Bozenta telling him he was fired. When this point was reached, Madame Modjeska became the peacemaker, going to each in turn and enveloping him in her soothing warmth of spirit.

Maurice's creative instincts were stimulated by Modjeska, and he announced his intention of writing a play for her. He churned out a fiercely melodramatic opus called *Nadjeska* which dealt with a Polish princess who left her native land and became a courtesan on the Riviera, where she fell in with some rich Americans and captured the heart and soul of a millionaire. The play had over tones of profound Slavic gloom. As presented in New York at the Star Theater in 1884, it was billed as "an entirely new and original play in Prologue and Three Acts by Maurice H. Barrymore, with orchestral selections and calcium and gas effects." Modjeska's role was so demanding that playing it for the two weeks of the New York run brought her close to exhaustion. Even though the critical reaction was poor, Modjeska was roundly applauded for her fiery performance. The play was taken to Boston, where after a few performances Modjeska informed Maurice that she could not do nightly performances of the play because of its taxing physical demands on her. She offered to do it three times a week instead. Maurice responded by withdrawing the play entirely.

A Victorian aunt of Maurice's obligingly died at about this moment and remembered her nephew in her will. Maurice announced to Modjeska that he was ending his association with her. He took his family to London where, with the dead aunt's bequest, he put on *Nadjeska* at the Haymarket. The production didn't last long, but while in London Maurice wrote another play and sent it to the transcendent Sarah Bernhardt, who returned it to him. A few years later Bernhardt achieved one of her largest triumphs in Sardou's *La Tosca*, which struck Maurice as suspiciously resembling the play he had sent her. He entered suit against Sardou, but it was never settled. Miss Bernhardt, upon hearing of the suit, remarked: "If a great man gets the germ of an idea from some obscure source, what does it matter?"

Maurice's response to her remark was: "Any man who takes your cane out of your house and builds an umbrella out of it is no less a thief." This was the only satisfaction he gained, however. He watched in anguish the mounting royalties Sardou received from *La Tosca*, and more salt was rubbed in his wound when Puccini based an opera on the Sardou play and *Tosca* entered into the operatic repertoire.

In London Maurice acted in several other productions at the Haymarket, but then responded to Modjeska's pleading messages to return to her company. He spent only part of a season with her. Count Bozenta "fired" him one day, and this time Maurice, instead of waiting for Modjeska to woo him back, abruptly left the company. His career after this became uneven, even though he was still much

21

sought after as a leading man. He toured for a season with Mrs. Langtry, then was managed by A. M. Palmer, and spent a few years with Georgie under a new young manager, Charles Frohman. It was being said about Maurice that he could bring an audience to its feet with applause and also send it home in disgust. He seemed to be constantly on the brink of splendid achievement. But if he managed to be at his peak in one performance, at the very next one he would walk through his part, forget his lines, and ad-lib in inspired, if not entirely appropriate, wit.

Georgie's acting was done for the most part in Maurice's shadow, but as he wavered she began coming into her own. Particularly noticeable was her sense of timing when it came to delivering an amusing line. She also became known for a display of wit when the occasion called for it. An exchange of telegrams between Georgie and Charles Frohman was widely quoted. She was touring with her husband in a Frohman company, reached San Francisco, and noticed that her costumes had lost their freshness. She explained her difficulty to Frohman in a lengthy telegram, mentioning the number of dresses that had become frayed and discolored. Would he kindly remit to her enough money to replace the worn costumes? In a money-saving mood, Frohman tersely wired back: "NO."

Georgie sent him another wire. This one said: "OH."

Upon which Frohman was softened, and he sent her the money.

Maurice's energies extended beyond the theater to convivial drinking, much recounting of anecdotes, and, if the mood struck him, to indulgences with members of the opposite sex. After one Saturday evening performance he stayed out all night, and still attired in his dinner clothes arrived home on a bright Sunday morning. He met Georgie just as she was leaving the front door, dressed in her handsomest. "Where are you going, my dear?" Maurice asked her in his most gentlemanly manner.

"I am going to Mass," she replied firmly, drawing on her gloves, "and you can go to hell."

By 1889, when he moved his family to New York for a brief period, Maurice was one of the most popular members of the crowd that frequented such upper-crust haunts as the Hoffman House and Delmonico's. At The Lambs club, frequented by actors and playwrights, he was held in high regard as a bon vivant and a brilliant phrase-maker. During this year he made a success in an Australian play, *Captain Swift,* and in the window of almost every stationery shop and jeweler his likeness was displayed in a silver frame, usually holding a saucer and demitasse in his hands with proud gentlemanly bearing.

It was at this time that he also became noted for his peculiarities. He kept a collection of animals, and, as he added to the assortment, took to keeping them in a dilapidated small farm on Staten Island. He kept up his mode of dress, but it began to be noticed that he wore the wrong coat and trousers for the time of day. Sometimes he would appear in the morning wearing dinner jacket, striped trousers, and a fresh boutonniere in his lapel. It began to be noticed, too, that his linen was not always of the freshest. As clever as his mind was, he seemed not so much to mature as to regress to a boyish level. Augustus Thomas met Barrymore for the first time to discuss a play he wanted him for and received from the actor a playful jab in the ribs by way of introduction. "It was like making the acquaintance of a ten-year-old boy," he said.

Yet his mind was usually alert, keen, and articulate. He once described to Thomas a fight between his pet mongoose and a cat, saying, "All you saw was an acrobatic cat and a halo of mongoose." When his remarks had too keen a cutting edge, he would disarm his hearers with a smile and a charming, gentle manner. If his anger was aroused, he could take care of a heckler with his fists, but usually found a suitable remark to make that served almost the same purpose. He listened politely one evening to a Londoner, new in New York, who began comparing the British and American armies. "The British," he said, "could come over and lick this country overnight."

"What, again?" Maurice asked, in mild protest.

There was an occasion when his friends felt he *should* have used his fists. A man had made a disparaging remark about one of Barrymore's woman acquaintances, and Barrymore did not bother to reply. He was asked to explain this example of self-discipline. "Every blow struck in defense of a woman," he said, "is a dent in her reputation."

He and Augustus Thomas became close friends during the tryout period and run of *The Burglar,* a play that Barrymore starred in and that established Thomas as a playwright. When the play opened in Boston the morning papers were less than kind. "Boston, my boy!" he cried, whacking Thomas on the shoulder to give him fortitude. "Pay no attention to it. What is it? A city of Malvolios."

Sidney Drew was in the cast, too, and also attempted to comfort Thomas. "Now, Gus," he said, "I've been in too many first nights."

"You have, Mr. Drew, you have," his brother-in-law told him.

When *The Burglar* was a success in New York, as Barrymore had promised, Thomas took a room on Twenty-fifth Street, above a small restaurant run by an Italian, and was particularly pleased with the table d'hôte dinner served below for thirty-five cents, a price that included a bottle of red wine. He invited Barrymore to sample this bargain meal with him. "An excellent buy for the money, don't you think?" Thomas commented when finished.

"Great," Barrymore enthused, eying the empty wine bottle. "Let's have another."

Maurice thought that Thomas's room above the restaurant, permeated as it was by rich Italian cooking odors, was an excellent place to write. When he found that the adjoining room was for rent he took it at once, and on the same day brought in reams of writing paper and several dozen sharpened pencils. "Tomorrow morning I begin a play," he told Thomas.

Thomas met Georgie later that same day and told her of Maurice's decision to become creative. "He won't be there in the morning," she predicted. "Our own apartment, wherever it happens to be, is always strewn with stray pages on each of which is written: 'Act One, Scene One: A ruined garden.'" Maurice did not come the next morning, and, in fact, appeared there only once in all the time Thomas stayed on Twenty-fifth Street. Several years later Maurice brought Thomas, then ensconced in far handsomer quarters, a play that he had finished. He wanted to read it to his friend. It began: "Act One, Scene One: A ruined garden . . ."

It was not altogether surprising that Maurice did not use the room, for it was during that period that Maurice had, including the above, four legitimate addresses in New York City. One was in a house on Twenty-eighth Street, run by Mrs. Higgins, which he mainly used to store his trunks of costumes, in the event he needed something for a play at a moment's notice. Barrymore never slept in the room, which was almost bereft of furnishings, but he gave the house as his address to people for whom he did not particularly care. If anyone called, Mrs. Higgins had orders to say that he was out; sometimes he allowed one or another of his transient friends to sleep there. The place he preferred to sleep in was an apartment on Fourth Avenue, which he rented cooperatively with two of his actor friends. Georgie, who had reached her prime as a comic actress, traveled frequently, but when she was in the city, Maurice took a suite with her in a hotel called Sturtevant House.

Young Ethel was given permission one weekend to leave her convent school in Philadelphia and visit her mother. This meant there was no bed space that weekend at Sturtevant House for Maurice. It should not have been a problem to him, but it was. His share of the Fourth Avenue apartment had already been lent to one of his actor friends. The room at Mrs. Higgins's was impassable because of the stores of belongings he kept there. This meant that he would have to use the room next to the one inhabited by Augustus Thomas. As it turned out, Thomas had lent the room to a destitute young man who had asked Thomas for a handout when he was returning from The Lambs club to Twenty-fifth Street. The night was miserably snowy and slushy, and Maurice had not been near the place for weeks.

Thomas was awakened at three in the morning by Maurice, dripping from the wet snow. *"What* is that in my room?" Maurice demanded.

Thomas said that the boy had no place to sleep, and that a man with four addresses to his name certainly ought to be able to spare one. Maurice explained his own difficulties. "Old chap," Thomas said, with not much sympathy, "I don't know what you're going to do."

"I do," Maurice said. Grimly he shed his wet outer clothes and climbed into bed with Augustus Thomas.

Maurice's perambulations in New York could be easily traced, since much of his life centered around the Madison Square area, then both the fashionable and theatrical center of the city. When not playing at one of the theaters in the vicinity (Daly's, Palmer's,

or The Lyceum), he was close by at The Lambs on Thirty-sixth
Street, west of Broadway, or Delmonico's, on the corner of Twenty-
sixth and Broadway, or at the Hoffman House café, across from
Madison Square. Everyone either knew Maurice or recognized
him as he strolled by, and his quips were passed around with
relish.

The *Police Gazette,* which in those days was found in more
barber shops than *Playboy* is today, had a drama critic who brassily
called to Maurice in the street one day: "Did you see the piece I had
on you in the *Gazette* this week?"

"No," Maurice said, with hardly a pause in his step. "I shave
myself."

If his morning coat did not always go with his trousers, if the
fresh flower in his buttonhole seemed out of place, he nevertheless
was fastidious. Leaving the Hoffman House bar one evening, he
was stopped by a stranger who asked him for a light. Maurice
politely handed the man his cigar, which was less than half smoked,
and the stranger puffed at his own until lit, then handed Maurice's
back to him. Maurice walked a step away and threw it in the gutter.

Not even Sarah Bernhardt, known for her acid remarks, could
quite cope with Barry, as he was familiarly called. He happened to
be seated next to her at a dinner one evening and was the recipient
of several of her barbs. He allowed them to remain ignored until she
happened to mention that she had a son who, coincidentally, was
named Maurice. "He was educated at Harrow," she said proudly.

"Yes," the forty-five-year-old Barrymore said with a sudden show of
enthusiasm, "we were playmates together at Harrow. He is well,
Madame, I venture to hope?"

On the stage he divided the critics. Amy Leslie, a critic of the
time, could write rhapsodically: "To look upon, to listen to Maurice
Barrymore in a congenial part is to behold nature in her liveliest
temper of pleasantness. He is about as near a desirable man to see
across the footlights as the stage shall ever grant us." Other critics
complained about his extemporizing lines, even when they were
witty, about his uneven performances, and his English accent. On
the other hand, when he acted in London, the English critics regarded his accent as too American. "Good Lord," Maurice said after

26

reading those notices, "am I to be condemned to giving recitations on ocean liners for the rest of my life?"

A playwright told Maurice at The Lambs that he would never become a great actor "unless you undergo a great sorrow or some harrowing experience."

"Then write me a play," Maurice replied, "and I'll undergo both."

One of the more scathing critical attacks on him came from William Winter, who was regarded as the dean of drama critics. Winter, after jabbing away at Maurice's acting, then went to work on his morals. The actor was wounded enough to compose a letter to Winter, which he read to a friend, James Huneker. "Sir," went the letter, "In your column this morning you allude to me as an immoral actor, who should not be allowed to blister the gaze of the theater-going public. Sir, I never kissed your daughter."

Huneker was shocked. "Barry, people don't write such letters!"

"Oh, but they do," Maurice said. "They not only write them, but they mail them." He sealed the letter, dropped it in a mailbox, and added, "Of course, you know, the old hedgehog has no daughter."

But it turned out that Winter did have a daughter, and upon hearing this Maurice said with great regret, "I wouldn't have written it if I had known."

Maurice's fondness for animals became obsessive during a cross-country tour he took in 1893 with a Charles Frohman company. He brought with him his favorite, a Clydesdale terrier, winner of several blue ribbons at dog shows. In Chicago, where he stopped off to take a look at the World's Fair, his fancy was caught by a pair of skunks in a sideshow, and he bought them. At every stop along the way he added to his collection. Frohman was bothered by the presence of so many pets, and said the tour would halt for Barrymore at once if he didn't send the animals home. Maurice arranged to have them quartered in a baggage car, where animal fights broke out frequently and delayed the train. By the time they arrived in San Francisco he had with him (in addition to the Clydesdale terrier and the skunks) three dogs, two mountain lions, eight birds, each of a different species, six prairie dogs, and three weasels. When the hotel manager refused to house the pets, Maurice reluctantly shipped the lot to the small farm on Staten Island.

By the time he arrived in Seattle he was lonely for animal companionship. He took a walk outside the town and came across a tramp who owned an awkward, wobbling bear that caught beer bottles tossed to him, pulled out the corks with his teeth, and drank the contents. Maurice, entranced, bought the bear for ten dollars.

The owner of the hotel rebelled at putting up the bear, so Maurice prowled around Seattle until he found a boardinghouse keeper, with no boarders, who reluctantly agreed to keep the big animal in a backyard. One Sunday evening Maurice gave a boxing exhibition between himself and the bear for the cast. In the third round the bear jabbed Maurice's shoulder and drew blood. Claiming that the bear's claws presented an unfair advantage, Maurice borrowed a heavy pair of shears, but at the first snip the bear let out a roar, which scattered the crowd of onlookers, and caught his owner in a bear hug. Maurice slipped out of the hold and shot through an open door, followed by the enraged animal. Inside the house the bear threshed around, tearing down mantels, smashing chairs, tables, and lamps, and altogether running up a large damage bill against Maurice. The original bear tamer had to be sent for before the animal became docile enough to be led away.

Maurice's entire collection of animals at the farm on Staten Island —all except Belle of Clyde, his medal-winning terrier—disappeared in 1895 when vandals set fire to the sheds in which they were kept. Barrymore was hollow-eyed and unshaven for days, and he broke into tears when he told about the tragedy to friends. After that he and Belle of Clyde were inseparable.

In the late nineties critics noted with distress that Barrymore was not the captivating actor of his former days. More often than before he had embarrassing lapses on the stage and his improvisations seemed like the stumblings of a ham actor. When The Lambs put on an annual burlesque and used Barrymore's starring vehicle, *Captain Swift,* as their take-off, Augustus Thomas was the hit of the show as, made up to resemble Barrymore, he pretended to forget every one of his lines. Maurice's own play-writing efforts, which included a musical extravaganza, failed miserably. He made an abortive comeback in an all-star production of *Becky Sharp,* and won some praise for his vivid portrayal of Rawdon Crawley, but his last days were spent almost entirely in vaudeville.

It was common later on for stage stars to do dramatic turns on the vaudeville stage, but Maurice Barrymore's appearance in vaudeville was considered revolutionary. Five hundred dollars a week was the bait which persuaded this star of the stage to do a serious playlet, *A Man of the World,* at Keith's Union Square Theater in 1894. He was something of a novelty to the vaudeville audience, and Maurice basked in their applause, and settled for his new-found affluence. But his friends shook their heads and murmured that Maurice had committed artistic suicide. He was regarded as a man who had wasted large talents. Wilton Lackaye, an actor whose wit was said to sparkle every bit as much as Barrymore's, sat across from him at a table one day and scribbled an epitaph for the father of the Barrymores:

> I talked beneath the moon
> And slept beneath the sun;
> I lived a life of going-to-do,
> And died with nothing done.

Maurice, for once, had no satisfactory reply.

A CROP OF BARRYMORES / *chapter III*

THE FIRST GROUP picture ever taken of Lionel, Ethel, and John (probably in 1887) shows their three small heads arranged nicely around their mother's. Ethel, wearing bangs, and her long hair in flowing curls, has large eyes of a pensive cast; her chin rests in her palm, which in turn rests upon her mother's full shoulder. Lionel's hair is like a mop on his head, and his face has a slightly rebellious look. John is perhaps four or five in this photograph; his face wears a dreamy expression, and already one eyebrow is lifted quizzically. All three, at the time of the taking of this picture, lived in their grandmother's house at 140 North Twelfth Street, which Georgie referred to as "the tomb of the Capulets" because a carver of tombstones lived and worked across the street and kept his samples in an open yard.

To the children the house seemed large and cavernous, with its big attic and a cellar which had been converted into a dining room. It was, in fact, a solid but ordinary red brick Philadelphia row house with three white stone steps up which one climbed to the front door. The house was roomy enough for the several branches of Mrs. Drew's family. Her mother, Mrs. Eliza Kinlock, had the large front bedroom on the second floor, in which she lay most of the day, tinkling a small bell to obtain the attentions she was entitled to by her past labors and her advanced years. Another of the bedrooms belonged to John Drew, but he was almost never home, since most of the time he acted in New York. The little Barrymores would glance into the well-kept room with awe. In the same house was a room for Georgie and Maurice, for Sidney Drew, and for Adine Stevens, the little girl the elder John Drew had brought back with him from Australia. She was now Aunt Tibby to the children.

Servants' wages being what they were, and while Mrs. Drew's Arch Street Theatre still did well, the house was attended by a cook, a maid, and a housekeeper who saw to the children's needs when the elder Barrymores and Mrs. Drew were acting out of the city. But because of the feast-or-famine nature of their parents' occupation, the children were often uncertain in their early years as to whether to feel rich or poor. Part of the confusion was due no doubt to Maurice Barrymore's sometimes forgetting, when he was out on tour, to send money home. When money was plentiful, they had fine clothes, but because it was Maurice's habit to spend money capriciously, the children often had to make their worn clothes do for extended periods.

When at home, Mrs. Drew set the tone of the household. The children were expected to keep silent in the presence of their elders. They were shy enough, though, by nature, and Ethel obeyed Mrs. Drew's injunctions to such an extreme that her eyes seemed always to be studying the floor. At such moments some member of the family would say sternly, "Look up, Pauline!" This was a line from Bulwer-Lytton's *The Lady of Lyons*. The use of quotations was common in the household. "Stand not upon the order of your going, but go at once!" was the way in which the children were ordered to bed. "Our manners," Ethel recalled later, "were shaped in terms of theater dialogue."

When away from their elders the children were normally mischievous. Lionel took to keeping a secret family of white mice in Uncle Googan's room. In "The Annex," their attic playroom, John imagined himself a pirate chief and pirated a good many glittering objects he found lying around the house, storing them in an old chest. A detective visited the house one day, and John paled when he heard his grandmother describe the valuable articles of jewelry that were missing. Mrs. Drew noticed John's expression as the detective made his notes, and later obtained a confession on her own from the pirate chief.

When she was led to his cache, she said severely, "Do you realize that I might be locked up as a receiver of stolen goods?"

At the age of five John recorded his first overindulgence in alcoholic beverages. A big family dinner had taken place, to which the children had been barred. After the elders retired to the parlor on the main floor, John explored the leavings on the table. The remnants of food had been removed by the servants, but not the glasses, in which small amounts of liquid remained. John sampled the various wines, liquors, and brandies, and soon developed symptoms that alarmed the family greatly. His look became glassy-eyed, he was noticeably pale, his physical movements were uncertain, and he threw up. A doctor was summoned to the house to examine John, and after a few minutes gave Mrs. Drew his diagnosis. "The boy is drunk," he said.

The talk around them was always about the theater. Mrs. Drew and her mother, Mrs. Kinlock, would often talk of their past days and cast scorn on the new methods that were modernizing the theater. They talked of Edwin Forrest as a young man, and of the father of Joseph Jefferson. That, they claimed, was the golden era of acting. Ethel was shown a letter that Abraham Lincoln had written to Mrs. Drew, regretting that he could not attend a performance at the Arch Street Theatre, as business kept him in Washington. John Wilkes Booth, who assassinated him a year later, had played on Mrs. Drew's stage more than once.

When Mrs. Drew instituted matinees at her theater, she let the children occupy the Drew box for Saturday afternoon performances; and when the great Edwin Booth came to play an engagement at the Arch Street, she allowed the children to watch one evening from backstage. Ethel, from her vantage point in the wings, noticed that Booth fell silent in the middle of a speech as though he had forgotten his lines. The audience appeared to hold its collective breath. Then Booth resumed and finished the act, to tumultuous applause.

"I was a good actor tonight," he informed the small Ethel between the acts, taking her on his lap.

"No," Ethel told him accusingly, "you stuck dead."

"I had to," he explained. "The audience wasn't alive until I did. If they show signs of dying again I'll have to tumble over a chair. They'll think I've been drinking and watch me like cats."

Toward the end of 1885 the children were taken to London by their parents for Maurice's production of his *Nadjeska*. The Blythes and the Waces got a chance to meet their son's actress wife (they had not looked kindly upon his marrying into an acting family) and his children. During dinner with their relatives Lionel wandered in to ask, "Where in the hell did someone put my suspenders?"

Maurice looked at his wife and said severely, "Georgie, have the children been allowed to stray into the coachman's quarters again?"

The house they resided in while in London was in St. John's Wood. It was pleasant, roomy, and had a garden surrounded by a tall brick wall. Maurice, who had begun collecting animals, kept several dogs and a monkey in the garden. Ethel liked to wrestle with the dogs, and also with her older brother Lionel, usually managing to hold her own with him. Lionel enjoyed peering out of the window of the third-floor nursery with a spyglass. Lord's cricket grounds were not far off, and he could see the matches in progress.

Maurice spent his inheritance lavishly, entertaining Oscar Wilde, Herbert Beerbohm-Tree (who appeared in the production of *Nadjeska*), and Alma Tadema among their brilliant coterie of guests. Georgie made it Ethel's duty at tea time to pass around the little cakes. One day she brought the cakes to a stranger sitting on the sofa, keeping her eyes downcast as usual. Her mother called out, "Look up, Pauline!" and Ethel, looking up, saw the huge white face of Oscar Wilde. She shrieked in fright, dropped the plate, and ran up the stairs to the nursery. Her mother found her there later and applied the family form of punishment known as the green slipper, a felt shoe with which they were spanked.

Lionel, in London, was old enough to start school, and was entered at the Gilmore School in Warrington Crescent. The educations of Ethel and John did not begin until their return to the United States toward the end of 1886. Georgie, who by this time was a converted Catholic, insisted that the children must attend Catholic schools. Ethel was boarded not far from home at the Academy of Notre Dame in Rittenhouse Square, a convent school run by an order of Belgian nuns. Lionel was sent to a Catholic boys' school on the Hudson, St. Vincent's Academy. Both children had acquired British accents during their stay in London. Lionel's got him in trouble with his fellow students, and being naturally combative, he was often to be found on the floor underneath a pile of boys. He ran away from school twice, following the railroad tracks into New York City. After the second flight he was placed in Seton Hall Academy at East Orange, New Jersey. John later attended Seton Hall, too, but first he was sent to a school for small boys that was attached to Ethel's school. In the afternoons he was allowed to trot home to his grandmother's.

Their education can hardly have been said to have fitted them for their later careers as actors. None was a particularly good student, and Lionel claimed that at Seton Hall he had set an all-time record for resistance to knowledge. When he left the school at fifteen it ended his formal education. Ethel took piano and singing lessons at the convent, and was given special dancing lessons. The latter, along with her newly acquired British accent, made her an object of curiosity to her schoolmates, who were aware, too, of her theater connections. At school Ethel was painfully self-conscious and blushed if called upon to recite. She developed a passionate desire to be a nun, and then developed an even more passionate desire to become a concert pianist, practicing as much as five hours a day, and winning the school's silver medal for music for her playing of a Beethoven sonata.

At a school entertainment, to which Maurice came with Georgie, she took part in a two-piano performance, and Maurice was so astonished at his daughter's ability that he listened spellbound. He at once promised that she would go to Salzburg to study, a promise that Ethel took seriously. But that was the last she ever heard of it.

John spent three years at the boys' annex to Ethel's convent school. Once he got into a fight with a schoolmate and threw a hard-boiled egg at him. "You may be an actor someday," one of the sisters told him, "and have an egg thrown at you." For punishment she made him sit and look at Doré's fearsome illustrations for a large volume of Dante's *Inferno*. Instead of resenting the discipline, he found himself fascinated by the drawings, and said later that it was this incident that was responsible for his artistic ambitions, and that Doré had been the influence for his own macabre drawings.

Before joining Lionel at Seton Hall, he was sent to Georgetown Academy, where he soon ran into trouble. The older boys celebrated the evening of Washington's Birthday by taking John along for a visit to a brothel. A suspicious priest pulled a raid but was able to collar only John, the rest of the boys having fled. John took the First and Fifth amendments when pressed to reveal the names of his companions, and was sent home in disgrace. An explanatory letter went to his father. John said the accusations were false; he hadn't done "anything."

"Why in God's name not?" Maurice thundered. "Aren't you a Barrymore?"

John made an interesting start at Seton Hall. One of the fathers, trying to interest him in athletics, took him to the gymnasium, pointing out the rings, horses, and parallel bars. John tried the parallel bars, and several odd items fell from his pockets, including a set of brass knuckles, a pack of cigarettes, and a half pint of cheap whiskey.

From the school, not long after he was enrolled, John sent his grandmother an impassioned letter that told how a priest had felled him to the ground "with a blow." The Episcopalian Mrs. Drew immediately sent the letter on to her son-in-law, with the implication that this was what might be expected from a "Catholic school," and advising him to go there at once from New York, where he was playing, to investigate. Maurice, imbued with parental indignation, went to East Orange, where he was greeted by a gracious, gentle priest. The two became involved in an absorbing discussion of a recent murder case that had filled the newspapers. Hours went by, and Maurice barely had time to catch his train back to New York. He forgot to mention the incident that had brought him to the school.

The Barrymore children's schooling was incomplete, but their minds were lively, nevertheless, and all three were omnivorous readers. They were also fed by the voluminous fund of information possessed by Maurice, who regaled the boys during the periods he spent with them with a repertoire that ranged from classical literature to a thrilling recital of the siege of Fort Agra.

Their mother was a somewhat distant figure in their memories

35

of childhood. "I looked at her in worship and silence as a small girl," Ethel remembered, "longing to talk with her, but fearing out of the very shyness of my nature to speak to her." Lionel and John's closeness to Georgie was even less. Although Ethel could remember having seen her once or twice on the stage, Lionel remembered neither her nor his father in any of their performances. John made only one remark about Georgie in all the various "confessions" and reminiscent series by him and about him that appeared during his career. "My mother died when I was eleven," he wrote in *Confessions of an Actor,* "and I remember her only vaguely." Much more clear to him was the elderly Mrs. Drew, to whom he was extremely attached during his childhood.

Their summer vacations were more likely to be spent with Mrs. Drew than with their parents. One of their summers was spent in a boardinghouse at Fort Wadsworth, Staten Island, where Mrs. Drew paid regular visits. Under Ethel's direction the three put on a performance of *Camille,* for which Ethel practiced a magnificent cough and John wore a long, droopy black mustache. Mrs. Drew heard Ethel coughing and coughing away in the bathroom and became upset. "Something must be done about that child," she said; "she's started to bark like a dog." So far as can be determined, this was the only occasion on which the young Barrymores showed any leanings toward the stage.

Another summer Ethel went to Buzzard's Bay for several weeks with her grandmother, while John and Lionel stayed at the ramshackle farmhouse Maurice owned on Staten Island. They were left in the care of an old Negro who looked after the farm and the animals Maurice kept there, including thirty-five dogs. When Maurice forgot to send money for their food, Edward, the hired hand, managed to get enough supplies on credit from the local grocery to keep the boys alive. While they were there a letter came from Mrs. Drew which, they thought, said that she would pay them a visit. They scrubbed up the place and themselves and put on their best clothes. All day long they waited on the porch for her, but their grandmother did not appear. The next day a telegram came from Mrs. Drew asking why they hadn't come to Long Branch, New Jersey, where she had gone, taking Ethel with her. The boys read her letter again and realized that they had been invited to her house. John wrote a reply, saying that they didn't have any money, and Mrs. Drew sent him enough for one ticket to Long Branch.

"I remember," John said later, "that as I drove away in the hack, Lionel and Edward were standing on the porch waving at me. There was a big lump in my throat and I wanted to cry. It seemed unfair, as if I were being taken away from Lionel forever. It was a cruel thing to do to Lionel, who was only thirteen and sensitive. My grandmother's favoritism had built a wall between us. It was years before he forgot." But Mrs. Drew, that season, had been able to spare enough money for only one of the boys.

Slowly, inexorably, Mrs. Drew's house in Philadelphia lost its place as the family center. Eliza Kinlock quietly passed away and was buried in Glenwood Cemetery; Aunt Tibby died young. John Drew was a major actor, married to an actress, Josephine Baker (the Barrymore children called her Aunt Dodo) and living in New York. Uncle Googan had moved to New York, too, after marrying Gladys Rankin. Both acted in vaudeville and on the legitimate stage. It was to be expected that New York now became the home city of the Barrymores. In 1889 the Twelfth Street house was vacated, and Mrs. Drew went to live with her son, John Drew, in New York. The Barrymore children were taken there too, staying for a time in the apartment rented by Georgie and Maurice at 1564 Broadway (where the Palace Theater is now located). Later the Barrymores moved to an apartment on West Ninetieth Street.

However, there was not much home life for Ethel, Lionel, and John. When it was school season Ethel returned to the convent on Rittenhouse Square, and Lionel and John went back to Seton Hall. It seems even the apartment was given up in favor of a permanent hotel suite for Georgie (who lived there when she had her greatest success, in 1890, in *Mrs. Wilkinson's Widows.*) Maurice kept the three other residences mentioned earlier.

Good times were in store for the children the year that Maurice starred in *Captain Swift* and Georgie in *Mrs. Wilkinson's Widows.* The expansive Maurice took them to the Central Park Zoo, introduced them to John L. Sullivan during a stroll along Broadway.

Lionel was judged old enough to accompany his father on a visit to the Hoffman House bar. Maurice knew and was known by everyone. He introduced Lionel to a Mr. Samuel Clemens. Lionel remained silent and unawed until it was explained to him that Mr. Clemens was also known by the name of Mark Twain.

This information excited Lionel so much that he began to tell the author all about Huckleberry Finn and Jim, relating one episode practically verbatim. There were tears in Mark Twain's eyes when Lionel finished. He beckoned a waiter and ordered a drink for him that contained an apple, spice, and hot water, but omitting the brandy. Lionel was vastly pleased with himself.

It would appear that from the age of ten onward Ethel had no great amount of affection for her father. It can be assumed that this was due to what she regarded as his poor treatment of her mother. The effect of his forgetfulness and his unexplained absences on Georgie would certainly explain Ethel's attitude, coupled with the fact that Georgie's health began increasingly to fail. But it was traditional in the Drew family that the private and the personal were exactly that—not to be revealed to others. Stoicism was encouraged, and even within the family any showing of emotion was likely to be met by one of those play quotations that took the revealer down a peg.

During the windy and bitterly cold winter of Ethel's eleventh year, Georgie caught a cold that hung on stubbornly and worsened. She developed a racking cough and ran a constant temperature. The doctors advised a trip to the Windward Islands for her, and she went there alone, returning in the spring beautifully tanned and seemingly in good health again. Consumption may have been suspected by the doctors, but, if so, Georgie was not told of this.

She had reached her prime as an actress. She made an enormous hit in *The Senator,* and a reviewer wrote about her: "Georgie Drew had been promising for several seasons to take the lead as a comedienne. Now she has taken it, handsome as a picture, brimming over with fun. An actress to the tip of her fingers, she captivated the audience at once, and kept them in roars of laughter and applause."

But now Georgie's health failed again, and in 1892 the doctors at last admitted that she had a serious case of consumption, and she was advised to seek the drier air of California. Ethel was taken from the convent school to accompany her there. When she arrived in New York she was told only that her mother was ill with bronchitis and that she was to take a long trip with her by boat to the Isthmus of Panama, which they would cross by train, following which they would take another boat north to Santa Barbara by way of the Pacific. Ethel was vastly excited by the prospect of the journey. But just before the boat sailed she witnessed her mother's leavetaking of Maurice, as Georgie begged him not to forget her. A momentary chill came over Ethel, but she quickly recovered her gaiety and waved cheerfully to her father and two brothers from the rail of the ship.

The trip to California took three weeks. Georgie had the lower berth on the sea voyage to Panama and Ethel the upper. At night Ethel would hear her mother coughing and coughing, not loudly, before at last the exhausted woman would fall asleep. Ethel woke up one night to hear her mother saying, "What's going to happen to my children?" Ethel was frightened, but did not tell her mother she had heard. On the train, as they crossed Panama, she saw the huge abandoned machinery of the de Lesseps attempt to build a canal. On the Pacific side they took another boat, which stopped at several small Mexican ports before it reached Santa Barbara. Within a day they found a small, comfortable house covered with climbing roses, and engaged an elderly Chinese cook.

The doctor Georgie had been referred to came to examine her. He listened to her cough and asked quietly: "Who is going to take care of you, Mrs. Barrymore?"

"My little girl," Georgie said.

"What I meant," the doctor said, "is who will be looking after you?"

"My little girl," Georgie repeated.

The doctor nodded, but Ethel was never to forget the odd expression that came over his face, nor the panic with which it filled her. The doctor, she realized later, was indignant that Georgie's eastern doctor would send a woman so far to die, with only a child to care for her. But there were some happy times left for thirty-six-year-old Georgie Barrymore and her thirteen-year-old daughter. The

39

climate was ideal, and their neighbors in Santa Barabara were friendly.

Georgie's health appeared to improve, so much so that one Sunday she accepted the mayor's invitation to take a drive in his carriage. Ethel went to morning Mass, and assuming her mother was out driving, did not hurry back, deciding to return home by a roundabout way. A child came hurrying toward her as she approached the house, crying, "Hurry, Ethel, hurry! Your mother's had a hemorrhage." By the time Ethel reached the house, Georgie Barrymore was unconscious, and died without recognizing her daughter.

The Chinese gentleman cleaned up the room so that there was no look of death. Friends were extremely kind to Ethel as she went about the grim business of packing up her mother's clothes and sorting out the personal effects she felt the family would want to retain. She had not cried much until then, but the sight of her mother's pretty things suddenly brought on tears that would not stop. When she stopped crying, it was as though she had suddenly become a mature person. She sent telegrams to her father and to her Uncle Googan, telling them to notify John and Lionel. She made arrangements for the undertaking, and had just enough money left to transport herself and the coffin by train back to New York. There was no money for conventional mourning clothes, so she put up her hair severely and wore her black convent uniform.

At Los Angeles, on the way back, there was a wait of a few hours while changing trains. Madame Modjeska, who was living then at nearby Anaheim, met her at the station, and to distract the child, talked of everything but Georgie. Then she took her to a restaurant and bought her ice cream before putting her on the eastbound train.

The train ride to Chicago took four days and four nights, and Ethel spent all of them sitting in the day coach. There being no dining car on the train, the bewildered girl did not know what to do about eating until passengers pointed out the station lunchrooms along the way. She had a number of books with her, and she read four and five of them a day, methodically turning over the pages but not comprehending what she read. She did not cry because she did not want to show emotion before strangers. At Chicago her father met her and continued the rest of the way with her to New

York, but not until Ethel made the transportation arrangements for them and the coffin that contained her mother's body. Maurice was in a state of near hysteria. The news had been a frightful shock to him.

Mrs. Drew met them at the station in New York. She was seemingly calm, but Georgie had been her favorite, and her death was the greatest sorrow of her life. She took charge from that point on, and although Georgie had been a Catholic, the services were held at St. Stephen's Episcopal Church in Philadelphia in deference to Mrs. Drew's wishes. The church was thronged on that warm July Wednesday. Maurice walked behind the coffin with Ethel on his arm. Lionel walked with his Aunt Gladys. Maurice trembled during the ride to Glenwood Cemetery. "It's not true," he kept saying, "it's not true."

Mrs. Drew took charge of the children for the remainder of the summer. She had by now relinquished her hold on the Arch Street Theatre and was preparing for another tour as Mrs. Malaprop in *The Rivals,* with her son Sidney in charge of the company. Meanwhile she stayed at a boardinghouse on Staten Island, with the destinies of her grandchildren uppermost in her thoughts. Maurice, it was quite clear, could not be counted on as a trustworthy guardian. Things had not been going well for him; not only had his own playwriting efforts failed, but the shows he acted in were for the most part unfortunate ventures, too. Ethel, Mrs. Drew decided, would return to the convent school in Philadelphia, Lionel she would take along with her on her approaching tour, and eleven-year-old Jack would stay for the time being with his Uncle John Drew and his Aunt Dodo. John Drew, now firmly established as the most popular exponent of the drawing room manner, had come under the management of Charles Frohman and was to play an important part in developing that producer's extraordinary managerial career. Young Jack was John Drew's favorite and was given quarters at Hotel Marlborough in Manhattan, where the Drews stayed, and also at a small cottage in East Hampton, where Jack spent much of his time during the warm months.

At the convent Ethel again took to the piano seriously. With family funds at a low ebb, Mrs. Drew saw that the chances of Ethel's finishing her musical education were slim, nor had Lionel shown any real aptitude as a scholar. She talked to Lionel about the stage as a possible career for him. Lionel told her grandly that he would enjoy designing scenery. "First," Mrs. Drew said, "you will become an actor." They were in Kansas City on tour with *The Rivals* when the moment was chosen for his debut. The part entrusted to him, short but not easy, was that of Thomas the coachman.

Lionel was overcome by an agony of embarrassment when he went on for an afternoon performance. He repeated the words he had learned, but without expression. In the evening he tried again, without improvement. When Mrs. Drew passed him in the wings on her way to her dressing room she gave her grandson not so much as a glance. Knowing he was in disgrace, Lionel wandered the streets of Kansas City for an hour before returning to his hotel room. There he found a note propped on the bureau, written in his grandmother's hand.

> My dear Lionel,
>
> You must forgive your Uncle Sidney and me for not realizing that when Sheridan wrote the part of Thomas he had a much older actor in mind. We feel that we were remiss in not taking cognizance of this, although we are both happy that you are not at the advanced age you would have to be in order to be good in this part. We think, therefore, that the play as a whole would be bettered by the elimination of the front scene and have decided to do without it after this evening's performance.
>
> . . . With deep affection,
> your grandmother,
> Mrs. Drew

Lionel habitually called at his grandmother's room to say good night. Relieved that he would not have to play the hated role again, he knocked at her door. Mrs. Drew sat before a fire, enjoying a light supper and her usual dram of whisky. Her eyes filled with tears when she saw Lionel, and she opened her arms so that the boy could come into them for comfort. But suddenly she noticed an amused expression on his face and asked why he took the occasion so lightly.

"But I agree with you about the scene," Lionel said. "Of course it ought to be eliminated. Don't mind about me."

"And what are we to do with you now?" Mrs. Drew asked.

"I'd still like to paint scenery," he said. "Or I suppose I could go back home."

Home, Mrs. Drew reminded the sixteen-year-old boy, was no longer in Philadelphia, nor anywhere, unfortunately, but where she was. Besides, it was time that he faced the problem of earning his upkeep. "You can do odd jobs around the company," she told him firmly, "until such time as we find something else for you to do on stage." Lionel mainly proved useful to his Uncle Googan, who liked martinis, although he had been warned about their being bad for his health. Lionel learned to mix the drink, tasted it to make sure it had the requisite taste and potency, and would smuggle it to his uncle. Sidney Drew kept Lionel around for several years and man- aged—in self-defense, as Lionel put it—to teach him a few things about acting.

When she was about to finish her term at the convent school in May of 1894, Ethel was sent for by her grandmother, who was tour- ing *The Rivals* in Canada. It was now necessary for Ethel to face up to realities. Her mother was dead; she had learned from a news- paper clipping someone had shown her that her father was reputedly remarried; the Arch Street Theatre had passed from Mrs. Drew's management. There was no house to return to and there was no money. Maurice undoubtedly could have supplied enough for her to continue with her schooling, if he had been more of a dependable sort, but Mrs. Drew had long ceased putting any dependency upon him.

So Ethel packed her trunk and took the train for Montreal, where the company was playing. When she joined the company, her fifteenth birthday still some months off, her hair still hung down her back and was tied with the customary large black bow. A small part in *The Rivals,* Julia, usually eliminated in most productions, was reinstated by Mrs. Drew for Ethel, and she was given forty dollars to purchase her costume. It was the only money she received during that tour.

Ethel did not receive instructions for her first appearance on a stage other than being given the lines she was to learn. Just before going on, Mrs. Drew visited her backstage. "What is that you have on your face?" Mrs. Drew asked. Ethel, knowing nothing about make-up, had plastered it on the way she had watched others do.

"Make-up," she said.

"Well, go and scrub it off," Mrs. Drew ordered.

Ethel had her first experience of stage fright as she went out before the Montreal audience. She sat on a small sofa with Gladys Rankin, who was playing Lydia Languish. Ethel said her first line and noticed a glazed look appear on her aunt's face. The part of Julia was, after all, new to the performance, and Gladys Rankin hadn't properly memorized her own responses. Ethel conquered her terror and began asking herself questions and answering them, until at last Aunt Gladys began to respond.

Her grandmother, as Mrs. Malaprop, sat there on the stage while this was going on, slowly, calmly waving her fan, pretending not to be at all nervous for Ethel. Then Ethel saw her lay the fan in her lap and give a little nod, as much as to say, "That's all right."

When she was back in her dressing room, having survived her trial by fire, Ethel found a large red apple awaiting her. No one of the family was ever able to tell precisely how the custom started, but when any member of the Drew family had an important first night, an apple was placed in the dressing room. The tradition persisted as long as Drews were on the stage. Through the years Ethel, Lionel, and John received their apples, sent by one member or another of the family. It was the opinion of their uncle, John Drew, that the custom had something to do with a child's nursery rhyme: "Speak your piece prettily, and I'll give you a big red apple." Ethel was judged to have spoken her first piece prettily.

Ethel had hardly broken into her role when Mrs. Drew left the company and traveled to New York. It is likely that the reason for this was that family matters needed attending to. Lionel had been sent back to New York to make contact with his father—the reason he and Ethel did not cross paths at this point—and reported that Maurice had indeed married Mamie Floyd, the pretty daughter of a vaudeville stage manager. After locating his father at The Lambs, Lionel had been taken uptown to a Ninety-seventh Street apartment, where he was introduced, in an agony of embarrassment on all sides, to his stepmother. John Drew was at this time completing an engagement in London, and Lionel was instructed to go to East Hampton, where John Drew's wife, Aunt Dodo, would look after him for the summer. His younger brother was already there.

In Canada Mrs. McKee Rankin supplanted Mrs. Drew as Lady Malaprop, and, with her son-in-law, Sidney Drew, was to look after Ethel. The tour from this point on took on the air of melodrama. Mrs. Rankin had no drawing power, and Sidney Drew, in charge of the company, began meeting severe difficulties in paying salaries and bills, especially hotel bills. In one town the orchestra deserted, and Ethel was hurried down to the stifling pit and bidden to play the piano in lieu of entr'acte music. Finishing, she raced backstage to be in time for her entrance. At Halifax it was decided to give a new bill, and cast and stagehands worked frantically all night to put on a Sidney Drew version of *Oliver Twist*. Having reached St. John, New Brunswick, after a series of disastrous one-night stands, the company discovered that funds were nonexistent. It was time to elude the sheriff. Ethel's aunt and uncle were familiar with such situations, but to Ethel it was quite novel, and she didn't fully comprehend what was meant when she was instructed to dress thoroughly at the hotel before leaving for the theater.

After the final curtain everyone was told to remain in the theater until after midnight. Then, in the dark, they trooped to the train station, leaving their trunks behind at the hotel. To Ethel this meant cutting herself off from her former life; the trunk had contained her entire, though small, store of possessions. Aunt Gladys, she noticed while walking to the station, seemed to have a certain rigidity to her carriage that was unfamiliar. On the other hand, Aunt Gladys remarked on how little in the way of clothes Ethel was wearing. "Only one waist, and one skirt?" she exclaimed. She showed Ethel the proper attire for such emergencies, no less than five dresses, and such other small objects as could be secreted on her person.

Returning to New York—Philadelphia was never again to be the home of the Drews and the Barrymores—Ethel found her grandmother living at the Sherman Square Hotel on Broadway, where John Drew, returned from Europe, kept an apartment. There Ethel found she was to stay, in a tiny, dark room next to her grandmother's. And Ethel also found that she was now expected to seek her fortune in the theater. So every morning the tall, slender girl would leave the little room and make the rounds of the theatrical agencies. Day after day the answer given to Ethel Barrymore was the same: nothing today.

It was suggested to Lionel Barrymore, too, that he look for work on the stage, and when his search proved as fruitless as Ethel's, he faced his grandmother and his Uncle John and received their permission to enroll at the Art Students League, where, he assured them, he would very quickly demonstrate masterly gifts as an artist. He was admitted to the class of a well-known painter of the nineties, John Twachtman. The atmosphere was all that the nearly seventeen-year-old youth might wish: a class full of easels, talented young men painting busily away, pretty girls in bright-colored smocks, and conversation full of such heady expressions as Impressionism, and Art Nouveau.

Lionel enjoyed it thoroughly until one day in Twachtman's class he got into an argument with a young painter called Ferdinand Pinney Earle. Lionel's combative instincts were roused quickly, and in no time at all the two were crashing into easels and splattering color everywhere. Both were thereafter barred from Twachtman's class, but, humble and contrite, were admitted to the class of the fine painter, Kenyon Cox. There Lionel applied himself diligently for more than a year, until pressures again mounted for him to earn some income. Sidney Drew and McKee Rankin had gotten together to put on a comedy called *The Bachelor's Baby,* and for Lionel there was a part called Sergeant Jones. He acquitted himself creditably enough this time, and McKee Rankin, who toured frequently, used Lionel after that whenever he could.

When John was fourteen, he began to see more of his father than formerly. Maurice was now in vaudeville and was preparing *A Man of the World* for opening at Hammerstein's Olympia Theatre on Broadway. John, like Lionel, claimed artistic ambitions, and doodled and drew a great deal—sometimes on his Aunt Dodo's tablecloths. "Nonsense," his father told him. "Artists starve. You'll do much better on the stage." In vaudeville Maurice was earning five hundred dollars weekly, more money than he had ever made before. Thinking that it might now be time to interest his young son in so lucrative a profession, he suggested to John that he play the part of a youth in the sketch. John agreed.

Maurice, on the night of the tryout in Coytesville, New Jersey, rushed into the dressing room, with only minutes to spare, and made up. He applied the large black mustache his role called for and left the dressing room for his cue. John had not been told anything about make-up and decided the safe thing to do was copy exactly what his father had done. He, too, applied a mustache, covering half of his face with it. This Maurice didn't notice until John made his entrance. John became aware that his father had turned to the audience and made some remark about him, for he was greeted with shouts of laughter. He stood there, grinning foolishly, knowing only that he was the butt of a joke. The experience was painful enough to cure him of any incipient affection he might have felt for the stage. For his part, Maurice made no further effort to encourage John to learn the trade.

Ethel summed up the feeling of all three young Barrymores: "We became actors not because we wanted to go on the stage, but because it was the thing we could do best." But it took several years and much trial and error before either John or Lionel decided that acting was, after all, the only thing they could do best.

ETHEL BEGINS / *chapter IV*

ETHEL BARRYMORE, at the age of fifteen, would board a five-cent horsecar every morning near the Sherman Square Hotel and get off at Broadway in the mid-thirties, which in 1894 was the heart of the theatrical district. Methodically she would trod from agency to agency, seeking parts in plays. She waited in airless outer reception rooms with other actors who were "at liberty," and she quickly learned to keep a blank, unconcerned expression on her face when she was told there was nothing for her.

But she dreaded the fruitless, tiring rounds, and it was painful to have to return each day to the hotel to face the questioning glance of her grandmother. Ethel had not even the spur of stage ambition to keep her spirits up. Mrs. Drew was bewildered. A member of the Drew family unable to get so much as a small job in the theater! She could not understand it. Times were changing so fast and confusingly. These were the days of the Syndicate, a theatrical trust which booked shows and organized traveling companies for the entire country, and individual enterprise no longer seemed possible. These were the days of "stars," around whom whole spectacular productions were built. A handful of important producers were now running Broadway and entwining thousands of formerly independent theaters around the country in their grasp. Not only was Mrs. Drew unable to understand the new situation, there was nothing she could do to help Ethel. Her own touring days had come to an end, her theater in

Philadelphia was only a memory, and for the first time in her life she was a dependent and needed her son John to keep and care for her.

"But instead of drooping," Ethel remembered, "her back seemed to get straighter and straighter as she gazed out over the sinister rooftops of New York."

John Drew, however, saw to it that his graceful, slender niece received her opportunities. It was earlier in this same year that he had left the Augustin Daly stock company, in which he was highlighted with a group of three other actors that included the delightful Ada Rehan, to come under the management of the young and enterprising Charles Frohman, whose important booking organization had just joined together with the Syndicate and who was becoming known as a theatrical producer of consequence. Drew was already one of the most popular actors in the country; under Frohman he was now about to take his place as a great star.

To his apartment at the Sherman Square Hotel came such friends as Charles Dana Gibson (creator of the Gibson Girl), the young and brilliant Richard Harding Davis, and Arthur Leigh, who was later to become Lord Leigh and to give his house, Chequers, as the official residency of the British prime minister. Through John Drew, Ethel met "Dick" Davis, and Davis took it upon himself to introduce her to the young social set. If Ethel found the stage barred to her, there was no barrier to her attending important social functions. She met and made friends with a much-written-about debutante, Nancy Langhorne, and once shared a drawing room with Nancy on a trip to a brilliant wedding in Richmond. It was apparent that the name Drew in her lineage did count for something after all.

But now it was not her grandmother who gave luster to the name, but John Drew, who was thought of as the very best of "modern" actors, a dashing chap with an elegant mustache who interpreted the new concept of "gentleman" in modern plays. His forte was drawing room drama, and in real life he carried himself fully as proudly, dressed as impeccably as when on the stage.

His association with Charles Frohman strengthened his position immeasurably. Frohman, at the time he lured John Drew away from the venerable Augustin Daly, was still regarded as something of an interloper in the theatrical hierarchy. But Frohman, although only in his early thirties at the time, had a remarkable amount of experience in show business. While still in his teens he had traveled the country many times as "advance agent" for minstrel shows; at twenty he had managed one of the best and most popular of these shows, and had coined the phrase associated with such shows: "Forty—count 'em—forty." In 1890 he had produced a smash hit, *Shenandoah,* and in 1893 he had opened the Empire Theatre at Fortieth Street and Broadway, thus accelerating the movement of Broadway theater uptown.

Frohman, it might be mentioned, was one of the first to become aware of a change in America's theatrical structure. Nearly all of the famous independent actor-managers, who produced their own shows and managed their own bookings, were aging and due for retirement. The great days of Edwin Forrest, Madame Modjeska, and Clara Morris were all but over. Edwin Booth and Joseph Jefferson were about to quit the stage. Frohman sensed that the public was ready for new stars, for younger people with glowing personalities and stage magnetism. John Drew, as a matter of fact, was one of the cornerstones of his future plans.

Ethel could not possibly know that her future would someday be dictated by Charles Frohman, but it was the creation of the "star system" that prepared the ground for her own eventual emergence as a star. At the time all she could do was to doggedly persevere in her efforts to get work.

Frohman had recognized the fact that the public was captivated as much by personality as by acting accomplishment. They wanted to watch, he felt, fascinating people in productions that would "type" their best assets. Instead of taking under management the rounded actors of the past, who played a relatively small number of well-tried roles in play after play, he built a system of favorite stars who could be counted upon, year after year, to open in new and glittering productions. To Frohman the play was not so much the thing as the player. His experience in advertising and publicizing plays gave him the means to quickly accelerate the advance into stardom of someone he regarded as having star quality. No longer necessary was the long schooling in the theater, the laborious and endless touring, the many years required to reach a peak of recognition. Frohman became known as the star-maker.

He was a small man, somewhat rotund, with a genial, moonlike face. He was laconic, but his remarks were well chosen and pithy. The son of a German-Jewish cigar maker who had owned a cigar store in the heart of the downtown theatrical district, he had conceived a love for the theater before he was in his teens, and had posted bills for the same Charles Vandenhoff who was responsible for bringing Maurice Barrymore to this country. He had employed both Georgie and Maurice in some of the companies he had booked on road tours, and had given Georgie the second leading role in *Mrs. Wilkinson's Widows,* in which she made a hit shortly before she died.

When he acquired John Drew as a star, he paired him with a new young actress, Maude Adams. For their first vehicle he chose a French farce, *The Masked Ball,* and was prescient enough to have it adapted by a clever young playwright, whose name was Clyde Fitch, and who was later to provide the vehicle for Ethel's first venture into stardom. Frohman, Fitch, Drew, and Maude Adams all were "made" by *The Masked Ball.* Another of the stars he brought under his banner was William Gillette, both a playwright and a popular actor. Gillette wrote a melodrama for Frohman called *Secret Service,* the leading part of which was tried out on the road by Maurice Barrymore. However, it was Gillette who filled the role for its opening at the Garrick in New York; both he and the play made an instantaneous hit.

Through John Drew's influence Ethel's first good opportunity came in *The Bauble Shop,* a Frohman production that starred John Drew and Maude Adams with Elsie De Wolfe in support. Frohman consented to Drew's request that Ethel be given a job as tea-tray carrier on stage and as understudy to Miss De Wolfe off-stage. The assignment gave Ethel a weekly salary of thirty dollars, enough for her to support herself and to buy her own clothes, at age fifteen.

Probably the reason her dignified Uncle Jack went to such lengths on her behalf had something to do with the change in his own family plans. It had been decided to send his daughter, Louise, to France for her schooling, and for his wife and mother to accompany her there and chaperone her for a time. This meant that Ethel would have to be entirely on her own, and she needed money to live on. The salary she received from her job with *The Bauble Shop* enabled her to take a room at Mrs. Wilson's, a respectable theatrical boarding-house located at 162 West Thirty-sixth Street, where Maude Adams stayed with her mother. John Drew recommended the place to her, and for nine dollars a week she was given a hall bedroom and three meals a day. Also at Mrs. Wilson's was Ethel's cousin, Georgie Mendum, the daughter of Georgie Barrymore's sister, who had died in 1894. The two girls became devoted to each other, and Georgie Mendum remained more or less of a fixture in Ethel's life from then on.

When *The Bauble Shop,* after a three-month run, was scheduled for a tour, Elsie De Wolfe decided to stay in New York, leaving open the part of Lady Kate Fennell. John Drew was worried about leaving his niece alone in New York, so he asked Frohman to let Ethel replace Miss De Wolfe on the road. Although the part was written by Arthur Henry Jones as a fashionable lady of thirty-two, and Ethel was not yet sixteen, Drew pointed out that there was really not much in the part except sitting and standing around wearing fine clothes. Ethel played a matinee during the final days of the New York run, and Frohman decided that the tall fair-haired girl, wearing her hair in the latest French style and fitting nicely into Miss De Wolfe's fine costumes, provided a reasonable facsimile of Lady Kate.

Off Ethel went to tour Boston, Philadelphia, Chicago, and St. Louis. In Chicago she actually drew a line from a critic, who referred to her as "an opalescent dream named Ethel Barrymore that came on and played Lady Kate." She was an opalescent dream, indeed, possessed of a willowy figure, a radiant complexion, and large eyes, the color of which no one ever seemed to be fully certain, although they were usually described as blue, green, or a mixture of both. Her voice was full-throated and on the deep side. While in Baltimore she was invited to the swank Hunt Ball. One of the guests became drunkenly amorous and so frightened the shy girl that she fled in the snow all the way back to her hotel. In Washington her Uncle Jack took her to the British Embassy for a luncheon. In Cincinnati she met the prominent Longworths. And in Milwaukee she nearly lost her young life. Mistaking a knob for one that turned off the gaslight, she turned on the gas instead and was found in the morning unconscious. There were no long-lasting effects, however.

In Chicago she met the McCormacks and the Fields, and also George Ade and Finley Peter Dunne. Barely sixteen, she came out into the great world, and actually had a sort of debut at a debutante's ball. Her friends insisted that she go, even though her uncle objected to this strenuously. Her dream of becoming a concert pianist evaporated during the excitement of traveling and meeting people. How, she often asked afterward, did she manage to meet and become friends with so many? She never quite understood it herself, but she somehow, in spite of her shyness, exuded warmth. She carried herself at this young age straight and proudly.

A society reporter commented about Ethel in 1896: "Her manners are unaffected, and she has a frank unconventionality which is refreshing without being bizarre." Everyone, it seemed, loved Ethel, and how brave of her at so young an age to attempt to carry on the Drew-Barrymore tradition.

John Drew's next play was *The Imprudent Young Couple,* and Ethel appeared in it in a one-line part. "I wish I had a needle," she said, and for this was paid her same thirty dollars a week. The following season she was given the slightly larger part of a serving maid in *Rosemary,* which starred John Drew and Maude Adams.

"Your words r-oll and r-oll and r-oll," she said to her master in that play, and it was the first time the audience became aware of what was to become the famous Ethel Barrymore drawl. Even though the part was small, Ethel made enough of it to cause the critics to notice her, and not merely because she looked like an opalescent dream. The audience noticed her too, for on her entrance and exit she was applauded, a clear indication that they knew her to be a new member of the Drew-Barrymore stage family. Elderly Mrs. Drew, returned from Paris, came to see her granddaughter perform in *Rosemary.* "Please tell me how I did, Mum Mum," Ethel begged.

"You would have done very well," Mrs. Drew said with her customary severity, "If it had been possible to understand a word you said."

It was Ethel's great ambition now to go to London. She had

memories of that place as a small child, and the reading she had done—particularly Dickens—had created for her a romantic impression of the city. She had begun to have secret crushes, especially on William Gillette, the star of *Secret Service*. Luckily he held his matinees Thursday instead of the usual Wednesday, and Ethel was in admiring attendance at the theater at each one of those matinees, thrilling to the sight of his handsome, craggy profile. She had even bought his photograph, dipping into the little hoard of savings which she hoped would pile up enough to afford her a trip to London.

One night in St. Louis, while touring in *Rosemary,* John Drew called her to his dressing room. He handed Ethel a telegram. It read: WOULD ETHEL LIKE TO GO TO LONDON WITH GILLETTE IN SECRET SERVICE? It was signed: FROHMAN.

"I don't suppose you'd want to go," Drew said.

Her excitement was so great she could barely get the words out to the effect that this was a chance greater than any other that could possibly happen in the world. Ethel waited impatiently until Drew found someone to replace her and then took a train for New York, but not before writing to her father for letters of introduction both to Gillette and to people in London. Maurice greeted her in New York, told her he couldn't have been more pleased with the news, promised her the letters to friends in London, and said he would appear personally at the dock to introduce her to Gillette. He of course never appeared—at least not by sailing time.

But Ethel was still too high in the clouds to mind this disappointment. She went on board by herself and stood by the rail with Harry Woodruff, another actor in the company. Strolling along the deck came William Gillette, he of the chiseled profile and weary manner. "I don't *know* him," Ethel told Woodruff in an agony of expectation.

"Oh," Woodruff said, "why don't I introduce you?"

Gillette took her hand and bowed over it. What happened then was one of those tenuous, ineffable moments of significance, almost nothing at all, and yet something of shattering importance to Ethel. Gillette held the pretty girl's hand merely a half second too long. When he released it, Ethel's great crush was over. Oh, no, she thought, that isn't what I meant at all. Gillette, in that moment, was metamorphosed from a God into an ordinary male mortal.

But England did not disappoint. If she had fallen out of love with William Gillette, she immediately, upon coming out of Waterloo Station into a soft rain, fell in love with London. She found lodgings in Chapel Street. Her good friend Richard Harding Davis had sent letters to his friends, and they looked her up and took her out. Her part as Miss Kittredge in *Secret Service* was very small, but she had been engaged primarily as an understudy to the ingenue, Odette Tyler, and one night Miss Tyler conveniently fainted just before making her entrance. The curtain was rung down. Luckily Ethel's crush on Gillette, and her constant attendance at matinees, had made her thoroughly familiar with the part. Miss Tyler was taken off to the hospital wearing her stage clothes, and Ethel had to play the part in the clothes she was wearing. The next day she played it again, dressed as she was supposed to be. Word having gotten round that she was charming, some London critics came to see her, and praised her in print.

Odette Tyler was too ill to continue, and Ethel envisioned herself playing on and on in the role; but a new actress had meanwhile been sent for, and back Ethel went to the small old part, heartbroken, but at least she could remain in London. Her admiring friends told her she was wonderful, that she was much better than the new actress, and even advised her to stay in London, because they foresaw a brilliant future for her. Among those who were kindest to her were Ben Webster, an important actor, and his wife, May Whitty. The group Dick Davis had introduced her to included several literary lights, and, in her youthfulness, Ethel took it almost as a matter of course that she should be able to move in their circle. A young man, Laurence Irving (the son of the great actor, Sir Henry Irving), began paying marked attention to her. She met the Duke of York at one party, and the future king of England said to her: "Aren't you the little girl I saw in *Secret Service?*"

She gasped out that she was, and he told her that he had seen the play twice, had come back expressly, after seeing her in it, to take in her performance again, and was disappointed that someone not nearly so good was in her place. Yes, England was the place for her to be! And when *Secret Service* closed and the company sailed for home, Ethel was not with them. She had made up her mind to remain in London.

For her participation in the social life of the city she had two dresses, one black and one white. Sewing on and changing bits of trimming, she made them do. She paid for her lodgings with her small savings, and unless asked out for dinner subsisted on meals of dates, which she had discovered kept her from starving. But the triumphs that were supposed to be on their way did not come, much less jobs and money. Meanwhile John Drew came to London, and Ethel went to him and confessed her dire economic position. Was it too much to ask if she could return with him? Her imperturbable uncle told her that of course he would see to her passage and told her to pack. As she packed, Ethel's tears fell on one of her well-worn dresses. She had put the other aside to wear to a dinner party given as a farewell by Anthony Hope to her Uncle Jack.

A hansom cab stopped at the door of her rooming house. The cabbie had a note for her (it was *de rigueur* in London society to send messages by hansom cab) from Ellen Terry, asking Ethel to "come down to the theater tonight to say good-by to Sir Henry Irving and me."

At the Lyceum Theatre Ellen Terry said to Ethel: "Sir Henry wants to say good-by to you."

She went into the actor's dressing room. Irving said: "You're going back to America, I hear. Wouldn't you like to stay in England?"

"Oh, of course," Ethel said.

"Would you like to play with me?" he asked.

She had all she could do to keep from fainting before him, but she remained erect and said "Ye-es!"

Irving told her he had a part for her in *The Bells,* the play he was about to do with his co-star Ellen Terry, and that contracts were ready for her to sign in the manager's office. Ethel floated from the theater to the supper party. Mrs. Patrick Campbell, one of the guests, called to Ethel in her deep-throated voice that she had heard she was sailing the next day, and Ethel answered in her own deep tones: "Oh, but I'm not!"

The table was all inquiries. Her uncle asked her what she intended to do in London, and Ethel was able to inform him that she had just signed a contract with Sir Henry Irving and Ellen Terry. She was unaware, however, of the matchmaking role being played by Ellen Terry. Laurence Irving, Sir Henry's son, had fallen hopelessly in love with Ethel, and the compassionate Miss Terry had seen to it that he have his chance with the charming American girl.

During the several weeks of free time in London before she was to begin rehearsing with Sir Henry Irving, Ethel heard that her grandmother had taken seriously ill. She decided she would make a quick trip home to see her. But how to do this was a problem, because no salary was as yet coming in. In desperation she cabled Richard Harding Davis in New York, and almost at once the hundred dollars was wired back. What she did not know was that Davis was away, and that his father had read the cable and sent the money.

Mrs. Drew by this time, the spring of 1897, had moved to a boardinghouse in Larchmont, New York, taking John Barrymore to stay with her. The family was, as usual, scattered, and few of them knew—because of her habitual reticence—how much her health had failed. John brought her the paper-backed novels she liked to read, arranged her cushions for her, and before tucking her in bed at night would rub her feet.

Ethel stayed at Larchmont for a week, and during that time she vowed to herself that when her salary of ten pounds a week began coming in she would have her grandmother moved from her third-floor room to a lower floor so that it wouldn't be necessary for her to climb the stairs each day. She noticed how pleasant a rapport had been established between the old woman and young Jack who listened patiently to the tangled thread of his grandmother's reminiscences. Jack told Ethel how pleased Mrs. Drew was that she was going to play with Sir Henry, but the only reference made by the seventy-seven-year-old trouper directly to Ethel was: "Can you always understand what he says?"

One evening, not long after Ethel had hurried back to England, Jack helped his grandmother as usual up to her room. He tucked her coverlets about her, and just before falling asleep she reached out and patted his arm. She fell asleep, but never awakened.

A sister of Mrs. Drew attended to the funeral arrangements. Telegrams and cablegrams went everywhere: to Salt Lake City, where John Drew was playing in *Rosemary*; to Lionel, who was acting a minor part on the road; to Uncle Googan, who was touring in Australia; and to Ethel in London.

The cable reached her just as she was about to leave for the theater for her first rehearsal with Irving, and she took some time to compose herself, thus committing the all but unforgivable sin of being late. Henry Irving gave her a cold look as she quietly joined the rest of the company on the stage, and she explained to him that she had just received some very bad news.

"What was it?" he asked.

"A cable just came," she said, "telling me my grandmother has died."

"Mrs. John Drew?" he asked.

"Yes."

"Go home, my dear," Henry Irving said gently. "There will be no rehearsal for you today."

Mrs. Drew was buried next to Georgie in Glenwood Cemetery, Philadelphia. She had left instructions that a verse be inscribed on her tomb, and John Drew obeyed them. The epitaph read:

> *Life! we've been long together,*
> *Through pleasant and through cloudy weather;*
> *'Tis hard to part when friends are dear;*
> *Perhaps 'twill cause a sigh, a tear;*
> *Then steal away, give little warning,*
>   *Choose thine own time;*
>   *Say not Good-Night, but in some brighter clime,*
>   *Bid me Good-morning.*

Being part of Sir Henry Irving's company proved to be fully as exciting to Ethel as she had hoped. She had parts in both *The Bells* and a play that Irving's son, Laurence, had written, called *Peter the Great*, which were alternated in London and also during a tour of the English towns. She admired Sir Henry immensely, and was drawn toward his son. Laurence as a student had been sent to Russia, where he became infected with typical Russian literary somberness, one fruit of which was his melancholy play about Peter. In London he often took tea with Ethel in a flat she shared with an American friend, Suzanne Sheldon. Ethel was entranced by his gently solemn moods, and played melancholy Russian pieces for him on the piano. She found their brooding seances so delightful, not to say original, that she accepted his offer of marriage.

She at once sent a cable to her father with the news of her engagement, and Maurice cabled back: CONGRATULATIONS LOVE FATHER.

As soon as it was officially confirmed to Laurence that Ethel was his bride-to-be, his dark mood lifted, and he revealed another personality, one which disappointed Ethel. She had been prepared to lead a life full of brown, tragically beautiful moods, and here was her partner, suddenly cheerful and hearty. In that mood she simply couldn't bear him. It took all her courage to tell first Laurence and then Sir Henry that she had made a mistake. Sir Henry was perfectly understanding, if Laurence was not.

Ethel once more went to the cable office, and sent her father the news of her broken engagement. Maurice cabled back: CONGRATULATIONS LOVE FATHER.

But the gay, stimulating life she led in London soon produced another fiancé for Ethel. This was Gerald du Maurier, son of George du Maurier, the creator of Trilby and Peter Ibbetson. The two were seen everywhere together, and it was taken as a matter of course that there could be no hindrance to their wedding. According to Ethel, Gerald had charm, wit, and gaiety to make up for his lack of good looks. His family was delighted with his choice, and spoke of having the wedding as soon as possible.

In June of 1898 the New York *Morning Telegraph* publicly revealed some of its own qualms about the approaching wedding. "Mr. du Maurier," wrote a correspondent, "impressed most of those who beheld him as being scarcely ripe. His physique was frail to the point of attenuation, his legs looked for all the world like a couple of sectional gas-pipes with abrupt bony projections midway between the floor and their jointure to the trunk." As for Ethel, the following comment was made: "She, in all the radiance of her young loveliness, will be far and away the spectacular feature of the wedding."

But suddenly Ethel felt she must make a trip home. For what? wondered the bewildered mother of Gerald. Ethel did not explain, and off she went, with Gerald taking her to the train, and tears streaming down her cheeks at what she knew was a final good-by to him.

The New York *Telegraph* had come very close to guessing at the truth. Ethel broke off the engagement when Mrs. du Maurier began to tell her how to take care of Gerald, what to make him wear in winter, and what it was best for him to eat. She knew that she had to leave.

The heartbroken Gerald eventually married someone else and had a daughter named Daphne, who, when she wrote a book about her father, had this to say of Ethel at the time of his courtship of her: "She wore her hair in a pig-tail, with a crimson tam-o-shanter, and looked elfin and adorable, and never more than fourteen."

The news was a matter of public comment in the United States well before she had arrived. "Americans are being kept in a continual state of suspense over the matrimonial prospects of Ethel Barrymore," said the New York *Telegraph*. "Tidings have come that she has broken the engagement to Gerald du Maurier."

Ethel had missed the ship she was supposed to take at Liverpool, and had gotten on the Canada-bound *Vancouver* instead, which dropped her off at Quebec. From there she had to take the night train to New York. Arriving at Grand Central Station she found she had exactly one quarter in her bag. She gave this grandly to the redcap who carried her bag to a hansom outside. "Where to, miss?" asked the cab driver. Her London training was such that she immediately thought of the then most expensive hotel in the world, the Waldorf. "Drive me to the Waldorf," she said imperiously. At the hotel several clerks greeted her with pleased smiles at her entrance, and she thought for a moment they had mistaken her for someone else. But she was addressed as Miss Barrymore and told how happy they were to have her. And it turned out her uncle, John Drew, was also in the hotel. "I'll have a room," she said, with relief. "And," she added languidly, "will you pay my cab, please?"

A little later she discussed her situation with her uncle, who was surprised to find her in New York. Ethel wanted some work in a play, and John Drew said he would arrange for her to see Charles Frohman. Although she had been in the great manager's employ before going to England, she had never been noticed by him (so she thought) and was in awe of him. Her uncle took her to Frohman's office the next day, her first visit to a place that was to become very familiar to her.

Frohman was kind. "You look like your mother," he said. "I was always very fond of her." He had a play going into rehearsal called *Catherine,* and there was a small part . . . Ethel took it, and on the assurance of a salary of thirty-five dollars a week moved back into Mrs. Wilson's boardinghouse on Thirty-sixth Street. She spoke only a few lines in the play—although she wore two beautiful dresses, which had to be paid for out of her own earnings—and yet when she walked on stage she received an ovation from the audience.

The ovation embarrassed her, for there seemed nothing to justify it, except her dress. But the audience seemed satisfied merely to see her. The stories that had come out of London had whetted their interest in this nineteen-year-old girl. Ethel, without knowing it, without having heard the term before, had become a glamour girl! She continued to live frugally, however, saving her money for a trip back to her beloved England.

When *Catherine* went on tour the applause continued for Ethel. On a few occasions she was allowed to play the leading role, which she understudied. Charles Frohman said to a friend: "There is going to be a big development in one of my companies before long. There's a daughter of Barry who gets a big reception wherever she goes. She has the real stuff in her."

THE ABNORMAL
SPROUTS

chapter V

"IT WAS CONCEDED in our acting family," Lionel said, "that Jack and I were abnormal sprouts, slow to blossom, but eventually due to floriate by the nature of our seed pods." This floriation was a slow process and in no way resembled the exciting rise of their sister. In fact, Lionel and John spent their youth searching for ways to avoid the family fate, and picked art as their preference. Lionel spent three years studying at the Art Students League, a period interrupted by several attempts at acting. When Sidney Drew joined the McKee Rankin Stock Company, after the retirement of Mrs. Drew, he persuaded Rankin to employ Lionel. Rankin was married to a popular actress, Kitty Blanchard, from whom he had separated after she bore him two children—Gladys (who married Sidney Drew) and Phyllis (who became the wife of Harry Davenport, a well-known actor). During the period of separation, Rankin had another daughter, Doris, and when he and his wife came together again, Kitty Blanchard adopted the little girl as their own.

Lionel appeared in *Magda* as Max, a young officer, and as it turned out, John played the same part several years later when he made his formal debut on the stage. Usually Lionel appeared in any role for which no one else was available. Gradually he came to feel more at home on the stage, and absorbed the necessary technique by simple observation. He discovered as the company moved on from city to city that he was getting better parts. In Rankin's own adaptation of *Oliver Twist,* Lionel was given two parts, Joey and Toby Crockett. Fast at memorizing, he learned both parts quickly and felt competent in the roles, even though it had become necessary for some reason to cancel the full dress rehearsal. But in one of his scenes, during the first performance in Minneapolis, he was shocked to discover that *both* his characters were supposed to be on stage at the same time.

He rallied and made the best of the situation. As Toby he talked to the supposed Joey through a window of the set. He made up another voice for Joey to answer back with. McKee Rankin was delighted with Lionel's ventriloquistic ability and told him to keep doing the scene that way. This saved him from having to hire another actor.

His roommate and companion during the tour was a former newspaperman, Frank Butler, who had become an actor. Butler was an ebullient near-alcoholic, and Lionel had companionable sessions with him at various saloons and bars. But Butler was unable to stop drinking in time to give sober performances on the stage, and in Minneapolis Rankin decided to let him go. Butler visited a local newspaper, charmed the city editor, and was given a job—as the paper's dramatic critic. He wasted no time in concentrating his diatribes on the Rankin season in Minneapolis. Even Lionel was not immune.

Lionel picked up the paper one morning in his hotel room and read:

> There is one performance that manages to stand out more loathesomely than the others. A dreadful young actor, whose name I believe is Barrymore, was so hideously inept in his role that when at last he left the stage the audience remained in continual terror that he might return.

Butler, still Lionel's roommate, regarded the review as a wonderful joke, but a bad notice was a bad notice, and Lionel did not appreciate it. Butler did not last long in Minneapolis. He was fired from the paper for directing his criticism at the entire city.

In the smaller towns, where they played one-night stands, Lionel liked to take long walks into the relative freedom of the country.

One afternoon in Gainesville, Texas, he wandered out of town along a prairie road. A girl and a boy in a buggy drawn by two horses overtook him and offered him a lift. He climbed in and discovered they were headed for a local sport known as rabbit chasing. At the rendezvous point several horsemen were waiting, and other young people were in various vehicles drawn by horses.

They went after several rabbits that had been let loose, and Lionel's driver managed to maintain a lead, with the girl laughing and screaming and the boy urging his horses on like a jockey. The rabbits were never caught, but everyone had a marvelous time. There were drinks passed around when the chase was over, and then everyone jogged back toward Gainesville. Lionel had never felt such a sense of well-being and happiness. The boy companionably asked him what business he was in.

"I'm an actor," Lionel said.

The girl and the boy became noticeably cool, and from then on they addressed Lionel as "sir." The buggy was stopped at the edge of town, and the boy remained silent, as though tongue-tied. The girl said: "Sir, we are not allowed to be seen with show people."

Lionel got out and sadly shook hands with them.

At the end of the century one of the most popular plays on Broadway was *Arizona* by Augustus Thomas. When a play was a success of magnitude in New York, several road companies were usually sent out to cross and crisscross the country, exploiting its popularity until every last penny was milked from it. One of these road companies employed Lionel, who, although only twenty-one, had become reasonably adept at playing character parts. In *Arizona* he played a man seventy years of age, even though he had the good looks to play romantic leads if he had wanted to. But Lionel was content to disguise himself in any and every get-up. He didn't take the theater seriously enough to have any great ambitions in it, and character parts he thought of as more enjoyable. They formed a perfect foil for his shy, reserved nature, and he had an unusual facility for developing the different voices needed.

A New York producer, James A. Herne, happened to see Lionel perform in *Arizona*, thought him good, and went backstage to meet him. He was astonished to meet, instead of an old man, a young, husky actor, about six feet tall, with the compelling eyes of the Drew family. Herne told Lionel that he was wasting himself as a doddering old man in a second-rate production of *Arizona;* furthermore, he said, he was willing to use him in a New York production, soon to be gotten under way, of a play called *Sag Harbor.* Lionel, although a veteran of several years on the stage by this time, had never performed before a New York audience and was hesitant about giving up the security of the long-running and ever popular play he was in. He was flattered to be considered a good actor, but told Herne he didn't think he ought to leave.

"I'll give you more money," Herne said, and that was the clincher. The offer came to a salary of thirty-five dollars a week, considerably more than Lionel was then earning.

Sag Harbor came to the Republic Theater in New York on September 27, 1900, and provided Lionel with his Broadway debut. For almost the first time, Lionel acted his real age on the stage and failed to impress a single one of the New York critics. The experience convinced him that he couldn't play a young man, no matter how well he could play old men. It was a puzzling thing, but even Herne realized he was a complete fizzle in his pink-cheeked role, and after a few performances he admitted to Lionel that he had led him astray. To soften the blow he said that the part was an impossible one anyway.

But there were other circumstances besides bad acting to account for Lionel's abrupt dismissal. Herne had two attractive daughters. Lionel took a fancy to both, and they to him, and Herne felt that the young man's method of courtship was too fiery and might lead to unfortunate results. He wanted Lionel out of the way before any real damage was done. "I suggest," said Herne, "you take a vacation, think things over. It's my guess if you handle yourself right you'll have a brilliant career."

With nothing else in sight for him, Lionel was forced to take a vacation, and, his salary cut off, took to sharing rooms in a tenement on Thirtieth Street with two friends, Jack Gallatin and William Carpenter Camp, both young men of good family but just as short of dollars as he was. From this headquarters he began making the rounds of the theatrical agencies in earnest. The thing he could do best was acting, and so acting it would be, that is, until he could find a convenient way of escaping from the profession. He heard of three brothers who were in the process of carving out a theatrical empire for themselves, Jake, Lee, and Sam Shubert by name, and applied to Sam Shubert for a job. When the small, busy man asked him what his salary was, Lionel took a deep breath, reminded himself he was a Barrymore, and named the dizzy figure of seventy-five dollars a week.

Shubert, also aware that he would be getting a Barrymore, agreed to the seventy-five-dollar figure but held out for Lionel's supplying his own dress clothes for the part he had in mind for him. These Lionel borrowed from one of his roommates, who received in return a share of the actor's salary. The play, *The Brixton Burglary*, had forty-eight performances at the Herald Square. During off hours Lionel played sandlot baseball, well enough to be eyed by minor league scouts, kept at his painting, and took up a new pursuit, music. A friend of the family, Thomas G. Patten (later the post-master of New York City), had a fine player piano. During visits to him Lionel would place his fingers in the depressions of the keys as the piano operated and in a short time he learned to play pass-ably. Deciding to follow up this new talent, he took lessons from a Mrs. Agnes Morgan. After some progress had been made in this new direction he approached a famous composer of the period, Henry Hadley, and demonstrated to him his pianistic gifts.

"One thing certain," Hadley told him, "you're never going to make a pianist. You'd better take up composing." This Lionel did, and he kept it up for the rest of his life.

Lionel made news in another way at about this time. A newspaper headline read: NOTED YOUNG ACTOR KNOCKED OUT BY SULLIVAN. The event took place at a restaurant called Jack's which Lionel patronized with other young New York actors. One evening after finishing a performance of *The Brixton Burglary* Lionel dropped in at Jack's wearing the typical hat of the time, a derby. He kept it on, as was the practice at Jack's. John L. Sullivan's idea of a joke was to walk up to some unsuspecting chap, take a swing at his derby, strike it just above the wearer's head, and sail it across the restaurant.

Lionel was standing at the bar, engaged in talk, when Sullivan came in and took a swing at his derby. Lionel tried to dodge, and woke up half an hour later. In trying to avoid what he thought was a real blow he threw Sullivan's timing off. Sullivan was apologetic, an unusual thing in itself, and bought everyone drinks for the rest of the evening.

Lionel decided the experience was salutary on the whole. He came to the conclusion that he had been hit because he had gotten slow from too much drinking, eating too heavily, and keeping irregular hours. He made up his mind to keep himself in condition thereafter, and the next day took up boxing and wrestling at a gymnasium. There were periods when he let down, but he kept up his interest in boxing for a great many years, and made it a point to know most of the boxing champions as they came along. There were several stories of how he came to be afflicted with a bad knee in later life, but one fairly credible one had to do with his wrestling workouts with a champion of the day, Stanislaus Zybysko. Lionel broke his kneecap in one of these friendly bouts and neglected to allow it to heal properly. Lameness eventually set in, but even in advanced middle age, with a leg that could give way on him at any time, he would keep at the punching bag.

And it was always a point of pride with him that he had been knocked out by Sullivan.

John was sent to England by Maurice, after the death of Mrs. Drew, to acquire a good British education. At age fifteen he was entered in King's College, Wimbledon, where Maurice's brother-in-law, Henry Wace, was the headmaster. John made little headway in his studies but attracted notice on the football (rugby) field as goalkeeper. Bringing to the game a knowledge of American football, he tackled fiercely, covered himself with mud and glory, and was immensely admired by his teammates. The teachers seem to have thought less of him, for he remained at King's for only a year—long enough, however, for him to acquire a fondness for the official jacket of the college, which he wore proudly many years later. At sixteen he was a boy of slightly less than average height, on the skinny side, but enormously good-looking none the less. His hair at this age was worn wild and long, and this gave him a poetic appearance. He was precocious at drinking and also at romance. A young married duchess was rumored to be extremely fond of him.

Ben Webster and May Whitty let him use the spare sofa-bed in their Bedford Street flat when he was not in school, which was often. He had a habit at this time of wheedling small sums of money from his friends and relatives. Once he borrowed two pounds from May Whitty on the vague excuse that he was supposed to meet his sister at Waterloo Station. He disappeared for three days, driving Ethel frantic, and when he wandered back gave no explanation of where he had been. After he left King's College, the Waces took him in for a time.

Ethel determined to keep a watchful eye on John, and took him with her to large parties in the hope that he would get to meet a wholesome group of people. This helped little, for John was shy at parties, and would usually hide himself away in inconspicuous corners or talk to the servants, with whom he felt more at home. An elderly man who seemed to be a butler got into a conversation with him, and John spent a pleasant hour chattering away.

"What did you talk about all evening with Henry James?" Ethel asked curiously, later.

Ethel also, seeing that her younger brother was serious about his artistic ambitions, persuaded him to enroll at the Slade School of Art in London. Aubrey Beardsley was the prevailing influence on young artists at the time, and Jack modeled his efforts on the effete master's style. He received some encouragement at the Slade School, for he showed a mild talent for water colors.

John stayed alone in London throughout the winter and spring of 1899, for his sister was on tour in *Catherine* in the United States. After finishing the tour, Ethel, mustering up her courage, asked Charles Frohman for the leading role in *His Excellency, the Governor,* a play she had seen in England. A comic adventuress called Stella de Gex was the part she wanted. "I would like to play Stella," she told Frohman.

"Really?" asked Frohman, with a discreet smile. "So does Ellen Terry." He told Ethel he doubted she was quite ripe enough in age, face, and figure to play Stella, but if she wanted to rehearse the part and show it to him he would take a look at her.

Ethel studied the role and went alone on the stage of the Empire one morning. One dim light hung down from the ceiling and her audience of one was Charles Frohman. "You're very much like your mother, my dear," Frohman told her, using almost the same words he had used once before. Ethel didn't know if she had been given the part or not and waited hopefully for the cast list to be announced. When the list came out her name was nowhere to be found on it. Frohman hadn't had the heart to turn her down then and there.

But with her savings from the tour of *Catherine* she headed straight for London again, where she found John had lost some of his shyness and made some friends of his own, including a wizened little jockey, Ted Sloan, who had won several big races. She took rooms for herself and John for a few weeks at Cockham. She, too, made new friends. One of these was Millie, the young, beautiful, and fabulously wealthy Duchess of Sutherland. She was invited to stay at Stafford House, the great house of the Sutherlands in London, and at Dunrobin, their famous castle in Scotland. Through Millie Sutherland she met Margot and Henry Asquith, Herbert and Dolly Gladstone, and Arthur Balfour. John went along with her to Dunrobin and distinguished himself by outdiving two famous women swimmers and divers who gave an exhibition for the house guests. By the end of the summer Ethel's savings were gone. It was time to head for home and work, and she decided to take John with her. Her seventeen-year-old brother had gotten himself involved in a liaison with a titled married woman twice his age, and there were already rumblings of legal action by the outraged husband. E. Lestocq, the manager of Frohman's London interests, advanced the money for their passages.

Back in New York, John Barrymore persuaded his father to pay for a year's tuition for him at the Art Students League, but managed to turn up for only one class. When his absences were reported to Maurice, the elder Barrymore merely said: "I can't understand how you managed to go even once." John next decided that the peculiar

nature of his artistic genius demanded studies at a school run by
the famous American painter, George Bridgman. Bridgman took an
interest in John, both in class and out, and John later gave him much
credit for teaching him about both art and life. When his enthusiasm
was aroused, John was capable of hard, serious work; and when
members of his family began to notice his devoted attention to
drawing and painting, they conquered their suspicion of any other
work besides acting and saw to it that he had the means to continue.

John Drew took a room for him, for a time, at the Algonquin
Hotel, where he himself was then staying, and then Ethel suggested
that it would be cheaper for the boy to stay at Mrs. Wilson's, where
a small room was available at reasonable rent. Ethel paid for this
room, as she did for another room for Lionel during one of his
periodic "vacations." Once established at Mrs. Wilson's, John
promptly fell in love with the star boarder, Maude Adams. Miss
Adams was a remote personage, a full ten years older than her suitor,
and she treated John's ardor as one more symptom of the general
adulation she took as a matter of course.

Hardly discouraged, John next turned his attention to the beautiful, willowy Ida Conquest, an important star who also lived at the
theatrical boardinghouse. She was a more worldly sort of woman
than Maude Adams, and considerately she explained to John that
she had neither the time nor inclination to help raise a young boy
to manhood.

John, in his eighteenth year, conceived an intense admiration for
his uncle's manner—imitating it in a half-mocking way—and also
for his uncle's wardrobe. When he received an invitation to a large
party given at a house of consequence, he went to his uncle's apartment and helped himself to the clothes he thought most suitable
for the occasion. Unfortunately he selected the very dinner jacket
that John Drew was planning to wear the same evening. If Drew
had known that his nephew was wearing the jacket he would have
chosen another, but his valet, upon receiving orders for the clothes
he was to lay out for the evening, rushed after John, invaded the
house where the party was in progress, and informed his quarry
that the jacket was to be immediately relinquished. John agreed, on
condition that the valet give him his own jacket in place of Drew's.

"Good God, man," John said. "Do you realize that the honor of the Drew family is at stake?"

John returned to the gathering and explained that a poor acquaintance had asked for his jacket, and that out of compunction he had given it up. As Ethel put it: "Around this time Jack lost his shyness."

It was also at this time that John conceived his admiration for newspapermen and the life they led. In the evenings he sought the company of the newspapermen who gathered at a boardinghouse on Thirty-fourth Street run by a warm-hearted woman, Minnie Hay.

Minnie Hay's was the place where it was possible to meet almost anyone who wrote or drew for the newspapers. On Saturday nights the revels were particularly festive, and guests were expected by the hostess to bring some contribution. John, being penniless most of the time, was not able to add anything in the way of drink or food and felt bad about it. But Ethel had happened to tell him about the odd gift sent her by Colonel John Jacob Astor, whom she had met at a supper party.

During a conversation with her, Astor inquired as to whether she liked grapefruit. Indeed she did, she said. Grapefruit were still regarded as a novelty, and the next morning a whole crate of the fruit arrived at her boardinghouse. While she was out one Saturday, John and a friend "borrowed" the entire crate and transported it to Minnie Hay's. John basked in a warm glow of approval for the whole evening.

At Minnie Hay's he met Frank Butler, who had shared a room with Lionel in Minneapolis, and who was presently working as a reporter for the New York *Morning Telegraph*. Butler decided one evening, after a dinner that had included several rounds of drinks, that the Victory figure on top of the Dewey Arch in Madison Square needed improvement. This figure held a sword in its hand. With two newspaper artists, Carl Decker and Rip Anthony, also good friends of John, an expedition was mounted to the arch. John, being the youngest and most agile, was boosted part way up the statue, and climbed the remainder of the height by himself. He came down triumphantly bearing the sword and the four men paraded up

Broadway with it. At each bar they entered, the story of the exploit was told and retold, and John was the hero of the hour.

But because John labored industriously by day at his drawing, Ethel was impressed with him. She once discussed her brother with a friend of hers, Cissie Loftus, a celebrated young leading woman. "It's too bad Jack can't get started seriously in his career," Ethel said loyally. "He's talented, but he needs the recognition."

"But what does he do?" Miss Loftus asked, not aware that John was working at anything.

Upon being told that he was an artist, Cissie Loftus spoke to Daniel Frohman, the brother of Charles Frohman, under whose management she was. Frohman, with the ready generosity always reserved for a Barrymore or a Drew, commissioned John to do a poster for *If I Were King,* the play about Francois Villon. Bridgman helped him with the poster, which turned out very well and was displayed prominently. John's pay for this fledgling effort was ten dollars, the usual fee.

Encouraged, he entered some drawings in an exhibition at The Press Artists' League. One, a drawing of a hangman walking a road and casting a shadow that suggested a gallows, was purchased for ten dollars. Jack asked the name of the purchaser who had recognized his talent, and learned it was Andrew Carnegie, the multimillionaire.

John was sensitive to art, and his knowledge of it was voluminous. Whenever he had a spare dollar he collected prints and pen and ink drawings. He knew the names of even the most obscure artists, and could identify their work at a glance. To get extra money both John and Lionel hired themselves out as artists models. John posed for a lean, young artist with a beard, the aforementioned Rip Anthony, who usually paid by taking his model out for meals. Lionel, through Augustus Thomas, met Frederic Remington and impressed the famous artist of the West with his ability to mimic the faces of the men in his paintings. Remington asked Lionel to pose for him, and although Lionel is not recognizable, he portrayed Indians, settlers, and cavalry officers in several paintings by Remington.

"In those years," Lionel said, "Jack and I practiced similar techniques. We associated with friends who had no more money than we and made certain that we met people who might be charmed or persuaded into buying us food and drink."

John, after a while, was able to count on selling an occasional advertising drawing to a clothing firm. He came across a small studio for rent on Fourteenth Street near Sixth Avenue, and kept up the bare, cold place with handouts from Ethel and odd jobs he found occasionally. One of these was obtaining testimonials for a shaving lotion called Schaeferine. He got the job because he was the nephew of John Drew and could unconditionally guarantee a testimonial for the product from the famous actor. John, who received five dollars per testimonial, suggested that the preparation might also be advertised as a general face lotion. Acting on this, the company felt a testimonial from Ethel Barrymore would be worth the five-dollar fee. She was out on tour, but John sent her a wire and waited impatiently for her testimonial to arrive so he could earn his five dollars.

At last it came: "To the owners of Schaeferine Water: I have used your very palatable beverage, and henceforth will have no other water served at my table."

Young Barrymore approached other celebrities, among them Nat Goodwin, the actor. Goodwin enabled the boy to earn his five dollars by sending a testimonial, but wrote John a personal note: "I have used Schaeferine. My lawyer will see you in the morning."

Ethel was finally able to report to her friends that John had obtained regular employment. He was hired by the New York *Journal* to illustrate Arthur Brisbane's weekly column of editorial comment. He did other drawings for the paper, including illustrations of verses by Ella Wheeler Wilcox. The sentimental Miss Wilcox, dismayed by the gloomy, heavily symbolic cast of Jack's drawings, wondered if she couldn't have someone younger and less pessimistic than that elderly fellow Barrymore to do her illustrations.

Brisbane told Jack to pay her a visit. He went to the Hoffman House where she was living and told her that he was Barrymore.

"Your father should have come here himself," she reprimanded him.

When he explained that he was the artist, Miss Wilcox invited him in, and after a long talk was charmed enough to call Brisbane and tell him that no one but Jack Barrymore was to do her drawings.

73

Some weeks later he was given the assignment of covering a distinguished wedding between an American society girl and a French-
man of noble pedigree. The city editor, a man named Carvalho,
impressed upon Jack the necessity of delivering the sketches to him in
person, because he wanted to beat the other papers. John covered the
wedding, did his drawings, strolled into Keen's Chop House, met
friends in the grillroom, then, with the drawings still under his arms,
went into The Lambs next door and after that stopped at Rector's.
Long after midnight he found himself in front of Carvalho's residence
on Riverside Drive. He had remembered to deliver the sketches in
person. He rang the bell, got no response, rattled the door, and, in
desperation, tossed stones at the upper windows. A window opened
and a head peered out.

"Is that you, Mr. Carvalho?" John asked.

"Yes. What do you mean disturbing me at this hour?"

"I'm Barrymore—with the sketches."

"You're discharged—with the sketches," Carvalho shouted, and
banged down the window.

John's newspaper career ended at this point, but he continued to
live the life of a bohemian, though well-connected, artist. One of
his projects was the compiling of a folio of his pen and ink drawings,
and these were evidently displayed in an art gallery, for a critique
of the artistic work of John Barrymore appeared in *Cosmopolitan*
magazine, the issue of January, 1902, along with four illustrations
called "Despair," "Unrest," "Fear," and "Jealousy."

The critic wrote: "Mr. Barrymore displays considerable power of
thought and technique. The anatomy of his work is correct, and his
work is well ordered. The emotions he portrays are the strong emotions
of strong men. Mr. Barrymore's pictures give great promise for his
future . . ." There was more, and it seems not to have been realized
by the critic that he was discussing the efforts of a youth who had
not yet reached his twenty-first birthday.

John Drew was asked about the drawings in this folio and gave
another kind of estimation. "I remember one," he said, "entitled 'The
Web of Life,' in which a lot of weird people were trying to get across
some place. It was accompanied by an explanation which began,
'This is not an unpleasant picture when looked at properly.' "

Gene Fowler mentioned in *Good Night, Sweet Prince* that John summed up his talent himself by saying, "I might have been, but I wasn't."

Fowler went on to say that John had "an abiding passion for art, a driving imagination, a compelling sense of color. Yet he never approached, in terms of technique and fulfillment, the earnest accomplishments of Lionel, either in oils or at etching, mediums in which Lionel excelled. His water colors were rather successful, several of them indicating superior taste and feeling. In none of Barrymore's drawings can there be found a line of pornography, real or implied, whether among the crowded, random pencilings of the walls of his telephone nooks, or among his papers or canvases. This from a man deemed blatantly erotic by so many commentators."

This amounts to a negative sort of praise for John Barrymore's artistic efforts, which to present-day eyes do reveal less genuine talent and proficiency than clues to his youthful mental states. He seems for the most part to have called upon his nightmares for subject matter: monsters and weird half-human forms struggling to emerge from deep and dark chasms. Through most of his life he spoke wistfully about the career in art he had abandoned and that he felt would have given him a much greater sense of fulfillment than acting. But the evidence is lacking in his youthful work that he would have been anything more than a proficient illustrator.

When John was twenty-one the evidence that he had a future as an actor was lacking too. He was twenty when he wandered onto a stage for the first time as an adult, and he did little other than deliberately make a fool of himself. Frohman happened to be a witness on this occasion, and the canny little producer saw certain possibilities in the youngest Barrymore. He knew a good potential comedian when he saw one. In fact, Frohman was the one who recognized the potentialities of all three Barrymores, although in 1901 it was Ethel who claimed most of his attention. Lionel and John had to wait until Ethel made the grade. Until then they remained in her shadow.

Mrs. John Drew, the grandmother of the three Barrymores. Born Louisa Lane, she was a celebrated actress, manager of the Arch Street Theatre in Philadelphia and the founder of an American acting dynasty.

John Drew, Jr., son of Mrs. John Drew. An excellent light comedian, known as "The Gentleman Actor," he was the brother of Georgie Drew and the celebrated uncle of the Barrymores.

The Arch Street Theatre in Philadelphia, which Mrs. John Drew managed for nearly a quarter of a century. Many of America's great actors played here, among them Edwin Booth and Madame Helena Modjeska.

Maurice Barrymore, the transplanted Englishman whose real name was Herbert Blythe. He risked the wrath of Mrs. John Drew by marrying Georgie Drew and became the father of Lionel, Ethel and John Barrymore.

Georgie Drew Barrymore. The gifted mother of the Barrymores was a captivating comedienne and a woman known for her resourceful wit. She died shortly after reaching her full flower as a leading lady in comedy.

Georgie Drew Barrymore, in a rare photograph taken with her children probably in 1887. Lionel is at her right, and the dreamy-eyed boy just below him is John Barrymore, age five.

Ethel Barrymore came to stardom at the age of twenty-one in *Captain Jinks of the Horse Marines*, after being groomed by producer and star-maker, Charles Frohman. Above is a poster announcing Ethel in a play at the Garrick Theatre.

Ethel, at twenty-one, as she appeared in Act I of *Captain Jinks*. She played Madame Trentoni, an opera singer from Europe visiting American shores for the first time, and reputed to be of great wealth.

The three Barrymores were seldom photographed together during their early stage years. The picture above was probably not posed, but instead the result of joining two separate photographs.

Ethel displayed her versatility in 1903 by playing a lonely French boy in a curtain-raiser called *Carrots* and a young Englishwoman in a lengthier play called *A Country Mouse* given on the same bill.

Ethel in Pinero's *Mid-Channel*, with H. Reeves-Smith as the Honorable Peter Mottram, and Charles Dalton as Theodore Blundell. Prognostications for the success of this 1910 Frohman production were not favorable, but Ethel's performance as Zoë Blundell made it into a hit.

John Barrymore in *The Fortune Hunter* (1909). John is here seen as a clerk in a small-town drug store, the role which established him as one of Broadway's favorite light comedians.

Lionel Barrymore as an old clown *Pantaloon*, a short Barrie piece played with his brother in 1905-6 Almost four years intervened until was seen on the stage again, for duri that period he led the life of a bo mian student-painter in Paris.

Lionel was the first of the Barrymores to try movie-acting. Here he appears in a vintage 1911 D. W. Griffith one-reeler called *Fighting Blood*.

John Barrymore in 1910, around the time of his first marriage.

Doris Rankin, Lionel's first wife. She was the daughter of McKee Rankin and some unknown stage actress, but was brought up by Rankin's wife. Lionel fell in love with her when she was sixteen. Their two children, both girls, did not survive childhood.

Katherine Harris, first wife of John Barrymore. Her fascination with stage people and stage life bored John, who often found it necessary to escape from her to out-of-the-way saloons. The marriage lasted seven years.

part TWO

Part Two

ETHEL CLAIMS
HER BIRTHRIGHT

chapter VI

AS THE NINETEENTH CENTURY turned into the twentieth, headlines like the following in American newspapers were common: ETHEL BARRYMORE THE MOST ENGAGED GIRL IN AMERICA. The Sunday supplements were the worst offenders of Ethel's delicate sensibilities. She *deplored* such stories, she told the newspapermen who were sent to check on the constant rumors. There was a report that she had become engaged to a young socialite, Charles Delevan Witmore, and another that the lucky man was Ernest Lawford, the pirate captain in Maude Adams' *Peter Pan*. Not true, Ethel said despairingly, simply not true.

"It maddens me," she said, "when I see my pictures alongside Madame Sarah's and Duse's in the photographers' windows, and selling, mind you, just because I have a certain kind of face, and a father who is famous, and a mother who was loved!" Her indignation was lovely to behold.

Was the rotund little Charles Frohman behind this undoubtedly valuable publicity? Some unkind reporters for the drama pages hinted at this. "We have had our pulses quickened so often by these rumors," wrote one, "that we are beginning to be a bit blasé. Miss Barrymore is really not worth the newspaper space, judged by coldly reasonable standards."

For the avid readers of these glamorous goings-on, Ethel was described again and again. She was tracked down to a "bohemian gathering, where, without urging or eagerness, she sat down and made the piano keys talk, first chucking away her *cigarette!*"

When *His Excellency, The Governor* was about to go on tour, Frohman gave Ethel the part of Stella de Gex, although he still had qualms about her being of proper vintage to play a thirty-year-old adventuress who had lived too well and dangerously. Ethel found herself a gorgeous red wig that made her look older, bought a black gown of extreme daring, borrowed some elegant costumes from Frohman's stock, and toured eight weeks of one-night stands. She had been raised to the munificent salary of eighty dollars a week. The hinterlands, agog from the fabulous stories of engagements and her conquest of England's highest social circles, were delighted with her.

Her arrival in Detroit was not so much a theatrical as a social occasion. "One could never forget her first appearance in a private house in this city," wrote a social editor. "Several of the handsomest women of the town were there to receive her. When the door opened, there, instead of the woman of the world, Stella de Gex, stood a dainty girlish figure draped in somber close-fitting velvet [Ethel's only good dress]. No ornament relieved the almost puritan severity of costume, save where strings of pearls shimmered above the high collar; no color showed, save where the bloom of youth and health gleamed pink through clear, childishly soft cheeks. Big eyes that were luminous and appealing turned rapidly from one to another, as with the air of a debutante she stood beside her chaperone to receive necessary introductions. The actress was gone."

Or was she?

During this tour Ethel discovered a trick about acting. Instead of heavily stressing a comic line, as was common practice on the stage, she tossed the line away as though it had no point. She had noticed her mother doing this seemingly artless bit of business in *The Senator* and remembered how natural the effect seemed. She remembered, too, what Sir Arthur Pinero, the English playwright, had told her after he had seen her perform with Sir Henry Irving. "My dear child," he enthused, "you're the most natural thing I've ever seen on the stage."

Although she was too young and still too inexperienced to know what was happening generally, styles of acting on the stage were going through an accelerated change. Bombast was disappearing, as was the attitudinizing habitual to the older actors. There was soon to be a cry for more realism in the way life was treated on the stage. Ethel was lucky enough to possess the naturalness and ease of movement that audiences were beginning to prefer. She, without knowing it, was *au courant*. She knew, however, that good acting required from the actor more than appearances. To be seemingly at ease took hard work and thorough understanding of a role. Ethel had the will to work and the artistic sense that enabled her to cover up the cogs and wheels behind her performance.

On this tour she saved enough to afford another summer in England. Frohman, who made frequent trips to England, was in London when she arrived, and she went to pay a courtesy call on him at the suite he maintained at the Savoy on the Strand. "Where are you staying?" he asked her.

"I'm about to look around for a room," she said.

"You can't be roaming around," he said. "Get yourself a room here."

She knew it was tacitly understood that the Frohman office would take care of the tab, a clear sign that she was now beyond being an ordinary actress.

But within a day or two her friend, the Duchess of Sutherland, invited Ethel to move from the Savoy into her own home, the baronial Stafford House. From that imposing headquarters she ventured again a round of social activity, meeting some of the most distinguished people in England. Duchess Millie attracted around her some of the leading literary lights of the period, and Ethel met and conquered such personages as Hilaire Belloc, G. K. Chesterton, and Max Beerbohm.

When it was time for the Sutherlands to leave London and move on to their castle in Scotland, Dunrobin, Ethel went there, too. She noticed less gaiety in the social whirl than the year before. The Boer War had taken its toll, and many of her friends had lost sons, brothers, and husbands. She met the young Winston Churchill at Dunrobin, and his name, too, appeared on the list of her rumored engagements. During this time she made up her mind that in the future America would be her place of work. England was to be reserved for enjoyment and stimulation, and she vowed that every summer she would return.

She had begun to feel irked by what she regarded as her lack of advancement in her unchosen field of endeavor. She had gained a respect for the acting profession and now, well known and feted as she was, it was less for her acting than for her social graces.

She imagined people saying: "That's Georgie Drew's daughter (or John Drew's niece). But she can't act at all, can she?" She was not an actress, she was not a star; all she was, really, was something of a celebrity. Two people knew differently. One was Charles Frohman and the other was America's most successful playwright, Clyde Fitch. Neither had overtly communicated to her their belief that she was headed for great things. Frohman, for one, was distinctly not the communicative sort and preferred to let actions speak instead of words. As for Fitch, he saw in young Miss Barrymore a new jewel of a young glamorous star being polished. Now while writing a play called *Captain Jinks of the Horse Marines* he allowed it to be bruited about that he was writing it for young Ethel Barrymore.

In the fall of 1900 Ethel, just home from London, paid Frohman a visit, and he told her that Mr. Fitch had turned in his new play with a fine part in it for a young woman. He cautioned Ethel that neither he nor Fitch was certain she could play it, but they would take a chance on her. As a matter of fact, Frohman did not regard the play as any great shakes, but Fitch already had two plays running on Broadway and wanted to have a third. The gossamer play, however, needed a vivacious, fresh personality; it was Frohman's guess and gamble that Ethel had the qualities to lift it above the routine.

All that was required of Ethel was that she sparkle as a comedienne, act with pathos, and dance and sing as well. Her role in the play was Madame Trentoni, a famous European opera star who has come to America to add to her riches. The news of her coming has reached three young American officers (of the Horse Marines), and they agree to pool their small assets for a romantic pursuit of the lady, whom they haven't yet seen but assume to be forbidding in person. The winning lover upon obtaining the diva's hand in marriage will, according to agreement, divide her fortune with the two unsuccessful rivals. Captain Jinks, however, is immediately smitten by Madame Trentoni, the very personification of charm and grace, and abandons his contract with his fellow officers. True love wins the day.

Flowers greeted Ethel in her dressing room on opening night in Philadelphia. Standing in the wings before making her entrance she saw a crowded house and suddenly began to tremble. It was like making a plunge into cold water to go out on stage, and once before the footlights she was attacked by that old shyness, and unconsciously lowered her head. Suddenly someone in the gallery cried out to her: "Speak up, Ethel! All the Drews are good actors!" She rallied as her stage fright began to vanish, and sought to give the play the lightness that was essential to it.

When she was back at the Stenton Hotel where she was staying, there were friends who assured her that everything had gone splendidly. But the morning papers assured her of quite the opposite. "Mr. Fitch's play is a comic opera with the music left out," a critic wrote. "Miss Barrymore's interpretation of a role is to dress it and look it and leave the rest to providence and the imagination of her audience." The review went on to say that she posed prettily, sang and danced badly, and acted not at all. Another critic put the blame for what he regarded as the play's inevitable failure squarely on Ethel's shoulders: "If the young lady who plays Madame Trentoni had possessed beauty, charm, or talent, this play might have been a success." Ethel remembered that review, word for word, all her life.

Hiding her bruised feelings, Ethel played the remainder of the week in Philadelphia to half empty houses, and Frohman, sensing his young actress had lost her confidence, sent the play on the road for three weeks. She went through a series of single performances in several towns and cities along the Eastern seaboard, and Ethel, fearing the light of failure might blaze fiercely indeed on Broadway, begged Frohman not to take the play to New York. Here Fitch's vanity intervened. He was captivated by the prospect of having three plays running simultaneously and prevailed upon Frohman to bring in *Captain Jinks*. Frohman scheduled it at the Garrick for a brief two-week run. The opening night was February 4, 1901.

Ethel felt for the first time the terrible sense of responsibility that was to assail her often later. First nights never failed to fill her with an agony of terror that was like a fear of dying. Philadelphia had not been as bad, nor had her road tour in *His Excellency, The Governor*. In her dressing room at the Garrick was the traditional red apple sent ahead of time by her Uncle Jack. Perhaps, she thought, a sudden heart attack or the need for an emergency appendectomy would rescue her from having to go on stage and face friends and, afterwards, the crushing reviews.

For the first few minutes on stage she felt awkward and stiff. Her gaze, as in her childhood, kept going to the floor. But all at once (and there were many witnesses to attest to this) it was as though the ghosts of all the Drews of the past had come to her rescue. Suddenly Ethel was her enchanting self, her voice took on a rich confidence, and she sailed through the performance with a radiance that drew bravos and cheers at the play's conclusion.

Ethel did not learn until many years later that Maurice Barrymore had stood with Augustus Thomas all through the play leaning on the back rail of the orchestra. At the end Maurice turned to Thomas, his eyes filled with tears, and said, "My God, isn't she sweet?" He was among the throng of well-wishers backstage afterwards, but all he said after kissing his daughter was, "You were wonderful, darling," and he faded out of sight.

The papers next day happily reported the clapping of hands, the beating of the floor with canes and umbrellas, and the shouts of approbation. A little lady of the finest theatrical stock, said the New York *World*, had aimed at a shining mark and hit the bull's-eye, even though she had earned her applause in what he described as "a whimsical little comedy."

The important critic Alan Dale wrote:

> A girl who seems to have plighted her troth to half the population of this rock-bound isle is certainly interesting as a phenomenon, but not necessarily to the stage. Let me try and treat her as the comely daughter of her admirable father, Maurice Barrymore, and of her gifted mother. As the prima donna in the play, she was quite a surprise. There was a good deal of natural charm in her work, and in spite of a lack of proper experience, she made a very pleasing impression. She was judged as an

actress and she was not applauded until she had done something good.

Other critics were less lukewarm, and as for the public, it took Ethel and the play to heart. "Dear Miss Barrymore . . . *Dear* Miss Barrymore," a critic wrote in a follow-up, "New York is at your feet." The play's run was extended to three months and then to six. Every evening during those months a large bouquet of red roses arrived for Ethel backstage at the Garrick, her admirer preferring to remain anonymous, and there was someone else who sent her the little old-fashioned bouquet of gardenias she carried on stage in the last act. The card with the bouquet said: "L'inconnu." Ethel tried to discover the identity of her admirers. When she asked her escorts if they by chance had sent her flowers, each naturally answered: "Oh, I'm so glad you got them."

A fashion writer took note of Ethel's popularity. "There is a real Barrymore cult among the girls, who model themselves on her." Ethel's hair-do was illustrated in the papers and described as follows: ". . . combed back and then falling far forward over her forehead, forming a golden brown aureole."

Ethel maintained her equilibrium in spite of her spectacular success. She continued living at Mrs. Wilson's boardinghouse on Thirty-sixth Street opposite The Lambs and walked each evening the short distance to the Garrick Theatre on the corner of Thirty-fifth Street and Broadway. One evening John escorted her to the theater. As the two of them turned onto Broadway, Ethel glanced at the sign blazing over the Garrick and clutched her brother's arm. "Oh, lord, look at that," she said to John. He looked up and saw Ethel's name in electric lights. She couldn't stop crying the rest of the way to the theater.

The next day she made sure to be in Charles Frohman's office to thank him. "I didn't do it," Frohman told her. He gestured toward the window, toward the people walking by outside. "They did it," he said.

From that day forward Ethel was never anything less than a star.

But Ethel's glory was to have its accompanying dark cloud. Maurice Barrymore's behavior had become more noticeably erratic, and reports of it reached Ethel by word of mouth and the newspapers. There was nothing she could do about it, and it was not something that could be handled by Lionel, who was usually touring away from the city and whom she saw seldom. As for John, she was in the habit of looking after him rather than the opposite. While the Barrymores lived they said little about the collapse of their father, but it weighed heavily on them all and was to have a noticeable effect on John in his later life. Gene Fowler, when he wrote *Good Night, Sweet Prince,* took the feelings of Ethel and Lionel into account when writing about the tragic last days of Maurice and fabricated a gentle little fable about Maurice's being found sitting on some brownstone steps, not quite conscious of his whereabouts, and being led by a reporter to Bellevue, where it was decided to keep him under observation. He gave the date of this event as 1903. The actual occurrences were far more stark and bizarre, and harrowing to Maurice's sons and daughter.

In the autumn of 1900 Maurice had been persuaded to leave vaudeville long enough to support a well-known actress, Marie Burroughs, in a national tour of a play called *Battle of the Strong.* The first performance was given in Louisville on November 29, 1900. Within a week or two rumors became current in New York that Barrymore was on the verge of a breakdown. It was said, for one thing, that he had been barely able to walk through his part and that the other actors complained strongly about having to act with him. The New York *Telegraph* printed the following: "His memory, it is said, is so far gone that he forgot his lines and did business that had never been rehearsed. His cues fell on empty ears, and he had to be told his entrances and exits. As the play went on to other cities on its tour, reports of his amazing acting filtered ahead of him and almost empty houses were the result."

This report received some substantiation when he was given his notice by Marie Burroughs in St. Louis. Maurice composed a long letter which he sent off to the *Telegraph.* The rumors about him, he said, applied only insofar as the play was in the process of being continually rewritten. "It is notorious," he went on, "that I have the misfortune to be a very poor study and have often been well nigh flayed alive for apparent indifference and neglect, when in point of fact I have worked harder and often hopelessly to acquire my lines, devoting more time and labor to the task than the entire company. Mere memory, however, is not the first or most essential quality of an actor. I played with Edwin Booth at the Fifth Avenue Theatre when he stuck eight times in his first speech of seven lines in *Richard III*, after ten years of the profoundest preparation.

"There was nothing to justify the reporter's statement (from St. Louis) that I was either drunk or paretic." He claimed the failures in his lines were only momentary. The strange letter was lucid enough to cause the *Telegraph* to print it and add a note to the effect that the published allegations about Barrymore were exaggerated. "The letter proves that his intellect has not undergone any change for the worse."

But on his way back to New York, Maurice stopped off in Pittsburgh, where he purchased twenty identical suits of clothes at fourteen dollars each. He went back to doing vaudeville, which he felt was in parlous need of all his efforts in its behalf, mainly because the vaudevillians, through their organization popularly known as the White Rats, were attempting to get higher salaries from the theatrical managers. Maurice made no bones about his hatred for theatrical managers, and to them he ascribed the failures of his own plays and others in which he had appeared. Offered the role of the dark-skinned Prince of Morocco in Abe Erlanger's all-star production of *The Merchant of Venice*, he turned it down in a letter that said he was not yet ready to go into "Negro minstrelsy."

He wrote other letters on behalf of the White Rats, made speeches at their rallies, and composed messages for circulars, which he ordered printed on large sheets and posted everywhere in New York. He was enraged when this was not done, and held theatrical managers responsible. The time for decisive action had come, he felt, on an evening in late March, 1901, when on a vaudeville stage in what is now Harlem he stopped in the middle of his performance, advanced to the footlights, and began haranguing the audience about the machinations of theatrical managers and the dangers the Jews represented to the theater and the world. The audience held its collective breath in astonishment.

When he left the stage, he told his associates he was going to a chophouse for a late dinner. Instead he took a ferry to Coytesville,

New Jersey, where he owned a house. Missing for over twenty-four hours, he came back to New York with a wild, unsubstantiated tale of a fight he'd had with a policeman on the ferry, and mentioned casually that he had killed a bystander who had intervened. He wandered about The Lambs for the next two days, talking incessantly of gigantic schemes that he had and of triumphs that would be his in the future.

"I'll build the largest theater in the world!" he shouted, banging the mahogany bar. When the theater was finished, he would plaster the city with posters, announcing that all theater managers (he named them all, including Charles Frohman) were jealous of Maurice Barrymore, who had brains. If his talk was insane, some of The Lambs' members were held spellbound by flashes of his old sparkle and epigrammatic speech. But an epigram would be followed by a confidence in lowered tones that he was going to see to it that power and influence in his huge theater, covering many city blocks, would go to the White Rats.

Ethel and John, who lived just across the street from The Lambs at Mrs. Wilson's, were kept informed of Maurice's peculiar behavior. In fact, on the night of his speech at the vaudeville house, she canceled a late dinner invitation after her performance, dreading whatever further developments might come. She heard that her father had returned to The Lambs and was shouting, and that The Lambs management feared for its furniture. She was too paralyzed by shock to make a decision.

The next morning the doorbell at Mrs. Wilson's rang, and Maurice pushed aside the servant who answered and ran up to Ethel's room. "I'm the greatest theatrical manager in the world," he shouted, according to the account of a newspaper reporter who had been dispatched to The Lambs and who subsequently wrote the following lurid dispatch:

> "William C. Whitney has promised to build me the biggest theater in America on Amsterdam Avenue next fall," Maurice told his daughter. "Death to the syndicate." He strode about her room, declaiming old parts from his plays. Whenever he talked about the theatrical syndicate he grew violent. "Charles Frohman is dead, the White Rats have killed him," he screamed.

He shook Ethel. "John Golden is greater than Christ, and I'm his vice-regent."

"That's true, Father," Ethel said.

While he talked, his restless hands grabbed her throat. "The trust is doomed," he yelled.

The girl kept on smiling. Then danger passed as Jack Barrymore came in. After Maurice had talked of a comedy he was writing he put on his hat and ran out across the street to The Lambs club, Jack following.

When John rejoined Ethel she told him she had consulted with Maurice's close friend, Augustus Thomas, and that he had suggested talking with their attorney, Joseph D. Redding. Redding and Thomas helped Ethel and John work out the details of what they had sadly decided was necessary, a commitment to an institution for the insane. The nineteen-year-old John, given the responsibility of handling Maurice, did it well. He convinced his father that he ought to make a complaint against the policeman he had said he had fought with. He and John went off in a horse-driven cab, presumably on their way to a police headquarters. Instead it was Bellevue that John took his father to, and guards were waiting for them on their arrival.

When Maurice realized he was at a hospital, he smiled and said: "My son has an exaggerated idea about my condition."

After a thorough examination of their celebrated patient, the doctors reported the details of his condition to the waiting reporters. He was suffering at the moment "from absinthe and incipient paresis," one said. A Dr. Stafford Newton revealed that Maurice had suffered a similar, but not so acute, attack two years before and had pulled through, and he offered hope that the actor would pull through again. The trouble this time, however, was that Maurice's formerly strong constitution was shattered, and he was all but emaciated from lack of proper nutrition.

Further reports came from Bellevue in the days that followed, among them that he would break down into incoherence and immoderate laughter, that he had said once, "Oh, Ethel, Ethel . . . Don't talk to your father that way." His mood changing, he called for pen and paper and wrote about a hundred stanzas on a half-dozen pages. Maurice turned, in his torment, to writing a drama about an

Indian princess which soon changed into a dissertation on the social evils of New York. Then came incoherence, and then docility. His second wife, Mary Floyd, who had just returned from a trip to Europe, visited him, and he recognized her, as he did his son John when the latter brought him a bundle of clothing. He was able to read the newspaper story about his having nearly choked Ethel, and this caused him to break into a violent spell of weeping.

"He begged me piteously to have it corrected," Dr. Stewart told reporters.

Maurice seemed aware that his mental faculties were impaired and controlled his behavior to the extent of shaving daily, changing his linen regularly, and having his shoes polished. But his docile phase passed, and he knocked out an attendant by hitting him on the head with a table. The physicians decided that his illness had reached the homicidal phase, that he was now hopelessly insane and incurable, and that he could not live more than six months. "His paresis is in an advanced phase," was the final diagnosis, "and there is no possible way for the disease to be checked."

Ethel's salary at this time was not very large—in the area of a hundred dollars weekly—and hard upon the scandalous reports in the newspapers, Frohman sent for her and told her that her salary was to be greatly increased. He said, too, that he was off for Europe, and that in the event she needed emergency funds he was leaving instructions at his business office that she was free to draw whatever sums of money she needed and whenever it suited her.

Thus Ethel was able to manage the costs of his stay in Bellevue and to provide her father with comfortable facilities in an Amityville, Long Island, rest home for mental cases. Ethel's burden of care for her father was not to last six months, as the doctors had prophesied, but four years.

The veteran actor went to the Amityville sanitarium under the delusion that he was to fulfill an engagement in Philadelphia. He made a sad figure as he passed through corridors mumbling passages from old roles, bowing to fancied compliments and applause. Ethel visited him regularly, and he was always tractable in her presence; she seemed to have a remarkable power over him. What Ethel felt about these visits it was not in her nature to divulge. His appearance at her opening in *Captain Jinks* had been her only glimpse of him in three months. She stoically, however, bore the costs of his Amityville confinement, never mentioned them, never complained.

Lionel and Jack saw Maurice only seldom during his last years; they, too, were always reticent about the nature of their father's illness. Lionel did mention a remark his father made to him shortly before his death in 1905. Lionel had said that he was about to head west for San Francisco. "You're a damned liar," Maurice said. "Everyone knows that San Francisco has been destroyed by earthquake and fire." Nothing unusual about the remark, perhaps, for one in his state, except that it was made a full year before the great earthquake in San Francisco, and, as it happened, John Barrymore was to be there at the time.

Lionel did mention something about the effect of Maurice Barrymore's collapse on their brother John: "That collapse, following Mum Mum's and his mother's death, had a lasting effect on him. I believe that Jack was haunted, in those dark moments that come to all men, by the fear that he too would collapse; and I have been told that it is psychologically sound that the thing you most fear is precisely the thing that is most likely to happen to you."

Captain Jinks played on at capacity until well after the Fourth of July. Symptomatic of Ethel's new status was her move from the hall bedroom at Mrs. Wilson's to the much grander second floor front, which consisted of a bedroom plus an alcove, which she thought of as her sitting room. She was happy at Mrs. Wilson's, and while she accepted many of the invitations that showered upon her, she enjoyed as much and more the quiet evenings she spent with her cousin, Georgie Mendum, and her good friends, the Kearneys. Mr. Kearney was the stage manager for *Captain Jinks* (and was to be Ethel's stage manager for many years after), and Mrs. Kearney had a small role as a ballet dancer in the same play. The Kearneys, Georgie Mendum and Ethel remained inseparable well on into the twenties.

But when the play closed during the heat of summer, Ethel fled to London again to put behind her the hard work and the stress of her father's mental collapse. As soon as she arrived it was assumed by her friends that she had been away for no more than a weekend. Henry Asquith was now Prime Minister of England and the company she associated so familiarly with was august indeed. "When you go to dinner in England," she said afterward (for anyone who may have needed the advice), "you must take with you all your mentality, for you are sure to need it." Her English friends seemed to think Ethel was on the stage purely as a pastime, and had no real idea that she had become so prominent. One young man of title asked Elsie Janis (who later made a success imitating Ethel) if she had ever heard of a friend of his who did a bit of acting in America. Her name, he said, was Ethel Barrymore. Elsie Janis gave him a withering glance.

Ethel learned to play golf near a castle rented for the summer by the Asquiths, attended "wonderful" dinners, and being only twenty-two took it as a matter of course that she should have such interesting friends as Lord Balfour at one side of her at the table and G. K. Chesterton on the other. If a touch of grandness came into her manners as her career proceeded, this becomes understandable in view of the company she kept in England. Nor did her English socializing do her a bit of harm with the American public. It was only right and proper that their adored Ethel should conquer English society.

But the time came to leave again, and Frohman sent Ethel out on the road with *Captain Jinks.* Her salary was raised to $250 a week, as befitted an important star, and when *Captain Jinks* arrived in Philadelphia again for a two-week run, her name was up in lights over the new Garrick Theatre. She broke the house record in the same play and with the same cast that had been treated so disdainfully several months earlier. The chastened Philadelphia critics now had only the kindest words for Ethel.

LIONEL TAKES
HIS TURN

chapter VII

DURING THAT SUMMER of 1901 Ethel made a brief trip to Paris. She was entertained at dinner by Charles Frohman and his associate, Charles Dillingham. Frohman's major weakness was for sweets and pastries of all kinds, and while he was sampling some Parisian fantasies and feeling blissfully mellow, Ethel asked: "What are you going to do about Lionel?" Her concern was justified. Lionel's theatrical career had reached a low ebb; about the best he could do in the way of finding jobs was an engagement for a split week in some out-of-the-way place such as Elmira or Binghamton. Frohman had no particular reason to feel dutiful toward Lionel, but Ethel somehow made him feel that they shared a common responsibility for this unsuccessful young Barrymore.

Frohman dug methodically into an orange ice and said: "I'll put him in *The Second in Command*." The matter was settled. The play referred to was a London success by Robert Marshall that Frohman was scheduling as a John Drew vehicle for the fall season. Lionel made his second Broadway appearance as Lieutenant Barker of the 10th Dragoon Guards, escaped unharmed by any critical venom, and during seventy-six performances had the opportunity to observe his uncle's solid acting workmanship at close hand. In Drew's view, from the time the curtain rose until the time it fell an actor was out on stage earning a living. He made it clear to Lionel that nothing but his best was expected from him while performing for an audience.

There is no record of what Frohman thought of Lionel's work in this play. Probably the appearance of a secondary actor in a secondary role was of no great importance to a man whose theatrical enterprises then included some fifteen or twenty productions each year in New York, another eight or ten in London, and several in Paris, as well as the management of several of the stage's most important stars. When Lionel finished in *The Second in Command* he was again out of work, with nothing on the horizon.

Ethel interceded for him once more, with some help from John Drew. In June of 1902 Frohman offered Ethel a large bonus instead of a salary raise to which she was entitled. His reasoning was that any salary given Ethel was bound to disappear, especially with the drain on it from her two brothers, but a large sum could be put aside for investment or stowed away in a bank. Instead of accepting the bonus, Ethel made Frohman a counteroffer, a part for Lionel in John Drew's next play, *The Mummy and the Humming Bird*. Drew had sent her the play, with a notation that an important character role in it might be a good one for Lionel.

Frohman agreed, but mentioned that the part was more challenging than any Lionel had yet had to handle; as an Italian organ grinder he not only had to play the contraption itself, but also come up with a convincing accent. Lionel by now knew that a good actor had to prepare himself thoroughly. He first of all sought help from an experienced actor, George Barnum, who had supported Ethel in *Captain Jinks* and was a warm and sympathetic person. Lionel had him read the part of Giuseppe, the organ grinder, and was gratified when Barnum assured him that the role was an actor's dream in that it was colorful and filled with passion.

"But what about the Italian accent?" Lionel asked.

"Try it," Barnum suggested.

Barnum listened to Lionel's attempt at the accent and decided more assistance was needed. One of his actor friends, Ralph Delmore, was of Italian descent and would know how one ought to sound. Delmore was called in, was amused by the notion of grooming another Barrymore, and now the two took Lionel in tow. They trained him to talk, scream, and cry in Italian accents and gestures. Barnum, carried away by the project of turning Lionel into a great actor, brought in a genuine Italian organ grinder for Lionel to watch and imitate.

But Lionel concentrated mainly on imitating two good actors: Barnum and Delmore. Through them he made his first discoveries of how to play a part, and also began the practice he later always used—to consult as many as three or four other people for assistance in preparing a role. The work with Delmore and Barnum lasted three weeks. As he developed the role, he included in his observation several Italian waiters in small restaurants around the city and was soon able to detect the shades of difference between Neapolitan, Umbrian, and Sicilian Italians. He eventually chose Sicily as Giuseppe's place of origin.

Drew was to play an aristocratic scientist too immersed in his laboratory work to notice his young and beautiful wife was about to be seduced by an amorous, unscrupulous Italian poet. Giuseppe, an organ grinder in London in search of the villainous poet, saves the wife from her dreadful fate. At the end of one of Giuseppe's scenes, Lionel had to take a knife from his belt, kiss it fiercely, and cry, "Vendetta! Vendetta!" and then collapse in wild sobs on a chair as the curtain descended. The audience was to gather from this that the knife would soon be plunged into the Italian poet.

At the dress rehearsal Lionel was set to reveal his new virtuosity to Frohman and his partner, Dillingham. Crying genuine tears, he threw himself toward the chair and missed it completely. On picking himself up he half expected to hear derisive laughter but heard only the sound of Frohman's quiet voice saying: "I'm glad you did that tonight, Barrymore, because now I know you won't do it again."

The next night it was Lionel's turn to find a red apple on the dressing table. His audience was nothing less than the most fashionable of the season, not because of the importance of the play, or his being in it, but because John Drew's annual opening at the Empire now rivaled the glittering first night at the Metropolitan as a social occasion.

The *Telegraph* headlined its article: STAR'S NEPHEW SUR-PRISES FASHIONABLE EMPIRE AUDIENCE BY HIS CLEVER WORK IN THE MUMMY AND THE HUMMING BIRD. The newspaper also recorded the fact that Ethel Barrymore sat among the audience, "in intense excitement" as her brother made his mark. Actually she was in mid-ocean at the time, her hectic social life in England having delayed her departure for home.

The critics were now aware that Barrymore talent had flared up in another member of the family. Lionel's was not the most important role of the play, but he received the most attention:

> His eyes reflect wonder at his strange surroundings. It is with difficulty that he is urged to come into the room. When he speaks it is as if he is afraid his voice may do damage to the dignified appointments of the place. It is just such a voice as one would expect to hear from such a man, and in its tones are the peculiar mingling of the guttural and the musical. The Barrymore talent has made it a little work of art.

On the other hand, it was generally agreed that John Drew had taken for himself a thankless role. But he had known this from the beginning and had probably resolved that if anyone was going to outshine him it would be his nephew.

Drew pretended to be annoyed by the success Lionel had made in the play. When someone inquired about his health one day at The Players, he said testily: "I'm very well, thank you, considering that every night I now have to play second fiddle to that nephew of mine."

For his next play, *The Best of Friends*, Lionel developed his own characterization for the part he played, a sturdy old commandant in the Boer army. The play ran for sixty-five performances, good enough for the time, but on his next outing, in *The Other Girl*, he was in a smash hit that was forced to move twice to different theaters during its hundred and sixty performances. This play was the work of his father's friend, and now his own, Augustus Thomas. It required him to do a take-off on Kid McCoy, a famous fighter with whom he also became fast friends. Lionel trained for the role in a gymnasium with McCoy as his helpful mentor and developed a fondness for amateur sparring. The morning following the opening of the play, he was referred to by a critic as "one of the greatest of American character actors."

"So now at last here it was," he said in his autobiography. "Nudged by Ethel, favored by Charles Frohman, taught by Delmore and Barnum, I had got my feet planted firmly on Broadway."

He was twenty-six years old, was able to live decently for the first time since he had begun his acting career ten years before, and yet he continued to regard acting as something which he must escape from. He longed to paint instead.

He had also become prominent enough to merit engagement rumors. It was said he was about to marry Angela McCaull, daughter of the manager of a comic opera company. Ethel approved the match, so the paper said, but it never took place, and Lionel was hardly the type to provide reasons why or why not.

During his early period of wandering around the country with McKee Rankin and Sidney Drew he had been vaguely aware of little Doris Rankin, a tot of three or four when he first saw her. After a lapse of many years he met her again at an upstate New York farm owned by Harry Davenport, who had married another Rankin girl, Phyllis. Doris was now sixteen, adorably pretty and sweet. In no time at all Lionel was in love with her. They saw each other for a year, then became engaged and were married in June of 1904 at St. Xavier's Catholic Church in New York. Ethel was not present; she had already gone abroad for her London visit. But John was a witness, as were McKee Rankin and Lionel's Uncle Sidney and Aunt Gladys.

Doris, too, had been around the stage and stage people all her life, and was not in the least touched by any of its reputed glamour. If Lionel wanted to paint she saw no reason why he shouldn't go back to the Art Students League and start once again. But Lionel took his responsibilities as a married man seriously. He found a small house for Doris and himself on Long Island, away from the bustle of New York, and paid for their upkeep by continuing to act.

Ethel had also helped arrange for John's stage debut. She made a successful tour of the eastern part of the country in *Captain Jinks*, and the company then headed to Philadelphia for the third and final appearance there of the play. In that city one of the actors was notified that his mother had died, and he abruptly left the company

97

to attend her funeral. No understudy was available for him, so Ethel, seeing a chance for gainful employment for her younger brother, wired him to immediately take the train for Philadelphia. Frohman came to Philadelphia, too, probably curious as to whether a third Barrymore had any qualifications for the stage.

John was told to memorize his part, that of a lieutenant of the Horse Marines, during the train ride. When he arrived at the theater he donned his costume and went on as nonchalantly as though going to a dinner party, modeling his aplomb after that of his uncle, John Drew. He, however, not only lacked similar experience but had not taken the trouble to thoroughly learn what he was to say. He had made a cursory examination of the words, assumed he had committed them to memory, and that was that. Once on stage he found it was not only important to know one's lines but also where exactly to stand. In the middle of the first act, shortly after going on, he said to a fellow officer of the Horse Marines: "I've blown up, old chap. Where do we go from here?" He cheerfully improvised the scene while the other actors floundered, and the fond Ethel, standing in the wings, thought her brother so funny she became all but helpless with laughter.

At the end of the next act, which finished with Ethel doing her little dance "with a breaking heart," it was customary to bring the entire company out on stage for a curtain call. The applause was for Ethel, who then would take it upon herself to bring the others out to share it. Somehow, when the curtain went up for this call, John found himself all alone on stage. Hearing applause, he bowed low, graciously went to the wings and brought Ethel forward, bowed to her and then to the audience. The audience took the charade as part of the fun of the play, and Ethel was too amused to be able to do much chiding of her brother. Frohman, far from being angry, told John afterward that he might make a comedian someday but would have to work on improving his memory.

John's more formal debut didn't take place until the following year. The date was October 31, 1903, the place was Cleveland's Theatre on Wabash Avenue in Chicago, the play was Sudermann's *Magda,* and the role was Max. (Lionel had played it several years before.) In fact it was the same McKee Rankin production of the play, and family intervention can once more be seen in John's being hired. It may very well have been Lionel's uniform he wore, for Lionel was several inches taller than his brother and more heavily built. In any event, it was at once apparent that the German military frock coat was too large for John and that it would be simpler to build the actor up than take in the uniform. Various items from wardrobe were stuffed inside the coat, but hardly had John walked out on the stage when the stuffing began to change position, most of it settling in the area around the stomach.

John did his best, moving about as little as possible so as not to cause further movement of the stuffing of his uniform. He sat up all night with friends in a warm saloon waiting for what the morning papers might say about his debut performance. Only one review greeted the play, but an important critic, Amy Leslie, had written it. She said about John: "The part of Max was essayed by a young actor who calls himself Mr. John Barrymore. He walked about the stage as if he had been all dressed up and forgotten."

John was crushed enough by this first reference to his acting in print, but what bothered him more was that friends of Ethel's in Chicago, to whom she had thoughtfully written to look out for her brother in the city, were anxious to see him act. When they came in a body one night and howled impolitely at his delivery of his lines, he decided he was through with the stage and ran to the nearest telegraph office. In duress, it was always Ethel who was good for money, but it took a message of dire urgency to bring it. "For Christ's sake," he penciled out, "send me fifty dollars." The operator said company rules forbade sending so blasphemous a message, but Jack explained that a man in Rankin's company called George W. Christ had taken ill and was the one who needed the money. The message was sent and Ethel came through with the fifty dollars.

On December 28, 1903, John made his New York debut in a Clyde Fitch comedy, *Glad of It,* about which a critic commented: "The last of the Barrymores, Young Jack, made a successful debut as a press agent, but *Glad of It* is no more than a half-baked success." Another critic summed up the play as "too much of it." William Collier, a famous comedian, watched John in the show and was convinced that something could be made of this third Barrymore.

John was hired for a Collier starring production, *The Dictator,* and for the next year and a half learned his ropes as a comic actor in that play.

Ethel was in Philadelphia, appearing in *Sunday* when on March 25, 1905, Maurice Barrymore slipped into a coma at the sanitarium in Amityville, Long Island, and died without regaining consciousness. Two weeks before, the hallucinations that had plagued him suddenly disappeared, and he had become placid and obedient, like a child stricken with a mild illness. Alf Hayman, a manager for Frohman, waited until Ethel finished her matinee performance before telling her the news of her father's death, then closed the theater for a few days to allow her time to make the funeral arrangements. She hurried to New York, where she was met by John, and together they sent off a wire to Lionel, who was well across the country on a train bound for Los Angeles. Lionel turned around immediately and headed back, but he arrived too late for the funeral.

Services for Maurice were held in the chapel of a burial firm located at Nineteenth Street and Eighth Avenue in New York, and Ethel gave strict orders that no one outside the immediate family was to be permitted to view the ravaged face and wasted body. She obtained her uncle's permission to have her father buried in the Drew family plot in Philadelphia, and she and John traveled there together. At graveside they were the only two family members present (two of Mrs. John Drew's old servants also turned up) as the coffin containing the hulk of an old actor, who had died mad and penniless, was slipped into the earth.

Lionel returned to the West Coast, bypassing Los Angeles, where his play, *The Other Girl,* went on without him, and going directly to the next point on the tour, San Francisco. Ashton Stevens, stage critic for the San Francisco *Examiner,* interviewed the young actor, now thoroughly seasoned and professional. Stevens, in the piece he wrote, commented on Lionel's casual, slouching manner which, he said, belied his seriousness.

"It's all very well to take yourself seriously," Lionel told him, "but when the first night comes and the audience shuffles in and the orchestra scrapes the overture—oh!—it's a nightmare. It takes me two nights to know what happened on the first."

"The morning papers might help you know a little earlier," Stevens said.

Lionel gave a hearty laugh. "Good notices in the papers are valuable and instructive only in that they help you with your beliefs about yourself."

"What about bad notices?"

"Bad notices disturb you. Many of them, if they are pointed in the same direction, are apt to make you unhappy, and what's more, they're apt to make you alter your performance. Unless a man is the Great Actor himself, he cannot stand continuous pen-pricking on one spot. But on the whole, I regard newspaper criticism as befuddling, unless all the criticisms are good. And I hope you realize how beneficial to the audience they are."

Stevens asked him to describe that Great Actor type he had mentioned. Lionel obliged him with the following portrait: "The Great Actor must always act. He must make a ceremony of waking up in the morning. He must sit in his room and act so that his whole body vibrates to the thrill of it. Forever he must be a poseur. To the very last second of his life it must be pose and posture. He must be such a poseur as to be blinded against all rational points of view. He must live in roles and love them. He must be another fellow. Ridicule must pass him by. If by chance it grazes him, the Great Actor must view it with pitying kindness. His last week's failure must be more than forgotten—it never happened. Above all, the Great Actor must have no sense of humor. When he looks at himself in a mirror he must use a telescope. Everything admirable that he reads or sees or hears must be his. Let the most profound, the most classic line fall from his lips, and he must be unconscious of the fact that he is not the author of it."

It should be remarked here that in all their long careers, never did the Barrymores take on any of the coloration of the Great Actor type so neatly described by Lionel. All three had excellent senses of humor which they applied to themselves as well as others.

Lionel confessed to Stevens that he felt guilty when he first saw his name in larger type than the title of his play. "I daresay," he said, "that I know less about acting than any other man in the business, because practically all the time since I was a kid I've been on the stage, winter and summer, and have had very few chances to sit in front of performances." He felt himself lucky to play what he called "the character man." "The leading man has to carry the whole play," he explained, "and almost invariably his part is long and bad. And usually when it is at its worst, the character man comes on with a selected situation and captures the works." He added, offhandedly, that he didn't think it mattered particularly who played the character part.

"Just how far does the Barrymore name carry?" the critic asked.

"How far will the name carry?" Lionel drawled, a glimmer of amusement in his eyes. "It might not be wise for me to tell you this, but my father died in the east while I was on the way to California. I got here barely in time for the San Francisco opening. But meanwhile *The Other Girl* company opened in Los Angeles. Our stage manager, Tully Marshall, played my part and was called not only 'great' but 'Barrymore.' Mind you, I'm not saying that Marshall wasn't great, but—well, there's your answer."

Lionel sat back in his chair in the lobby of the St. Francis Hotel and casually lit a cigarette.

From San Francisco Lionel went on to Denver with *The Other Girl* company, and there manifested signs of a nervous condition that was to result eventually in his leaving the stage for a long period. The first sign was a wire he sent Frohman, saying he needed fifteen hundred dollars desperately. He wasn't making enough money, he told other actors; he wasn't getting the kind of salary that justified the hard work he was doing. Frohman, not given any reason for such an advance, refused to send the money. Lionel angrily left the company in Denver, saying he was ill, and returned east. Behind all this was a nervous terror of acting that Lionel had begun to develop. Although he was always letter perfect in his lines, he had become obsessed with a fear that he would forget them. The death of Maurice some weeks earlier had affected him, most likely, more than he realized. In New York, during the late summer and early autumn of 1905, he was seen haunting concert halls. He carried with him the scores of Beethoven symphonies and concertos, and assiduously pored over them during the performances.

When Frohman put on the Barrie twin bill, *Pantaloon* and *Alice*

Sit-by-the-Fire, with Ethel as the star of the latter play, Lionel was persuaded by his sister to take the part of Pantaloon in the curtain raiser. All his instincts were against it, but he acceded to her request, making it known to her that at every performance he still had that terror of losing his lines. The critics noticed none of this and commented on the magnificent performance he gave. His "old man" voice was so perfectly lifelike that not even his closest friends recognized it. John won praise, too, as Harlequin in *Pantaloon.* He demonstrated some astounding acrobatic abilities, at one point leaping across a room and landing cross-legged on a table, a feat no one had suspected he could perform. In the longer play John appeared with Ethel in a small part. It was the only time all three Barrymores shared a stage together, although Lionel had taken off his make-up for the night by the time *Alice Sit-by-the-Fire* went on.

Lionel played during the New York run and performed for two additional weeks in Philadelphia. Closing there, the play was due to move on to Boston. Lionel, the last night, visited Ethel in her dressing room and told her he could continue no longer. He was through with the stage.

An all-night talk session between the two ensued. What, Ethel asked him, did he intend to do if he gave up acting. Lionel said he might take his chances at painting, perhaps at composing. He wasn't so bad at the latter, he reminded his sister, citing the composition for piano that he had done that was being played between the two Barrie plays for the tour.

"How will you live?" was Ethel's practical question.

Lionel told her that Doris was agreeable to living simply, and that it was her suggestion he go back to the Art Students League, that is, if Ethel would lend him the necessary money.

"But why there?" asked Ethel. "You've already studied there. Wouldn't Paris be a better place?"

That was beyond his means, Lionel said. The two bent their heads together to see how much it would take for Lionel to live with Doris in Paris and study painting. They agreed on a modest figure, and Ethel said, simply, that she would send him a stipend every month. As was usual with the Barrymores, they were reticent about what they had decided. Lionel left the company without a word being said, took Doris to their small home at Rocky Point, Long Island, and began packing up for their Paris adventure.

More rumors appeared in the newspapers about Lionel's "nervous breakdown," upon which Ethel had the Frohman office give out a story that he was recuperating from a mild attack of pneumonia at Rocky Point. In May of 1906 Lionel and Doris quietly boarded a small ship and sailed for Europe without benefit of reporters, champagne, or bon voyages from members of the family. John Drew, for one, could only look with coolness on a member of the family who had deserted the trade.

ETHEL IN A
GOLDFISH BOWL

chapter VIII

"HOW DOES SHE manage it?" blazed a headline over a large, illustrated feature story in a newspaper of 1903. "She watches the cup races from the deck of Mrs. John Jacob Astor's yacht; she automobiles with the Goelets; she dines or lunches at Sherry's with Mrs. Herman Oelrichs, with Mrs. Stuyvesant Fish, with Mrs. Cooper Hewitt." The one who watched cup races and lunched or dined with the socially prominent was Ethel Barrymore, and all eyes in this age of the glorified American Girl were upon her, as though what happened to Ethel could happen to any pretty, healthy, intelligent young woman.

How did she manage it? The answer lay, according to this article, in "the same peculiar, bewildering charm that has made of her a successful star." But it was also thought that at twenty-four Ethel was in no sense a great actress. "She is not as good," the article firmly stated, "as nine-tenths of the young women acting on the stage today."

It was admitted that she was beautiful, "that she has big eyes that are as blue as a deep sea," and it was predicted that stage historians of the future would never be able to understand the phenomenal success of the young woman, because "no one can adequately describe the charm of the one who has accomplished it all."

Feature pieces such as these about Ethel were common during the first six or seven years of the new century, and it especially galled her that her prominence was ascribed more to something called "personality," and later to "glamour," than to great acting talent.

Some years after she had played with Sir Henry Irving in England, she met the actor again during his farewell tour of America. "And so you're a great star now," Sir Henry said to her.

"Oh, no," she explained. "You see, that's the system in this country." And she confessed to him that she was bothered by critical carping at her.

"What do they say about you?" Sir Henry asked.

"They say that I'm good and that I look right, but that I'm always Ethel Barrymore."

Sir Henry took her arm and gave her an intent look. "See to it," he said, "that they never say anything else."

Ethel took the advice and resolved that she would not let reviews make her miserable. Yet she did not lack admirers of her artistry. When Frohman in early 1903 starred her in a double bill made up of a curtain raiser called *Carrots* and a longer piece, *A Country Mouse,* a critic thought it time to announce: "Miss Barrymore as a star is no longer an experiment. Her success in the double bill has established her versatility." Versatility! She did nothing less in *Carrots* than play a boy, and a lonely misunderstood French boy at that!

As for the social success of Frohman's new luminary, there was never the slightest doubt. "All this week," it was chronicled, "the Savoy Theatre has had the aspect of a Fifth Avenue drawing room." On opening night the boxes and the front rows in the orchestra were occupied by some of the august names in "Society."

Ethel noticed after several weeks that the response of New York audiences to *A Country Mouse,* a typical light drawing room comedy of the day, was less than enthusiastic; she responded by becoming ill. So sudden was this indisposition that ticket holders to an evening performance found the lobby lighted when they arrived but the doors to the auditorium securely barred. Ethel was showing signs of temperament. After a rest in a quiet resort at Lakewood, New Jersey, she agreed to take the two plays to Chicago, where audiences were always gratifyingly receptive to her. Chicago was her favorite acting city for a long time; the critics there always appreciated both her talents and her charm.

In the summer of 1903 she sailed for England, where she established herself more firmly than ever as the darling of London society. A rich American, Clarence Jones, gave a dinner at the Carlton in her honor; the women who attended were given hand-painted Venetian fans, and the male guests were presented with gold watch chains. The room and the tables were decorated with "a profusion of American Beauty roses." The cost of the dinner alone, it was cabled to waiting readers in America, "came to fifteen hundred dollars!" This can be considered expensive even by today's standards in view of the fact that the guest list was limited to twenty people.

Ethel, during that stay, attended the then famous fancy dress ball given by the Duchess of Devonshire; at another party she was introduced to the Prince of Wales; and the Duchess of Devonshire—a beautiful and brilliant woman, regarded as one of the cleverest in England—gave the following tidbit to a society columnist: "Ethel Barrymore's London season is one of the pleasures of the year to which I look forward."

That season there was another and highly newsworthy romance for Ethel. She kept meeting at the houses of friends the charming Harry Graham, a captain in the Coldstream Guards, writer of books of verse, and author of a witty book called *Misrepresentative Men*. Together as weekend guests at various country houses, they would sit on the grass and sing the themes of symphonies to each other; each had to guess what the other was singing. "It was great fun," Ethel remembered afterward.

Ethel felt that she *ought* to be married and hoped that she could let marriage happen to her. Her friends thought a match with Harry Graham would be ideal. Ethel supposed that if she could marry anyone it would be Harry, and she allowed herself to become engaged to him. The engagement was announced and again she broke it. In her *Memories* she wrote: "I really agonized about not going through with it, because it was a fine and rare human being that I was hurting." But she was not yet as sure of herself as she wanted to be, and because she wasn't fully sure of who she was and what she was to become, "I knew I might have hurt him far more if I married him."

In New York later that year she was given the honor of opening a new theater, the Hudson, in a play written for her called *Cousin Kate*. Theatrical New York was heading uptown, and this West Forty-fourth Street theater was described as being of severe Renaissance-style architecture with unique concealed lighting effects and an absence of pillars for the support of the balcony and gallery. The foyer and promenade were lighted by disks of Tiffany glass set in the panel squares of the ceiling.

She had become the favorite star of college students, and groups of them would come to watch Ethel at the Hudson. Once a body of Yale youths came and chanted: "What's the matter with Ethel?" Their own answer was: "SHE'S ALL RIGHT!"

The play was called "a charming trifle," and it was Ethel who provided the charm.

She had finally moved from Mrs. Wilson's to an apartment of her own on Park Avenue near Fortieth Street with room enough for Lionel and Jack when they were not out of town in plays. Her own "studio-den" overlooked Park Avenue, and she furnished the spacious room with books, bearskins, a piano, prints, and pieces of decorative pottery. A visitor for an interview described it as "one of those pretty, contradictory rooms one calls expressive. It was full of sunshine, brightness and comfort."

She told the interviewer: "Remember, I come from a family of actors. The stage is in my blood. I love it." Forgotten now was her plaint that she had never wanted to go on the stage.

"What an actress wants to do," she said, "is to give only the fullest expression of her temperament. But she must think only of the author's intent and meaning and of the character she is helping him create."

The conversation was brought around to playwrights. She admired Ibsen's "power and skill as a playwright," but thought his themes and characters were perverted, even false." (This was a year or so before she played Nora in *A Doll's House* for several performances.) As for that upcoming English-Irish playwright, George Bernard Shaw, she admired his wit, but disliked everything else about him. "Shaw," she declared, "is trivial. He has reverence for nothing—always the indication of a small intellect. I don't believe he could do anything great. Brilliant, yes. He makes you laugh, of course, but afterward you reproach yourself for your frivolity. Think of the fuss made over *Candida*. People talked solemnly over something they did not for an instant understand—because there was nothing to understand."

The visitor noticed that under the grand piano was a pile of music: Bach, Beethoven, Grieg, Chopin, and Liszt, and also a piano edition of *The Prince of Pilsen*, a light opera that had caught the popular fancy.

The following spring Charles Frohman decided the moment was propitious to make Ethel a star in London, too. He chose as her vehicle *Cynthia*, a comedy by H. H. Davies that gave her the part of an extremely young, innocent wife, which Elsie De Wolfe had played during the New York run without much success. Ethel didn't really like the play, and she would have preferred a meatier role for a London opening. The audience that turned out to greet her at the Wyndham Theatre on May 15, 1904, included such notables as W. S. Gilbert, Sir Arthur Pinero, James Barrie, the Duchess of Sutherland and her society cohorts, and the American ambassador. Ethel faced this imposing group with unmistakable signs of nervousness.

The English audience was different from those she was used to; it seemed cold, almost indifferent. She lost her nervousness after the first act, but the chill lasted through another act, and only in the third act did the usual applause for Ethel begin to be heard. The next day the play received a roasting in the London newspapers, and it managed to last through only four of its scheduled six weeks of performances.

Max Beerbohm devoted one of his *Saturday Review* pieces to a rather curious analysis of Ethel's quality.

> Miss Barrymore evidently depends very much on her personality and very little on her instinct for the art of acting, and very little on her experience in that art. The only question is whether she is a fascinating person on the stage, and the only answer to that question is a loud and unqualified yes.

Her charm is rather hard to analyse. It is not a simple straightforward charm. It has no solidity and seems to vanish delicately at the first attempt to explain it. Womanly is the last epithet one would apply to Miss Barrymore. She reminds one from moment to moment of many various things—of a bird, a fairy, a flower, a child, a terrier, a what not, but of a woman, never. Protean, she shirks that one metamorphosis, content to be something more and something less.

Perhaps she can best be summed up as a Pierrot. Take it in its original sense and you will have some notion of Miss Barrymore's charm. Pierrot's gaiety and Pierrot's sadness were inhuman; they had no roots in common life, they were shallow and transient . . . and yet, or therefore Pierrot was irresistible and we mourn him. In Miss Barrymore surely he has come to life again.

Yes, here for the first time on the modern stage is Pierrot himself. In modern real life he is not at all rare, and it is usually into the body of a woman that his soul enters. Pierrot women—women whose defect and charm alike are in their detachment from the realities of life—women who sadden us and delight us by their incapacity for ought but trifles are as common in New York and London now as in the court of Louis Quinze. They are indeed a salient type of the age. They differ of course from their forerunners. They are not artificial (There is little time for artifice in the wear and tear of modern life; the motor car has swept much before it.) and they have that new freedom and frankness of manner that comes of being (as women now are, more or less) taken seriously.

No play has yet been written with the modern Pierrot woman as central figure, but if ever written there is one person to play it, and Miss Barrymore is that person.

Miss Barrymore, if she ever read this analysis of her essential quality by Max Beerbohm, could only have been nonplussed. She didn't stay as long in London this time. Frohman had a new play called *Sunday* for her to do in New York. It was written by three actors using the joint name of Thomas Raceward, in the manner of the stories of Bret Harte. Ethel played a foundling who had been brought up by four rough miners, and had to invent a Western drawl for the occasion.

The second act took place in England; the foundling was back with her relatives there, and the four miners had composed a letter to her which she read to her aunts. She stopped reading the letter at a part that was supposed to be too personal for the aunts to hear, and one of the aunts said, "Go on, Sunday."

The script had Ethel run off the stage without answering. While Frohman was watching a rehearsal, Ethel said to him: "I think I ought to say something to the aunt, not just run off like that."

Frohman, a little annoyed, asked her what line she wanted to say.

"Oh," Ethel said, "maybe something like 'That's all there is. There isn't any more.'"

"Yes," Frohman said, "that will do fine."

Thereafter Ethel's drawling way of ending the scene with "That's all there is. There isn't any more," brought down the house, and that line of added dialogue became virtually her trademark—to a degree annoying to her, because satirizers like Cissie Loftus and Elsie Janis were merciless about using the words for their Ethel Barrymore imitations.

Another grand Frohman tour of the country followed the New York success of *Sunday.* Ethel arrived in San Francisco shortly after Ashton Stevens had interviewed Lionel, and because she was grateful for any favorable attention paid to her brothers, she invited the critic to her suite at the St. Francis Hotel. "However," she told Stevens, "I plan to be the interviewer." She promised, too, to get her copy in on time.

> The following dialogue took place:
> *Ethel:* Mr. Stevens, do you think dramatic criticism has any value?
> *Ashton:* It's of great value to me.
> *Ethel:* Bernard Shaw said that some time ago.
> *Ashton:* I'm glad that Shaw and I agree on one point. As a matter of fact, I take great pleasure in going to the theater. I'm a most enthusiastic audience.
> *Ethel:* A "deadhead" though?
> *Ashton:* No, at Mr. Hearst's expense. I'm the best customer of the box office in San Francisco. I find a wonderful satisfaction in being by nature a passionate playgoer and in being able to talk about the play to four or 500,000 people the next morning. I think the most pleasant form of fiction is—
> *Ethel:* Dramatic criticism?
> *Ashton:* No, the drama. I think it is ridiculous that a popular

public demands so much newspaper space for actors rather than plays. Actors (dreamily) are the pianoforte upon which the composer plays.

Ethel: Luckily for the composer he seldom plays his own composition.

Ashton: For that matter, all actors are not Steinways.

Ethel: And very few authors are Beethoven. Mr. Stevens, has it ever struck you that the writing time a dramatic critic devotes to a first night—from forty minutes to two hours, depending on the newspaper—is inadequate for a just consideration of a performance that has taken the dramatist a year to write, the manager several months to arrange, and the actor as many months to study and rehearse?

Ashton: The critic's contribution of time is much greater than the audience's, for the latter's verdict is immediate. In this country, unfortunately, the hiss and boo are barred. He who pays for his seat is privileged to demonstrate only approval.

Ethel: You perhaps don't recognize that an actor is a sensitive creature. It doesn't take great demonstrations of sound to convey to his mind that he is a success or a failure. There is no sound so terrible to an actor as silence. To a mummer who sees across the footlights a sea of eager, intelligent faces, or—which more often happens, even to the greatest—a sea of dead masks—such conveys to the actor infinitely more than the vulgar, blatant demonstrations from the galleries of countries where hissing and booing are not only tolerated but encouraged.

Ethel was less good-humored about dramatic critics and criticism in later years, but Ashton Stevens remained an exception. He was a loyal admirer of all three Barrymores during their stage careers.

In London the following summer Ethel was advised by Frohman (who was, as usual, staying at the Savoy) to get an advance look at her next vehicle, Barrie's *Alice Sit-by-the-Fire,* in which Ellen Terry and Irene Vanbrugh were starred as mother and daughter, respectively. After seeing the play, Ethel visited Frohman who asked her whether she preferred to play the mother or the daughter. Ethel thought herself suited only for the younger role.

The telephone rang in Frohman's suite as though on cue. The playwright was on the other end of the line, asking how Frohman planned to cast the New York production. "I was just talking it over with Miss Barrymore," Frohman said.

"I'd prefer her to do the mother," Barrie said.

This was relayed to Ethel, who took the telephone and asked Barrie how he was able to visualize her as a woman well past forty. "I see you playing it and hear you saying all those things in the last act," Barrie said. "You have the 'mother thing,' you know."

It was in return for her agreement to play a woman with gray hair that Frohman agreed to let Lionel and John do the curtain raiser, *Pantaloon*, and John play a role in *Alice Sit-by-the-Fire*. Frohman was later credited with having the perspicacity to see that all the Barrymores possessed star quality, but it was the "mother thing" in Ethel that made her find opportunities for her brothers. It also accounted for her inability to save much of her considerable earnings. A remark made by Finley Peter Dunne around this time shows how well known she was for her handouts to John and Lionel. Dunne, a friend of Ethel's, was asked during the period of her engagement to Captain Harry Graham if the Englishman would be able to support the reputedly extravagant Ethel. "Don't worry," Dunne said. "Lionel and Jack will support them on the money Ethel gives to Lionel and Jack."

Ethel's following saw her as a creature of all lightness and charm, and Frohman's choice of her plays was dictated accordingly. Yet now and then she attempted to break out of the mold, as when in May of 1905 she played a brief revival of Ibsen's *A Doll's House* for a few weeks in New York and Boston. The critics were seemingly unresponsive to this more serious side of her ability, for as her popularity increased, notes of protest from the aisle-sitters became more pronounced. At the end of 1907 she appeared in another of Clyde Fitch's gossamer plays, *Her Sister*, which featured smart drawing room conversation and Ethel's very fashionable clothes.

"Miss Barrymore," wrote one critical observer, "is the victim of her own charms." He went on to say that to know her was a delight, merely to be presented to her a genuine distinction, but "it is complained that the young woman has never learned to act, and that it is time she should."

Ethel was quick to answer the slight on her abilities. "I wonder what it is the critics cry for," she said. "I think I discovered it when I saw a well-praised actress tear everything to pieces, unbare every emotion. There was nothing 'covered' in her acting, and you could see every cog and wheel of her emotion. *That* seems to be what the critics admire, what they rave about. They want to see the machinery. Never mind what is art or not. If the critics only realized what an easy thing it is to tear scenery to tatters and to murder diction in an attempt to act, they would not stress it so much." She would go her own way, she declared, and ignore the carpers.

But the carpers now thought the cult of her fame and success had been carried too far. And it did seem true that in *Her Sister* Frohman had chosen a most inane play for Ethel. Its heroine, which she played, was a poor woman who suceeded in staying virtuous despite all temptations that Fitch (and his co-author, Cosmo Gordon Lennox) could devise, and in the end this formidably virtuous creature was rewarded with a handsome, rich, and simon-pure husband.

"The deepest impression it left on me," wrote a critic, "was one of profound respect for the courage of the man who had dared to present it to the manager."

But the play deterred Ethel's fans not one whit. "Her following has become a veritable Frankensteinian monster," worried the critic. The first act, he noted, had already begun and ten whole rows of orchestra seats gaped emptily.

> Suddenly, all the doors burst open at once and a vast human tide came swarming in through the lobby; canes rattling, tongues chattering, silks rustling, and throats laughing. Noisily the flood surged and eddied about me, climbing over me, talking across me, looking through me, and finally subsiding into a sea of white necks, black broadcloth, showy shirt fronts, chiffons, and flowers.
>
> The ten empty rows were now filled with wealth and fashion and beauty. Isn't Ethel looking sweet tonight? a young woman exclaimed.
>
> Another young woman, after a thorough and critical examination, gave her opinion. I never saw her as handsome.
>
> A fretful, high-pitched voice was heard. Oh, please . . . *please* tell me what the play is about. But—I don't think I *like* her in that dress.

The critics were bothered because they made a distinction between what they regarded as a following and something vastly more important, an audience. The "following," they claimed, was not interested in Ethel as an actress but looked upon her merely as an ornamental young woman who wore a golden halo of fame. Two others had public followings of equal magnitude: they were George M. Cohan and Maude Adams. It was time, her true believers felt, that she assert herself as an actress.

Ethel, her scorn for her critics notwithstanding, determined to make them eat their words. At first she announced that Rosalind in *As You Like It* would be her next role. But Frohman was of a different mind. *Her Sister* was doing well at the Hudson, and the play, with Ethel in it, was wanted in other large cities of the country. Ethel's practical sense asserted itself (she was now receiving a percentage of the box-office receipts in addition to her salary) and she still had Lionel to support in Paris and Jack to rescue from his frequent states of impecuniousness, and off she went on tour.

According to Cornelia Otis Skinner, who knew Ethel well, "Ethel Barrymore was one star who knew the wisdom of building up a road following. She considered it no hardship, for to her every tour was an adventure." If some of the tours were on the rugged side, due to conditions on trains and in hotels that lacked the latest conveniences, Ethel, on the whole, lived comfortably. She spared no expense. She liked elegance; above all, she thought it important to live with taste. She was friendly with other members of the cast but maintained just enough reserve to emphasize her position as the star. On the stage she was uncommonly generous toward other actors, helping them to get their laughs, holding up her own lines if there was a chance another actor might get some applause on his exit.

She thought the public on the road preferable to the New York public, which "has such a superior air and its attitude that of trying to find out how bad a play can really be. It goes to carp, not to laugh and cry." But in other cities, she said, people came out to be amused and entertained.

"Where will you make your first appearance as Rosalind?" a rapt provincial interviewer asked.

"Not in New York, thank you. There's no telling what would be written and said about me. It might even be claimed I had the play written *for* me. And how could I survive that responsibility?"

Rosalind had to wait, for following her tour, Ethel dashed off to London and there saw *Lady Frederick,* a new play by young Somerset Maugham. She and Frohman at once decided that it would be her next play, and in September of 1909 she was in New York for the rehearsals. She had been invited to spend a weekend with Uncle Jack in East Hampton, and before leaving for the Long Island resort lunched at Sherry's with him. Included in the party were John Drew's wife, Ethel's Aunt Dodo, and a few other young people "coming down" for the weekend. A young man walked by the table and Drew called to him. "Hello! Sit down."

The young man sat down. He was introduced as Mr. Russell Colt. It turned out he too was going to East Hampton for the weekend. They all took the same train, and Ethel found him exceedingly attractive, so much so that she invited him to call on her at Uncle Jack's. Later that evening, after dinner, he called. "And after that," as Ethel described it, "well, it just happened."

Russell Griswold Colt was twenty-six at the time he met Ethel. He was the son of the millionaire president of the United States Rubber Company, Samuel Pomeroy Colt, who was also the president of the Industrial Trust Company, of Providence, Rhode Island. The younger Colt had some vague interest in finance, was well educated, well traveled, had a charming sense of humor, and with so rich a father was not particularly troubled by what might otherwise have been regarded as his irresponsibility. He played an excellent game of bridge and belonged to a set that gravitated between Newport and Palm Beach. Ethel determined that this time there would be no announcement of an engagement. The inevitable rumors spread, but they were not taken very seriously, if only because Ethel was a mature three years older than the millionaire's son.

She busied herself with *Lady Frederick,* described by a critic as "a brilliant, somewhat metallic, but exceedingly entertaining comedy of manners in which an Irish widow makes all the men she meets fall in love with her, then makes some of them fall out again." This woman, all glint, all metal, has been turned into what she seems to be by the effects of ten years of married hell and the loss of her only child.

An entranced young man says to her: "Do you suppose that I see nothing but the color in your cheeks—that I don't know beneath all this artificiality there isn't the dearest, warmest-hearted little woman in the world?"

Maugham, who was then thirty-three, and described as a "delightful, affable chap, not unlike Clyde Fitch in looks," had created a character that Ethel could not resist in spite of the critical complaint that she was devoting too much of her time to light, ephemeral plays. Any actress would have dearly loved to play the scene in which Lady Frederick must disenchant the callow young Lord Mereston, who has made the mistake of proposing to this experienced, dangerously radiant woman of title but no money. She arranges for him to learn the shabby mysteries of her beauty preparations by having him call on her at ten in the morning.

Ethel played it to the hilt. The audience saw her clad in dressing gown and slippers, her hair frowsy. Her maid dresses her, and Lady Frederick deliberately lets the young man see how much of her glorious hair must be attached to her head, and in his very presence she produces "a bloom of youth" with rosaline and powder.

Maugham provided the scene with lines that reportedly sent quivers and gasps through the women of the audience. "Just at present I can make a decent enough show by taking infinite pains," Ethel told the tortured suitor, in rich tones leavened by the trace of an Irish brogue, "and my hand's not so heavy that the innocent eyes of your sex can discover how much of me is due to art. But in ten years you'll be only thirty-two, and then, if I married you, my whole life would be a mortal struggle to preserve some semblance of youth."

Her impassioned speech and demonstrations of art and make-up cure the youthful lord, and he lets out a sigh of relief when she releases him from his proposal. But must Lady Frederick face the oncoming of a lonely middle age? Not at all. She promptly marries the youth's rich uncle.

This was the fare that Ethel took on a tryout tour before opening at the Hudson in New York. Wherever she went, whether it was Poughkeepsie or St. Louis, bundles of roses from Russell Colt arrived for her on stage, always after the second act curtain. But perhaps all was not going smoothly with this romance. The impassioned, devoted Colt had, it seemed, a roving eye for other women. Can we ascribe to her knowledge of some passing fancy of his the interview Ethel gave a young woman reporter in St. Louis?

"Women of wealth," she was quoted as saying scornfully, "are merely piggish and selfish, utterly content with comfortable living quarters, a good dinner, a little polo or bridge, a rapid automobile or two. They are empty shells and perfectly meaningless and useless to the country . . .

"Never, never," she continued, "will I marry the son of a millionaire! The millionaire would be bad enough, but the son of one—no. He hasn't any purpose in his existence. He never enters the world of affairs, the political arena, or a career of any kind, as English gentlemen consider it their duty to follow. [The American heirs] lie around in a luxurious club, bask in the glory of their fathers' dollars with infinite leisure. I will marry none other than a poor man."

Now the question became: did Ethel really *say* those words?

In the furor that followed the published interview, society leaders in the large cities claimed to be shocked by the Barrymore tirade. It was recalled that Ethel, the previous year, had been equally cruel in her remarks about critics. In newspaper articles it was wondered whether "society" was, in truth, as useless as Ethel reported it to be. She, the darling of society, should certainly be the one to know.

Telegrams flew back and forth between Charles Frohman and Ethel. He issued a denial of the "interview" published in St. Louis. "Miss Barrymore," he told reporters, "has been greatly upset by a railway accident on her way to St. Louis." (There was such an accident, but Ethel was unhurt.) "It left her in a nervous condition, and she is greatly shocked over the publication of the alleged interview."

Frohman made public a wire that Ethel had sent him in which she professed herself to be horrified at what had appeared in the papers. She had seen a young woman from the newspaper, she admitted, but had been cruelly and wrongly misquoted. "Not for words," said Ethel, "would I utter a statement about my American sisters that is so absolutely false and low."

The reporter, thus chastized, never uttered a peep. Ethel was far too grand a young lady, too esteemed, to take on in combat. And Ethel's real point was that even if she had spoken so, in a moment of agitation, no *lady* would have printed her words.

Society was mollified by Ethel's denial. In Chicago such august leaders as Mrs. LaVerne Noyes, the Princess Eugalitcheff, and Mrs. Edward Leight joined together in a statement. They said they were certain it was a dastardly Frohman press agent and not Ethel who had cast aspersions on the Four Hundred. Russell Colt, publicly, said not a word.

A series of ratifications of society's forgiveness of her took place as she continued *Lady Frederick* on its pre-Broadway run. The Chicago Press League gave her a "beauty banquet." The pathway to her place of honor at the head table was a carpet made from petals of American Beauty roses, into which Ethel sank ankle-deep as she walked. The luncheon, replete with speeches exalting beauty in women, art, and music, threw Ethel into a daze from which she recovered enough to notice that the ladies gathered up the bruised rose petals afterward and sold them as souvenirs.

The Indianapolis *Star* printed a poem by Clarence J. Bulleit that extolled her as follows:

> *A voice whose haunting melody would move*
> *Grim Pluto to yield up the Orphean dead;*
> *Eyes in whose radiance the god of love,*
> *Awed from his pranks, would hesitate to tread!*

After several more verses, the poem ended with a couplet:

> *Should men, as in the Pagan Age, adore,*
> *One goddess would be Ethel Barrymore!*

When she came to New York with *Lady Frederick* in November, 1908, Ethel was received with general applause. Society turned out as usual, and a headline in the *Des Moines Register* gave the important news of the opening to the Mid-West: PATRICIAN NEW YORK FORGIVES BARRYMORE.

Presumably Ethel had forgiven Russell Colt, too, for during the 104 nights that she played at the Hudson there was always one empty seat in a front row that she played to—unless it happened to be filled, as was frequent, by Russell Colt. He had bought the seat for the entire run. Each afternoon or evening that she entered her dressing room she found a huge bouquet waiting for her and attached to it a letter from Russell. The infatuated Ethel took the unusual step of having a private telephone installed in her dressing room. If the seat in front was empty, she would hurry after each act from the stage to the dressing room, pick up the receiver, and find the line open, with Russell at the other end. It was reported that she had paid forty dollars in a single month for calls to Boston.

After the New York run, Ethel took *Lady Frederick* to Boston, and it was in that city that the announcement of her engagement to Russell Colt was made on March 9, 1909. Never, never would she marry the son of a millionaire. Well, hardly ever. Colonel Samuel Pomeroy Colt asked Ethel to come to see him when he first received word that his son and Ethel were contemplating marriage. He was concerned because Wall Street was going through a mild panic, and he felt considerably poorer than usual. "I can't understand why you would want to marry my son," he told Ethel in the gloomy parlor of the old Holland House where he stayed when in New York. "I have no money." This was an indirect way of saying that Russell had none either.

Ethel, fixing a frank gaze on the old gentleman, gave the standard reply that she was marrying not for money but for love. Her statement may have sounded like a cliché, but it was true. Could she provide the income for the marriage? the colonel asked.

"I make enough money for the two of us," Ethel said.

And how much was that? The colonel was very blunt.

"About a hundred thousand a year," she replied. "But I think it would be a good thing if Russell had some sort of job."

The colonel saw to it that Russell joined the firm of H. L. Horton and Company, a Wall Street brokerage in which he had an interest, and stipulated that once his son buckled down to his career he would be made a junior partner of the firm.

When their engagement was reported, two of Ethel's friends showed skepticism. "Do you really believe she'll marry him?" one asked.

"It is possible," the other answered, "but it isn't customary."

However, the marriage took place sooner than anyone expected, even though several church dispensations were necessary because of the fact that Russell was not Catholic. Finally Ethel went directly to a friend, Bishop O'Connell of Boston, to hurry matters up. Russell was charmed by the bishop (who later became a cardinal) and wondered if he ought to give up Protestantism and turn Catholic. It was just a thought; he remained a Protestant and Ethel remained a Catholic. On Sunday morning, March 14, 1909, the two were married, as secretively as possible, at the Church of the Most Sacred Blood in Hyde Park, twelve miles from Boston. Another dispensation had been required to get married during Lent. The two witnesses were John Barrymore and Russell's brother, Roswell Colt. There was a wedding breakfast at the home of the John Fairchilds in Dedham, and Ethel resumed acting the following evening.

On that day Russell was reached by reporters. "It'll be a funny honeymoon," he said cheerfully, "the bride working and the husband loafing. But our honeymoon is going to last so long that Ethel will have all the various changes from work to ease she may need. Don't think for a moment I'm going to be left behind when she goes on tour to the Coast. One of my pre-engagement promises was that I would in no way interfere with her business or professional plans. Why were we so quiet about the wedding? There's a 'secret society' reason why I can't divulge it. I might say that Miss Barrymore and I form the secret society."

Russell went west with her for the tour; the two shared a private railway car, a wedding present from Colonel Colt. Shortly before they returned to New York it was announced that the celebrated English playwright, Sir Arthur Pinero, was writing his next play for Ethel. And in June Charles Frohman further announced that a distinct change would take place in her theatrical career; henceforth there would be no more light plays for her. She would only do strong dramatic work. "When a play of power comes along," he said, "she shall have it."

The play of power had already arrived in June of 1909, Pinero's *Mid-Channel*, which was of a distinctly dark, not to say gloomy, cast.

"You may not want to do it," Frohman told Ethel in his office. As was his habit he partly told, partly acted out the story.

"You're quite wrong," Ethel said. "I want to play the part very much,"

The canny Frohman had, of course, known that the moment was propitious for Ethel to turn serious but was unsure whether or not Ethel would require some convincing.

Ethel, who was pregnant, expected that her baby would arrive in early January, and there was then a wrangle over whether or not the play should open in September. Frohman wanted full speed ahead, whereas Ethel wanted a quiet summer away from the city. The dispute reached the newspapers, both Ethel and Frohman made mutual declarations of loyalty to each other, and Pinero finally declared that he would wait a year, if necessary, for Ethel to do the play.

Ethel and Russell took a house for the summer in Greenwich, Connecticut, with Jack and Lionel frequent visitors. Russell, meanwhile, had taken to commuting to Wall Street from Greenwich. "What train do you take?" a friend asked him.

"I usually miss the ten thirty-seven," Russell replied.

In the fall the Colts rented the August Belmont, Jr., town house on Thirty-fourth Street, and it was there that Master Samuel Colt was born during the night of November 28, 1909. Ethel had been introduced to the joys of watching football by her husband that autumn, and she said afterward that her first child had nearly been born in Princeton Stadium. The Ethel Barrymore public couldn't have been happier over this new event in its idol's life. Periodicals, newspapers everywhere, printed pictures of young mother and infant, a lace cap on Ethel's head. It was not even commented upon that Ethel in these pictures looked decidedly plump. She had survived marriage, motherhood, and her thirtieth birthday, and still her public loved her.

A CONVULSION OF NATURE

chapter IX

ACTING, romance, and drinking occupied John Barrymore about equally after he put aside his artistic ambitions. If Ethel had started him off as an actor, it was Willie Collier who was his true discoverer. Collier was a popular comedian at Weber and Fields Music Hall, a friend of John Drew's, a baseball companion of Lionel's. When Frohman intrigued him away from his vaudeville following to star in Richard Harding Davis's *The Dictator,* Collier suggested John for the part of an absent-minded telegrapher. Ethel immediately seconded the proposal and Frohman gave way; he hired John at the quite handsome salary of thirty-five dollars a week. *The Dictator* kept him employed for the better part of 1904 and 1905; he toured Australia and England with it, and established himself as the attractive light comedian that Collier (and Frohman earlier) had envisioned.

But John at this period of his life made more news in another field—the field of romance. He began his career precociously, rumor having it that he was started off on the path of sexual adventure at the age of fourteen by his father's second wife, Mamie Floyd. Rumor also had it that this early seduction had had its traumatic effect on him. If so, he gave little evidence of it during the first years of the twentieth century. He was only nineteen when he kept Ethel and her friends at Mrs. Wilson's boardinghouse highly amused by his habit of using Ethel's telephone to call up several girls in a row (usually of some chorus or other) and employing the same conversational gambit with each. "It was quite an education for me," Ethel recalled later.

He attracted attention around town when he temporarily monopolized Bonny Maginn, a chubby little dancer at Weber and Fields. She was one of the toasts of Rector's—a more lively Sardi's of that day—and she and John were seen there together almost every night. After a while John switched his affections to Vivian Blackburn, a beautiful showgirl and model. Vivian ditched him for the son of a vice-presidential candidate. When the pert singer and dancer, Elsie Janis, reached Broadway as a star, John was her frequent escort, and rumors spread of their engagement. But Elsie had a vigilant and terrifying watchdog of a mother, and John was soon shooed away.

By far the most sensational of these romances of his early phase was with Evelyn Nesbit, still a teen-ager when she became known as "the Toast of Broadway." She became known, too, as the protégée of Stanford White, the famous architect who later was shot to death by Harry K. Thaw in a dispute over the same Miss Nesbit. Barrymore met her at a Stanford White luncheon in his "tower apartment" in the old Madison Square Garden. John was twenty-one, Evelyn seventeen.

Evelyn Nesbit testified to John's courtship methods when she was a witness at Thaw's trial. "Barrymore," she said, "kept pinching at his thin mustache, throwing me covert, admiring glances; and once, when our host left the room to answer the telephone, he leaned forward and whispered, 'Quick! Your address and telephone number.'" Evelyn obliged the handsome fellow with the information and he scribbled it on his starched white cuff. The evening of the same day he sent a tender bunch of violets to her dressing room and a note surrounded by several funny little sketches. Evelyn's fancy was more tickled by these than by the several hundred dollars worth of orchids Stanford White had sent to her dressing room.

"He called for me at the stage door every night," said Evelyn, "without fail, and took me to Rector's for supper. He would order me a glass of milk, set a rose leaf on its surface, and say, 'that is your mouth.'" To reporters who queried him as to his intentions, he said: "She is a quivering pink poppy in a golden windswept space."

Another statement was slightly more down to earth: "She possesses the most perfectly modeled foot since Venus."

Youth flamed sweetly. One night John and the exquisite Evelyn dined and drank red wine at a small Italian restaurant. Evelyn drank too fully, and John suggested she recuperate at his rooms before he took her home to her mother. "The rooms were not even decently warm," Evelyn recalled indignantly. John wrapped her in an old cloak of his father's, and she stretched out on the floor and fell asleep. John folded himself up somewhere in the vicinity. Both slept a long, dreamless sleep (or so they declared) and awoke to find it was early afternoon of the next day. Terror set in, both of Evelyn's mother and of the hovering "benefactor," Stanford White. John bravely volunteered to accompany her home. He was met by screams from mother Nesbit that he had ruined her daughter's reputation. Stanford White was there, too, glowering at him.

John was dismissed, only to be bidden to appear before White in his apartment atop Madison Square Garden later in the day. What White really wanted to know was whether or not John had besmirched the girl. John assured him gallantly otherwise, and just as gallantly offered to marry Evelyn. The offer was refused by White on his and Mrs. Nesbit's behalf. But because John kept repeating the offer at frequent intervals, White suggested that Evelyn be sent to an out-of-town school. And Evelyn was so sent.

But a few years later, in June of 1906, Evelyn was involved in one of the century's most sensational crimes. She had married a socialite millionaire, Harry K. Thaw, who, suspecting that White was still paying court to Evelyn, shot him down on the roof of Madison Square Garden. Thaw's family spent enormous sums to paint a picture for the public of Thaw's virtue and White's blackheartedness. The district attorney tried, on the other hand, to prove that Thaw could hardly fail to at least know something about his wife's past and attempted to find John Barrymore to testify about his former (and perhaps continuing) romance with Evelyn. John faked a nervous breakdown and managed not to appear in court. Thaw was convicted of murder but escaped the death penalty. Upon which

John Barrymore was suddenly seen in New York again, looking the very picture of health.

William Collier at times regretted his sponsorship of John as an actor, although he did much to pass on to him his own sense of comic timing. When opening night for *The Dictator* came at the Criterion in New York, John failed to appear, and the stage manager was hastily called upon to take his place. John had taken some friendly drinks at The Lambs and quite forgot about his opening until around the time the last-act curtain came down. Collier forgave him this lapse but added some dire warnings should anything of the same sort occur in the future.

John did manage to make his opening curtains by a hairsbreadth, and to save time usually slept in his costume. On tour he was late for train calls, sometimes managing to jump aboard a car as it was leaving the station, at other times catching the next train. In Cincinnati Collier asked him to leave a wake-up call at his hotel because the next train to their destination wouldn't leave until twenty-four hours later. John caught the train at the last moment, dressed in evening clothes. Fuming, Collier asked why he hadn't left the call at his hotel, and John explained that he distinctly had left calls at *six* hotels, just to be sure. "I didn't manage to hit the right one," he said apologetically.

Collier eventually decided to fire John and wired Frohman that he would do so. "Don't do it, Willie," Frohman hastily wired back. "It will break Ethel's heart." Collier replied: "If I keep him it will break mine."

John, like Lionel, was interviewed by Ashton Stevens in San Francisco. "Don't overlook my good fortune in being the nephew of John Drew and the brother of Ethel," John told him. "It helps fabulously. . . .

"But in a way I do take acting seriously. Acting is a great stunt, you know, if you can succeed in it. No man is old nowadays until he is thirty. You are either a live member of society or a dead one by the time you are thirty—a success or a failure.

"Through the kindness of Charles Frohman—there's a brain for you—I first appeared in *Glad of It,* and again through the kindness of Frohman in *The Dictator.* I'm inclined to believe the ancient and honorable saying that good parts make good actors. At the same time, I am also of the belief that you don't know how good an actor is until you see him in a bad part. The actorial family tree with its prestige and a moderate share of the center of the stage will, for a time, make the young actor a point of attraction. But he's got to make good later on. He's got to justify the tremendous start in his favor. And he's got to take the thing seriously."

Here we find the first recorded indication that John Barrymore was beginning to take the stage seriously. He had something, also, to say about audiences.

"Audiences? No; the plural is impossible. Whether it be in Butte or Broadway, it's an audience. The same great hulking monster with four thousand eyes and forty thousand teeth. What a wonderful monster it is, with a hide that might have been torn from a battleship, with warts on it like hills, just like those bug-house cartoons I used to draw. And that monster unit with one mind makes or breaks men like me. The narcotic of acting is that it comes easy and pays well." John's salary had just been raised to forty dollars a week.

John left *The Dictator* company to play on the road briefly with Ethel in *Sunday* and later in the double bill of *Pantaloon* and *Alice Sit-by-the-Fire*. One reason Ethel wanted John with her, it was said, was because he had continued his romantic escapades in London when he was there with Collier, and she wanted to keep him from the clutches of some ardent married aristocrats. Collier, deciding to take *The Dictator* to Australia, offered John his old part back, and they arrived again in San Francisco just in time for the great earthquake of April, 1906.

While waiting to board ship, John went to see *Carmen* at the Grand Opera House, with Caruso in the cast. At a late supper party after the opera he met a man who invited him home to see his newly arrived collection of old Chinese porcelain, and John decided to sleep the rest of the night there rather than walk back to the St. Francis Hotel. He had been in bed for only a few minutes when the first shock tossed him out of it to the floor.

Slightly perturbed, John put on his dinner clothes again, noticed the collection of crockery had been shattered, and woke his host who slept soundly. "Come and see what's happened to the Ming Dynasty,"

John shouted, to get the man's eyes firmly open. They left the partially demolished house and walked toward the center of town, noticing that several houses had whole walls missing. Many of the embarrassed occupants covered themselves from public view with sheets.

As John neared the St. Francis, William Collier saw him and shouted cheerfully: "Go west, young man, and blow up with the country!" Collier was perched on a pile of baggage amid the rubble, still wearing bedroom slippers and a dressing gown. John noticed Madame Alba of the opera company wearing a flimsy wrapper and, because she looked chilled, gallantly offered to bring her a warming drink. He found a place open, purchased a glass of brandy, and carefully carried it back to Madame Alba. Diamond Jim Brady saw him en route and told admiring stories afterward about how John wandered around the quake-stricken city in the early morning hours dressed in evening clothes and delicately holding a drink. A second shock came. The St. Francis held firm, so John retired for the balance of the night. He slept until his nostrils told him something was burning. It turned out to be San Francisco.

He joined friends in a suburb, Burlingame, and stayed for six days, meanwhile hoping that the Collier company had gone on to Australia. He had lost his zest for the trip. It was suggested that he at least get word to his family and to Frohman, so he borrowed a bicycle and headed for San Francisco. He also borrowed a police badge to get him through the various cordons set up to prevent looting. Before he reached the Oakland ferry, some soldiers overseeing a gang of men sorting and piling debris assumed that John was the sort of man to take charge of the operation, especially with the badge displayed so prominently. John bossed the gang for eight hours before being allowed to proceed.

In Oakland John ran into Ashton Stevens, who informed him his company was to sail from Vancouver in three days and that he still had time to make the trip. Another member of the company appeared, hailed Jack, and there was nothing to do but head for Vancouver. From there he wrote a long letter describing his experiences, considerably embellishing them in the process, and Ethel, reading the letter sympathetically to her Uncle Jack, noticed that he seemed quiet. "Don't you believe it?" she asked him.

"Every word," Drew responded. "It took a convulsion of nature to get him out of bed and the United States Army to make him go to work."

After returning from Australia, where naturally he encountered a beautiful woman, singer Grace Palotta, and where he only made the return ship because Collier held his ticket and threatened to abandon him if he didn't get aboard on time, John appeared briefly in two plays. In one of these, *Toddles*, he was actually the star, but the Clyde Fitch trifle was demolished by the critics, and John was out of work and, as usual, broke. Fortune was heading his way, however, in the person of Mort Singer, a Chicago producer of musical shows who had read some pleasant notices of John's work in *Toddles*. Singer took a train east to try to interest John in a Chicago production of a musical called *A Stubborn Cinderella*, found that his quarry had gone to Atlantic City with friends of rather poor repute, and journeyed to the boardwalk town.

John was alone at his hotel by the time Singer got there and would have returned to New York if he could have hit on a way of paying his hotel bill. Singer found him sitting moodily in front of a plateful of shrimp bisque which served as his dinner. John listened to the story of *A Stubborn Cinderella*, and his eyes opened wide when Singer offered him a weekly salary of a hundred and fifty dollars. "Make it one seventy-five," Singer said, thinking that John was hesitant. "A handshake on the deal gets you another hundred in advance." John gulped and shook hands.

John co-starred in *A Stubborn Cinderella* with Sallie Fisher, who was billed as the prima donna and played an English girl of overwhelming innocence. John played a madcap, convivial collegian. As insubstantial a bit of fluff as the show was, it turned out to be one of the biggest hits in the history of Chicago, which was then a major theatrical center.

Julia Warwick, whose mother was the wardrobe mistress, still recalls John in the show. "He did not collect guffaws, but his wit and clever delivery were sustained. One scene was his solely. He was supposed to be sculpting a bust of Sallie Fisher. The prop man rigged up an elliptical bust on a stand on which was piled modeling clay shaped to resemble a head. In the act, with a spatula-like tool, he gouged out two holes for eyes, made a nose of the two balls removed, shaved here, dug there, for ears' material, during which he had some side-splitting chatter, along with ad-libs about everything on his mind, some of which was heard out front."

As was true from then on, no two performances were alike. "He had remarkable hands," said Mrs. Warwick. "He could stand stock-still, with his head cocked sideways, and get more out of his hands than from a page of dialogue. He did a recitative to music, during which he shuffled, tripped, and bounced, which could not by any means be called a song and dance, but he was nimble, exceedingly graceful and different. It went over."

The Chicago critics were delighted with him, finding him "as fascinating as his father in his palmiest days." They said he had inherited the grace of his lovely mother, the magnetism of his erratic father, and the fascination of John Drew. "Of course he can't sing, but he dances like a jumping Jack endowed with brains." Clearly it was in Chicago that John found his abilities at last. He also found financial stability for the first time. Once the show was a roaring hit, Mort Singer gave him heavy rises in salary in order to keep the young star with him as long as possible. Jack never missed a performance, although Julia Warwick remembers those perspiring moments back-stage before the curtain was due to rise, with everyone waiting until Barrymore made his "last inning, last-minute home run for his first entrance on stage. His timing was perfect; he arrived at the theater just as the overture was being played."

The press agents were busy touting an "engagement" between Jack Barrymore and Sallie Fisher, but Julia Warwick described the talk as nonsense. "In the very early days of their working together she may have had a slight crush on him because he could be charming, thoughtful, and he had impeccable manners. But Miss Fisher was not his cup of tea—she was a decent lady. Nor was working with him a bed of roses. I remember one evening. I was sitting on my perch—a wardrobe trunk near the stairs—with one of the chorus girls. Barrymore was going upstairs for the last scene. The chorus girl said: 'Poor Sallie Fisher. She'll have to hold him up again to be kissed. And that will be like propping up a mashed juniper tree.' "

Mrs. Warwick also remembered Ethel, who was in Chicago briefly during the tour of *Lady Frederick,* being out front one night to watch her brother. "She came backstage after the show," Mrs. Warwick said, "and midway down the stairs (backstage was the basement) she shouted, 'Jack-k-k, Jack! Come and *get* me.' Well, it had the desired effect. Every dressing room door opened and was cluttered with heads. Miss Barrymore made her majestic trek down the long hall to Jack's dressing room, smiling and greeting all of them."

New York was much less friendly to *A Stubborn Cinderella* when its Chicago success prompted a Broadway opening. One critic even suggested that John had been miscast, preferring to blame the material. After playing a barker at Coney Island for a few weeks in a play that collapsed quickly, John was tapped for Winchell Smith's comedy, *The Fortune Hunter.* Fortune was now hunting John Barrymore down, even though the producers were doubtful about his ability to carry the play after it opened to a chilly reception in New Haven.

He played the part of a down-and-out profligate who is advised by a friend that his only way of recouping is to head for a small town, stop drinking, smoking, and swearing, attend local church functions, and create a general belief in himself as a young man of exemplary virtue. He will then be able to pick out the richest girl in town to marry. Naturally none of the plan works. The young man is moved to help an impoverished old druggist, marries *his* daughter, but eventually, finding the exemplary life more to his liking, becomes a prosperous tradesman.

Lionel had returned from Paris in time for John's opening night on September 4, 1909, but Ethel, in an advanced stage of pregnancy, had decided not to chance the muggy weather and sent a red apple in her place. Seats were at a premium for the opening—as though word had gotten out that this would be another big Barrymore event —and Lionel had to stand at the back of the house, accompanied by Kid McCoy, the boxer he had gotten to know well while imitating him in *The Other Girl.* John was faultless that evening. He had all the glibness and buoyancy the role demanded, and when a hint of pathos was required, he managed that too. Backstage after the performance was crowded as it had never been before.

"What the hell happened?" John asked his brother. He seemed almost frightened. Escaping from the crowd of well-wishers, he, Lionel, and Kid McCoy found an out-of-the-way café and celebrated over champagne.

John explained his fear. "I heard thunder in the applause," he said. He was disturbed and saddened because it occurred to him that he now had a career that could no longer be taken lightly. "It was good-by to the irresponsibilities of youth," he wrote in his *Confessions,* "I had happened to be fairly good at them."

John's stardom was assured when crowds stormed the Gaiety Theatre night after night to see him in *The Fortune Hunter.* Ethel took in a performance two weeks later and told him backstage, "Jack, you're the biggest Barrymore yet." Less than a month after the opening his name went up in lights, and the producers, George M. Cohan and Sam H. Harris, redecorated his dressing room in prevailing tones of blue at a cost of a thousand dollars.

He recalled what Kid McCoy had told him over the champagne following opening night: "Remember what Bill Mizner said, son—'Be awfully nice to them going up, because you're bound to meet them all coming down.'" Two months later John bought out the entire house for a matinee and invited everyone he knew in the theatrical profession. The theater was packed, and John made a speech, addressing the audience as his "fellow unfortunates." The Friars returned the favor in January of 1910 by throwing a dinner in his honor at the Astor, taking over the north ballroom. "John Barrymore," a theatrical columnist enthused afterward, "is now the youngest male star in the country."

In April Sam Harris, aware of the long-running potential of the play, and aware too of the steadily increasing number of scented letters sent to John by female admirers, attempted to negotiate with Lloyd's of London for a $50,000 policy against John's marrying within a year. The reason for this was, a statement from his office (and presumably concocted by a press agent) said, "that married, Jack Barrymore will be worth only half of what he is now." John solemnly filed an affidavit to the effect that he was not now and did not intend to become engaged.

A few months later the *New York Times* carried a lengthy announcement of his engagement to a youthful girl, Katherine Corri Harris, who had recently made her debuts in Newport and New York society.

The engagement provided the public with several enthralling tidbits of gossip. John had met Katherine when he was invited to the ball given by Katherine's mother, Kitty Harris, in honor of her daughter's New York debut. Mrs. Harris was a stage-struck woman, who had hoped herself to become a star. She had even played with John Drew in *Rosemary*. The Barrymores and the Drews were more fascinating to her than the wealthy society of which she was part, and John's reputation as a Lothario did not bother her in the least. Her divorced husband, Sidney Harris, who was a prominent lawyer with practices in Paris and New York, was a good deal less impressed with John as a prospective son-in-law. He was aware of John's involvement in the Thaw case and knew of John's subsequent romances, including one with Irene Frizzell, a chorus girl who became known as "the Pocket Venus." Irene had ditched John for Jay Ward, a Wall Street financier and man-about-town, then married Felix Isman, a real estate and shipping magnate. She kept to the stage, changed her name to Irene Fenwick, and many years later became the second wife of Lionel Barrymore.

Sidney Harris was the son of Miriam Coles Harris, who wrote sweet novels about the perils and pleasures of chastity. Kitty, his wife, had first been known as one of the beautiful Brady sisters, daughters of New York Supreme Court Justice John R. Brady. The other daughter, May, became Mrs. Stevens Harriman of the fabulously wealthy Harriman stock. Both daughters inherited trust funds from a rich uncle, Charles Daly, but Kitty Harris, after her divorce, was able to keep up her style of living mainly from the large alimony Sidney Harris had been ordered to pay. Sidney's objections to John were further based on the rumors of his intemperateness and on the ten-year difference in age between the Broadway star and Katherine.

He made the mistake of ordering his divorced wife to take their daughter to France and put her in a convent school. Mrs. Harris, perhaps thinking of the alimony she received regularly, complied. But this had the effect of deepening Jack's passion for little Kitty, who was a lovely creature with taffy-colored hair, eyes described as a "saucer-like blue," and the possessor of what an admirer called "a fashionable Riverside Drive lisp." He was inconsolable over her absence, his letters told Katherine.

It was Katherine's grandmother, Gabbie Lydig Brady, who came to the rescue of the lovers. The elderly lady wrote her granddaughter as follows:

> DEAR KITTY:
>
> Don't let your father keep you over there. Come back with your mother. You cannot be shut up. The more he is against Jack Barrymore, the more you will like him. Do not be afraid of Mr. Harris. He helped to bring you into the world. That was all.
>
> Aunt May and Uncle Herbert [the Harrimans] are bitterly against Jack, but don't you care. Come home to see him. A lady told me today that the Barrymores go everywhere in Philadelphia. Excellent family. Excellent position.
>
> Jack looks as if he wants a woman's care. I saw him in the street. He is so handsome. If I were a young woman, I would be crazy about him myself.

The letter was written immediately after John was pointed out to Mrs. Brady on the street. Perhaps but for this accident his matrimonial career would have taken a different turn. As it was, the letter turned the tide, and an absurd little real-life comedy then ensued. Taking advantage of Sidney Harris's temporary presence in New York (he spent most of his time in Paris), the mother helped her daughter jump convent and went westbound with her on the *Oceanic* to New York. Hearing rumors of revolt, Sidney Harris had already taken ship for Paris. Upon arriving there and finding mother and daughter gone, he turned around and took the first steamship he could get on back to New York.

While Harris was still on the high seas heading west, John met Kitty Harris the elder and Kitty Harris the younger when the *Oceanic* docked. He kissed each affectionately, took them to their Madison Avenue hotel, the Brayton, and the following day Mrs.

Harris formally announced the engagement. Katherine's being engaged to one of New York's most notorious names displeased the Harrimans mightily, and miffed at her own mother's role in the affair, the rich May Brady Harriman withdrew, according to the newspapers, a large income that she had settled on Gabbie Brady. Later Mrs. Harris had to sue her former husband for unpaid alimony. He too had presumably taken the most chastening form of revenge.

When John was approached for statements on his forthcoming nuptials, he gave the following worldly-wise opinions: "A couple who want to get married should appear before a judge for a license. The judge should relate the hardships of marriage and then send them home to think it over. If nothing shakes their resolutions, let them appear before a judge and get the license. If they're able to stand all those preliminaries, they'll probably be able to stand matrimony, too."

He and Katherine appeared at the City Hall marriage license bureau in early August, 1910, the day before Mr. Harris's ship, *La Provence*, docked. Sidney Harris was met by rumors that the couple had run off and secretly married. It was reported that his face showed an expression of extreme distaste. At any event, married or not, there was nothing he could do to prevent a marriage, he said. "The law says my daughter is old enough to marry."

For some reason Katherine gave her age as nineteen on the license, although that birthday was still some months away. John's address was given as 228 West 42 Street—the address of a well-known restaurant, Murray's. John had an apartment over the restaurant.

One of the casualties of the wedding announcement was the fiction about a Lloyd's policy insuring his singleness. Sam Harris did not collect the supposed $50,000 indemnity, and when the play opened for its second year's run in September, an enthusiastic audience wildly cheered the newly married Jack.

The marriage had taken place on the evening of September 1, a Thursday, in the Church of St. Francis Xavier. John left immediately to appear on the stage, and Katherine left with Ethel to the home she and Russell Colt had recently purchased in Mamaroneck. Ethel had been a witness at the ceremony as had, fittingly, the bride's grandmother, Mrs. Brady. Since John's bachelor quarters were not suitable for a married couple and because Katherine's abode was still the Brayton Hotel, it was announced they would stay temporarily with the Colts in Mamaroneck.

It was not long before John had something to say publicly about the state of marriage. "A true sporting spirit is indispensable to a happy marriage. The married sportsman does not believe that his wife is to forsake her old friends and devote herself exclusively to him. He knows that she will still require friends and amusements. The married sportsman will not nag or scold, and petty fault-finding will be beneath him. The husband with the sporting spirit will give his wife mental, financial, and social freedom . . ."

As for the husband's rights of freedom in marriage he had no comment. But hardly a week after his marriage it was rumored on Broadway that Katherine complained she saw her new husband all too infrequently.

LIONEL AT LARGE / *chapter X*

IN 1906, newly arrived in Paris, Lionel and Doris found their first place to live on the sixth floor of a house on Rue Bonaparte, taking over the studio of Raymond Duncan who, even then, wore his Greek-style toga for which—along with the fact that he was Isadora's brother—he became increasingly famous. The rooms cost $135 a year in rent and were not much of a bargain, for they lacked conveniences, and the Barrymores soon discovered that the walls exuded moisture. May Irwin, a well-known comedienne and friend of the Barrymores, visited Doris and Lionel there and reported to Ethel on her return: "You ought to see those dear young things beginning a painter's life in the Latin Quarter. I didn't know whether to laugh or cry."

But Lionel was supremely happy and so was Doris, who loved being in Paris and experimenting with French cookery over her small stove. Lionel registered at the Academie Julien, an atelier presided over by a noted academic painter, Jean-Paul Laurens, who completely awed the would-be artist because one of his works hung in the Panthéon. Checks from Ethel arrived with unfailing regularity. Lionel and Doris made an enthusiastic exploration of the artistic-bohemian life; they congregated with painters and writers, drank cheap red wine, talked art late into the night.

Lionel seldom completed a painting, but that was only to be

expected of a student at the Academie Julien, where at the end of each week it was customary for the students to scrape the paint off their canvases, clean their brushes and palettes, and start afresh on Monday. Praise was doled out sparingly, and Lionel seems to have received none at all from his instructors. He wasn't bothered by this, for he knew no one else who received praise at the Academie. The Laurens precepts were faithfully followed by Lionel, but he was too shy to show his work to the master who came once a week on Saturdays to criticize. On that day Lionel would stay away. But one day Laurens came on a Wednesday, and he looked at the work on Lionel's easel. He asked Lionel who he was, looked at the work again, said, "Ha!" and that was all. This only added to Lionel's appreciation of Paris, where the Barrymore name was not automatically associated with actors and acting.

He and Doris during a three-year period of residence in the Latin Quarter tried several places of abode, all with an eye to low rental and high creative atmosphere. One such was a large studio over a printing shop, rented at a surprisingly low figure. They soon discovered what the catch was. Below them the printing presses thumped all day, rattling the entire building. So rapt was Lionel in his painting that he grew used to the continual tremors and noise and so did the patient, adaptable Doris. The proprietor rewarded them, while they were away on a trip to the country, by redecorating the entire apartment for them free of charge.

Sixteen months after they had left the United States they made a brief visit home, traveling on the *Bremen*. Ethel met them at the dock in Hoboken. Lionel shaved off the shaggy, black beard he had grown in Paris so as not to shock his sister, but he could not hide the fact that he had grown stout, and Ethel hardly recognized his moonlike face. The rigors of the stage and his boxing and wrestling workouts in gymnasiums had kept Lionel reasonably slim in the past, but French food and wine and too little physical activity accounted for the weight increase. If Ethel had hopes that Lionel might be persuaded to go back to the stage, they were dashed by his appearance, suitable only for genuine heavies. After a month of family visits, Lionel and Doris sailed back to Paris.

In another couple of months Doris became pregnant, and the child was born in midsummer of 1908. Ethel rushed over to see her niece, who was named Ethel Barrymore II, in obvious gratitude as well as honor, and immediately took an apartment on fashionable Avenue Marceau to help Doris during the nursing period.

Lionel continued with his painting for another year. He developed enthusiasms for the work of painters such as Le Didaner, Prinet, and Dauchez, aligning himself not with the avant-garde, as can be seen, but with the academicians. Picasso was in Paris, was already being talked about, and Lionel noticed him at the Dôme in Montparnasse and heard about him, too, from Gertrude Stein, whose acquaintance he had made. He failed to see much in another new painter, Matisse, and continued his academic exercises, not much aware of the painting that would soon become dominant. Yet, as his etchings in later life showed, he had unusual ability and sensitivity.

When Ethel suddenly married Russell Colt in 1909, Lionel realized his time was up in Paris. He had not been "discovered," and he could no longer expect that Ethel, the main breadwinner of her own marriage, would want to continue her monthly remittances to him. He and Doris sailed for home on the *Pennsylvania* in late July, 1909, and docked in Hoboken on August 6. Only one ship's reporter recognized the heavy young man who disembarked with his wife and year-old daughter. Lionel was asked what his plans were, and he replied, in all honesty, that they were indefinite. "Do you contemplate a talk with Charles Frohman?" the reporter asked.

"Yes," Lionel said, "I'll have a talk with Mr. Frohman."

In one last attempt to escape his fate, Lionel prepared several drawings in the hope of interesting magazine editors in him as an illustrator. But he soon discovered that prominent members of the American "Ash-Can School," Glackens, Sloan, and Luks, were also the artists preferred by such popular magazines as *Collier's*. He was not only out of the swim in Paris but here too. It was back to acting and he went to see Frohman, who, as usual, came to the rescue. Frohman was about to send out on the road (before bringing it to New York) a play by A. Conan Doyle called *The Fires of Fate*. There was the role of Abdulla that Lionel could have. Abdulla, as it turned out, was written as a fat, loquacious, unctuous dragoman employed as a guide by an Englishman touring the Middle East.

The Fires of Fate opened in Chicago in December, 1909. The astonished reviewers commented on Lionel's remarkable girth, but were kind to him nevertheless. "We are led," one said, "to the enthusiastic impression that Lionel Barrymore is the most skillful character actor of this stage." Not long after the Chicago opening Lionel came down with appendicitis, requiring an emergency operation. Whether this operation ever occurred is not known for certain, but one thing is certain: Lionel made a rapid and remarkable recovery. Hardly a week after he left the play he appeared with Sidney and Gladys Drew in a vaudeville sketch. A good guess is that Lionel was unwilling to face the New York remarks on his new appearance and decided to take advantage of his uncle's offer of a vaudeville job. Ethel opposed his doing this, but he was stubborn about it.

He stayed in vaudeville for a year and a half, performing in sketches written by his Aunt Gladys and by himself. None of these were intentionally humorous, although they might seem so now. One, of Gladys Rankin authorship, went over particularly well and was called *The Still Voice*. The story dealt with a rich man who tyrannized his family. Over a fireplace in his home hung a recently purchased painting of Christ. All at once, during the course of the sketch, a sepulchral voice (Lionel's) issued from the fireplace, over which hung the painting. The voice gave the rich man and his family all sorts of needed advice.

For a change of bill Aunt Gladys wrote another sketch, *The Jail Bird*, a piece that was talked out mainly by McKee Rankin. When the vaudeville audiences proved restive at so much talk, Lionel wrote another, *The White Slave*, which contained parts for himself, his wife, Doris, and her father, McKee Rankin. In it a coal man, come to deliver coal to a girl kept in white slavery, recognizes the girl as his own daughter from the locket she wears, and when her keeper comes to collect her earnings he gets instead, as his due reward, a stiletto driven into his breast by the coal man. This went over well on the Keith and Proctor vaudeville circuits, and Lionel found himself reviewed favorably as an author.

But the tour came to an end and Lionel, ready to try Broadway again, found that no one had anything to offer him. The talk at The Players and at Gilsey's bar, where free lunch was served, was frequently about that new thing, motion pictures. He happened to meet a chap at lunch whose name was D. W. Griffith and learned that he was making one-reelers at 11 East Fourteenth Street in New York City. Lionel paid him a call and offered his services, which were met with immediate suspicion by Griffith, who told Lionel, "I don't employ stage stars." Griffith thought that stage people took themselves too seriously and were liable to put on airs if they worked in such a lowly medium as the movies.

Lionel immediately disclaimed any excessive amount of attachment to the stage, said he by no means regarded himself as a star, and was mainly interested in a job that provided steady work. Griffith put him on at ten dollars a day with the stipulation that he bring his own dress suit for his first one-reeler. This was called *Friends;* it marked Lionel Barrymore's debut in motion pictures, and he appeared in it in a borrowed dress suit.

Griffith was then cranking out at least one movie a week with titles such as *Love at First Sight, Two Days Later,* and *Came the Dawn*. Production was done in Fort Lee, New Jersey, and later in Coytesville, New Jersey. On and behind the bluffs that overlooked the Hudson he was able to indulge his liking for spectacle, though on an admittedly small scale. Mary Pickford, a pretty little thing, worked for Griffith at about the same time, and she and Lionel appeared together in *The New York Hat,* a story by another diminutive girl whose name was Anita Loos. She received fifteen dollars in full payment for the tale.

Ethel took a dim view of Lionel's sacrificing his stage talent for the steadier movie work. He hooted her objections away, told her he enjoyed appearing in movies and enjoyed even more the regular paychecks, which rose to fifteen dollars soon enough. He was able to pick up extra remuneration by writing one and two-reeler scenarios, for which Griffith had an endless need. One of Lionel's first such efforts was called *The Tenderhearted,* built from an actual incident he had observed. A butcher boy in Port Jefferson, Long Island, where Lionel had taken a small house, kind-heartedly left little cuts of meat with a poverty-stricken old woman. The woman, it turned out, had hoarded a large sum of money and willed it to the boy when she died. The story was worth twenty-five dollars to Lionel, who related it to Griffith at lunch one day and was told to put it on paper.

The camera that Lionel faced then was a heavy square box with machinery driven by bicycle chains and that made a noise something like a gasping flivver. Scenery was painted cloth, not dissimilar to that used on the stage. For illumination direct sunlight was the only source, and the harsh shadows it caused made an actor's eyes look like black craters in his face.

Griffith began spending six months of the year in the wider spaces and more mellow sunlight of California. He first considered Florida, which might, if he had followed through, have become a movie capital perhaps the equal of Hollywood. Several of his regular players were scheduled to go with him on his first movie-making junket in the west, and Lionel discovered, to his dismay, that his name was not on the list. One of the most prominent actresses of the stage at that period, Minnie Maddern Fiske, unwittingly played a part in the development of Lionel's film career. She had let it be known that she was considering him for a part in her new production, not realizing that Lionel was much stouter than when she had seen him perform some years before. But Lionel used this interest to get to California. He contrived to have her stage manager (and a friend of his) get her to telephone him at a restaurant used for lunch by Griffith and his actors in Coytesville.

Lionel, when he took the call, spoke loudly and assured Mrs. Fiske he would be delighted to appear in her play and would be ready to rehearse at a moment's notice.

Griffith rose to the bait. "Barrymore," he said, "how about coming to California with me?"

Lionel gave his regrets to Mrs. Fiske and in 1911 made his first pioneering visit to Hollywood, then not much more than a vast expanse of empty lots. Shooting was done in some of these rented lots and in the streets of downtown Los Angeles. For dressing rooms canvas tents were put up. Lionel crisscrossed the country from New York to Hollywood several times during the next five years, making what was to him the satisfactory income of $125 a week.

His early Hollywood films included the long-since-forgotten *An Adventure in the Autumn, Oil and Water, The Sheriff's Baby, The Wanderer,* and *The Yacqui Cur.* While making these Lionel lived in rented rooms and cheap hotels. Although other pioneer Hollywood actors, such as Donald Crisp, saw the chance for real estate speculation in the growth of the movie community, Lionel remained above such practical matters and failed to accumulate what might easily have become a fortune.

He was more concerned with pursuing his efforts at musical composition, continued to do some painting in his spare time, and to get his weight down worked out in gymnasiums. The strenuous dashing about on foot and on the backs of horses also helped to get him slim again. In Griffith's *Judith of Bethalia,* a 1913 spectacle that ran for four reels, he played several parts in various disguises. The picture was regarded as important for the technical innovations it introduced; its success made important screen stars out of Henry B. Walthall and Blanche Sweet. But Lionel, who was busy in practically every scene, was only recognizable as himself for a brief moment.

By 1915 stage actors had lost their snobbishness about appearing in movies, and Lionel was joined by others, including his sister. The pay that lured her was far more than any given Lionel at that time, but he was well satisfied with his situation, mainly because it kept him from appearing on the stage, which he still cordially hated. He was cast in *Exploits of Elaine* with Pearl White and became a movie star in his own right. These serials were packed with lurid action for which doubles were mainly used, although Lionel did some of his own acrobatics, until his kneecap injury prevented it.

He joined the Metro organization (then known as Metro-Rolfe) in 1915 and starred in *The Flaming Sword* with Jane Grey. The title had little to do with its subject, a dramatic tale of Maine fishermen, done partly on location. Lionel was now kept busy. In *The Yellow Streak* he played a crazed financier who assumes the double life of a priest and a highwayman, alternately christening babies and robbing stagecoaches. In *The Brand of Cowardice* he played five reels as a wealthy New York idler who becomes a private at a Mexican border camp, rescues a girl from a bandit chief, and single-handedly holds off the whole Mexican Army. In *Dorian's Divorce* he was a doting young husband who, although divorced by his wife, takes responsibility for a crime he thinks she has committed; in the course of events he disappears from public view and later re-emerges as a stoker on a yacht aboard which his former wife is a guest!

Metro now claimed him proudly as one of the studio's important stars. In quick succession he made *The Quitters, The Upheaval,* and *The End of the Tour,* all with astonishingly inventive, if incredible, plots. Yet with all the success he was having in movies, and the security they represented for him and Doris, the old trouper in him responded when a call came for him to return to the stage. And he made one long go at it before returning to the movies for the rest of his life.

TURMOIL IN PARADISE / *chapter XI*

MARRIAGE AND MOTHERHOOD only increased the flow of Sunday news-paper articles about Ethel Barrymore. Most of these were of a senti-mental nature; it was said that Ethel in the part of a mother was playing the most becoming role of her career. Others, via headlines, wondered if in Ethel's case marriage and a career could be success-fully combined. Ashton Stevens, who came to visit her while she and Russell Colt lived in the Belmont town house, asked her the question outright. "I was born," Ethel replied, in reference to the fact that stage careers and marriage were commonplace in her family, "so were my brothers, and so, I've always understood, was my mother."

Russell had greeted Stevens, showed him to the small elevator that led to an upstairs sitting room, and swiftly disappeared, as though to demonstrate to Stevens that he played no part in his wife's profes-sional life. Ethel sat in a room with its inevitable grand piano, vases of flowers, and family photographs on mantels and shelves. She assured Stevens, as she assured other interviewers who came to see her, that marriage and a career mixed very well. But the truth was something else. Ethel of course hoped for success in marriage, be-lieved that it could be attained, but was never able to do much more than construct a charming façade.

Russell, she soon learned, had little interest in the theater, and cared not a bit about his wife's career. Theater people bored him and from boredom eventually grew resentment and hatred of all Ethel's theatrical associations. A blight was put upon the marriage from which it was never fully to recover, although it rallied from time to time.

It soon became clear, too, that the financial burden of the marriage was to be borne by Ethel. Russell's father, Colonel Colt, was in no mood to support a son he regarded as somewhat shiftless; by purchasing for him a small share in a brokerage he made it possible for his son to rise through initiative and enterprise, but not to become a tycoon at one swoop. He did promise to buy Russell and Ethel a country house if they located one he thought suitable. Ethel came across an old house in Mamaroneck, twenty miles from New York, considered then a good distance. The barn-red structure was on Taylor's Lane, looked out on Long Island Sound, had ten acres, and was surrounded by woods. Russell thought the color of the house was horrible, but Ethel convinced him that it would be very pretty if painted white with green shutters. Colonel Colt not only approved of Ethel's choice but thought it an excellent real estate investment.

After Samuel Colt was born (named in honor of Russell's grandfather, the inventor of the famous .45-caliber revolver), Ethel was anxious to go to work again. Pinero's *Mid-Channel* was still waiting for her, but by this time it had opened in London and had failed, and Frohman's brother Daniel had brought back word that it had not only depressed audiences but seemed deficient in stagecraft. Frohman reported this to Ethel, but by now she had fallen in love with the character she was to play, Zoë Blundell, unhappily married Englishwoman of thirty-seven. Frohman scheduled the play for a brief five-week run at the Empire. The opening took place on February 1, 1910.

With this role Ethel forever put to rest all doubts about her maturity as an actress, even though in the tryout period before it was brought to New York the out-of-town critics agreed with the London estimates. In Cleveland, the *Plain Dealer* reported: "A more miserable, depressing, and unpleasant drama than this has never been sent across the water. The audience detested the play thoroughly, and Ethel Barrymore's public will never care to see her in so intensely disagreeable and depressing a play."

What was this miserable, intensely disagreeable drama? It was the story of a wealthy English couple married for thirteen years, years which failed to weld them together. Zoë insists that Theodore, the husband, neglects her; Theodore claims that Zoë is petulant, restless, too eager for change and excitement. Things might have been different, she charges, if he would have allowed her to have children, but no, he wants no offspring to encumber his comfortable life. They have become a miserable, nagging couple, ready to fly apart when the convenient opportunity arrives. When Edward Albee used the same theme in his *Who's Afraid of Virginia Woolf* some fifty years later, Albee, too, was accused of being depressing in devoting so many hours to his miserable, nagging couple. Yet the theme was hardly that new or challenging, for Strindberg had been over similar ground before.

Fifty years can make a difference in stage conventions. Where the couple in the Albee play found it necessary to interrupt their quarrels with frequent gulps of vodka and bourbon, tea was the liquid medium used by Pinero. A carper felt it necessary to complain that "every step of the play is interrupted by tea. Before the husband can quarrel with his wife he must have tea. Before Ethel can nag at her husband she must rush off for the teapot. Every fresh scandal in the family must have its tea obligato."

At the end of the play, having endured too much in the way of insults from first her husband and next her lover, Zoë decides to end it all by throwing herself (or did she merely fall?) from a balcony.

The morning after the premiere performance at the Empire Ethel awoke to find herself the talk of New York again, for she had carried the play to a triumph. If her charm had made *Captain Jinks* a success, what counted most now was what one critic called "her genuine dramatic work." Her sparkle and charm was "combined with a nervous intensity, a fire and pathos, which, though it may have been latent, has not been called forth before. She takes a new place on a stage she has long adorned."

She could not have had better reviews if she had written them herself, and the supposedly gloomy play had its run extended at the Empire and was subsequently sent on another tour of the outlying cities. This time, preceded by Broadway approval, she encountered only enthusiasm.

It was noticed, though, that not only had her art rounded out but her figure, too. "The poster Ethel Barrymore has gone," one observer wrote. "Gone are pose of sublime thirstiness, her length, and her 'exploring neck,' which has bulged in the back. Width has set in—in unexpected places. We now get a somewhat heavy woman who can act considerably, shed damp tears, and suggest dry ones. She no longer 'decorates' Grieg at the piano. She no longer cranes— she surges!" There are always those waiting to notice the exact moment when a "public" beauty has slipped a bit. Some were generous enough to ascribe her new figure to her recent motherhood and to proclaim her to be in her fullest bloom.

In November of 1910, while Ethel played in *Mid-Channel* in New Orleans, there were the first reports of quarreling between Ethel and her husband. The story was emphatically denied by her attorneys, but when reporters sought her out for a denial from her own lips, she gave them the denial but became hysterical while doing so.

The following July the rumors of discord flared up again. Ethel had gone on a long repertory tour, playing Barrie's *Alice Sit-by-the-Fire* and his new playlet, *The Twelve Pound Look,* and on other nights doing Pinero's *Mid-Channel* and *Trelawney of the Wells.* Attendance was poor, and this may have also contributed to Ethel's state of nerves. Suddenly, while appearing at the Mason Opera House in Los Angeles, Ethel—accompanied by Louise Drew (John Drew's daughter) and Georgie Mendum (who was in the company with her and was now Ethel's constant companion)—visited a lawyer and a notary for the purpose of beginning an action for divorce. Or so the rumors went, and this time Ethel didn't deny them. It was reported that a young woman's name was included in the bill of particulars, and though the name itself did not appear in the papers, it was said to belong to "a prominent society woman."

"Friends" talked freely. They said that Ethel had considered taking such a step before but had forgiven her husband each time. Her husband, they stated, was not only of no assistance to her in her work but, further, that he annoyed her and made it doubly hard with his objections and opinions. A "Mid-Channel" sort of married life, in other words. Ethel still loved her husband, but his unfaithfulness, combined with the anguish he caused her, had led to her taking this drastic step. Her brother Jack had been consulted with and so had her uncle, John Drew. In fact, Louise Drew (Bee) was with her because of her upset over Russell's behavior. For the next several weeks the rumor mill operated. Her lawyers, when contacted, confirmed that a possible suit for divorce was in the works, and that it was also possible a "number of women will figure in the case."

Ethel returned to New York by way of Chicago and then went up to St. John in New Brunswick. Meanwhile Russell denied "all." In fact, he was so anxious to get to St. John to see Ethel that he was stopped for speeding on a Long Island parkway. He had been spending the day in Bayshore, he said, and the young woman in the car with him was his secretary. (This was later revised to a nurse he was bringing for the baby.)

On August 14 Russell and Ethel were back at Mamaroneck, and suddenly all was well. The two gave out the following statement to reporters: "We have never parted, never have quarreled, and never have contemplated any legal proceedings."

Puzzled city editors dispatched reporters to Mamaroneck, and one came back with the following:

> The lights were on brightly in the old Taylor Homestead, as Colt came to the door. "All lies," he said angrily.
> There came a voice from the drawing room: "Now, Russell, don't become so angry." She stepped to the threshold, smiling pacifically. "Really, the public has been misinformed as to our domestic relations. You see, the stories have grown and grown, because neither of us have thought it worthwhile to say anything."
> "But you did have divorce papers served on Mr. Colt?"
> "Goodness, no. There is absolutely no truth in that."
> "But your attorney admitted it."
> "He simply couldn't have admitted it, because I didn't have the papers drawn up."

So there it was. All lies, nasty rumors, and possibly, for all anyone knew, a dastardly plot on the part of Frohman's press agents, for "the whole thing," the newspapers said, "was expected to enhance Ethel's popularity." Of course, in years to come, it became plain that Ethel's marriage had seldom run smoothly. But it ran smoothly enough for two more children to be produced during the next few years. In 1912 her daughter, Ethel Barrymore Colt, was born, and in 1913 her son John. While the children were growing up they were called Sammy, Sister, and Jackie.

About fifty years later her daughter, now Ethel Colt Miglietta, said: "I don't think it possible for a great woman star to make a complete success of her marriage unless her husband gives up everything for her career, or subordinates his own desires to its necessities. Between my mother and father there was absolute incompatibility. It was the most terrible life in the world for a man. On the other side, he did not behave well and was the kind of 'Palm Beach' person my mother, ordinarily, would have found hard to bear. She really did *not* regard herself as a dedicated career girl, and when she found the marriage wasn't working, she was miserable."

And what about Ethel as a mother? The younger Ethel remembered: "Her relations with us were extraordinary in spite of the fact that we were put under the care of governesses and were sent to boarding schools because she was away a good deal of the time. We would see her, after babyhood, at the Ritz in Boston, in Chicago at Christmas, Atlantic City in Easter. We weren't over-mothered by any means. She was a goddess to us. She was wonderful and warm, but let's face it, she did not change our pants."

THE FIRST SEVEN
YEARS

chapter XII

JOHN'S MARRIAGE to Katherine Corri Harris lasted seven years, produced no offspring, and worked out even less well than Ethel's marriage to the Newport socialite. The problem here was, in a way, the opposite of Ethel's. Katherine thought the stage and people of the theater very glamorous and was willing to join her husband in his work, which, very shortly, she did. But in spite of this apparent mutuality of interests they quarreled frequently. John blamed many of these quarrels on the fact that he desired domesticity, while his young wife desired the excitement she thought herself entitled to as the consort of one of the stage's leading matinee idols. The conflict proved irreconcilable.

When he returned from his road tour in *The Fortune Hunter*, the couple rented an apartment on Gramercy Park with a balcony that overlooked the fenced-in park. Their not infrequent quarrels penetrated the walls of neighboring apartments in the building, and several tenants joined together in a letter of complaint to the landlord. As a committee marched out of the building to mail the letter they noticed the Barrymores walking arm-in-arm in the little park, cooing and chattering away like doves. They hadn't the heart to mail the letter.

John had become a good friend of James Montgomery Flagg, the illustrator, and loved to spend long afternoons poring over Flagg's collection of art books. He usually arrived in a taxi, told the driver to wait, and would become so absorbed that he would forget about the meter of the cab ticking away. Sooner or later Katherine would drift in at Flagg's studio.

Flagg thought Katherine as lovely a creature as he had ever seen and invited her to pose for him. He made a portrait of her and then used her as a model for several of his illustrations. John eventually became annoyed by the amount of time his wife spent in Flagg's studio and once growled to his friend: "Who the hell is she married to anyway?"

John alternated between possessiveness toward Katherine and annoyance with her habits. She was bored easily and after half an hour in one place wanted to go somewhere else. John mockingly called her "The Mental Giantess." At the same time, he snapped at her if men gave her admiring looks, and he claimed she *flirted*. He thought the lipstick she wore was unbecoming and would sometimes take out his handkerchief and wipe the stuff off her lips, regardless of who was present. He sometimes went with her, under protest, to the balls and parties to which they were constantly invited by Katherine's society friends, but once there would not dance with her. His excuse was that he was not an accomplished social dancer; on the other hand, dancing would have prevented his frequent visits to the bar. After these visits he would take her to task for dancing with other men. It was not an easy life for Katherine.

Sometimes he would be among the missing for days on end and when located would be found in some Bowery saloon. Katherine dispatched friends in search of him when his drunken outings became too prolonged. He proclaimed to her and to his friends that he could stop drinking any time he wanted to, but he seldom wanted to. It began to be said that John's marital unhappiness was caused by his fondness for alcohol. But John told Gene Fowler, his biographer: "Unhappiness increased the drink, and drink increased the unhappiness."

Katherine made her first appearance on the stage with John in a weak comedy called *Uncle Sam*. The play opened in Chicago in September of 1911. A review mentioned Katherine Blythe in a small part and said she "did it easily and gracefully." But two months later, when the play opened in New York, it was roasted and closed down at once.

John's stage appearances for the next few years, if they brought him more fame, hardly added to his development. But even during this period, in which he made little progress as an actor, he had good luck dogging him in spite of his growing reputation for alcoholic indulgence. The luck turned up in the form of Edward Sheldon, a young Harvard-bred playwright who had electrified Broadway a few years earlier with a realistic play called *Salvation Nell,* and later with stark melodramas called *Nigger* and *The Boss.* Sheldon helped bring a mood of social realism to the theater, contrived and hackneyed though his plays seem now. He more than anyone else was responsible for turning John Barrymore in more serious directions.

Jack was cast in the role of a young New York millionaire for Sheldon's *Princess Zim-Zim,* which dealt with the millionaire's fascination with a snake charmer at Coney Island. The play opened in Boston on December 20, 1911, and proved to be so creaky a vehicle that it never managed the journey to New York. But a strong friendship sprang up between the young playwright and the young actor, a friendship that was to bear strange and wondrous fruit.

On the surface the two men seemed to have little in common. The playwright was poised, in an unassuming way; Barrymore was unstable and quixotic. Sheldon's doting mother once asked him what he saw in the actor, and he answered, dryly, that he liked to be with him. What caused the attraction? They had a mutual love for beautiful things—or things they thought beautiful—and they both had a passion for "living." Sheldon sensed that for all the mannerism, the outward cynicism, Barrymore was a man badly in need of protection. During the short run of *Princess Zim-Zim* Sheldon would visit John's dressing room after the performance, and while the actor removed his make-up the two would have long discussions about a myriad of subjects. Over beers, over early morning breakfasts of pancakes and coffee, they would continue their talks. When the bleak December light filled the eastern sky the two could be found sitting on a park bench, engaged in endless argument. In New York

John took to visiting Ned's elegant apartment, which also overlooked Gramercy Park.

John dawdled through several more plays. One of these was *Half a Husband* in which Katherine appeared with him, and another was Arthur Schnitzler's *The Affairs of Anatol.* The latter play was not appreciated to any degree, although John drew the comment that his Anatol was "acted lightly and intelligently." Katherine played Hilda, the purest of the several heroines. While marking time, John appeared in a Barrie curtain raiser, *A Slice of Life,* with Ethel, who had revived *Cousin Kate* at the Empire. The short play, supposed to be a burlesque of "the modern play," ridiculed the conventions of drawing room realism. John's contribution was clearly an imitation of his uncle, John Drew. Later an actress named Hattie Williams imitated Ethel in the same little play, drawing down Ethel's ire on Charles Frohman, whom she thought had allowed it to happen.

In 1913 John and Katherine moved to a house in Rockville Centre, Long Island. He received good reviews in a comedy called *Believe Me, Xantippe,* but this did not survive for long. Perhaps under Sheldon's influence he made an effort to get himself in hand, particularly in the direction of controlling the drinking. Within a few years he had managed to stop drinking entirely, which lasted until a second marital venture started him again. But in 1913 he was the very model of exemplary behavior. He and Katherine gravitated between Rockville Centre and the Gramercy Square apartment, played tennis at the West Side Tennis Club, loafed on Long Island during the weekends. Now and then he did some weekend painting, which he never showed, but which made him happy. He announced that he was through with his former life, and that he intended to put it all down in a book which would deal mainly with his after-hours Broadway adventures.

He began his screen career in 1913 when he played the lead role in a movie made from Nat Goodwin's comedy success, *An American Citizen.* "The film," he announced, "determines an actor's ability, absolutely, conclusively. It is the surest test of an actor's qualities. Mental impressions can be conveyed by the screen more quickly than vocally. The moving picture is not a business, it is an art."

His marriage to Katherine threw John into a state of extreme depression in 1914, and the cure he took was a trip to Italy where he joined his friend Ned Sheldon. The marriage lasted another three years, in name at least, but all intimacy between John and Katherine ceased with his flight to Italy.

The previous year Sheldon had had his greatest success as a playwright with *Romance,* which told of a glamorous opera star who sweeps a young clergyman off his balance and reduces him to a state in which he is willing to sacrifice his churchly career to his grand passion. The opera star then, in a grandiloquent gesture of renunciation, sends him back to his parish, this gesture being made while the clergyman's parishioners carol in Christmas snow outside the lovers' window. The play enthralled audiences all over the world for many years and made an important star of the beautiful actress, Doris Keane, for whom Sheldon had written the play. He had offered the part of the clergyman to John, who turned it down.

Sheldon's contention was that John would never get serious regard as an actor until he performed in a play of a serious nature. John's frivolous reply was that a serious role would require him to shave off the mustache he prized almost more than anything on earth. Besides, would the audience accept the comic madcap he was supposed to be in so sepulchral an emotional involvement?

Sheldon had been engaged to marry Doris Keane; when she broke the engagement, he left for Europe to try to forget what had been for him a shattering experience. Venice attracted him most, and John met him there. The city's pellucid light, the charm of its waterways, its restful silence, the narrow, flagstoned streets through which the two friends wandered—all acted to restore the spirits of both. Ned put aside his own problems to listen sympathetically to the tale John gave of his. He again made the suggestion that John act in serious plays instead of farce comedies, most of which couldn't be expected to be better than mediocre. John listened, but only half convinced.

Ned's feeling for Venice he could share completely, however. Their troubles and confusions seemed to evaporate as they meandered through the Accademia delle Belle Arti and the ancient palazzi. They sat at the Florian and Quadro cafés in the Piazza San Marco and listened to music, watched the walls of the Doges' Palace take on a rose glow in the light of the setting sun. Next they went to Rome, where Ned insisted on their visiting the grave of Keats in the English Cemetery and browsing among the volumes of the Vatican Library. At night they were attracted by the singing of a fiery young girl who sang in a little café. They took long walks and studied the stone reminders of the Roman past. On they went to Florence, the Renaissance spirit of which John found most suited to his mood. John made the suggestion early one morning that they climb to a cupola on the roof of their hotel and watch the sunrise. The Arno turned into the green bronze of Florentine painting, the sun lit up the Ponte Vecchio, and as the bells of the city's churches began to peal all around them, John, noticing he and Ned were still in pajamas, said: "All this seems highly improbable."

The following day John left for home, feeling thoroughly restored. He was hardly back when he was offered a role in a melodrama by Al Woods, a producer. The play, formerly called *Birds of Prey,* was retitled *Kick In.* Several of John's friends advised him against leaving the field of comedy, in which he was so well established, but Sheldon had hurried home when it looked as though Europe would soon be engulfed in a war, and he reiterated his advice that John turn to more serious acting. While *Kick In* wasn't of much consequence as a play, it would serve as a vehicle in which to break away from farce. Meanwhile Sheldon promised to search for just the right sort of serious play for John.

Sheldon was too modest ever to take the slightest credit for the turnabout in John's career. He insisted that John had his own theatrical genius, that though he might listen to the suggestions of others, the final decisions were made by him alone. John, on the other hand, admitted several times the help given him by Sheldon. "In fact," he said, "I'm not sure that he didn't make me a serious actor."

Ethel, meanwhile, had taken a surprising turn in her own career; she went into vaudeville. Several months after the small Ethel was born an economic pinch began to be felt in the Colt household. Russell's father, provoked by his son's indolent ways, cut him off from any share in the wealthy Colt estate. It was up to Ethel to provide most of the money needed to maintain the Mamaroneck house, to pay the maid, the housekeeper, the chauffeur, and the butler their salaries.

And Ethel had become provoked with Charles Frohman. Not only had he allowed one of his stars, Hattie Williams, to play *Slice of Life* in a quite conscious parody of Ethel's performance; worse, he had announced Ethel for the starring role in *Bella Donna* and then had given it to the glamorous Nazimova. A report in *Variety* in 1912 mentioned that Ethel had approached those new powers in the theater, the Shuberts, but they, friendly with Frohman, had refused to take her under their management.

Ethel let it be publicly known that Frohman had not offered her anything for the fall season of 1912 that she regarded as suitable, and it was for this reason that she had suggested taking James Barrie's *The Twelve Pound Look* on a vaudeville tour. Vaudeville salaries had risen to a dizzying level, with a few favored headliners earning as much as $2500 weekly. Lionel, before busying himself with the movies, had managed to collect $850 a week on the vaudeville circuit, although out of this had undoubtedly come salaries for the others in the cast.

Frohman was upset by the idea of Ethel's appearing in vaudeville, but under her prodding he sent her to Martin Beck, who arranged the tour and offered her nothing less than the highest salary yet paid to a performer in vaudeville, three thousand dollars a week. Ethel did not collect all of it; a thousand a week went to Frohman to repay him for the loss of her services. She took her cousin Georgie Mendum and her niece, Louise Drew, along with her on the tour and made sure that the presentation was a highly professional one, with a good actor, Charles Dalton, in her support.

Ethel rehearsed the cast herself, using a method all her own. *The Twelve Pound Look* was a charming one-act play about a divorced woman who supports herself with a typewriter. The woman decides to give up the security of marriage with a selfish, overbearing husband after learning that a woman can always earn twelve pounds a week by pounding a typewriter, especially if she dresses herself in the severe garb of a secretary. She puts on the proper look to get a job and thus secures her independence. The play was popular because it caught the mood of an emergent suffrage-conscious woman-hood, although Ethel herself never became a militant suffragette.

"A play," Ethel announced, "should appeal to the eye and the ear." She made her actors rehearse behind a thin black curtain and sat out front to judge how well the voice alone brought out the play's dramatic values. Next, she would have the curtain raised and ask the actors to do the play only in pantomime. This directorial method was supposed to guarantee beautiful voice quality and grace-ful movement on the stage.

Ethel played in vaudeville as far west as California on the Orpheum Circuit, and then, overcoming Frohman's objections to her playing in the east, appeared in the Keith houses on the Atlantic seaboard. She found vaudeville houses all over the country often more beautiful and better designed than legitimate playhouses, with good dressing-room facilities. She enjoyed standing in the wings and watching the other star turns, the acrobats, dancers, singers, and monologists and gained respect for their professionalism.

"I kept on working," she told a friend later, who was surprised by her activity during a period in which Ethel gave birth to three children. "I *had* to work."

"But why?" the friend asked.

"Dough," Ethel answered.

To add to her income she also tried movies. "Movies are really becoming the thing," she was quoted in a magazine article as saying. "We people of the theater realize that. Those of us who are well known are constantly being approached by the various companies and they make such attractive propositions!" One such proposition was made by All Star. The bait was fifteen thousand dollars and a script called *The Nightingale,* especially written for Ethel's movie debut by Augustus Thomas.

"Girls!" wrote a lady reporter, "we're sure moving pictures are all right now, aren't we? Nothing lowbrow about them if Miss Barry-more loves them, is there? Our taste is vindicated."

Movies, first regarded as entertainment solely for the working class, had begun to appeal to the middle class audience, and Ethel was aware of this change in taste. "Oh, I want to do things in pictures!" she enthused, even though she was less than enthusiastic about the way *The Nightingale* turned out. Instead of the static, statuesque posing required of her by that film she wanted to be "given something *really* to do. Since lines count for nothing, actions should count for everything."

But movies amounted to little more than a lucrative sideline for her. She and Frohman had made up their differences, especially when Frohman made public announcement of the fact that he was having a popular novel called *Tante* especially adapted for Ethel by Haddon Chambers. While the writing of this play was in progress Ethel was pregnant with her third child and gave birth on September 15, 1913, to John Drew Colt, immediately and thenceforth called Jackie.

Two weeks later she was rehearsing *Tante*, which was presented in New York and Washington and in which the critics found her to be doing "some of the best work of her career." Said one: "She is now the first actress of our stage." Critics always seemed to be reiterating, as though reminding themselves, that Ethel had become "the first lady," "the first actress," and that those awful terms formerly used to characterize her—*charm* and *delightful personality*—were no longer suitable for so important an actress.

Her maternal appearance drew increasing comment, too. Not that it mattered for the role she played in *Tante*, that of an unlovely woman, all of forty-eight, an eccentric, affected, frankly selfish genius of the keyboard. Ethel played it for comedy, and Alan Dale thought her "delicious." But *Tante* did not last for long, and in May, 1914, she was back at the Empire playing with John Drew in a revival of a musty Sardou play, *A Scrap of Paper*. Frohman had prudently scheduled this production for four weeks to round out the Empire season. It was the first time uncle and niece had been together in eighteen years, and the bland, affable John Drew led Ethel to the footlights after the curtain, beaming on her with avuncular pride.

A carper wrote: "Other actresses may acquire avoirdupois and the addition be accepted humorously, but in the case of Miss Barrymore it is really resented." Ethel was advised to take a lesson from her uncle on the secrets of staying slim. She took the advice and embarked on a weight reducing program. During the summer of 1914 she shed seventy-five pounds. What method had she used? "Not eating," she replied.

Armies clashed in Europe that summer, but the atmosphere of Long Island Sound was pastoral. The Mamaroneck house and grounds had become one of the Westchester County showplaces. Ethel took her children on picnics, bathed with them at Rye Beach. She bought a pony cart for the children and kept a kennel filled with fine dogs. But she became particularly fond of a mongrel puppy.

"Is he a full-blooded animal?" a friend asked politely.

"Don't speak so loudly," Ethel whispered. "He isn't, but he thinks he is."

An interviewer came to see her for one of those inevitable Sunday supplement pieces, and her eye was caught by a portrait of Ethel done by John Singer Sargent. Several years before, during her slim, high-necked period, she had performed in Boston while Sargent was staying there. He requested a sitting and did the portrait in an afternoon. Her swanlike neck and uplifted chin were emphasized by Sargent, but it was hardly a faithful likeness. The interviewer asked if Ethel thought Sargent had caught her as she really looked.

"Well, yes," Ethel said. "It must have been as Sargent saw me."

"One might say, then, it is Miss Barrymore plus Sargent?"

"And minus the resemblance," Ethel said. But as time enhanced the portrait's charm, Ethel came to regard it as her finest art possession.

Ethel soon lost her optimism about motion picture work, though she continued to do it for the "dough." Relations with Russell Colt were decidedly strained, although it was second nature with her to continue to hope for the success of the marriage. While on location in Georgia during the making of a gypsy epic, *The Call of Her People,* she decided that it was her wifely duty to share Russell's Palm Beach life, which he pursued during the colder months. She played bridge for a week, was soon made aware of the presence of a young woman who was obviously Russell's current romantic interest, and rushed back to Mamaroneck to be with her children and to resume her working life. From 1914 to 1918 she made thirteen movies, including one in which she played an Alaskan dancehall vampire. In 1915 she signed with Metro for four pictures a year, at forty thousand dollars each. She despised all but one, *The Awak-ening of Helen Ritchie*. Lionel directed her for Metro in 1917 in *Life's Whirlpool*, a story of his own.

Metro's studio facilities were then located in New York at Broad-way and Sixty-first Street. Bosley Crowther, in *The Lion's Share*, described the studio atmosphere in which Ethel and Lionel worked.

> The studio was above a garage, a vast chamber, more than 200 feet long, with the shooting stage in the middle and offices around the sides. It was in this primitive atelier—a veritable crazy house of painted scenery, jumbled furniture, old-fashioned arc lights and hand-cranked cameras—that the stars per-formed . . .

In one of Ethel's films she played a Russian princess. A Russian émigré, Leon Trotsky, was among the extras; he was a tailor who earned extra money in movies before turning his attention to the Russian Revolution. Many years later, in the first sound film she made, Ethel played the Czarina whom Trotsky had helped to elimi-nate.

As movies more and more captured the mass audience, John Barrymore found himself in increasing demand for this relatively easy, well paying work. He signed with Famous Players in 1914, and during the next four years made a series of ten film farces. They were a sideline for him but a satisfying one, and he thoroughly enjoyed inventing the kind of pratfall that caused some critics to compare him with Charles Chaplin. In *Nearly a King*, a comic variation on the theme of *The Prisoner of Zenda*, he cavorted to the point of ridiculousness. He played a double role as a Balkan prince and an irresponsible American; this less than notable film marked the film debut of his wife Katherine. She played a crown princess. Katherine, still trying to adapt herself to the rigors of married life with John, was willing to forsake society for the chance to be with John in his five-reelers. She appeared with him again in *The Lost Bridegroom*, in which, said the conscientious film reviewer for *The Dramatic Mirror*, "she pleased more than in any picture in which we have seen her." In this film John, the bridegroom, was hit on the head by a thug, woke up not knowing who he was, joined a gang of crooks, and burglarized his fiancée's home. Another crack on the head brought him to his senses and to the church on time.

Some of these films still have an antique charm. A particularly pleasant one was *Raffles, the Amateur Cracksman,* which appeared successfully in 1917. John, as the gentleman jewel thief, gave a smooth, deft performance while outwitting a master detective, breaking into safes, and showing both athletic and romantic prowess.

John said of his screen work in those days: "I found that I overacted many of the scenes, that missing the stimulus of the audience I became indiscreet . . . I had been forewarned, but I had a feeling that if I worked hard enough I could make the electricians and the cameramen laugh and they would take the place of a theater audience. The result was woeful and unreal." He was harsher on himself than he needed to be. These five- and seven-reel movies were making him almost as known throughout the country as was Ethel. Lionel, appearing opposite Pearl White in her weekly adventures, was also paving the way for his eventual fame. No matter how the Barrymores twisted and turned, their dynastic destinies seemed inescapable. And if they looked down on their screen work, the public looked up to them all the more.

Edward (Ned) Sheldon, the young playwright who convinced John Barrymore that he should play serious roles, who talked Lionel into returning to the stage and who adapted a version of *Camille* for Ethel. At the peak of his success he was stricken with a crippling disease, and was an invalid for the remainder of his life.

Russell Colt, who married Ethel in 1910. He was not at all fascinated with stage people and stage life, and Ethel's years with him were seldom happy, although the marriage gave her three children.

Charles Frohman, the diminutive rotund producer who had much to do with advancing the careers of all three Barrymores. He built the Empire Theatre, in which Ethel performed frequently, as did her uncle John Drew.

Ethel starred with her uncle John Drew in a revival of Sardou's *A Scrap of Paper* at the Empire Theatre in 1914. Audiences were delighted to see them together, but the play was roasted for being "out of date."

Ethel in a scene from *Tante,* in which she played a spoiled, eccentric pianist of genius. She had no trouble with the moments required at the keyboard for she was an accomplished pianist herself. By now, 1913, critics had taken to calling her the "first lady of the theater."

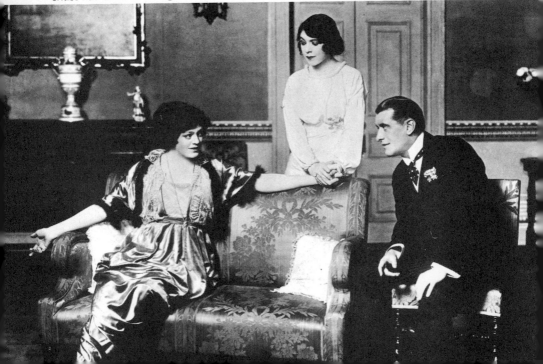

In a scene from *The Shadow,* Ethel, after years spent in a wheelchair, learns that she can walk and therefore has an excruciating decision to make. This 1915 performance caused copious tears to flow in the audience.

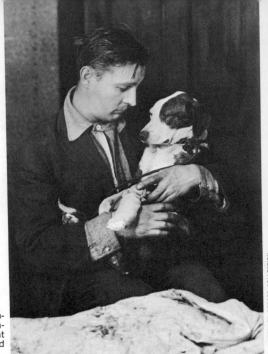

John Barrymore's fame throughout the country increased when he turned to screen comedy. This scene shows him in a Paramount picture called *The Lost Bridegroom*, released in 1916.

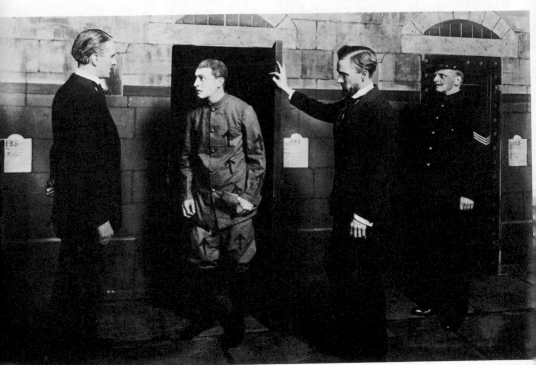

That same year he stunned playgoers on Broadway with his powerful performance in John Galsworthy's *Justice*, a play that Edward Sheldon had urged him to do.

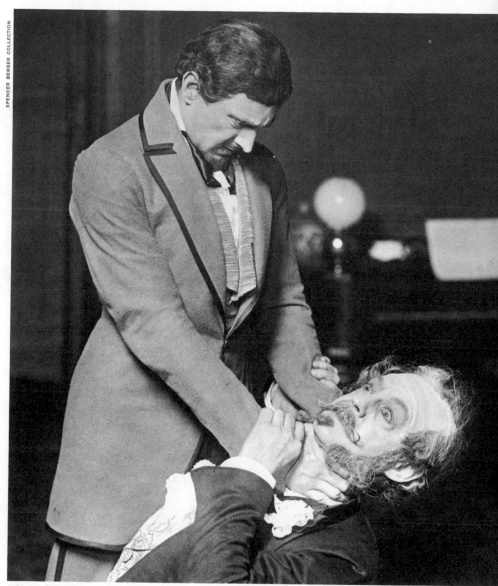

John as Peter Ibbetson, throttles Lionel as the vile Colonel Ibbetson. The play was adapted from the George du Maurier novel and was a great success for the brothers Barrymore at a time when the United States had just entered World War I. Ethel helped in the staging.

Lionel became known as America's greatest character actor after his performance as Milt Shanks in *The Copperhead* (1918).

The Jest, brought to the stage by Arthur Hopkins, made the 1919 theater season memorable, and no limit was placed on the future careers of Lionel and John by the critics, so impressive were their performances. Lionel, as the brutish Neri, and John, as the effeminate poet Gianetto, are seen above with Maude Hanaford and Arthur Forrest. Robert Edmond Jones provided the Florentine setting.

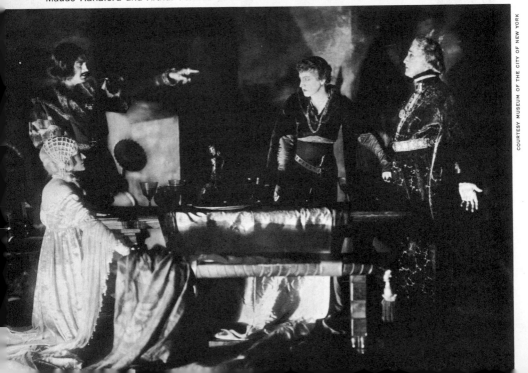

Lionel as Neri in *The Jest*. Dorothy Parker, the young reviewer for *Vanity Fair*, thought it one of the wonders of the age that Lionel's voice should bear up for a full evening under the roars of rage and the bellows of laughter required from him.

John as Gianetto in *The Jest*. Edward Sheldon had come across the play by the Italian Sem Benelli in 1913 and had always regarded it as perfect for the Barrymore brothers. He adapted it into free verse while lying in his sickbed, and further touches were added by John and Lionel. In Europe the Gianetto role had been played by a woman.

Michael Strange, second wife of John Barrymore and mother of Diana Barrymore. Michael was born Blanche Oelrichs on the same day as John's first wife Katherine. This marriage, too, lasted seven years.

Portrait of Arthur Hopkins, who produced and staged John Barrymore's *Richard III* and *Hamlet*. He was less successful with Lionel's *Macbeth* and Ethel's *Romeo and Juliet*.

John and Michael, aboard ship and bound for Europe in 1921. Michael had ambitions of her own as poet, playwright and actress, and her temperament was able to match John's mood for mood.

part *THREE*

REACHING FOR GLORY

chapter XIII

THE YEARS OF WORLD WAR I WERE, on the whole, kind to the Barrymores. Ethel was more directly touched by the war in that her husband, Russell Colt, shortly after the outbreak of hostilities volunteered as an ambulance driver in France. He was overseas for a spell, returned unharmed, and when the United States entered the war went into officer's training and was commissioned at Plattsburg, New York. John also attempted to enlist in the American Expeditionary Force, but was rejected. Lionel's knee injury by this time had made him quite lame and it was to plague him all his life. A blow close to home was felt when the Barrymores' young cousin, Sidney Rankin Drew, who had joined the Lafayette Escadrille, perished in flames behind the German lines. Ethel read the casualty lists with special foreboding, for the sons of many of her English friends were at the front and some were lost.

Ethel's career, already in its fullest flower, took another step forward when she made an acting triumph for herself in *The Shadow*. The play had been originally written for the fine French actress, Réjane, but war had halted its production in Paris, and it was sent in adapted form to Charles Frohman. Ethel's role required her to do her entire performance immobilized in a wheelchair. During the course of the evening the paralyzed woman she played learned that her husband, whom she had thought supremely devoted to her, had all along been having an extramarital affair. Even more crushingly, she learned that her husband had sired a child with the unmarried woman. What to do? *What to do?* The matter was further complicated when Ethel learned, with mingled joy and sadness, that she could walk again. But did Ethel ever reveal to her husband that she faced the prospect of a whole and hearty womanhood? No, she did not. She pretended that she had never risen from her wheelchair and acceded to her husband's request for a divorce so that he could marry his mistress and give his child a name. Ethel dripped tears on stage. In the orchestra and the balcony the audiences shed tears with even fuller abandon. Critics thought the play rather somber, all in all, but Ethel, it was unanimous, rose in it to superb emotional heights.

While in rehearsal for *The Shadow* Ethel attended a house party on Long Island, and during an idle moment picked up a book of short stories, *Roast Beef Medium,* by Edna Ferber, a new young writer. Ethel was so entranced by the dramatic possibilities of the stories that she told the other guests at dinner she was going to see immediately about getting hold of the rights. Someone else had optioned them, but Frohman repurchased the rights. He telegraphed Miss Ferber, announcing that Miss Barrymore wanted to play Emma McChesney, the heroine of the stories, in a play which he hoped the author would write in collaboration with an experienced dramatist. Miss Ferber wasn't altogether sure that the grand Ethel Barrymore was altogether right for the down-to-earth saleslady, Emma McChesney, but she gave her consent and wrote the play with George Hobart. *Our Mrs. McChesney* was a hit, but Charles Frohman was never to see it on the stage.

Ethel's rotund little producer was now ailing. He had hurt his knee in a fall, and a bad bruise had developed into articular rheumatism, which soon affected all his joints. He became a virtual prisoner in his apartment at the Hotel Knickerbocker, suffering torment yet still insistent about directing his affairs from a bedside telephone. Because he could not go to the theater, the theater was brought to him. Barrie's *A Slice of Life* was rehearsed by Ethel and John in Frohman's rooms at the Knickerbocker. The producer thought the piece so excruciatingly funny that he would often call up the Empire and say: "Send Ethel over to rehearse. I want to forget my pains."

One of his comforts was a phonograph, and his favorite tune was a new one called "Alexander's Ragtime Band." His nurse would put the record on for him, and friends who dropped in had the chore of cranking the machine for replays as many as twenty in a night. By the end of 1914 he became well enough to walk around with the aid of a cane. The war obsessed him and he would talk constantly about its wantonness and waste of human life. In 1915, when the seas became infested with German submarines, he insisted on making his yearly trip to England because some litigation there needed his attention.

When his friends and business associates, Ethel among them, tried to dissuade him from embarking on the *Lusitania*, he would only smile at their warnings. Other warnings came, some by way of anonymous letters and telephone calls, and there was even an official one from a representative of the German government. But he was adamant about going. Ethel, who was in Boston playing in *The Shadow*, came down to New York to wish him bon voyage, and upon saying good-by to her he made a rare gesture: he kissed her on the cheek. He made sure before departing to arrange the entire theatrical schedule for the next season in which was included the setting up of the rehearsal period for *Our Mrs. McChesney*. "It's an ideal play for you," he assured Ethel. "It has womanliness and wholesome humor."

A friend was in his office the day before his departure, and Frohman, wanting to jot down something the man said, pulled out his red pocket notebook which contained reminders to himself. "Queer," he said. "There's no more room." That same day he asked his partner, Alf Hayman, if he really thought there was danger.

"Of course I do," Hayman said.

"Well, I must go, anyway," Frohman said, and pausing at the door added lightly, "Al, if you need to write to me, just address the letter care of German submarine U-4." That night, just as she was about to go on stage in Boston, a telegram arrived for Ethel: NICE TALK, ETHEL. GOODBY. CF.

Frohman's ship sailed for Europe at ten o'clock in the morning,

May 1, 1915, and for six days the voyage was uneventful. But at half past two, the afternoon of May 7, a German torpedo struck just as the ship had come in sight of the Irish coast. Frohman was on the upper promenade deck when the crash of the torpedo came. He had finished his luncheon and was talking with three acquaintances, among them an actress, Rita Jolivet. He kept on imperturbably smoking his cigar as lifebelts were obtained. "I didn't think they would do it," he told the others calmly. The liner gave a lurch, and Frohman suggested to Miss Jolivet, "You'd better hold on to the rail and save your strength."

Within a matter of minutes the dimensions of the tragedy became apparent; the list of the ship increased, and bodies and wreckage appeared on the crests of the waves. Frohman said, still smiling: "Why fear death? It is the most beautiful adventure of life." For some reason the four people moved closer and joined hands. A green mountain of water rose and towered over them, and again Frohman said, as though to comfort the others, "Why fear death?" At that moment the group was engulfed. Of the four, only Rita Jolivet survived, and she told the story of those last moments. The next day Frohman's body was recovered and reached New York two weeks later.

After finishing the engagement in Boston, Ethel had gone on to Chicago, where she was being entertained at luncheon with another of Frohman's stars, Elsie Ferguson. A friend called her to the telephone and said she had heard the most terrible news, that the *Lusitania* had been sunk with all on board. Ethel returned to the table and told the others what she had just heard. She and Elsie Ferguson just kept looking at each other and saying, "Mr. Frohman, Mr. Frohman."

No other loss during the war touched Ethel as much as the death of Charles Frohman.

Another associate of the Barrymores', Edward Sheldon, almost joined Frohman on that last voyage. Frohman had invited him to travel with him on the *Lusitania,* and Sheldon had made up his mind to go, and would have gone if a close friend, a former Harvard classmate, had not asked him to be his best man at his wedding on Sunday, May 11. Sheldon was unable to refuse the request.

His conviction that John Barrymore had all the essentials for stage greatness remained with him after their vacation together in Italy, and through the first half of 1915 Sheldon worked on a play for John called *The Lonely Heart*. But when summer came he had to abandon the writing of the play because of an arthritic condition. He traveled to Chicago to see his family, and there his condition was found to be far more serious than he realized. It was nothing less than a crippling progressive arthritis. Movements of the hips and shoulders caused him dreadful pain. He nevertheless insisted on regarding the illness as temporary and whiled away his recovery time by looking for a suitable play for John. He came across John Galsworthy's *Justice*, which when presented in England some years before had resulted in changes in England's penal system.

Justice told the story of William Falder, an underpaid bank clerk who forged a check to help a troubled friend. Imprisoned for the crime and kept in solitary confinement, Falder, when released, was driven to suicide by the persecutory and incessant surveillance of the police. The play was not only stark, it was harrowing tragedy.

When he felt well enough to travel, Sheldon returned to New York and sought out John Williams, a Harvard alumnus who was about to enter the producing field. Sheldon's idea was for Williams to announce a production and approach Barrymore to play the part of Falder. John was nervous about so drastic a switch from comedy, but agreed to take the role. He not only went to work on it but by opening night in New Haven had worked himself up to such a pitch of intensity that when called upon to pound the cell door in his prison, he broke through the grating—made of wood and painted black to resemble iron. A press agent who was to publicize the play in New York came to the New Haven opening and remarked that the play was too dull and too deep from Broadway success. "It has one good scene, though," he said. "That's the one where Barrymore busts down the prison door and makes his escape." From then on the cell door was securely reinforced.

John was so convinced he would fail in New York that when the Candler Theatre in New York placed posters out front with his name printed larger than the playwright's, he insisted on smaller type for himself. While the new posters were being printed up he took the precaution of pasting out his name on the old ones. For this act of what was regarded as obeisance to the author he was given much credit for modesty. But John wanted no "extra advertising" if his venture into tragedy did not come off.

Precautions were not necessary, as it turned out. John's first-night performance was an exciting revelation to the audience. In the early scenes he suggested reserves of passion and power which at last broke through during those unforgettable moments when Falder, his spirit about to break under the torture of solitary confinement, beat helplessly on the door of his cell. Instead of the engaging, debonair Barrymore, the audience saw the poor, gray little clerk who spoke a strain of cockney. By the end of the performance the audience was already saying that John Barrymore was America's greatest actor.

That night, so it was said, John Drew made a pilgrimage to his nephew's dressing room, carrying with him an Oregon apple of blue ribbon proportions.

The amazement was general, for this, after all, was the same man who, as one publication put it, "in a recent motion picture shows you himself falling downstairs in a manner which, although different from Chaplin, is just as amusing and amazing, and who, while descending those stairs on his elbows, neck, the small of his back, engages in a life-and-death fight that takes the breath out of the villain and also the audience." How could one actor embody in himself so many facets of ability? It was evident that here was a man who could range with surpassing ease between the two masks of theater, the comic and the tragic. He had been dragged unwillingly into the arena, but once there had proved himself. It had taken a tragic play, however, before the public was willing to bestow upon him the laurel wreath. Or rather, it should be said, a jury of his peers bestowed the wreath. *Justice* was too solemn and anguished a play for the general run of audiences and was not an enormous hit. But it did count with those who counted.

The *New York Times,* a week after the opening, commented: "For Barrymore the first night of *Justice* was a milestone. By his simple, eloquent, deeply touching performance as young Falder, he arrested the attention of the city and gained overnight a prestige which is priceless in the theater, a prestige all his work in trivial entertainment would not give him. It is what the theater can bestow on those who serve it loyally. This comes now to a player whose years in the theater have been lackadaisical."

What was next for this actor who had been so drastically re-modeled? One project considered was an adaptation of *La Cena delle Beffe,* a violent and colorful melodrama set during the period of the Medicis. Sheldon had discovered the play by the Italian playwright, Sem Benelli, during a trip he made to Italy in 1913; it struck him then as an excellent vehicle for two Barrymores, John and Lionel. John's part would be that of a sensitive young artist; Lionel, if he could ever be convinced to return to the stage, would play a domineering nobleman. John was agreeable about doing the play because of its Florentine background and because he thought it time for Lionel to return to the stage he had deserted for the easier life of the movies. In this latter goal Ethel was his ally. Sheldon worked on the adaptation, but his illness prevented him from making much headway. Closer to production status was *The Lonely Heart,* which he had begun the year before for John.

When the New York run of *Justice* ended in June, 1916, John went along with Ned Sheldon to California, because the change of air and scene was thought to be good for the latter. Katherine accompanied her husband on that trip, the last they were to be together. John set a fast social pace in Santa Barbara, and this, at least, helped to distract Sheldon from his ills. At the end of the summer John took *Justice* on a tour of the West while Katherine stayed behind in Santa Barbara, where she set up residence for an eventual divorce. By the time November rolled around, the tour of *Justice* had folded.

But there was a new play for John and Ned Sheldon to discuss. This was *Peter Ibbetson,* adapted from the George du Maurier novel by John Raphael, an English newspaperman turned war correspond-ent. Back from France, Raphael had encountered the English actress Constance Collier and mentioned that he had adapted the book some twenty years before. He had gotten nowhere with his efforts to have the play produced. Miss Collier asked Raphael to send her the manuscript, for she had always been charmed by the story of two lovers who, though separated, had managed uncannily to meet in their dreams through a process du Maurier had called "dreaming true." When the script reached her, she became so caught up in the idea of a production that she wasted no time in talking to her many friends in the theater and proposing to them that they do the play at a special matinee for some money-raising purposes having to do with the war effort. The one performance of the play, which now included some rewriting by Miss Collier, brought in two thousand pounds.

When she went, immediately after, to New York to fulfill a picture contract, she took the play with her and showed it to several American theatrical managers, who, one and all, found serious weaknesses in it and therefore deemed it unproduceable. She was a friend of Edward Sheldon's and asked him to read the script. Sheldon was as much of an Ibbetson addict as Miss Collier, and within a few days he notified her that he intended to ask John Barrymore to play the part of Peter. John was agreeable, but said he thought Sheldon's own play, *The Lonely Heart,* should be done first. Invariably the self-sacrificer, Sheldon insisted that *Peter Ibbetson* be done and asked John to help him convince Lionel to play the evil Colonel Ibbetson, bane of the young lovers. Constance Collier was more than willing to enact Constance, Duchess of Towers, with whom Peter communicated in his dreams, as well as stage the play.

Lionel in the winter of 1916–1917 was perfectly content with his movie work and was living quietly at the time with his wife and daughter in a home on Long Island. He was not known for his communicativeness. When a small boy next door intruded on his property in chase of a ball, he told his mother that Lionel Barrymore had talked to him. "What did he say?" the mother asked. "He said, 'Get off my grass,'" the boy reported.

Talks with Lionel about doing the play took place in Sheldon's romantically furnished apartment on Fifty-fourth Street where John, separated permanently from Katherine, was boarding for the time being. Ned was gently persuasive, but more than one talk was required. After one long evening, during which Lionel was mellowed by a large quantity of beer, he at last said Yes. A few days later he tried to retract the promise, but with the immaculately honorable Sheldon a promise, once given, was a contract. Sheldon had already busied himself strengthening the play; he not only rewrote most of it, but added a long and theatrically effective scene.

John, with Constance Collier, paid a visit to Al Woods, the producer who had helped aim John toward his more serious career by casting him in the melodramatic *Kick In*. Woods was not in the least interested in sensitive theatrical art, and knowing that a straight recital of the play was unlikely to build much enthusiasm in him, John said: "There's one scene in which Lionel calls me a bastard, then I club him over the head and knock him out. I kill him, as a matter of fact." This was enough to persuade Woods to put up a portion of the production money, about twelve thousand dollars worth. But the production had now grown ambitious, and Sheldon's version called for some highly unusual staging and lighting effects. The extra money needed proved beyond the financial capabilities of Woods, and Lee Shubert was called in to the rescue. By now *Peter Ibbetson* had become the favorite stepchild of many important theatrical people.

When rehearsals began it was hard to know exactly who was doing the staging. Ethel Barrymore and Edward Sheldon did much of it. Billie Burke Ziegfeld stole her husband's chief electrician away from the Florenz Ziegfeld revue, *Midnight Frolic*. Maude Adams volunteered to supervise the lighting. Committee conferences took place frequently between those on stage and those out front.

The Barrymore brothers were not always happy during rehearsals. Jack had been saddled with a foppish red wig and lilting lines such as, "There are no words of music to tell you what I feel . . ." Lionel, who liked having a model in mind for a part, could think of none for the vile Colonel Ibbetson. As he recalled it: "It was the most formidable character I ever read in a play. We were approaching the dress rehearsals, and I still didn't have the slightest conception of how to play it. One night, Constance virtually dragged me to see the great English actor, Sir Herbert Tree, in *Colonel Newcombe*. There, to the life, was Ibbetson."

The Thackeray colonel was, of course, the very opposite of Ibbetson in character.

"I copied every single thing Tree did," Lionel went on, "and it worked out. It was like doing an impersonation in vaudeville. Sir Herbert came to visit me backstage after seeing *Ibbetson* and said, 'I seem to know that old fellow very well.' 'I'm sure you do,' I said. 'Very flattering,' he replied. 'I trust this won't get around,' said I. 'I shan't say a word about it to anyone,' he solemnly promised, and he never did."

The difficulties of the production strained the resources of the stage of the Republic Theatre. One dream scene allowed only seven seconds for the whole stage setting to change. John had to lie down on a cot in his prison cell and arrange himself in the prescribed mystical attitude for "dreaming true," which, if successful, would allow him to join his beloved Duchess of Towers, who was also supposed to be "dreaming true" at the same moment. The mechanics of this had him falling asleep while the lights were slowly dimmed. The prison cell occupied only a part of the stage. Back of it, unseen, the scenery of a garden was to be already in place. The instant the stage became dark enough, Peter leaped from his cot, his place being taken by another man, a supernumerary, who simply lay there during the ensuing scene. Peter then ducked under the drop representing the back of his cell as that drop was being quickly raised. He further scrambled under a scrim drop immediately back of the prison wall drop and rushed out through the garden gate. Almost at once the lights came on, and Peter and the Duchess were seen walking into the garden through the gateway. The dreamlike effect was to be gained by the scrim drop, which, when the lights came on, put a soft transparent veil between the garden and the audience.

On opening night that scrim was all too plainly a wrinkled gauze screen and the illusion was destroyed. Throughout the performance the stagehands were either careless or confused, and between scenes John raged at them to the point of near violence. During one scene a storm was supposed to be in progress outside a French inn. The noise of rain and thunder was heard off-stage, but meanwhile bright sunlight shone through the windows. While this was going on, the back wall of the inn was supposed to melt away for the playing of a dream sequence. When the dream was over and the wall was supposed to reappear, the stagehands forgot to put it back. Action proceeded, with the stagehands in full view attempting to get the scenery back in place.

"It was supposed to be a dream play," one of the first nighters said, "but it seemed more like a nightmare."

And yet the audience sat through the series of mishaps which prolonged the play well toward the midnight hour, patient, sympathetic, and properly tearful. Jack's remarkable make-up provided perfectly the illusion of a sensitive lad just out of his teens, and he managed to subtly suggest the combination of traits he was supposed to have inherited from a French father and an English mother. Constance Collier was as delicate and noble as anyone could wish. As for Lionel, he was out to rival his brother's artistry, and his malignant colonel was superb. Said the *Times:* "The reappearance of the two gave a special quality to the evening, and at its great moments the Barrymore-Drew box wept as one tear duct."

A few days later, on April 22, again in the *Times,* the signature of Alexander Woollcott appeared over more laudatory words. Lionel, he wrote, "returns to us, a most welcome prodigal of the stage."

On the second night, there was another vast orgy of mishaps, but the public was not to be denied its Barrymores. The play survived for two years, lulling audiences with its dreamy escapes from the realities of war.

Later, much later, after John Barrymore astounded New York with his Hamlet, Woollcott wondered: "Would he ever have played the part at all had that critical first night of *Ibbetson* been greeted with levity? If, at the moment when Peter, drenched in sweet music, lifted the Duchess's flower to his lips and murmured '*Amour!*' into space, someone out front had laughed?"

Someone did laugh eventually and at the very moment described by Woollcott. As Barrymore raised the bouquet to his lips someone in the gallery gave out with a raucous laugh. The audience realized, with a sense of slow shock, that Barrymore was speaking—not in a raised tone of voice—but slowly, quietly. "This is not so easy to do," he said. "If you think it is you may come down here and try it." The curtain fell, to a dead silence.

Ladies saw in John, as Peter Ibbetson, a lyrical approximation of romance, and one confessed to having seen the play forty-five times.

But John, however lyrical he appeared on the stage, inwardly mocked the wistful, foppish soul he played. Immaculate under the lights, he seldom changed his underwear, as though in this way he could assert his real opinion of his posturing other self. Everyone who was to visit him in his dressing room when he appeared in succeeding plays commented on his callousness toward the condition of the clothes underneath the costumes.

John's greatest delight while in *Peter Ibbetson* was vying with Lionel. Lionel, to give greater reality to his loathsomeness as the colonel, had gone so far as to figure out what sort of horrible scent such a man would use—much to his brother's discomfort. John recalled a night when, in the scene which required him to kill Lionel with a cane, "the damned cane flew out of my hand into the footlights. The stage manager rang down the curtain, but pulled it up before I finished fishing it out. I got it and turned around expecting Lionel standing with the dagger about to finish me. Instead of that, he was lying on the couch dying of kidney trouble or adenoids or something. I hit him so he'd be sure to pass away and fully expected a bell to ring as I hit his head."

When the play moved on to Philadelphia, Ethel told her brothers that she vastly regretted not being able to go along to witness one of the great theatrical ovations of all time.

"Well," John told an interviewer, "we opened at the Lyric, and from my dressing room, which was up above, I called down to Lionel, telling him I was going to leave my door open to hear this big thing that was about to happen. Five minutes passed and there wasn't a sound. Finally I looked up at the rafters and decided that the theater had rotten acoustics. I waited because I figured that I could imagine the greeting I would get from the one they gave Lionel. When I went on a couple of ushers bumped into each other, the only sound in the whole house. If Ethel had been there our triumph would have been complete."

"What was the matter with them? Paralyzed or something?" the interviewer asked.

"No," John said, shaking his head, "just Philadelphia."

The two brothers toured *Peter Ibbetson* through the winter of 1917. In December of that year John was divorced in Santa

Barbara by Katherine, after she had lived her required year of residence in California. Although the details of her complaint against her husband were supposed to have been kept secret, the California papers supplied several details, including direct quotes from Katherine.

"John's life," she said, "was before the footlights, and there he lived it. When he arrived home after a performance, he had exhausted his humor and his interest and spent all the rest of the time in reading books and sleeping. Jack read all night frequently while I watched and waited for recognition; and he slept all day, leaving a call for just before the curtain was scheduled to rise. One night in New York he telephoned from a club that he wasn't coming home and later a friend brought word that all was off between us."

The likelihood is that the ever-ready Ned Sheldon was the intermediary, but when approached he was fair enough to have some sympathy for Katherine's point of view.

Katherine said she had thought "it would be grand to be the wife of such a man before I married him, and even when later he told me we were to part forever I tried to win him back. His only response was that our temperaments were too different and further living together was impossible."

"Katherine," John Barrymore admitted, "was much younger than I, a charming, delightful, ingenuous person. She looked upon Broadway as something not unlike the promised land. To her actors were jolly fellows whose amusing monkeyshines continued after the theater in gay restaurants, in bohemian studios, and even at the breakfast table before the coffee was served.

"Like most bums, I had a secret passion for domesticity. To me marriage meant escape from Broadway. To Katherine's intense bewilderment and dismay, this supposedly glamorous Broadway party hound turned out to be a dull goof who at once bought himself a pair of carpet slippers and put his dress suit away in moth balls.

"It is not fair to Katherine to indicate that this was her only complaint against me. I know that often I was a very trying person, and even now I cannot explain my irritatingly inconsistent conduct."

Hardly was John a free man when he had to face the prospect

of continuing the tour of *Peter Ibbetson* without Lionel to club to death every night. A new play called *The Copperhead* had been offered to Lionel, and he fell immediately in love with his part. He had the feeling it was too good to let slip by, and he ducked out of *Peter Ibbetson* in the midst of its New England tour and left his brother to carry on with a replacement.

When *Peter Ibbetson,* during its tour, reached Chicago in the Spring of 1918, John decided he had had enough of the play. He came to Constance Collier in her dressing room and told her, "I just can't go on." The decision was a devastating disappointment to Miss Collier and the others of the cast, for while Lionel had been replaceable, it was John who was the cardinal draw. He gave as his reasons fatigue that was both physical and mental, and this had some truth, for Jack was no theatrical trouper. No matter how great his subsequent triumphs, there would come a point when he would lose all will to continue. But we have the report of Arthur Hopkins, a producer whose career in entertainment had begun with the operation of a nickelodeon, and who then became responsible for much innovation in the American theater. John came to him while the tour of *Ibbetson* was still in progress, said he had heard Hopkins was contemplating a production of Tolstoy's *The Living Corpse* and that he wanted the part.

Hopkins had seen the play performed in Europe by a great Russian actor, Leo Moissi, and had decided he would do the play in English if ever he found the right actor. Barrymore was that actor, and Hopkins told him he would hold the play for him until he was ready to do it. It was on Sheldon's advice that John looked up Hopkins instead of accepting another offer to appear in the sure-fire *Dear Brutus* by Barrie. Hopkins didn't hear from John again until he returned from Chicago; they then had a luncheon meeting over which they discussed the play, to be retitled *Redemption.* The producer casually revealed a plan he had in mind. Through an arrangement with the Shuberts he had been offered the tenancy of the Plymouth Theatre for three years, during which time he could present such productions as he liked. Hopkins's plan was to open with *Redemption* and from there go on to the building of a repertoire that would involve two productions each season. The plan also included the association of Robert Edmond Jones, the most talented scenic designer of that day, in the project. Both Hopkins and Jones were agreed that they could not put their ambitious plans into effect until they had the ideal actor around which to build their repertory. Neither had the slightest doubt that John Barrymore was the actor they needed and wanted, and with him they undertook to make Broadway history.

But even before these talks began, Lionel Barrymore undertook to make Broadway history on his own. *The Copperhead,* the play which had so intrigued Lionel, had been fashioned for the stage by Augustus Thomas and dealt with the Civil War and its aftermath. It fitted into the war mood of Lionel's own day because of its unabashed patriotic theme. Lionel was not the first choice for the main role, and he would not have gotten it if Richard Bennett, a more important leading man of the stage than Lionel, had not read it and turned it down. The producer, John D. Williams, took it, at Augustus Thomas's suggestion, to Lionel, who knew in his bones that the part of Milt Shanks offered him the theatrical chance of a lifetime.

This was unusual perception, for on its surface the role of Milt Shanks was not that prepossessing, and in fact was a growly, surly chap in the first part of the play and later a cantankerous, hated old man.

"Copperhead" was the epithet applied to Milt Shanks, a young Illinois farmer who had once known Abraham Lincoln and who, during the Civil War, let it be known that his sympathies lay with the South and refused to fight on the side of the North, claiming he was a conscientious objector. For this he incurred the understandable loathing of his neighbors. Time passed. In fact, between the second and third acts, no less than forty years passed. Young Milt Shanks had become an old man, and the years had not made him less a pariah in his community. The audience learned that his son had died at Vicksburg, and that his wife had died soon after receiving the news from the front. There was only one person who did not shun Milt Shanks, and that was his pretty granddaughter (a role given to Doris Rankin), who lived with him. Now and then he would mumble to her something about knowing Lincoln and about having met General Grant, remarks that his grand-daughter took as evidence of approaching senility.

Milt Shanks might have gone to his death unsung, regarded always as that hated "Copperhead" if his granddaughter had not been turned down by the school board when she applied for a job as a teacher. The old fellow, realizing the shadow of his shame has fallen on his granddaughter, at last decides to speak, and it was the ensuing scene that Lionel saw as his great opportunity.

Milt Shanks has summoned his detractors to his home, and to them he now reveals the causes of his self-inflicted martyrdom. Back in 1861, said the old man, his voice alternately faltering and gaining strength, he had gone to the White House and taken an oath. He had sworn to Abraham Lincoln that he would go back to Illinois as his agent, mingle with the Copperheads as one of them, and defeat their nefarious schemes. But this mission, said the President, was never to be revealed to wife, son, or friend. For forty years, not until this moment, had Milt Shanks betrayed that oath. Upon which out from the crowd stepped the most bitter of his enemies. Tearing his Grand Army coat from his back, he shouts, "You should be wearing it!" and places it upon the back of Milt Shanks.

"And at that conclusion," wrote drama critic Burns Mantle, "the audience rose as an individual and cheered and cheered again—not the sentiment, not the melodramatic craftiness of the author, but the actor who had made the scene the finest, most moving bit of character portraiture any American actor had offered these many years. And, fittingly enough, the actor was Lionel Barrymore, the elder son of America's most famous family of actors."

Lionel had known all along that he was going to stand his audience on its collective ear. He went so far as to break his habitual reserve and to suggest to Ethel and John that they make sure to attend his opening night. Ethel, who was to perform at the Empire that evening (February 1, 1918) suddenly and conveniently came down with an attack of bronchitis, but instead of spending the evening in bed, sat inconspicuously in the balcony of the Shubert Theatre. John came down from Hartford. Instead of canceling his evening performance of *Peter Ibbetson*, he simply bought out the entire house, announcing to Lee Shubert that it would be futile to play to empty seats. Lee Shubert, who was easily touched by any gesture of sentiment involving a brother, later refused to accept John's check. John Drew was there, too, and proudly, beamingly, he presented Lionel with his apple.

At the end of the performance, Lionel kept a careful count of the curtain calls and was satisfied when the total came to fifteen. The shy, subdued beauty of his wife, Doris, came to the notice of the critics for the first time, for this was her first legitimate appearance; up to now, she had appeared only in vaudeville with her husband. In the same play a boy of sixteen, Chester Morris, made his debut. One evening he arrived at the theater practically mute because of a sudden attack of tonsilitis. He was late dashing in and had no way of telling Lionel about his condition. He went on stage, opened his mouth, and made some helpless gestures.

"What was that?" Lionel asked.

Chester made frantic motions, trying to indicate to Lionel that he had lost his voice.

"You mean to say . . ." Lionel said, nodding, and giving the boy's line.

Chester nodded vigorously.

"I suppose you also want to tell me," Lionel said sagely, "that . . ." and he gave Chester's next line.

Chester nodded again and the scene proceeded without further difficulty and with no need for words from anyone but Lionel. The boy's voice returned soon enough, but he never spoke a line in *The Copperhead*. It was Lionel's opinion that the scene was better if Chester remained mute, and it was merely incidental that he happened to gain some extra lines for himself thereby. No actor could have asked for more heralding or more renown than Lionel received for his playing in *The Copperhead*. It was hardly the best play he appeared in, but it was always his favorite, and so much did he enjoy delivering the Milt Shanks "soliloquy" in the last act that he toured that section of the play later in vaudeville. And it was *The Copperhead* that fixed his stage image as America's finest character actor, whose particular specialty was the ability to suggest the aging process.

When asked how he accomplished this, he broke his shyness

long enough to say: "Suppose a young man wants some salt. He doesn't stop to *think* about it. He simply reaches for the shaker, puts some salt on the food, and so on. But an old man goes through a conscious mental and physical process. He thinks he wants some salt. Where is the shaker? Oh, yes, over there, across the table. He may decide he doesn't want it enough to stretch out his hand for it. If he does, the motion is deliberate and conscious."

Lionel did not have the royal manner of his sister, nor did he have the personality, personableness, and flair of his brother, but like them he brought great intelligence to the playing of his roles. The theater was hard, grinding work to him, taking a double toll of energy because always he would rather have been doing something else. Yet when he saw the chance to grip an audience and to wring its emotions, he could call up the necessary power in himself. Ethel, although savagely fond of her younger brother, always thought Lionel had the greatest acting potential of anyone in the family. Lionel's problem was that he never thought it of much importance to achieve acting greatness.

THE POETESS
OF PASSION

chapter XIV

ON AN APRIL DAY in 1917 Mrs. Leonard M. Thomas, twenty-seven years old, a socialite, wife of a rich Philadelphia socialite, mother of two small boys, and a poetess writing under the assumed name of Michael Strange, entered Cartier's on Fifth Avenue to exchange a diamond tiara (similar to one worn by the Russian Czarina on informal occasions) for a rope of exquisitely matched pearls. As she was ushered to the private office of the proprietor, she passed John Barrymore, who was bent over a showcase examining its contents. He glanced up and their eyes met. Each was aware of who the other was. Michael Strange, as she preferred to be known, knew John as the sensationally successful star of *Peter Ibbetson,* which she had already attended twice. "I thought," she wrote later, "there was in his beauty a fatal kind of fineness, an unearthliness which you could not but see through tears." And John knew that Michael was the woman who, a few years back, had been proclaimed by Paul Helleu, a "society" etcher, as America's most beautiful woman, whose name and face was seen often in the society pages of papers and magazines, who had published a small book of verse called, simply, *Poems,* and who was said to be a budding playwright.

Whether they next met accidentally or whether John deftly arranged it is impossible to say. Shortly after that first exchange of glances Michael went to a party given by the Theatre Guild Group following the performance of an Andreyev play. Ned Sheldon and John Barrymore were there too. A few moments after her arrival, Michael was approached by one of the Theatre Guild members who told her that Mr. Barrymore wished to meet her. In her autobiography, written twenty years later, she said: "It came back to me, that passing Mr. Barrymore I had not only been conscious of the beauty of his profile but sensed how well he was able to look to one side of it without seeming to move his head. But here he was, bowing and smiling, looking very slim and nervously poetic, with greyish, greenish eyes of immense fascination because they seemed to mirror back oneself in flattering mischievous terms."

Their relationship is described somewhat hazily thereafter in her autobiography, but no matter, for their private storms of temperament and ego became virtually public over the next eight years. She was born Blanche Oelrichs, a mixture of Austrian, Hungarian, and German blood on one side, of Baltimore blue blood on the other. Her family was prominent in Newport society, and she had been born in that resort town on the same day as John Barrymore's previous wife, Katherine. Charles Oelrichs, her father, was a stockbroker whose financial position was not quite up to his social standing. Her elder sister became the Duchess of Mecklenberg-Schwerin, a name which proved somewhat embarrassing to the family after America's entry into World War I. While Michael was still known as Blanche, she married Leonard M. Thomas, who when she met him was liaison officer of the American Embassy in Paris; he was then an urbane chap in his thirties, handsome, reserved, and wealthy.

Prior to her marriage at the age of nineteen Blanche had been thought one of the better, and certainly most beautiful, catches among the new crop of Newport debutantes, although she had been regarded as something of a problem during her period of schooling. The chic and strict Brearley School had expelled her for her pranks, the most serious having been her furtive pouring of several ounces of Irish whisky into a teacher's luncheon soup. She was then placed in the Manhattanville Convent School, where she awoke at dawn one morning to find a nun in her room murmuring, "Jesus, Mary, and Joseph." Blanche cried out, "What the hell?" This exclamation was reported and frowned on officially, but the reason given for her expulsion from the convent school was her habit of eating chocolate creams in bed after lights out.

She began writing poetry shortly before her marriage; childbearing interrupted the poetic flow briefly; but after the birth of her second child the outpouring of verse came at gusher strength. Friends believed that this free flow of free verse indicated that all was not well with the marriage. And, true enough, Blanche did not exactly enjoy the endless routine of society life: the Newport season, the New York season, the Palm Beach season; balls given for this titled person and that high-ranking member of society; games of bridge; chatter at a succession of cocktail parties. She was driven about in a chauffered Rolls-Royce, had a large Newport house, and a roomy Park Avenue apartment. She had nurses for her children. But none of this was enough.

Two years after her marriage she was chosen as the young society queen to lead the march of the suffragettes, thousands strong, up Fifth Avenue. This gave her some sense of satisfaction, but a greater thrill came from seeing the occasional appearance of her poems in magazines. One of these ran:

> I wake in weariness
> and fall asleep in tears,
> Tell me, is this life's measure
> for all the future years?

The rumor was that Leonard Thomas did not like the intimation the poem gave that his wife was not happy. A row between the couple occurred, following which Mrs. Thomas took her two children, Robin and Leonard, Jr., to a New Jersey pinewood where she wrote a series of quatrains. When they appeared, her husband took more offense from the following:

> O come, my soul has lived a thousand nights
> Within a moment's dream of you, beloved
> So let us build this hour of delights
> And give our wrongs the title of our rights.

Her husband's rather humorless contention was that no one could live a thousand nights in a moment, and, in any case, no married woman should. When a publisher decided to bring out a volume of the poems, it was thought literature would best be served by placing a different name on them, else the author would be judged as an amateur and a society woman, and sensation might replace balanced criticism. Out of thin air Mrs. Thomas plucked (in a taxicab, she said) the name of Michael Strange.

During the summer of 1916 at Newport Michael disdained the usual entertaining while she cultivated writing and her artistic sensibilities. Invitations piled up unread on the hall table while she burned with the fever of poetic creation and dreamed up gorgeous plays that would combine poetry, music, and dance. Her husband diverted himself meanwhile at the Newport casino, on the beach, and in the homes of friends, for his own home was filled with poets, painters, and sculptors. Michael held readings of her poems to her guests but barred admittance to these matinees and soirees to her husband. It was reported that she had bobbed her beautiful brown hair (she later wore it even more boyishly) and she was actually seen in Newport streets nonchalantly puffing away at a cigarette.

It was this fascinating woman, willful as she was beautiful, who piqued John Barrymore's interest and then his passion. During the spring of 1917 he saw her at parties. In the summer he took to spending weekends at his uncle's East Hampton house. The Thomas's had taken a place in East Hampton, too, for the summer, during the midst of which Leonard Thomas left for France as an Army officer.

John, too, volunteered for war service but was rejected because of varicose veins. So disappointed was he that he and a friend, Jack Prescott, went on a mammoth drunk that evening and threw plates around the dining room of the Astor Hotel. This was one of John's infrequent lapses from sobriety during the years following his triumph in *Justice*. Ethel and Ned Sheldon encouraged him in this self-discipline, and Michael Strange had made it plain that she would not tolerate a drinking man.

In the fall of 1917 John moved from Sheldon's apartment to a top-floor studio in an old house at 132 East Fourth Street, off Washington Square. Ned Sheldon had gone off to California, hoping that dry air and sunshine would have a therapeutic effect on his ailments, and instead of returning to New York stayed in Chicago for treatments from his family physician. John was left at loose ends and kept busy by decorating his "garret," as he called it, in a heavily romantic style.

He used pieces that he had had sent from Italy while there with Sheldon, rebuilt the fireplace with Carrara marble, and replaced the panes of a bay window with blue Italian glass. He kept candles burning hour after hour in the apartment so that the gilded walls would take on a smoky, aged patina. To gain access to the roof he had a crooked, winding staircase built. The roof itself he planted with trees and flowers after first covering it with a few tons of soil. Eventually the ceiling beams weakened and sagged, and water ruined the walls of other apartments in the building. But for a time he was happy with his otherworldly quarters, a mixture of Renaissance Florence and twelfth-century Paris. The only woman ever allowed to invade these quarters was Michael Strange. In December of 1917 the news of a divorce decree granted to Katherine arrived, and he and Michael were seen together somewhat more openly, even though *she* was still tied to her husband.

The influence of Michael can be seen behind John's talks with Arthur Hopkins about doing Tolstoy's *Redemption*. In fact no sooner did Hopkins mention that he needed a translator and adapter for the play than John spoke to him of his friend, a charming, gifted poetess who, in turn, could supply someone to do a literal translation from which she could work. This "someone" turned out to be Joy Davidson, sister of Jo Davidson, the sculptor. Michael and Joy spent the sweltering summer of 1918 together, enthusiastically working without benefit of formal contract from Hopkins, who did not believe in formal contracts. Work in progress was read to John who offered suggestions and criticism.

As for Arthur Hopkins' plan for an important repertory theater, Barrymore admitted it sounded inviting but showed little optimism about its possibilities for fulfillment. There was again no formal contract when John agreed to participate with Hopkins and Robert Edmond Jones in their Plymouth Theatre project. He did, however, sign a contract with Paramount Pictures for several films. He had already made *Raffles* for an independent firm while still performing in *Peter Ibbetson,* and the picture received good reviews and did brisk business. Even today it shows John as an accomplished, polished light comedian.

When rehearsals for *Redemption* began in the late summer of 1918, Hopkins noticed that John had acquired a rich Russian accent with which to interpret his role of Fedya, a Russian searching for his soul through the mire of degradation. Dismissing the cast for lunch, Hopkins took John off to a quiet restaurant where he hesitated about bringing up what was in his mind.

"Something wrong?" John asked.

"Well, it's your accent," Hopkins said. "You see, you're a Russian among Russians, and all of you are, in effect, speaking Russian. But, if you're the only one with an accent, this makes you a foreigner among your own people, doesn't it?"

"I've been studying all summer to acquire the correct accent," John said. "A White Russian, no less. But I suppose I'd better drop it."

As rehearsals progressed, Hopkins became aware that John's accent, although no longer Russian, had taken on a slight Jewish intonation, but let it go. As Michael Strange put it, "Jack played an adorable Fedya with a slight Russian Jew accent that stood out with exotic poignancy from the simple mid-Western voices that surrounded him." Her name was not listed on the program the night of the opening, but Michael nevertheless felt "terror, delight, and a sense of guilt to hear whole sentences of mine spoken from the stage." A critic mentioned that "the aimless incoherence of the writing hampered Barrymore's performance," but reviews were mostly laudatory, even though much was made of the "Russian melancholy" of the evening. Business was dull for the first four weeks, and the play would undoubtedly have folded if it had not been for the carte blanche tenancy of the Plymouth given to Hopkins. He kept the play running in spite of small audiences and a flu epidemic which further hampered theater attendance. When the epidemic abated, a surprising turnabout came. Performances sold out after the fifth week and continued to do so for the remainder of the run.

John never thought *Redemption* one of his high points. "In the first act," he said, "when I should have been a human being I was given so many jewels and appurtenances to wear that I always seemed to myself a sweet-scented jackass. Occasionally, I think I was good in the last act."

The play lasted for thirty weeks and could have run another thirty, but it was suddenly taken off while at full capacity. A play of more moment was in prospect.

The Barrymore-Michael Strange love affair was in full bloom, although not as yet guessed at by those searching for newspaper gossip. It behooved both parties to keep the matter quiet, for Leonard Thomas was still patriotically in France on war duty. Meanwhile Michael discreetly paid visits to John's hideaway off Washington Square, and John saw her in the suite she had taken at the Ritz. Nurses looked after Michael's two small sons in other rooms.

It was a miracle that in his dire suffering, Ned Sheldon ever managed to finish his adaptation of *La Cena delle Beffe,* the Italian play by Sem Benelli he had visualized as a perfect vehicle for the combined talents of John and Lionel. Everything else of his writing in progress he had destroyed, tearing up and burning an entire trunkful of manuscripts, as though by doing this he could erase the past and prepare himself for a bleak future. His physical condition had grown much worse. Taken to Los Angeles for an operation to break up the calcification of his knee joints, he was put through a tormenting treatment that involved the stretching of his legs. The treatment was of no help, and the operation was a failure. He had not destroyed the Benelli adaptation simply because he did not regard it as his property but as John's. Somehow he managed to complete the English version, which he titled *The Jest.*

Set in the Florence of Lorenzo di Medici, the play dealt with the rivalry between Gianetto, an effeminate young poet, and Neri, a brutal, coarse nobleman who humiliated and tyrannized the poet. In Europe Gianetto was played by a woman, by Duse among others. Sheldon's version kept the flavor of the original, a poetic tragicomedy, but added to the beauty of the dialogue with flowing, highly colored free verse. As usual he took no credit for his work in the program, although it became known on Broadway that he had contributed to it.

With Sheldon in Los Angeles, the two Barrymores had to rely on their own wits to fill in gaps caused by missing emphases and stage directions. Hopkins' method of direction was so quiet, calm, and almost unobtrusive that the cast was never fully sure when he had begun to direct. "His company," Lionel said, "like a kaleidoscope, had no pattern whatsoever at the beginning but invariably fell into amazing designs which Mr. Hopkins apparently had nothing to do with."

About Lionel, Hopkins had this to say: "He had been playing for two seasons the part of Milt Shanks, the old bent soldier in *The Copperhead*. With us he was to play Neri, the powerful, ruthless, drunken mercenary. When he appeared for rehearsal, he was Milt Shanks, bent, gray and old, old in voice and manner. I was alarmed, for it was not until later that I was to know that this most chameleon of actors actually became the parts he played."

Hopkins thought Lionel as highly gifted as John, and he particularly respected John for his evident appreciation of Lionel. "There was no touch of envy," said Hopkins, "only complete admiration." John told Hopkins on one occasion, "What I envy in Lionel is not only his mind but his ability to believe. If he never found love, he would still believe there was such a thing."

And about John, Lionel said: "Jack's Gianetto was even more of a character part than mine, despite the fact that I was full of sweetbreads in the way of muscle. He was supposed to be an aesthetic, almost effeminate boy who achieved an enormous thrill out of being in personal danger. Then, as his character develops before your eyes, you see a person who is not physically supreme triumph over and kick the daylights out of a brute. This was Jack's personal interpretation of the part and his contribution to the writing of the role. He made his Gianetto bring about the absolute demolition of the great roaring heel Neri—then quailed when he saw how completely he had destroyed him."

"Never,' wrote Michael Strange, "will anyone who saw it forget the savage ranting and groaning of Lionel, while Jack skipped about him like a malicious blade of green lightning, robbing him of his girl, his manhood, his life."

Rehearsals began while John was still playing *Redemption* at night, and the production was worked out in a series of conferences between Hopkins, the actors, and Robert Edmond Jones, whose designs were suggestive settings that emphasized contrasts between

the magnificence of Renaissance artistic achievements and the decadent cruelty of its ways of life. Costumes were elaborate, and while
it was not expected the play would have a long life—such high-style
melodrama, mingled with free verse, was not thought to appeal to a
large public—money was spent freely, even extravagantly. Seven
hundred dollars was spent for one mink-collared cape that John wore.

Sometimes Michael was at rehearsals, and she had a way of tossing
in her ideas like valuable little jewels that would gleam brightly
against the general dross. When she was not there, John would leave
the stage the instant the break came and telephone her, the excuse
being, often, that he could not remember where they were expected
for dinner that night. Michael and John were in great demand, and
in Michael's circle it was well known that she and the actor were
deeply involved. It became a social coup to obtain the two of them
for dinner.

The brilliant opening of *The Jest* attracted a glittering first-night
audience made up of the rich, the greats of the theater, the social
world, and several representatives of the Italian Embassy, curious as
to how their countryman's play would be performed. This opening
took place on April 19, 1919. "The final curtain," wrote the bright
young reviewer for *Vanity Fair*, Dorothy Parker, "fell on *The Jest* at
11:45. Until that time not a coat is struggled into, not a hat is groped
for, not a suburbanite wedges himself out of his mid-row seat and
rushes out into the night to catch the 11:26." By the end of the
second act of the four-act play there were cheers from the audience.
When the final curtain fell, it was already being predicted that *The
Jest* was the biggest hit in a generation.

"The part of Gianetto," Miss Parker wrote, "exquisitely portrayed
no less by gesture and pose than by voice, is in its morbid ecstasies,
its impotent strivings, its subtle shadings, undoubtedly far more difficult than the blustering role of Neri. Yet the physical strain of
Lionel's performance must be in itself enormous. How his voice can
bear up all evening under Neri's hoarse roars of rage and reverber-
ating bellows of genialities is one of the great wonders of the age. Not
an extraordinarily big man in real life, he seems tremendous as he
swaggers about the stage."

Not that *The Jest* as produced at the Plymouth was quite the same play that Sem Benelli had written. Sheldon's adaptation, along with other changes and interpolations made by the two Barrymores and Hopkins, had washed out some of the amorality of the original. Some of the actions were motivated so differently that when John heard of the possibility of Sem Benelli's coming over to the United States to witness the American version, he howled out, "God forbid!" By this time a whole apocrypha of John's retorts and expostulations had sprung up. One night, it was said, when he could no longer bear what seemed the exasperating coughing of the entire audience, he got down on his knees during a praying scene and interpolated several remarks about "the barking seals out front." The late Charles MacArthur carried the story even further. He claimed that on another night John flung a five-pound sea bass out into the audience crying, "Busy yourself with this, you damned walruses!" There was, however, only MacArthur's word to take for the incident.

The critics, though, preferred to take *The Jest* as one of the more stunning events of the American theater. John Corbin of the *Times* declared that the play had "fallen across the sky of a declining season like a burst of sunset color." He found a touch of genius in Lionel's portrayal of Neri and took another evening to better appraise John's performance. "It is only on a second hearing that its involutions become clear," he wrote, and said John had invested the part with "a white flame of beauty." Another critic thought that John moved through the gore and passion of the play like "a green flame."

True to the early predictions, *The Jest* set a new box-office record for nonmusical shows in America, taking in a total of $550,000, an extraordinary figure for the time. Even so, it closed to standing room only, to make way for the next phase of the ambitious plan of Arthur Hopkins. "To the future of such actors," John Corbin wrote of Lionel and John, "it is impossible to set any limits." The lonely invalid, lying secluded and in pain in a Los Angeles hospital bed, felt comforted on reading these paeans of praise; but the pleasure was not unmixed with anguish, for he never saw the triumph he had helped to accomplish.

Michael Strange, important as she was in John's life and career at this moment, was not his only amorous object. A young, fetching actress from the South caught his eye. Her name was Tallulah Bankhead, and according to her recollection John's first glimpse of her took place while both were having lunch, at different tables, at the Algonquin. John requested an introduction, with Estelle Winwood serving as the intermediary. Shortly afterward Miss Bankhead received a note from the famous actor, asking that she call on him at his dressing room in the Plymouth following a matinee performance of *The Jest*.

The girl, having heard something of John's reputation as a lover, was not sure of the exact purpose of her call. But he had a legitimate offer to make. He was about to starting filming *Dr. Jekyll and Mr. Hyde*, he told her, and wondered if she would like to be his leading lady. The offer was turned down by Miss Bankhead with the explanation that she was entirely devoted to the stage. Now another offer came. In her own words, John began making "little animal noises." He took her by the hand and started leading her toward his dressing room couch. Tallulah thought it wise to decline this offer, too, and after a considerable amount of pleading on John's part and much determination to resist on hers, she managed to reach Forty-fifth Street, her virtue still unblemished. In spite of this, a long-lasting friendship between the two developed.

The Jest closed for the summer months of 1919 and delayed its fall opening because of the great actors' strike which closed most of the theaters in New York. With the strike settled, *The Jest* reopened to its usual brisk business. But by now the plans for the first Shakespeare production at the Plymouth were well under way. Robert Edmond Jones had spent the summer in London, studying the Tower and collecting armor and rare fabrics for an ambitious production of *Richard III*. Lionel left the cast of *The Jest* early to fulfill a commitment to star in a film version of *The Copperhead*, and John prepared himself for his foray into Shakespeare. The play, although presented by Hopkins, was of John's own choice, and his interest in the role of the monstrous Duke of Gloucester had been awakened again by Sheldon.

A few years before, he and Sheldon had toured the Bronx Zoo, and the two had found themselves absorbed in watching a large red tarantula with a gray bald spot on its back. John thought the insect was a sinister creature and that it seemed to convey the sense of a crawling, evil power. "It looks like Richard the Third," he commented.

"Why not play him?" Sheldon suggested.

Hopkins was fully confident that John now had the force and stature to try one of the classical roles, but the actor, in spite of his own choice of a play, had qualms, particularly fearing that he could not measure up to the voice demands made by Shakespeare's poetry. His voice, at this time, had a nasal quality, was of limited range, and was occasionally marred by slipshod diction. Shakespeare, John thought, would glaringly reveal these flaws.

A voice coach was the answer, and Michael Strange was responsible for finding an ideal one. She had gone to California at her husband's urging "to forget about Jack," as she put it, and had settled down in Santa Barbara where she became rapturously engaged in writing a verse-music-drama based on a Victor Hugo novel. Unabashed, she would sing the various musical parts to her friends and acquaintances, among them Margaret Carrington, who was a retired opera singer and voice coach. Mrs. Carrington was the sister of Walter Huston, the noted actor, and through her preparation of John for his Shakespearean chores was to meet and eventually marry Robert Edmond Jones.

But it was not of John that Michael thought when Mrs. Carrington told her that her voice had a nice quality but needed cultivation. It was of herself, and she immediately appeared at Mrs. Carrington's for lessons. When Mrs. Carrington left California for her country place in Connecticut, Michael, on her return, continued her lessons.

Forgetting John Barrymore had not proved easy for the poetess, and as soon as her train trip began from Grand Central Station her determination had weakened. When the train made its pause at the 125th Street station, a messenger came aboard with a gift box. Inside was a spray of scarlet camellias and beneath them a soulful-looking photograph of John, set in a small triangular frame of jade embossed with diamonds and sapphires. The leather case in which all this was contained was gold-stamped with the Cartier label. She returned to New York before the six months was up, immediately resumed her affair with John, and told her husband and her father she planned to marry him. Mr. Oelrichs sent the family lawyers to call upon her and explain the various and sundry risks she was running if she did not change her mind. John was kept in suspense by these negotiations. It is not clear whether he hoped more to marry Michael or not to marry her. Gossip had it that it was the former. Gene Fowler claimed in *Good Night, Sweet Prince* that it was the latter.

Perhaps more important to theatrical history is the fact that Michael introduced John to Mrs. Carrington, who found him tremulous over the task he was undertaking, shy and modest. "Through exhaustive study and practice," John said about Mrs. Carrington, "she had come to believe that it was possible to free the speaking voice to such an extent that one could hear the inner essence of the speaker, the self, the soul, speaking through him. Only a child or a saint or a genius could hold such a belief, and Mrs. Carrington was all of these."

John was a remarkable pupil. Mrs. Carrington discovered that his voice was tired and that its shortness of range was due to a complete lack of what she called breath control. He responded at once to her remedial work, not only the principles she taught, but the light she shed on every nuance and meaning in the text of *Richard III*. They spent six weeks together, and during that time managed nothing less than the transformation of his voice. "In my experience," she recalled later, "this kind of tour de force, through the use of will and imagination, has never been done by any other actor in so limited a time."

Arthur Hopkins, long after his association with Barrymore was over, called him the hardest-working actor he had ever known. He was the first to appear at rehearsals and the first to be in full command of his part. As rehearsals proceeded, John's exploration of the part would deepen. He maintained a self-deprecating sense of humor and, oddly, with it a residue of the bombastic kind of stage delivery more characteristic of his father's and grandmother's time than his own. Hopkins would say to John that he reminded him, now and then, of a certain actor, one John particularly despised. "There was quite a list of these," said Hopkins, "and in them a fairly complete catalogue of all the offenses against intelligent theater."

John, in preparing his Richard III, was indefatigable off the stage as well. In addition to the trips to Mrs. Carrington's he made continual expeditions to costumers, bootmakers, and wigmakers. Jones decided he needed special armor manufactured for John and located a former armorer in Newark who now ran a machine shop. The machinist manufactured two sets of armor for John, one black, the other copper in tone. It took several dozen trips across the river before these heavy suits fitted properly. Meanwhile John kept up a correspondence with armor authorities in the British Museum to make sure that authenticity was maintained. This authenticity extended to the sword he carried in the play, designed from a copy of a weapon carried during the War of the Roses.

Hopkins, through his study of the play, had decided that traditional treatment and interpretation of the play had put the author at some remove from the audience, and he was determined to present it as a work newly written. No books of the play or about the play were allowed on the stage. Actors received typewritten parts with no stage or voice directions. He suggested that *Richard* not be treated with funereal reverence but as a melodrama. All traditional stage business, all "Shakespearean" gesture, was to be thrown into discard. John, in complete sympathy with this nonreverent approach, set the example Hopkins needed.

John's own conception of Richard was as a spiritually warped character, a man of fine intelligence who was possessed also of a mysteriously sinister power. The deformed body was to be regarded as the outward sign of a crippled soul. He developed a swift, tarantula-like walk for Richard that suggested extreme deformity. Asked by Fowler how he was able to manage this, he explained, "I merely turned my right foot inward, pointing it toward the instep of my left foot. I let it stay in that position and then forgot all about it. I did not try to walk badly. I walked as *well* as I could . . ." He also told Fowler that it was the first time he had never actually gotten inside the character he played. "I mean, I thought I *was* the character, and in my dreams I *knew* that I was he."

The opening night performance on March 6, 1920, did not end until one o'clock, and by that time Ethel and Lionel, having finished their own performances, were in the audience, as was John Drew.

The coloring of the production matched the sinister mood established by John; black, blood-red, silver, and gold predominated, and the proceedings were played out against the cold gray of the stone walls of the Tower of London. The version followed had been compiled by Ned Sheldon with additions from the third part of *Henry VI*, which first brings Richard on the stage in Shakespeare's chronicle. The amplified role gave John more scope. "He was unforgettable," Hopkins said afterward. "He had fire, humor, beauty, cajolery, chilling cruelty. Shakespeare tragedy, for the first time in that period, became thrillingly alive. It was in *Richard* that John took his place in the classical gallery." Robert Edmond Jones added his own estimation: "There never has been such a great actor at any time, there never has been such shattering beauty in art, as there was in John Barrymore's."

Alexander Woollcott printed the definitive accolade. "Richard III at the Plymouth Theatre, Barrymore's first Shakespearean role, marks a measurable advance in the gradual process of bringing his technical fluency abreast with his winged imagination and his real genius for the theater. The highest point has been reached in the rapid, unexpected ascent which began six years ago, a rise which has been unparalleled in the theater of our time."

The box office of the Plymouth was stormed by a public eager for this unparalleled theater experience and Hopkins and Jones bubbled happily about forthcoming productions of *Hamlet, Cyrano, Faust,* and *Peer Gynt*, nothing less than the dreamed-of repertory which would first play the Plymouth and then tour the world. Suddenly, less than four weeks after *Richard III* had opened, the marquee of the Plymouth went dark, and the dream burst like a bubble grown too huge.

On Broadway there was a persistent rumor that the star, John Barrymore, had suffered a nervous breakdown. Hopkins merely announced that Barrymore was ill and gave no further details other than that the reopening of the play was postponed until the fall. Some of those who attended the last few performances said they had noticed Barrymore fumbling some of his lines.

John's breakdown appears to have been a complete physical and nervous exhaustion. While still appearing in *The Jest* and rehearsing for *Richard III*, he went every morning to a studio on Fifty-sixth Street to film *Dr. Jekyll and Mr. Hyde*. So exhausted was he by his various chores that the opening of *Richard* had been postponed five days to allow him to recuperate. Wearing armor in the play, he still managed some amazing physical feats, such as a complete backward flip-flop that ended in a fall. Matinees had to be eliminated because of the physical strain of each evening's performance. The emotional difficulties of his relationship with Michael were also overly strenuous. She had taken herself to Atlantic City, the better to cultivate her muse and sensibilities, and John often finished a performance, took a train to the resort, argued with Michael half the night, and came back for a performance the next day.

First making himself incommunicado at home, John then took Lionel's advice and put himself under the care of William Muldoon, former champion wrestler and friend of Maurice Barrymore's, who ran a sanitarium and training camp near White Plains. It was announced that John would stay there for two months and get himself back in shape. Muldoon insisted on a strict regime. John walked and jogged across fields in a gym suit, milked cows, was forbidden to drink or smoke or to use the telephone. Reading of anything but the newspapers was taboo. Even thinking was regarded as bad for the health. He rode horseback, sparred with other inmates, ate simple, wholesome meals, and went to bed early. After two weeks he had put on seventeen pounds. On May 1 he left Muldoon's, declaring that he would reopen in *Richard III* in September.

A reporter came to see him at his Washington Square hide-away, and while a centuries-old mechanical bird sang in a gilded cage, John discussed the fishing he said he would do in Florida during the summer and his desire to play Hamlet and Romeo, too. Meanwhile Leonard Thomas divorced Michael in Paris, and gossips wondered if she would marry John. Opinion was that neither John nor Michael would willingly part with their freedom. Ethel was openly opposed to a marriage, and not a single relative or friend of Michael's encouraged her to take John for her next husband.

In June of that year the film *Dr. Jekyll and Mr. Hyde* opened to much acclaim. In fact, the day of its first showing at the Rivoli a door and two windows were broken by crowds attempting to see the movie. "It will easily become the most talked of picture of the time," prophesied Burns Mantle. "Unquestionably it has lifted young Mr. Barrymore to the leadership of his contemporaries of the screen, as his Richard III has put him in the forefront of the advancing actors." Applause rang out in the Rivoli after each showing. "One leaves the theater," wrote a critic, "with the belief that motion pictures are on the verge of a new era."

To those who had seen *The Jest* there was a familiarity about the settings, and with good reason, for an entire set of rugs, draperies, mirrors, and other pieces from the palazzo designed by Robert Edmond Jones had been transported to the studio. Casting about for a girl to play the part of a Spanish dancer, John came across a chorus girl whose salary at the time was fifteen dollars a week. After her appearance in *Dr. Jekyll and Mr. Hyde*, Nita Naldi became a star. In this film John's penchant for the grotesque and the bizarre emerged. He managed the most striking malformation of his body and face, often without benefit of make-up. It was as though he did his utmost to distort his handsome features into the most fearsome ugliness.

St. John Ervine, the famous Anglo-Irish poet and playwright, paid a visit to John during mid-1920.

> We lunched together [he reported] with some friends in an old-fashioned house near Washington Square, and I found myself confronting a much more youthful man than I had expected to meet, with deep, dark eyes, not like the eyes of his sister, full of nervous disdain and elusive trouble, but full also of melancholy astonishment and some reproach. I imagine that Keats had eyes like Mr. Barrymore's, and I am certain that Hamlet, had he become an actual being, would have had his eyes, too. He talked much better than any actor I have ever listened to. Most actors can talk well enough about their craft, if they are not permitted to monopolize the conversation, but very seldom can they talk with interest or average intelligence about things outside their craft. But John Barrymore's talk interested me. I came away from luncheon with my problem still unsolved, whether Mr. Barrymore is an actor of supreme genius or merely a very clever actor, but I was in less dubiety than before. I felt that he was very likely to be an actor of supreme genius. I said to myself, "Certainly he can play Iago, but can he play Hamlet?"

as I greeted him when we were introduced, and when I said
good-by to him I said to myself, "Well, if he can't play Hamlet,
who can?" Only this is certain to me, that in this man there is
a unique power of expression that has not yet been fully revealed.

This power was to be revealed, but it would take some time. His
marriage to Michael Strange intervened, and in the light of subsequent history this marriage must be regarded as something of a
setback to John's development. Ethel ascribed to it a distinct change
in his career and personality. The marriage was celebrated on August
5, 1920, in a suite at the Ritz-Carlton belonging to one of Michael's
friends. One of her constant companions, Birdie Vanderbilt, was
conspicuously among the missing. There, on the other hand, were
her sister and brother, Ethel Barrymore, and Lionel and Doris. At
the marriage license bureau earlier, where they were first in line,
John gave his age incorrectly as thirty-seven (he was thirty-eight)
and Michael was honest about hers, twenty-nine.

The nuptials were celebrated none too soon, for less than seven
months later Michael gave birth to a girl first named Joan Strange
Blythe (in honor, Michael announced, of Joan of Arc), but whose
name was changed by Michael at the christening to Diana. John,
somewhat angered by this highhandedness on the part of his wife,
invented a nonsense name for his daughter. He called her Treepee-
wee. But it was as Diana Barrymore that she later, much later, became more celebrated—and notorious.

John did not return to the stage in the fall as he had promised.
He spent the remainder of the summer in East Hampton with
Michael, and in the fall moved to a cottage near White Plains that
he had purchased as a wedding gift for her. His wife, pregnant,
occupied herself with finishing her labors on her musical-verse-
drama, now called *Clair de Lune,* and John, rapturous over what he
seems to have regarded as this evidence of Michael's genius, devoted
himself to designing costumes and settings for its production. He
and Ethel would play in it, he declared enthusiastically. Ethel needed
some convincing and urging, but play in it she did. John's next
appearance on the stage was not in *Richard* or in *Hamlet* or as
Romeo, but in the play written and composed by his wife. This

fact alone gives an indication of the strength of Michael's personality and the sublime egotism that could allow one of the greatest of the world's actors to forsake Arthur Hopkins, and the grandiloquent repertory he was more than willing to activate, in favor of *Clair de Lune*. Yet, in all fairness, it was John who said that he would never have done *Richard III*, if it had not been for Michael's urging.

HOW BEAUTIFULLY
SHE DIES!

chapter XV

ETHEL WAS ALWAYS MORE ATTRACTED to the repertory idea than either of her brothers and was given her chance at it by Alf Hayman (who ran the Frohman enterprises after the producer's death). Having emerged from her eight-picture contract with Metro, she announced (1) that she would never devote herself exclusively to movies again, and (2) that her first repertory production at the Empire would be *Camille*.

"*Camille*," she said dreamily, "is the kind of play that sinks into the hearts of women. It is one of those plays that lingers for days after it has been seen, because it has the haunting elements of music. *Camille* wraps you around in the soft, soothing glow of dreams." Nevertheless, she sought Edward Sheldon's help in revamping the creaky play. He bravely, suffering pain as always, "modernized" it for her, although confined to his bed in Chicago. He based the new version on the novel, had the play begin after the heroine's death, and then allowed the story itself to unfold as a dream in Armand's mind. He thought music should be used to heighten the play's effect. The production opened in December of 1917 to something less than critical enthusiasm.

Although Sheldon's name was not on the program, his touches were recognized by the reviewers. One mentioned "Mr. Sheldon's inordinate affection for piccolos, fife and drum corps, love birds, harps, choirs, military bands, street organs, and Victrolas in the wings." It is to be assumed that most of these effects emanated from those Victrolas in the wings. Ethel looked ravishing, it was generally agreed. And there was so much crying in the audience that the stage was allowed to go dark for a full minute after one of the more pathetic climaxes so that noses could be blown and tears wiped away. Ethel loved playing Marguerite, and her faithful coterie of feminine admirers attended the matinees en masse. "Oh, let's go and see Ethel die!" they would twitter after their luncheons, and off they would rush to the theater. But the larger public failed to respond, and the play was taken off after five weeks. A modern comedy called *The Off Chance* took its place and following that a frothy farce by A. A. Milne called *Belinda*. So went the repertory venture.

During the summer of 1918, which Ethel spent at Mamaroneck with her children, she was asked by Alf Hayman to come to New York to see him because he had something wonderful for her to look at. The "something wonderful" turned out to be the first two acts of a new play called *Déclassée*. There were two acts yet to come, but Hayman prophesied that it was going to be her biggest hit of all.

Ethel took the two acts and drove back to Mamaroneck with her chauffeur, reading the play on the way. She finished as they were driving through New Rochelle and found herself so excited that she told the driver to turn around and drive back to Hayman's offices at the Empire. "Please," she pleaded with him, "make sure that nothing happens to interfere with my getting this play."

As it happened, Ethel had already met the author. The young Zoë Akins had written a long poem, *Ode to the Allies,* which it was hoped that Ethel Barrymore would like enough to recite at a war rally being held at New York University stadium. Elsa Maxwell brought Zoë to see Ethel in her dressing room at the Metro studio on Sixty-first Street, where she was still striving to fulfill her contract. Ethel thought the poem was glorious but awfully long, and instead of memorizing it prudently had it inscribed on a huge roll of parchment. Forty thousand people attended the rally. Ethel wore a long dress, a wreath of gold leaves in her hair, and recited the poem with tears in her eyes. The applause was tremendous. Like many others of the theatrical profession, Ethel was tireless about doing her "bit" for the war effort. With George M. Cohan, Jane Cowl, Annette Kellerman, and Nora Bayes, Ethel stood on flag-draped platforms and joined in the flag-waving and the bond-selling. At one big pageant of all the Allies in Madison Square Garden, Ethel was Belgium and was so effective that she continued being Belgium at pageants until the end of the war.

A new war loomed for her after World War I had ended. Ethel was all unaware of a coming struggle between the actors and the producers until it was about to break out. Zoë Akins had finished *Déclassée,* and Ethel, briefly vacationing at White Sulphur Springs during the summer of 1919, was looking forward to the start of rehearsals. Suddenly a telegram arrived from the Actors' Equity Association, of which she was a member, notifying her that a strike was to be called against the play producers of New York City. The telegram confused her. She had never heard of actors going on strike, and she couldn't imagine why a strike should apply to someone as well paid and without complaint as she was.

John Drew explained matters to her when she returned to Mamaroneck. The actors, he told her, sitting on the broad porch of her home, were going to stand firm against the producers and the managers; they were seeking more equitable contracts, better conditions in theaters, a shortening of the rehearsal period during which the actor traditionally worked without pay. He went into the complexities of the tangled situation, told her that the Drews and the Barrymores, and others who were classed as stars, had few problems, but that it was important for all actors to stand together. The support of leading stars was being marshalled by Equity, especially now that the producers had decided to refuse to recognize Equity as the official bargaining representative for the actors. A strike was imminent.

Ethel wrote a letter, which she gave her uncle to take back to Equity headquarters at 160 West Forty-fifth Street. It read: "While my entire theatrical career has been associated with but one management, from which I have received only fairness and consideration, I feel that the traditions of my family and my personal predilections ally me logically and irremediably with the members of my profession in the Actors' Equity Association."

The actors struck early in August, 1919. Seven shows were closed down (none of which employed any of the Barrymores, because of the summer hiatus) and rehearsals for several others were put off because of the refusal of the actors to work, among them Ethel. A few days after the strike began Ethel came to New York and visited her cousin Georgie Drew Mendum. Georgie asked her if she had been to strike headquarters.

"Oh, I sent them a letter," Ethel said, and asked her cousin if she thought anything more was needed from her.

Georgie's advice was that Ethel ought to go to strike headquarters and make it more physically plain on which side her sympathies lay. Ethel was not in the least convinced by any of Georgie's reasoning, but to please her drove toward the strike headquarters on Forty-fifth Street. As her car turned in from Sixth Avenue and headed toward Broadway she noticed that the entire block was so massed with people that it would be impossible for the car to make headway.

"What on earth is all that?" Ethel asked Georgie.

"The strike," Georgie said, and explained that the people were standing in front of the strike headquarters.

Ethel resolutely got out of the car and with Georgie started through the crowd with the object of pushing her way toward the brownstone which housed the strike committee. By the time she reached the steps of the building several in the crowd recognized her, and suddenly there was a loud, exultant shout, as though all the aspirations of America's actors had just then become focused in the person of Ethel Barrymore. They could not lose, not if Ethel was with them.

"It left me," Ethel recalled, "trembling from head to foot with a feeling of great happiness and exaltation."

From that moment on, Ethel gave her all to the strike. The doughty John Drew was already in the thick of battle; he had not only read Ethel's message to the throng that attended a meeting called at strike headquarters the previous evening, but announced that John and Lionel Barrymore, his nephews, had sent word that they stood firmly with Equity. Here was one case of a royal family on the side of the rebels.

Because of her efforts in the battle with the producers and their battery of lawyers, Ethel faced losing the play she now badly wanted to do. She had loved *Déclassée*—the story of a titled English lady who is tossed out of society after being unfaithful to her husband— and had waited impatiently for it to be finished. Now Hayman was anxious to get rehearsals started and sent Ethel a series of messages, commanding, cajoling, begging her to come to the theater. Such a thing was simply impossible, Ethel told him, for going to rehearsals would mean the same thing as playing. Hayman's position was that rehearsing was not acting before an audience on a stage. The more obdurate Ethel became, the more angry became Hayman. Finally he told his star that he could wait no longer and that he had already cabled Mrs. Patrick Campbell to come to New York and play the declassed Lady Helen.

"I'm sorry to lose the play," Ethel said in her sweetest tones, "and I'm sure Mrs. Campbell will be excellent in it."

To the crowds of strikers she spoke her feelings: "I don't know how to make a speech, really, but I am with you heart and soul and more than that. Don't be discouraged. Stick! It's coming out just the way it ought to for us."

As the strike deepened and broadened, every theater in New York was closed except for the Lexington Avenue Opera House, where performances were given to benefit the striking actors. The public, starved for theater, flocked in to see, among other pieces, the second act of *Camille,* given by Ethel Barrymore, with her brother Lionel as Duval and Conway Tearle as Armand. When Ethel made her entrance on opening night she was tendered a three-minute reception that rocked the theater.

An afternoon came when all the Equity forces, with support given by stagehands and motion picture projectionists, met at the Lexington Avenue Opera House to rally round the cause. The leaders of Equity made speeches. Suddenly Ethel sprang to her feet and asked for recognition from the chair.

"I know that we are all loyal," she cried, "and that we will win the strike, but our ammunition is money. I know a lot of persons here feel impoverished by recent events, but I think that some of us who have a little to spare should give this ammunition. If I can get one hundred and ninety-nine actors and actresses to give five hundred dollars each, I am ready to sign my check for that amount."

An enthusiastic rush to write checks followed this clarion call; the first to get his signature written out was Ed Wynn. Lionel handed his five-hundred-dollar check to Ethel. More than $20,000 was collected before the meeting was over, and Ethel Barrymore, together with Marie Dressler, was appointed to increase that amount to $100,000. In the theater while this was happening was Tallulah Bankhead, who had been made unemployed by the strike and was completely out of money as a result. She was so carried away by Ethel's gesture that she raced to the platform and whispered to the chairman that she wished to contribute a hundred dollars. "Miss Tallulah Bankhead will contribute one hundred dollars," the chairman boomed out, and the hall was thunderous with applause. She had to write to her grandfather, claiming that the honor of the South would be sullied if she did not produce the hundred dollars promised. Her grandfather not only came through with the money—no Yankee actor was going to outdo his little granddaughter—but sent her a beaded evening dress, too. Miss Bankhead's adventures with the Barrymores were not to end with this incident.

To honor her for her part in bringing the strike to a successful conclusion Ethel was appointed as one of the group to sign the five-year pact between actors and management. Her good friend, Augustus Thomas, presided at the meeting; another good friend, Arthur Hopkins, was the spokesman for the managers. The occasion lasted until three in the morning, and when Ethel left the meeting she had been signatory to the conclusion of a struggle she had hardly been aware of three weeks before!

She also learned, when the strike was settled, that Hayman had never cabled Mrs. Patrick Campbell, for she was told to proceed with rehearsals of *Déclassée*. Hayman was huffy and ill-humored, though, because of what he chose to regard as Ethel's betrayal. Charles Frohman, Incorporated, had become affiliated with Famous Players, a movie company, and when Ethel objected to the tacky nature of the settings and furnishings for the play, Hayman grumpily told her to clear anything else she wanted with Famous Players. Ethel at once went to Jesse L. Lasky, head of Famous Players, and got permission to buy a handsome sofa. She advanced the money for it herself and was never able to collect from either Hayman or Lasky. The "sofa incident" helped cause the bad feeling that was to result in Ethel's eventually leaving the Frohman management.

But apart from these "annoyances," as she termed them, Ethel was happy in the play and opened in it on October 6, 1919, to large acclaim. "As close to the manner of a Pinero drawing room drama as an American could be expected to get," Burns Mantle said. The slightly tarnished lady played by Ethel came to a sad end when she purposely walked out of the drawing room and got hit by a passing car. Zoë Akins, the author, thought Ethel's manner of doing this was one of the most memorable moments she had ever experienced in the theater, and she described it as follows:

> Lady Helen stands for a moment, a glass of champagne in her hand, thinking. Then she knows what she must do. She says a word to the butler, sets the glass back on its tray, and goes. As she walked from the beautiful room, the train of heavily beaded white dress rattled on the floor with the same glass and wood sound of windows rattled by the wind. The sound itself was ominous and dramatic, coming as it did out of that telling pause of decision. But it was the set of Ethel's head and shoulders, the swinging into desperate action, moving a little faster as she crossed the room to the door, after the tragic survey made by her eyes of past and future, which gave the moment its quality.

The play, however, became the target of the wits who had taken to frequenting the Algonquin dining room at luncheon hour. Ethel's manner of delivering certain of her lines were ripe for parody, and one of the more popular sayings of the day, as a result, was: "I never believe doctors, and I never believe lawyers, but I always believe fortune tellers."

Tallulah Bankhead, who had not yet made her own stage success, became a favorite guest at parties because of her ability to mimic Ethel in *Déclassée*. Frank Crowninshield, the editor of *Vanity Fair*, gave a party to which he thoughtfully invited both Ethel and Tallulah. During the course of the evening Tallulah allowed herself to be persuaded to do her Ethel Barrymore imitation for the guests. Courageously she performed her parody, with the subject of it sitting directly before her, but no sooner did she finish than she rushed up to Ethel and asked her to please forgive the impertinence. She would never have done it if . . . Ethel gave her the glance that withered. "But, my dear," she said, "you made me look so fat!"

"But, Miss Barrymore," Tallulah said, in mingled defiance and fear, "I was imitating *you*."

Upon which, Ethel smartly slapped Tallulah's face.

Déclassée turned out to be one of Ethel's greatest hits, running on and on at the Empire to standing room only. After her two hundredth performance she broke the Empire box-office record. The following year she took the play on tour with equal success, insisting that the high Broadway standard of performance be maintained. She noticed one night that an actor was badly off in his performance and asked her stage manager why this was happening. Upon being told the actor had a severe cold, she remarked contemptuously, "He has no right to have a cold on the stage! Let him have it off." She would have been equally merciless toward herself.

But it was during this tour of *Déclassée* that she had her most serious illness. One night in Cincinnati, when she was in the middle of the last act, she was seized by a pain that struck her back and all but paralyzed her. She was sitting on the famous sofa at the time, and it was just before she was due to leave the drawing room and get run over. The pain slowly moved upward, and with an extreme effort she was able to rise and leave the stage. Luckily her last entrance required her to be carried to the sofa by two strong young footmen, and she was able to proceed gracefully to die. When the curtain fell she collapsed and was taken by ambulance to a hospital.

The diagnosis at first was that Ethel had contracted a violent form of arthritis regarded as incurable. When it became clear that she would be many weeks in the hospital, she sent for her children and their nurse, had them established in a hotel, and saw them for a few minutes at a time whenever her pain lessened enough for her to put on a cheerful face. The arthritis eventually settled in her extremities, and she left for New York, where her train was met by

John Drew and John Barrymore. They sped her straight to Flower Hospital. After another series of consultations it was discovered that the cause of all her anguish was due to a streptococcic infection lodged in her tonsils. A major operation was necessitated, lasting an hour and a half. The arthritis had crippled one of her fingers, and on her way to the operating room she asked her doctors if she would ever be able to play the piano again. This, the doctor said, would be impossible. But it wasn't long before she was back to the piano, playing as well as ever.

During this period her marriage with Russell Colt was severed. Russell was openly involved with a young married woman, a rich, prominent socialite, and the affair was causing a considerable amount of scandal. Ethel decided, forthrightly, that it would be better for everyone concerned if her husband did not have to resort to such obviously clandestine meetings with his new beloved, and she let it be known publicly that she was seeking a separation.

She was resigned to the fact that her marriage could not be saved, and she went to see her old friend Cardinal Hayes in Boston to ask his advice about the possibility of her getting a divorce. He at first forbade it, then said: "All right, but you must not marry again."

Ethel had not considered the thought of ever marrying again, and she regarded the divorce as a mere legal formality. The legal separation was granted on the day she left Flower Hospital and the divorce took place two years later, in 1923, in Rhode Island without opposition and on the grounds of desertion and nonsupport. Ethel asked no alimony or support for herself but requested reimbursement for the education of her children.

Her oldest boy, Sammy, was at a boarding school in Canterbury, Connecticut, by now, and it was around this time that she enrolled little Ethel at the Notre Dame convent school now located in Moylan, outside Philadelphia. When she took her daughter there Ethel found the school much as it had been when she attended it, with even some of the sisters who had taught her still teaching the new generation. The smallest boy, Jackie, was also enrolled at a boarding school.

The actions for separation and divorce brought out publicly some alleged mistreatment of Ethel by Russell. As late as April, 1920, her maid, Anna Patterson, testified she had found Ethel suffering from nervous shock in her room, her face bleeding and her eyes discolored. If these allegations were true, it would appear that Russell Colt had quite a temper and that Ethel was as capable as John at creating stormy private scenes.

But after the divorce amiability between Ethel and Russell was the rule. Not only did she give him the right to see the children, but thought it would be better if they saw them together. So the custom was instituted for Russell to come to dinner once a week, whenever such a schedule was possible, and at other times to go out to dinner as a family. At Thanksgiving and Christmas dinners, when the family all came together, Russell was a permanent guest. Ethel, a great sports fan, went with Russell and the children to baseball games and, when the boys were old enough, to boxing matches at Madison Square Garden.

During her stay in Flower Hospital the calendar had been crowded with events of family importance. One was the birth of John's first child, Diana, on March 3, 1921; a few days later Ethel was awarded custody of *her* three children in her separation agreement with Russell. And a week later Lionel closed in an ill-fated production of *Macbeth,* one performance of which Ethel had raised herself from her hospital bed to attend.

Thwarted by John's breakdown from pursuing his Plymouth Theatre ambitions, Arthur Hopkins had turned to Lionel with a proposal that he play *Macbeth.* Lionel agreed to make his Shakespearean debut after finishing the film version of *The Copperhead,* but the production was postponed until he had completed a contract with Whitman Bennett for several pictures made at a Yonkers motion picture studio. In these, Lionel played, in order, a mental telepathist, a man who sacrificed his life to save some orphans from a fire, an impersonator of a dead valet, and a forger who reformed at the last moment of his life to save his daughter's reputation. None of these films made movie history, but they kept Lionel solvent. When Bennett failed to pick up his option, Lionel declared himself ready for *Macbeth.*

Robert Edmond Jones decided to give the production a spacious, abstract treatment. Hopkins was enthusiastic about his sketches. The playing space was ominous, witch-haunted. A sense of reality was purposely avoided, as figures came out of the dark into the light and faded into the dark again. A somber musical score enhanced the dank mood.

Lionel's voice was considered suitable for Shakespeare, and he took no special training as John had done for *Richard III*. According to Hopkins, Lionel's "tenancy of Macbeth produced an almost unbearable effect of horror. His eyes became those of a stricken madman, his voice a cry of writhing pain. As surely as Macbeth was possessed by the witches, Lionel was possessed by Macbeth. The result was something that had little relation to acting."

The dreadful deed was done, as Lionel put it, the night of February 17, 1921, at the Apollo Theatre. Heywood Broun's advice to the theatergoer the following day was "Lay on MacDuff, lay off MacBride." His reference was to the New York theatrical ticket agency. He headlined his review: MACBETH SEEN DIMLY THROUGH A HAZE OF ART. "Lionel's Macbeth," he wrote, "was a weary Neri." He called the castle setting of Jones "a curious sort of Stonehenge of jutting stones."

Kenneth Macgowan said the stage looked like "a glowing platform in space." Alexander Woollcott referred to "an Inverness that looks like a fiercely extracted tooth, a Dunsinane that suggests wastebasket cuttings strewn through space. The audience dispersed a little after midnight suffering chiefly from shock—shocked that Lionel Barrymore, while often good and occasionally very good, should never once have suffered greatness in all the length and breadth of the play." *Macbeth* left the Apollo after twenty-eight dismal performances, and the shock to Lionel contributed to his later decision to leave the stage for good.

And it was now time for the other Barrymores to get their lumps. Ethel, having returned hastily to her hospital bed after witnessing Lionel's Shakespearean downfall, was approached by her brother with the proposition that they play together in his wife's *Clair de Lune*. The play had already been turned aside by Arthur Hopkins, but Alf Hayman of the Frohman organization was willing to do it on condition that at least two Barrymores were starred. Ethel could never deny her brothers anything, and hardly was she out of the hospital before she was embroiled in rehearsals for *Clair de Lune,* which Michael Strange claimed she had written almost to completion before realizing she had dramatized Victor Hugo's *The Man Who Laughs.* (She later wrote a play about Edgar Allan Poe which was remarkably similar to one sent her husband by a woman playwright a year before.)

John, in Michael's words, "behaved in a frenzy of generosity" toward the play. He designed the scenery for the first and second acts and also designed the men's costumes. He chose the cast with great care and rehearsed the actors for long hours. Ethel, in the role of Queen Anne, was gowned in magnificent costumes and huge headdresses and surrounded by dwarfish lady's maids. John played the clown Gwymplane, whom, it was detailed in the script, mummers had stolen in childhood and slashed on one side of his face "so that he was hideous to behold." Only an author of the assurance of a Michael Strange could have employed John Barrymore in a role that for the most part required his profile, his whole figure, in fact, to be masked by a hooded cloak. Her script also called upon him to do a strange and difficult dance, including a triple *entrechat.* In spite of the fact that he would be unrecognizable by the audience, John tirelessly took lessons from a teacher of Russian ballet until he could execute the difficult steps. Naturally no one believed it was he who actually performed the terpsichorean feats.

Several dwarfs were required for the play, and John hired so many that Alf Hayman paled at the mounting costs of the production, for each extra dwarf had to be costumed in gold brocade. By opening night the costs of production were said to have reached $200,000, a monumental figure for the Broadway of that time.

Admission prices for *Clair de Lune* were lofted to a new high of five dollars at a time when other theaters were reducing prices. Interest mounted in the production as the stories of John's extravagance spread. And naturally all of society was agog with anticipation over the playwrighting debut of the society poetess. Seats for opening night were in heavy demand and scarce as a result. It was rumored that a pair down front brought as much as $250. The opening night audience, with the exception of those who bought their tickets through speculators, was selected with the same care given to the choosing of the cast. The smartest opening of the season, the society columns declared, was the unveiling of *Clair de Lune*.

"All the world and his wife," announced one New York paper, "and in a few remote cases someone else's wife, attended the opening" at the Empire the evening of April 18, 1921. The Jay Goulds were there, as was Mrs. Biddle Duke, and Mrs. Brady Harriman. But amid all the furry, bejeweled elegance, Mrs. John Barrymore arrived at the theater attired with becoming modesty in a simple afternoon frock of blue serge, embroidered in red silk, whipped up by her dressmaker for the occasion. She may have appeared cool to the onlookers, but she had dressed in such a flutter of nervousness that she had put the dress on backward.

Least impressed of all those in the audience were the newspaper critics who had difficulty describing the plot of the play to their readers the next day. "There seemed to be in the general moonlight of the whole proceedings," Heywood Broun commented, "a queen who was inclined to look with favor on the courtier about to marry her natural sister, a duchess. They were all in the park talking about it in the first scene. Then to this same park there entered a troupe of players. But it had been related by one of the courtiers earlier that a lackey, told to murder the illegitimate son of a duke, had instead attacked the real heir and sent him disfigured into the world. All these things seemed in moonlight to be in the play. It was all very vague."

Other critics, too, found their minds confused and their ears distressed by the language in which Michael Strange told the Victor Hugo story. Alexander Woollcott added the final note of insult by heading his review: FOR THE LOVE OF MIKE.

Ethel, while unable to shed much rationality on the events of the play, came off lightly. In her white wig, her rococo gown of silver and brocade, she was said never to have looked so lovely. "Her chiseled beauty seemed more than ever unsurpassable," noted an admiring critic. Michael Strange let it be known, however, that it was her opinion that Ethel neither had memorized nor understood all her lines. To this charge, Ethel never deigned to reply.

The critical scorn for the play so infuriated John that on the second night he came to Ethel's dressing room and told her he was going out in front of the curtain to make a speech in answer to the attacks. Ethel pleaded with him not to do it, and when the glowering John wouldn't listen, she called up Lionel at his home in Port Jefferson; Lionel on the telephone and Ethel in person took turns dissuading the irate star and husband from making the speech. The curtain was held until John agreed to take their advice. Nothing could stop him, though, from sending his complaint in letter form to the *Times* and *Tribune,* and it was relished mightily by readers a few days later.

> Upon reading Tuesday those notices of *Clair de Lune* written by the gentlemen of the *Tribune* and the *Times,* I became inclined to wonder if a malice so stark should be permitted to pass without comment . . . I am forced reluctantly to the conclusion that the gentleman of the *Tribune* is either jaded from forced attendance at the theater throughout a long season or that in his job he is, like Melisande, not happy.
>
> As for the *Times* reviewer, one cannot help wondering, while reading his odd cacophony of words, if he has ever dualized those two functions— which the public daily expect of him as a critic—of thinking and writing at the same time. . . .

More followed along the same lines, with Alexander Woollcott of the *Times* and Heywood Broun of the *Tribune* continually singled out for spanking.

Michael Strange received some comfort, as it turned out, from an unexpected quarter. The drama critic of the Boston *Transcript* journeyed to New York, saw the play, and wrote a flowery notice for his paper, one which the author chose to regard as the most honest evaluation. The play lasted for sixty-four performances, mostly because of the extra bonus of publicity that came from John's righteous and public wrath, and then expired into oblivion, although all concerned were later haunted by a parody revue calling itself *Clara da Loon.* John was always chivalrous toward *Clair de Lune* and later took the blame for its failure. "It seemed entirely filled," he said, "with dwarfs and Barrymores, and the only thing lacking to distract attention from the charming play was Lionel Barrymore's presence in it."

After the closing Ethel felt well enough to take *Déclassée* on tour again. She spent the summer in Mamaroneck and booked *Déclassée* for points as far west as California. Toward the end of the tour she made the decision to leave the Frohman management and join hands with Arthur Hopkins, who was somewhat surprised to receive the following telegram from her: I HAVE SEVERED MY CONNECTIONS WITH CHARLES FROHMAN, INC. DON'T YOU THINK YOU AND I MIGHT DO SOMETHING AMUSING TOGETHER?

Hopkins thought so, indeed, and replied: I CAN THINK OF NOTHING I WOULD LIKE BETTER.

This was their only contract, and if Ethel had regrets, they were caused by leaving her favorite theater, the Empire, and the stage-hands who had become her friends. At the end of Ethel's tour Hopkins had two "amusing" projects for her, Hauptmann's *Rose Bernd* and *Romeo and Juliet*, both of which would require her to die beautifully. Ethel was happy. Arthur Hopkins was the one pro-ducer who shared her dream of a New York repertory theater and, for the first time, all the Barrymores were to be under one manage-ment.

On September 26, 1922, she opened at the Longacre in *Rose Bernd* to decidedly mixed reviews. There had been some doubt as to whether Ethel could act the role of the peasant woman. These doubts were dispelled, although one critic said, "True, she was an Ethel Barrymore peasant." Heywood Broun thought that *Rose Bernd* was "probably her greatest achievement in the theater," but he did not admire Ludwig Lewisohn's translation of the play, which made it seem dour and hard and was kept tolerable only by Ethel's acting. Woollcott thought the speeches terrible, but Ethel's was a perform-ance "such as glorifies our stage only once in a long, long while."

The papers during the next few weeks ran some interesting letter exchanges between Hopkins and Ludwig Lewisohn and others who joined in the controversy as to whether the play had been miscast (as claimed by Lewisohn) or butchered in the translation (as claimed by Hopkins). Two months later *Rose Bernd* was taken off to make way for Ethel's Juliet.

Now an unprecedented race occurred between two rival produc-tions of *Romeo and Juliet,* one with Ethel, the other with the some-what more youthful Jane Cowl. Ethel won the race by a matter of a few days, but it was Jane Cowl who received the far more glowing reviews. And notice was taken of the fact, too, that Ethel outweighed Jane by a good many pounds. For several years thereafter no one dared to mention the name of Jane Cowl to Ethel.

Woollcott Gibbs, after calling Ethel "goddessy" in the role of Juliet, showered praise on Miss Cowl. Ethel was cut to the quick by this and for a long time was cool toward the portly little critic. And although she renewed her friendship with Miss Cowl, and never admitted how disturbing the Juliet episode was to her, she never quite forgave the other actress, who, she felt, might have waited for a more seemly time (presumably after the closing of the Hopkins production) before presenting her *Romeo and Juliet.* The ardor of the Ethel Barrymore following weakened considerably after both *Rose Bernd* and her Juliet were hastily taken from the boards, and it was once more, with the determination to win them back, that Ethel returned to the drawing room in *The Laughing Lady,* a play that Hopkins quickly dredged up for her. She made something of a hit, but now the critics who had not been joyful over her two previous serious efforts rebuked her for appearing in a work so trivial and frivolous. But Ethel knew her audiences, and especially when she took a play such as *The Laughing Lady* on tour, she knew she could count on loyal support. The role she played was that of a great lady in slight disrepute, and her lines were witty and delivered with spirit.

She managed to live down her Juliet which she had been brave enough (and perhaps foolhardy enough) to play at the age of forty-three, and she appreciated a letter from John, the brother she was fondest of, who wrote of that performance, "It really, really, is great— the finest thing you've ever done."

Her own sense of humor held firm. One of her few intimates among the drama critics was Percy Hammond, who was asked by a hotel owner in Chicago to recommend his accommodations to Ethel when she brought *The Laughing Lady* there. Dutifully Hammond relayed the request. Politely Ethel replied: "Be assured that if I don't stop at your hotel, I shall at another."

THE RAMPARTS OF ELSINORE

/ *chapter XVI*

From the *New York Times,* November 1, 1922—JOHN BARRY-MORE TO BE SEEN NOVEMBER 16. Arthur Hopkins' production of *Hamlet* with John Barrymore as its star will be seen at the Sam H. Harris Theatre on Thursday night, November 16. The principal roles have been assigned as follows: Ophelia, Rosalind Fuller; King, Tyrone Power; Queen, Blanche Yurka; Horatio, Frederick Lewis; Laertes, Sidney Mather; Polonius, John S. O'Brien; Ghost, Reginald Pole.

From the *New York Times,* Friday, November 17, 1922—A NEW HAMLET. The atmosphere of historic happening surrounded John Barrymore's appearance last night as the Prince of Denmark; it was as unmistakable as it was indefinable. It sprang from the quality and intensity of the applause, from the hushed murmurs that swept the audience at the most unexpected moments, from the silent crowds that all evening long swarmed about the entrance. It was nowhere—and everywhere. In all likelihood we have a new and lasting Hamlet.

"Then came Hamlet," as John Barrymore told it in *Confessions of an Actor,* as though it was the most natural and necessary of progressions for him. Booth's *Hamlet* had faded from living memory; the Forbes-Robertson *Hamlet* still lingered as the standard and the mark at which to aim. But before Barrymore was ready to make his supreme effort, he went through, not as an actor but as a man, some extraordinary emotional flounderings with his wife, Michael Strange.

Having given birth to a daughter and a play in 1921, she announced that she would make a trip alone to Europe. John agreeably said that he would take a fishing trip. But, suddenly, while Michael was at Newport saying good-by to her family, he called her from Boston, confessed to feeling lonely, joined her in Newport, made a friendly peace with the elder Oelrichs, and a few days later, on July 10, 1921, to be exact, sailed off with her to Europe. Ten days later they arrived in Paris and put up at the Crillon on Place de la Concorde.

At the Crillon they resumed their incessant and endless arguments. At one point John, angered that Michael could admire an elderly poet who was a known homosexual, swept all the glasses and dinnerware from a table in their suite. Above them, a moment later, came a horrendous crash, and in the silence that followed, John murmured, "Ah, professionals!" In the suite above them Isadora Duncan and her Russian poet husband had been having a quarrel of equal frenzy, and the Russian had suddenly leaped up, grasped the chandelier and torn its roots from the ceiling.

Both Michael and John habitually traded threats of suicide. On one occasion John announced to her that he was irrevocably determined to finish himself, and with the evident purpose of jumping in the Seine ran from the apartment that had been lent to them by a friend. A few minutes later the distracted Michael ran after him, but could find no sight of him on the quay or any floating body in the water. She went back to the apartment to sadly await word of the tragedy from the police and found John asleep in their bed.

Michael later countered with an equally implacable pledge to kill herself. She barricaded herself in the bathroom and through the door let it be known to her husband that she had just swallowed the contents of an iodine bottle. John cried out that he would break his head against the door unless she opened it. She refused. A horrible crash was heard. She flung open the door and saw John lying stretched out on the floor. When she knelt over him she could detect no sign of breathing and became hysterical, not realizing that John was adept at holding his breath and feigning death. John, satisfied with the ounce of compassion he had wrung from her, sat up morosely and resumed life.

So it went. And yet there was almost nothing John would not do to please her. "We are exactly alike in many respects," he told friends. Later he added: "Those respects separated us." Michael liked attracting attention and prevailed upon John to dress similarly to herself. "It just seemed to happen," she said artlessly when asked to explain their odd mode of dress. In Paris, wined and dined by the people who counted most to Michael, they wore the same felt hats. The pleatings and flutings of Michael's skirts were echoed on John's trousers which were sometimes made of strange materials, like black velvet. John let his hair grow longer. In response to Michael's suggestion he designed his shirts with long, flowing, pointed collars. Instantly the delighted Michael had a dozen copies made for herself.

These "idiotic" get-ups, according to Ethel, "embarrassed him to death," and she thought Michael was making a dreadful fool of him.

Michael's fascination with women often seemed to equal or exceed her fascination with men, and when a bosom friend, Iris Tree (daughter of the British actor Sir Herbert Tree) joined the quarrelsome couple at St. Moritz, where they had traveled, Michael enlisted her companionship on a walking trip from St. Moritz to Venice. She and John must breathe separate air for a time, she said. John decided to breathe the more rarified air of Chamonix and from that vantage point made a successful climb of Mont Blanc. In Venice Michael found herself entranced by a young British poet, and the forlorn Iris left the two of them alone. When John arrived and discovered what he assumed was a liaison (Michael always denied that the affair had been anything more than spiritual), he rent the air of Venice with his accusations. Both their voices were raised in fury until at last cries of "Shut up!" came from windows in the Grand Hotel.

John was scheduled to go to England to make a film version of *Sherlock Holmes*, and Michael took this opportunity to sail for home. In November John returned to the United States. Michael insisted on a temporary separation through the winter. Part of her distress with John was caused by his jealousy; if she danced with someone, he suspected the innocent man was her lover. A strange way to behave for a husband with whom she had agreed that each should maintain a personal freedom. And her distress was due, too, to his sporadic drinking which was also contrary to their agreement with each other. Once when she disposed of a bottle she found, he took revenge by consuming the alcoholic liquid in her curling-iron heater. Later, when they were together again in their New York brownstone on East Ninety-seventh Street, Michael discovered a cache of champagne and threw it all out. John retaliated by drinking a full bottle of her favorite cologne.

Early in 1922 John made *The Lotus Eaters* for First National on location in Miami with Colleen Moore as his co-star. In May he was in New York and stayed for a while with Ethel in her Mamaroneck home. Michael had sailed off for Europe again, where a new and fascinating friend, Cynthia Mosley, the wife of Sir Oswald Mosley (later to be the leader of the British blackshirts, a Fascist organization) joined her. John was bored. So Ethel took him off to French Lick, Indiana, with her, and there she said, "Here," and handed him a small copy of *Hamlet,* suggesting that he learn one or two of the soliloquies. Back at Mamaroneck, he walked around the grounds reciting from *Hamlet.*

John Drew Devereaux, the son of John Drew's daughter, Louise, was only four at the time that he paid a June, 1922, visit to his aunt's Mamaroneck home, but he was always to remember the first sight of his Uncle Jack.

"Aunt Ethel," he recalled in 1962, "had beautiful flower gardens, and my Uncle Jack had cut himself a stick as a cane and was walking up and down the flower beds saying things like, 'Now I am alone,' and whenever he came to something he wanted to emphasize, he would go swish with the stick and take off the top of one of those lovely flowers."

John now announced to Arthur Hopkins that he was ready for *Hamlet* and, with characteristic shyness, asked him if he would approach Margaret Carrington to assist him again. This Hopkins was glad to do, and Mrs. Carrington was happy to comply, insisting, though, that no date be set for the production. Hopkins, however, immediately commissioned Robert Edmond Jones to design the settings, and John took himself each day to Margaret Carrington's farm in Connecticut where he worked with her for six and eight hours at a stretch. Mrs. Carrington suggested that he throw away the texts he had obtained for more scholarly insights, and they worked only from the Temple edition of the play that Ethel had given him.

This small red volume is now in the possession of The Players, and there is an inscription on the flyleaf in John's handwriting which reads as follows: "To Margaret Carrington—with love & gratitude for her very great helpfulness & kindness. John Barrymore, 1923."

Below the inscription the following note (also in John's writing) appears: "This is the copy we worked from. It's a small copy—but God—how we worked!!"

This volume, used as a promptbook by John, shows the various cuts he made in the play and handwritten suggestions to himself on emphases and interpretations. The shape of the play as he presented it is very close to that of Laurence Olivier's film version. The cuts made by each actor would almost make one assume that either Olivier saw the promptbook or that the two came to identical conclusions about the material that should be eliminated for acting purposes. A few lines with the Barrymore notes are given below:

Frailty, thy name is woman! *Surprise*

I'll call thee Hamlet *Wait between words*

O all you host of heaven! *Sincerely (pitifully)*

Remember thee! (John crossed out the exclamation point after the second repetition.)

He that plays the king shall be welcome, (etc.) *In a sort of dream-like voice*

What's Hecuba to him, or he to Hecuba, That he should *weep* for her? *Down*

On the last page of the promptbook is John's drawing of Hamlet lying dead.

The rehearsals began in September at which time Hopkins announced the production. In staging the play, Hopkins ignored the previous interpretations. "We began with our own conception," he said, "and developed it in all parts of the play. I doubt if Hamlet had ever been given a clearer course to sail." And summing it up, he said: "To my mind, this was the great and crowning achievement of the modern theater. Never was one man more blessed with all the attributes of the complex, towering, haunting Dane—beauty, grace, eloquence, humor, pathos, and power."

Much was written during the weeks and months following the opening night performance about John's playing of the role, but there were some who claimed that his greatest performance of all took place at the dress rehearsal the day before. To accommodate Ethel, who had come to the Harris Theatre to see as much as she could of it before leaving for her own performance in *Rose Bernd,* John scheduled the last rehearsal early and did not wait to change into his costume. He played Hamlet in street clothes and gave, Ethel said, "the greatest experience I have ever had in a theater. . . . He . . . had in some mysterious way acquired that magical ease, as if he really were Hamlet."

On November 17, the critics burst forth in a paean of acclaim. In the *World,* Heywood Broun shouted out that "John Barrymore is far and away the finest Hamlet we have ever seen."

In the *World,* Alexander Woollcott called upon his most fateful rolling prose to describe the glory of what he had witnessed. "It lacked but twenty minutes of midnight last evening when the four tawny clad captains of Fortinbras lifted the slim young body of the dead Prince of Denmark to their mailed shoulders, bore it slowly up the great stone steps of Elsinore and out of the brilliant, gory, earthy castle into the cool of the moonlight beyond. They stood there for an instant, they had their burden silhouetted for us as a final memory. There was a wail of trumpets in the distance, the lights faded out and the curtain fell. Thus ended an evening that will be memorable in the history of the American theater."

John Corbin of the *Times* brought out *his* most flowery prose for the occasion. "The luminous, decadent profile of Mr. Barrymore's recent Italian and Russian impersonations had vanished and with it the exotic beauty that etched itself so unforgettably upon the memory. . . . This youth was wan and haggard but rightly manly and forthright . . ." In sum, Corbin thought this Hamlet thrilling.

The scenery for John's *Hamlet* occasioned not only much comment but controversy, the chief object of argument being the massive flight of steps Jones designed as the major playing area. He had built a forestage out over the orchestra pit and eliminated all foot-lights, stationing the lights from above the balcony. The steps led up to an opening which disclosed blue night sky. On the top level of these steps, against the night blue, the player king and queen performed in gold, and against that same backdrop Hamlet's sword hilt flashed as he followed the radiance shed by the ghostly king, his father. Further down the steps were massed the green, purple, and red of the costumes of other players. Some scenes were played before a delicately painted, formalized drop curtain. When Claudius prayed, it was before this curtain, facing the audience. Hamlet came from between the curtains and saw him there. The effect, so close to the audience as it was, gave a startling intimacy to Shakespeare.

Another point of discussion was the representation of the ghost as a stream of light falling on the actors, and it was complained that the voice speaking the lines from some invisible source did not always come from the same spot occupied by the light.

As much as Woollcott admired Barrymore's interpretation of the role, he could not keep a note of deadly humor from his description of the ghost. "Lo!" he wrote, "there appears against the deep blue midnight sky beyond the rampart of the Jones Elsinore a shifting and dissolving cloud of filmy white, in a state of tremulous flux, while from the wings issue the horrendous admonitions to the un-happy Prince . . ." Adjustments were made and Woollcott reported that "a week later the voice emerged crystal clear and neatly clipped in the manner of a lay-reader intoning the service."

Walter Prichard Eaton thought that the majestic set, which gave the effect of a vast domed chamber enclosing most of the stage, with the steps and platforms leading up through a lofty central arch, made the play seem "not unlike High Mass in a ritualist church, save that one is spared the incidental music. . . . The real hero of the piece might as well be the stairway, except that the latter performs no visible function unless to serve as an exit from which a character now and then leaps off into the wings." He had harsh words for the insubstantial, but well lighted ghost. "The majesty of murdered Denmark is represented by a floodlight and a voice. The straits to which the unfortunate star is put by this original device are worth mentioning. Having chased the floodlight up the steps and off left, Mr. Barrymore is obliged to pursue the elusive electricity in a sort of hide and seek around the wings and on again to the steps, where he collapses with exhaustion, as well he might."

Critics continued to be literal-minded in their discussion of this most original of *Hamlet* productions. "One cannot play Shakespeare up and down stairs," one stated categorically. A backdrop in the fore-stage which Jones designed to represent a room for one scene was allowed to represent the outdoors for another. Heywood Broun remarked: "Ophelia is buried in the front parlor, which seems to me a mistake."

But Jones received support from other quarters. Stark Young thought the architecture of the production "at once austere and princely, lyrical and enduring." Kenneth Macgowan regarded the settings, costumes, and lighting as having touched "the highest mark in Shakespearian production ever seen in America."

As for the star of the show, what did he think? John summed up the scenery as "Pennsylvania Station."

Nevertheless, excitement about the Barrymore *Hamlet* remained keen for several weeks. Ludwig Lewisohn, blistered only a few weeks previously by Hopkins for his translation of *Rose Bernd*, turned the other cheek and wrote a considered piece about *Hamlet* in *The Nation*. "Other actors can act Hamlet," he said, "but John Barrymore *is* Hamlet." All this helped of course to consolidate John's position as the greatest American actor of his time. And as time went on it became clear that he had set the pattern for the "modern" interpretations of *Hamlet* that followed years later. When John Gielgud and Maurice Evans performed the role on Broadway, Richard Watts, Jr., among other drama critics, referred back to still vivid memories of John Barrymore's interpretation.

When *Good Night, Sweet Prince* appeared in 1944 some who had seen John as Hamlet wondered why Gene Fowler had not discussed the quite evident incestuous nature of the scenes between Hamlet and the Queen. Dr. Harold Hyman, who had treated John for various of his illnesses in New York, wrote Fowler and asked him why he had not dealt more fully with the matter. "Not the least of Jack's achievements in *Hamlet*," said Dr. Hyman, "was his psychoanalytic concept of many of the incidents."

Fowler replied: "I am neither a psychologist nor an expert on the drama. . . . My views on psychoanalysis in general could not by any stretch of the imagination be regarded as more than the babblings of a layman. . . . I brought into my narrative a gallery of expert witnesses, just as an attorney for the defense does in a capital case. It was apparent that the incestuous motif was solidly lodged within the Barrymore *Hamlet*. Still, I ruled out his pre-play conferences with psychoanalysts. All the competent testimony pointed to the fact that Margaret Carrington was his principal and *only* real adviser in regard to this role. As to his reported hatred of his father, I, as a layman, would not presume to debate the point with the scientists. Personally, I don't believe it." Nor, he went on, did he believe John's purported seduction at age fourteen affected his attitude toward his father to that degree.

Fowler mentioned that he had discussed with John some of the subliminal aspects of his acting of Hamlet. "I must say," Fowler told Dr. Hyman, "that while Jack was giving the private *Hamlet* second soliloquy, translated by him into obscene and ghastly incestuous terms, it became a most startling and compelling performance."

To what extent John deliberately imbued his Hamlet with psychoanalytic implications can only be guessed at today. Dr. Hyman, in recalling his letter sent to Gene Fowler, said that he had not meant to imply that John's Freudian knowledge was profound, but rather that, more or less intuitively, the actor had felt his way towards the incestuous interpretation. "John," Dr. Hyman said, "had the capacity to make people believe he was a profound student of a subject when actually what he knew in the way of fact was superficial." (Apropos of this, the story still circulates of how John impressed Albert Einstein with his understanding of the theory of relativity.) John, so far as is known, did not consult pyschoanalysts; he did consult Dr. Pearce Bailey, a noted neurologist who taught at Columbia University and who had taken to dabbling with psychoanalysis. "He probably saw him no more than once or twice," said Dr. Hyman, then a colleague of Dr. Pearce at Columbia, "and whatever Dr. Bailey would have told him would have remained where the knowledge he gained usually stayed—on the top of his head." But it still seems a remarkable fact that John Barrymore should have antedated Laurence Olivier's Freudian version of *Hamlet* (the film he made in 1949) by so many years, and without the kind of consultations Olivier had had with the English authority on Freud, Dr. Ernest Jones.

"Barrymore," Lloyd Morris wrote, "was probably only transposing into art his most deeply felt personal experience." His theory was that it was John's grandmother, Mrs. Drew, whose ghost arose in the scene between Hamlet and the Queen. "It seems likely that in his closet scene with Hamlet's mother, Barrymore was acting out the only profound and permanent love in his life."

But whether or not images of his father, mother, or grandmother arose from his subconscious is really beside the point. Today it is commonplace to assume that a gifted man's personality would include a great many hidden or unexpressed urges, incestuous, latently homosexual, or whatever. The whole matter has become banal. Did John Barrymore unconsciously or consciously resent or hate his father? Who doesn't? Does hating a father or desiring a mother lie behind all examples of fine acting? Did Olivier also desire his own mother when he, as Hamlet, played the scene with the Queen so romantically? We can assume that John's interpretation came about through his intelligent study of the text, his sensitive awareness of the meaning of language, his finely developed instincts as an actor. He was blessed, at the time, with a keen ear, highly developed sensibilities, and some perception of the thought currents of the time, and he had arrived at precisely the right moment in his career when he was capable of a great Hamlet.

An acting performance begins to fade almost the moment after the curtain has rung down. If there is an argument, it must continue from the memory of the performance, for the document no longer exists. Too bad that John's Hamlet came during the silent-film period, else a record of it might have been preserved. As it was, John's achievement was wafted into thin air, living on mainly through its effect on others. John's Hamlet lived on in this way for a long time, as it became the standard of comparison with other, later Hamlets. Did they have John Barrymore's satiric, biting humor?

227

Did they have the Barrymore beauty of voice? The clarity, the intelligence? This was the real legacy of John's Hamlet.

John had thoughts of his own about performing *Hamlet*, these given in a newspaper interview about two months after the opening. "Hamlet is a great gentleman and has all the attributes of one," he said. "Hamlet is full of consideration for others; his history before his soul-shattering cataclysm is that of an enemy of restraint, suspicion, gloom or resentment. He has a sense of humor, is intensely human and, even when dreadfully wounded in spirit, he cloaks his feelings as is inevitable with people of finer instinct and breeding. Tortured and outraged from the very opening of the action, he has his hysterical outbursts, but he has too much charm, too much humanity, to be gloomy or lugubrious when he is in control. In his parting with Ophelia, with whom he is very deeply in love, he spares her the truth, and indeed his knowledge of her and his knowledge of most human beings, as is the case with every finely tuned spirit, is too deep for any explanation. Personally, I would say that Hamlet is every man with a fine spirit."

Asked about the cuts he had made, he explained, "In reading Shakespeare, every man is his own dramatist. He can visualize the action, and every speech, every scene has its significance. But in the projection on the stage it is found that portions of a certain speech cannot be used if the play is to retain its sweep and vitality." He gave the King's soliloquy on repentance in Act III as an example, pointing out that the first eleven lines sweep on "with rapidity and power. But now the current of thought turns in upon itself and the stream halts." The thought becomes involuted, and while "clear enough in the perusal, really serves to obstruct the forward movement in our acting version." He explained other flows and eddies of speech and referred to the "arbitrary scenery" used to accelerate the action. "What if Ophelia is buried in a crypt converted out of the throne room. We gain speed by the elimination of the stage wait."

Even so, the Barrymore *Hamlet* took up nearly four hours of playing time at the Harris Theatre. John was neither bothered by, he said, nor tired by spending this length of time on the stage. "*Hamlet* is much easier to play than *Richard III*. His emotions and reactions, although frighteningly poignant, are human and reasonable, and his scenes are marvelously paced. In *Richard* the actor must constantly project evil and do more or less of an 'act in one.' And he must be more and more violent as he disintegrates. If one tackles him as a steady diet one is apt to get in on the disintegrating one's self." He concluded: "The character of Hamlet has every attribute of humanity except compromise. And without compromise destruction is certain. And isn't is extraordinary that the most popular character ever written should apparently be defeated by life instead of transcending it?"

But, as the run continued, the question often became: which Hamlet did you see? John Barrymore's best performance, Arthur Hopkins claimed, was always the first one. The one hundred performances he gave at the Harris after the opening were hardly close copies. He had a habit of embroidering upon a part once he had successfully created it, and these embroideries seldom resulted in improvement. When in a relaxed mood, his good performance would come back. The trouble with the arguments over whether Barrymore was great or merely good was that seldom were the quarrelers discussing the same performance.

The Moscow Art Theatre Company played in New York at the time John gave his *Hamlet,* and Hopkins graciously invited the Russians to a *Hamlet* matinee. John, keyed up by his eagerness to impress the members of the great company, played with an hysterical fire he had never exhibited before and thereby lost his naturalness. Hopkins and Ethel (who was there) went backstage after the first scene and begged him to tone himself down. But it was too late. "The stampede was on," as Hopkins put it, "and he never got back into the corral all day."

The dazed Russians, Stanislavsky among them, came backstage afterward and stood in embarrassed silence around John, who glowed with his afternoon's achievement. One of the Russians, to break the silence, asked in awe, "Do you really do this *eight* times a week?"

Much was made of the "fact," at the time, that John, by playing 101 performances, broke Booth's record of one hundred. Strangely overlooked, amid all the hullabaloo surrounding that 101st performance, were the 102 performances given in New York ten years before by John E. Kellerd, and even the accurate *New York Times* fell prey to the excitement by headlining the event: BARRYMORE BREAKS HAMLET CENTURY RUN. The house for the closing night had been sold out for several weeks in advance, and the Harris Theatre management announced that standing room tickets would be put on sale at the box office on the evening of February 9, 1923. The line stretched from the theater along Forty-second Street for almost a full block. The box-office window closed down after three hundred tickets were sold, and the crowd slowly dispersed.

John vigorously denied to reporters the next day at the steamship pier, where he was about to board ship for Europe, that he had deliberately tried to break Booth's record, pointing out that his steamship reservation had been made for some weeks in advance and that it had therefore been necessary to close down the play on Friday night. But he failed to mention that he had played two extra matinees on Tuesdays to reach the 101 figure. And he seemed not to have known that the Booth record had already been broken. Why did he play exactly 101 performances then, when by the time he reached his sixtieth performance he had made it known that he was growing weary? Frank Case, manager of the Algonquin, offered Gene Fowler what he regarded as the true version, since John was not known for excessive egotism or conceit where his acting was concerned. It seems that several old gentlemen, dedicated to preserving the memory and accomplishments of Edwin Booth, had come to John's dressing room to request that he close after ninety-nine performances so as to leave Booth's "record" unsullied. John informed the gentlemen (Case claimed to have been an eyewitness of this) that he would play Hamlet exactly one hundred and one times.

But, it is probably true, too, that John regarded Hamlet as the one great professional challenge and accomplishment of his career up to then and, since he had already stood Broadway on its ears, why not wind it up neatly? As it was, he could have gone on for many more performances, since the house was sold out for several weeks beyond that Friday evening. Hopkins was forced to refund a large sum to ticket holders. But the loss was John's as well, for he participated in the profits. And Hopkins had his word that once he had had a long vacation, he would reopen the play. This he did in November of 1923, at the Manhattan Opera House.

When he sailed for Europe, it was to reconcile with Michael in Paris. So often did John and Michael sail to Europe and back during their marriage, sometimes with each other, more often without, that at a satirical revue at the Neighborhood Playhouse in Greenwich Village an actor began a soliloquy, "To sail or not to sail—that is the question," and parodied Shakespeare's lines with a summary of the Barrymore marital situation.

Hot on the heels of John's triumph in *Hamlet* in New York, a society portrait painter who went by the name of Zuloaga met Michael at a dinner in Paris and persuaded her to pose for him. When she went to his studio, she just happened to bring along a medieval boy's costume, and when Zuloaga exhibited the portrait of Michael at a New York exhibition he titled it "Hamlet." True enough, Michael looked in the portrait to be dressed exactly as John was in the play. Hoots of derision went up, but Michael always claimed foul and said she had been cruelly exploited by a painter in search of publicity.

The reconciliation between John and Michael was soon rent by arguments again. John was sure his wife had been entertaining a lover in the little mansion she had rented in Paris, and the accusations grew too much for Michael to bear. They agreed to separate, even drew up an agreement, but revoked it almost at once. John returned alone, to travel to Hollywood where he was to make *Beau Brummell* for Warner Brothers. He was obviously keeping up with the prettier new arrivals in pictures, for he requested seventeen-year-old Mary Astor, who had appeared in two small roles, for his leading lady.

He dallied with Mary while filming *Beau Brummell* but wasted no time, once the movie was shot, in climbing aboard a train for the East. He arrived in November, 1923, two days before he was scheduled to reopen *Hamlet* at the Manhattan Opera House. His appearance in the role was again regarded as distinguished, but the production was changed slightly in that the ghost appeared visibly on the stage this time. After three weeks in New York, he took *Hamlet* to Washington where President Coolidge saw the play and invited Barrymore and Arthur Hopkins to the White House the following day. The taciturn President warmed up to Barrymore enough to mention that he had seen E. H. Sothern in the same role and had thought Mr. Sothern's costume more interesting.

This revival lasted for three weeks more on the road and, because John had again grown weary, closed in Cleveland. Knowing that he was depriving the members of the cast of needed salary, John held a farewell party in Cleveland and made sure that a hundred dollar bill was under the plate of each of his co-workers. The wardrobe lady was included, too, in this largesse, and to her John had written a note: "Dear Jenny—This is not the price of our shame—for that— is priceless!"

If John soon tired of performing a part that he had created, he was not averse to accepting challenges. Booth had played *Hamlet* and conquered in London. To this aim John now dedicated himself and attempted to persuade Hopkins to give him an English production. Hopkins did go so far as to inquire of an English publisher friend what John's reception might be in London. "If Barrymore has the audacity to come to London in *Hamlet*," the publisher replied, "they'll kill him." Upon which John entered into negotiations on his own hook with theater managers in London. Even though he lined up an all-English cast that included Constance Collier as the Queen and Fay Compton as Ophelia, he met faint interest.

During two trips he made to London in 1924 it was pointed out to him by several theater managers that Shakespeare had not been particularly successful in the West End in recent years and that Shakespeare was being constantly and very satisfactorily played at the Old Vic. Constance Collier, who remembered that he had made her production of *Peter Ibbetson* possible in America, undertook to help him in his search for a theater and introduced him to Frederick Harrison, the owner of the Haymarket—where Maurice Barrymore had once played. Harrison agreed to give John the lease of the theater for six weeks, and John put up five thousand pounds toward the financing, risking, as he afterward confessed, almost all of his available capital. He served as his own director and producer, and in whipping the company into shape experienced as keen a pleasure as he had ever experienced in the theater.

Michael brought Diana and her two boys to England to be with John, living with him in Whistler's house in Cheyne Walk and cutting her usual wide social swath. Her escort at John's opening at the Haymarket the evening of February 19, 1925, was no less a personage than George Bernard Shaw, who the next morning wrote John a devastating letter about his forthright elimination of many passages in the text. Others at that first night included Lord Asquith, the Earl of Oxford and Lady Oxford, Arnold Bennett, George Moore, a multitude of social and theatrical celebrities in the stalls, and in the gallery the inveterate enthusiasts of Shakespearean performances at the Old Vic. The evening was an extraordinary success. The *New York Times* correspondent in London cabled that applause was warm and frequent and grew so enthusiastic at the end that John responded with a little speech. It was a proud evening for him, he said, to have played in "the foremost theater of the world."

Although first-night audience reactions were, in London, as well as elsewhere, unreliable barometers, the newspapers next day echoed the enthusiasm, and as days went on the acclaim grew. James Agate, in the Sunday edition of the London *Times,* wrote: "Mr. Barrymore's *Hamlet* draws fewer tears than Robertson's, but it is nearer to Shakespeare's whole creation than any I have ever seen."

He went on to discuss Barrymore's qualifications:

> Well, first a handsome face, intellectual as to the brow, a trifle womanish in the lower part . . . Next an agreeable voice, touching nobility here and there, but lacking the organ-note and in emotion running too easily to the head-notes of the tenor. Add the purest diction, perfect enunciation, and unexampled clarity. Now note a slim figure and the general illusion of princeliness and youth. All these are informed—and here is the key—by intellectual capacity of a rare order and analytical power of extreme cogency.

Other critics, while admitting the sincerity, unaffectedness, and clarity of the performance, missed in it warmth and passion. "Barrymore's *Hamlet*," said one, "is more brains than blood." But the praise far outweighed the caviling, and could any American actor have asked for more than to have an English critic say unequivocally: "It was a pleasure to hear verse spoken with such precision and without any accent, either of America, Oxford or Kensington. It was just Anglo-Saxon English."

The importance of John Barrymore's reception in London was not overlooked in his home country, for America through him had shown her cultural prowess (so it was said), and he thus contradicted a prevailing image of a land whose artists fled to the Left Bank of Paris. The scheduled six weeks at the Haymarket were quickly sold out, a demonstration to Londoners that Shakespeare *could* be successfully played in the West End, and Frederick Harrison was kind enough to postpone his following production to allow John to carry on for six weeks more.

During this period John and Michael split up irrevocably, and John moved from Cheyne Walk to a suite at the Ritz. John did not lack for company. He was a great favorite at the time of the Prince of Wales (afterward Edward VIII) and went to several clubs and parties with him.

The Prince was struck by John's seemingly limitless after-hours energy, especially after four hours of performing one of the most exhausting of all roles. How, the Prince asked, did he manage it? The recipe, John said, was fervor and champagne. Far more tiring were the lunches and dinners constantly being tendered him. One of these, held at a restaurant, had whitebait as the feature dish. John was persuaded to try the fish and was affected adversely by it later, in the midst of one of his soliloquies on stage. He rushed off-stage, relieved himself, and resumed a few moments later where he had left off. A critic happened to be in the audience, and wrote the next day in his paper about John's remarkable tradition-breaking bit of stage technique. This incident was elaborated by John and others in later years. John's claim was that his sickness had been caused by too much love-making just before a performance. He had lain siege to an attractive titled lady, and she had both capitulated and exhausted him on that day.

One of the more famous inhabitants of the Haymarket at the time he played there was a theater cat which was given the run of the house. During rehearsals the cat had a habit of crossing the stage and looking at John as he did a soliloquy. But one night during a performance the cat picked a careful path across the footlights. John casually crossed the stage, picked up the cat, and continued the soliloquy with the cat in his arms.

Ellen Terry took a box at the Haymarket for one of his performances, and by now stone-deaf, she repeated the lines of the play aloud from memory, often several lines ahead of John on the stage. Being deaf, she could not react to his interpolated sarcasm, and at last John, in a temper, tossed rapiers contemptuously about the stage. When reprimanded for this by Constance Collier, he retorted to her, "All the Barrymores have tempers. What do you think we are? Book ends?"

He, naturally, by the end of the twelve weeks, had become thoroughly tired of *Hamlet* and refused offers to take the production to Paris and Berlin. He did seriously consider, however, an offer to open *Richard III* in London the following year. But by this time Hollywood had beckoned to him again with sweet whispers of sunshine and much money. He vacationed in the fjords of Norway on a fishing expedition, and then, John Barrymore, the most triumphant American actor of his generation, returned home trailing almost visible clouds of glory.

The rest, for several years, was silent pictures.

John conceived his Richard III as "an evil, crawling thing" and his meticulous preparations for the role resulted in the most thrilling representation of Shakespearian tragedy yet seen in America.

Said Robert Edmond Jones, who designed the lavish production of *Richard III:* "There never has been such a great actor at any time, there never has been such shattering beauty in art, as there was in John Barrymore's."

While preparing *Richard III* John was also acting in a silent version of *Dr. Jekyll and Mr. Hyde*. When the film opened in April 1920 John had the distinction of being regarded as both the greatest stage actor and the greatest film actor of his generation. Above he is seen as Mr. Hyde.

As Gwymplane the clown, in Michael Strange's play *Clair de Lune* John was supposed to be "hideous to behold." He persuaded Ethel to appear in the play, but could not persuade the critics that the undertaking was worthwhile. One review was headlined: FOR THE LOVE OF MIKE.

During a period when John was breaking up and reconciling with Michael Strange he went to Hollywood to make *Beau Brummell* for Warner Brothers. He is seen (above) in 1923, clowning on the set with Charles Chaplin and Douglas Fairbanks.

Ethel achieved one of her greatest successes in *Déclassée*, written for her by Zoë Akins. She is seen, above (with Claude King), as the fated Lady Helen.

Lionel played *Macbeth* for Arthur Hopkins in 1921. Both the production and Lionel's performance in the role were singularly unsuccessful.

Ethel Barrymore as Juliet in the Arthur Hopkins production of *Romeo and Juliet* (1922). Jane Cowl opened a rival production the same week and received more flattering reviews, a blow which Ethel took silently but which registered nonetheless.

John's playing of his scenes with Gertrude, the queen in *Hamlet*, was regarded as having distinctly incestuous overtones. So Freudian an interpretation was regarded as novel and daring at the time. Gertrude was played by Blanche Yurka.

John reached the zenith of his career in *Hamlet* produced in 1922 by Arthur Hopkins. With him in this scene is John S. O'Brien as Polonius.

John Barrymore as Hamlet vacillates on whether or not to draw his sword on the praying Claudius (Tyrone Power, Sr.).

John's *Hamlet* was given 101 performances on Broadway and he revived it a few months later for six more weeks in New York and on the road. He could have gone on indefinitely, but decided to produce his version in London, against the advice of Arthur Hopkins. The English critics found his gloomy Dane brilliant on the whole, but Bernard Shaw reproached him for making cuts in the text.

The famous Moscow Art Players came to see John perform his Hamlet at a matinee during which Ethel was also present. The two people at the back are Nikita Balieff the impresario, and Olga Knipper-Tchekova, the wife of Anton Tchekov. In the front row from left to right are Morris Gest, an unidentifiable man, Ivan Moskvin, John Barrymore, Vassily Kachaloff, Constantin Stanislavsky, Ethel Barrymore, Arthur Hopkins and Robert Edmond Jones.

Ethel won new plaudits for her acting of the part of a nun in *The Kingdom of God*. With this play she opened in 1928 the new theater built by the Shuberts and named The Ethel Barrymore.

Among the actors whom Ethel Barrymore fancied was Louis Calhern, who is seen with her here in *The Love Duel* (1929).

Lionel began an extraordinary series of screen characterizations in 1926, after leaving Broadway irrevocably for Hollywood. His first important picture there was *The Barrier* in which he played a sea captain with a half-caste daughter.

In his last silent film (for MGM, 1929) Lionel played Captain Nemo in *The Mysterious Island.*

Gloria Swanson specifically requested Lionel from MGM, where he was under long-term contract, when in 1928 she produced for United Artists *Sadie Thompson,* the first, and silent, film version of the Maugham story. Lionel played the minister.

Ethel, while touring with *The Love Duel* in 1929, came to Los Angeles and stayed awhile at John's Tower Road home, where she was photographed (above).

Lionel's most famous etching, "Boatyard in Venice." The Society of American Etchers chose it to hang with its selection of the Hundred Prints of the Year, the country's best etchings.

This study of John Barrymore was taken in Hollywood in 1927, when he was at the height of his film stardom. It shows him as he preferred to see himself, and reveals the profile he considered his best, the left.

part FOUR

FROM EAST
TO WEST

chapter XVII

ALTHOUGH LIONEL'S MARITAL CAREER was never so spectacular as his brother's, he added his bit in the early 1920's to the Barrymore reputation for instability. In 1922 it became known on Broadway that Lionel was spending a good deal of his time with Irene Fenwick, the leading lady of his new play. Miss Fenwick (or Mrs. J. J. O'Brien, as she was known in private life) was in her middle thirties, blonde and slim, and an actress accustomed to featured billing. She was born in Chicago as Irene Frizzell, made a debut of sorts on Broadway in 1904 as a member of the chorus of *Peggy from Paris,* a musical show, and for a time was seen about a good deal with young John Barrymore when he was the mustached Lothario of Rector's.

Her petite figure and delicately pretty features soon caught the attention of many a roving eye; hardly a month after the opening of her show she was raised to featured status and billed as "The Pocket Venus." Fond as she was of John Barrymore, she left his side to become the wife of a real estate and shipping tycoon, Felix Isman. Not very much time passed before Isman brought suit for divorce, charged her with adultery (John was named as one of the correspondents, according to rumor), and won his case. Irene returned to the stage as a comedienne under Charles Frohman's management, now bearing the name of Irene Fenwick. She achieved considerable celebrity in both musical plays and comedies, found another wealthy husband in O'Brien, a handsome Wall Streeter, and met Lionel (presumably for the second time) when she was chosen by Arthur Hopkins to play opposite him in *The Claw*, a melodrama adapted from the French of Henri Bernstein.

Hopkins had quickly rushed *The Claw* into production as a form of therapy for Lionel after his unfortunate encounter with the witches of *Macbeth*. The play dealt with a middle-aged man, a French newspaper editor who is morally and physically destroyed by a grasping, unscrupulous young woman (played by Irene). Hopkins knew the play would show Lionel at his best, dealing as it did with a man who seems to age and wither before the audience's eyes.

For Doris Rankin, who played Lionel's daughter, the play offered another kind of spectacle, that of her husband falling violently in love with his co-star and combining stage passion with the real thing. Lionel's love for Irene began as an infatuation and turned into a life-long devotion. Photographs taken in 1922 show Doris to be rather more of a beauty than Irene, who was her elder by some four or five years. Doris, from the reports of all who knew her, was at this time a striking-looking woman in her early thirties with huge gray-green eyes that were accentuated by the whiteness of her face. Michael Strange, commenting on her old-fashioned way of dressing, thought she resembled Emily Brontë or Lorna Doone in a somber mood. By all we know of her, Doris was a sweet and self-effacing woman, almost slavishly devoted to her moody, hard-working actor-artist husband. She was to be seen constantly in the wings during rehearsals, encumbered with everything Lionel might need, from a pencil and notepaper to sandwiches she had made for him herself.

Lionel was a difficult man to live with, as he himself admitted. He cheerfully castigated himself later as abrupt, thankless, thoughtless, and sour. The frustrations of attempting to combine the arduous work of an actor with painting and musical composition caused him to vent his unhappiness on Doris, who was handiest. In addition to this, there was something he never spoke of: the death of his two daughters, one of whom lived well beyond infancy. Lionel worried over the influenza and polio epidemics that swept the East during and after World War I. He went so far as to disinfect himself in the basement of his Hempstead, Long Island, home upon returning from the city so as not to transmit any dangerous germs. In spite of this, the child contracted polio and died. Whether Lionel took to blaming Doris for this, no one knows, for he was not communicative even with close members of the family.

The Claw had a successful run, and the triangular situation did not erupt until the play went on tour. Then, on a train, the dreadful discovery was made, nothing less than that Lionel was in Irene's sleeping car when he should not have been. Doris left the cast of the play, and Michael Strange, proving to be a friend in need, took Doris off on a trip to Europe in the spring of 1922 in an attempt to lighten her sadness. When Doris returned in the late summer she had a meeting with Lionel, a reasonably amicable one, and agreed to obtain a divorce. The interlocutory decree was granted at Poughkeepsie, New York, on December 2 of that year. The newspapers gave the story considerable space but were unable to obtain copies of the testimony or the name of the correspondent. Irene Fenwick's name came into the stories nevertheless. When asked if she would marry Lionel, she mentioned the obvious fact that she was still married to J. J. O'Brien.

While refusing publicly to incriminate Irene as the stealer of Lionel's affections, Doris did say: "I have been married to Lionel Barrymore for seventeen years, but I would gladly give several years of my life if I could truthfully say that in all the seventeen years he looked at me just once in the same manner as I saw him look at that woman."

Ethel's sympathies were clearly with Doris, for she immediately employed Lionel's cast-off wife in the short-lived production of *Rose Bernd*. Following that, Doris went for a short period into vaudeville with a dramatic sketch, but her theatrical appearances were sporadic from then on, and by the end of the twenties she had disappeared from public view. She married again, sooner than anyone would have thought; her husband was Malcolm R. Mortimer, an English writer and dramatist, and the two lived quietly on a farm in Maryland.

Irene Fenwick obtained her divorce from J. J. O'Brien in April of 1923, and in June of the same year she and Lionel sailed off together for Europe on the liner *Paris*. Lionel was due in Rome to work in the Sam Goldwyn production of *The Eternal City* with co-stars Barbara La Marr, Bert Lytell, and Montague Love. On the afternoon of July 14, shooting was interrupted for the wedding of Lionel and Irene, and Sam Goldwyn canceled filming for several days to allow the couple to have a honeymoon in Venice.

During this period of marital upheaval and stage work, Lionel had never ceased making movies. In *The Master Mind* (1920) he was a mental telepathist; in *The Great Adventure* (1921) he impersonated a valet; in *Face in the Fog* (1922) he played Boston Blackie, reformed crook, and had a marvelous fight with Louis Wolheim, whom Lionel had persuaded to drop his academic career as a mathematics instructor and take up acting; in *Enemies of Women* (1923) he was seen as a profligate prince; in *Unseeing Eyes* (1923) he worked for Goldwyn as a heroic aviator. Although film production was rapidly shifting to the West Coast, Lionel was still in high demand for movies made in the East. In 1924 he worked for D. W. Griffith again, in *America,* a film about the American Revolution, and in which Lionel appeared as the wicked General Butler and gained acclaim.

His stock was high on the stage, too, for when he returned from Europe in the fall of 1923, he went almost at once into rehearsals for David Belasco's production of the Pagliacci story, *Laugh Clown, Laugh!* Irene Fenwick appeared with him in this play, and rumors were current on Broadway after the closing of *Laugh Clown, Laugh!* (it ran for 133 performances) that Lionel would not accept plays which did not include a role of equal magnitude for his wife. The rumor was denied, but it was nevertheless true that Lionel was not seen on the stage for several months, and when he appeared on Broadway again, it was in a forbidding little drama called *The Piker* in which Irene was also present.

This effort by Leon Gordon, the author of *White Cargo,* opened in January, 1925, was badly wounded by the critics, and closed six weeks later. Lionel's role was that of a sneak thief who steals an envelope that he thinks contains fifty dollars but instead holds fifty thousand dollars. His find turns him into an even more miserable person, and Percy Hammond termed this character "a tragic nitwit," a remark which must have nettled the actor to the extreme, for we find him breaking his customary reserve and writing an article of complaint about the play's reception for publication in the *Herald Tribune*. This attempt at self-justification was uncharacteristic of Lionel, who had cautioned John against just such actions in the past.

In the article Lionel explained that he had thought *The Piker* a masterpiece, that he had played it less for money than the art it represented, and that in spite of its reception he still considered it a masterpiece. When he wrote, "But an artichoke is evidently not a luxury if it grows in your own garden," he meant that New York audiences were incapable of taking kindly to a tragic play about New Yorkers. "A serious or tragic or important play about New York," he continued, "must open in Moscow and come to New York by way of Paris, Berlin, Balieff, and a subscription list. It seems a long diet of cabbage soup and sturgeon is necessary to make tragedy credible." His reference was to those who regarded the performances of the Moscow Art Players (who had recently impressed New York) as the quintessence of dramatic art.

After this burst of pique, Lionel subsided and went quickly into a new play called *Taps*. Actually it was not a new play. Lee Shubert, the producer, had not thought it necessary to mention the fact that *Taps* had been presented in New York some twenty years before, and the drama departments of the newspapers quickly ferreted out the information and reviewed the play as a revival. Lionel played an old German sergeant whose daughter (Irene Fenwick) did considerable damage to the regiment and was finally shot dead in a climactic courtroom scene by her father. Audiences were not yet in a German-loving mood and particularly did not care to see a cast full of German officers. "The play can rest in oblivion for another twenty years for all anyone cares," wrote one patriotic reviewer.

Lionel was blamed in another review for the miscasting of Irene Fenwick as "the youthful and supposedly buxom beauty of the regiment." Irene received a castigation of her own for the inadequacy of her portrayal. The play was withdrawn after four weeks and, seemingly a bear for punishment, Lionel at once went onto yet another play, this one a Jerome K. Jerome fantasy called *Man or*

Devil? Irene had been announced for it, but at the last moment she withdrew because of illness, and the newspapers printed a note that she would enter a hospital for a rest.

In *Man or Devil?* Lionel appeared as an old miser who persuaded a young man to swap souls with him, the story framed as a Dutch legend of the seventeenth century. Alexander Woollcott commented on Lionel's tireless and groping search for a play of his own caliber and found the new play—the third attempted by Lionel in a matter of four months—graceless and unimaginative. "Such stature as he has enjoyed in the American theater," Woollcott wrote in a warning that appeared solemnly directed straight at Lionel, "cannot long stand the whittling process of such a season as he has just passed through."

Lionel, whose retreat from the Broadway stage was lamented always by Arthur Hopkins and ascribed principally to his *Macbeth* experience, had good reason, as can be seen from the above, to forsake the theater and follow his brother, John, to Hollywood. He had been subjected to a critical barrage such as few actors of his standing had gone through, and here he was, a man who did not care for the stage in the first place! There was also the factor that Irene had begun to develop a series of real illnesses, and Lionel felt that the sun and the dryer air of California would provide a more healthful atmosphere for her.

The generous terms received by John Barrymore for signing a contract with Warner Brothers after arriving from his triumphal *Hamlet* season in London undoubtedly caused some extra cogitation in Lionel. The critical barrage he had just passed through made his situation in New York untenable; therefore the thing to do was to head west where movie gold might be mined and where he could present himself to new audiences in a revival of *The Copperhead*. It was not his intention at this time (nor was it John's) to break irretrievably with the Broadway stage and settle in the West, but he never returned to New York except for the briefest of visits.

Lionel and Irene followed John to the West Coast six weeks after he made the trip, but when they emerged from their sleeping car on July 14 they were not received with the fanfare which had greeted John. The circumstances were, of course, different. Even crass Hollywood was in a mood to lionize John for his *Hamlet* triumph in London, and his contract to make three pictures at a salary of $75,000 each entitled him to considerable promotion from the Warner Brothers publicists. Lionel, on the other hand, had no contract when he arrived; he had come on the promise of work from I. E. Chadwick, a small Eastern independent producer who had recently transferred his operations to the West. He was to make *The Bells,* that old Henry Irving standby, in which Lionel would enact a murderer with a virulent case of conscience. There was another difference between John and Lionel where movies were concerned. John was a star, his profile and his handsomeness more of an asset than his acting. Lionel had played character parts of late in his many films; he had worked for a salary and not on contract; and his stage reputation had begun to dim seriously, mainly because of his bad choice of plays. Therefore he came to seek and get what he could.

But Lionel and Irene had hardly unpacked their valises before his agent, Maury Small, had notified Paramount producer, Jesse L. Lasky, of the presence of another famed Barrymore in Hollywood, upon which Lasky rose to the bait and offered Lionel ten thousand dollars to play a featured role in *The Lucky Lady* with Greta Nissen as his co-star. Almost simultaneously, it would seem, he worked in another Paramount production, *The Girl Who Wouldn't Work,* and also kept his commitment with Chadwick. In fact, during his first year as a resident of Hollywood, Lionel appeared in no less than twelve feature films and managed to find time to do several two- and three-reel comedies as well. This astonishing amount of industry did his reputation practically no good at all, although the money he earned allowed him to live in excellent style and to support Irene near the style to which she was genuinely accustomed from her previous marriages to two rich men. At first they put up at what was then the most expensive and exclusive hotel in Hollywood, the Town House, (now the Sheraton West) on Wilshire Boulevard. Some months later Lionel purchased a house on Roxbury Drive, considered one of the best streets in Beverly Hills. Irene established their position among the society of movieland by giving a luncheon in this home on July 18, 1926. Among the guests who sat at a table turned into a bower of flowers were Jeanne Eagels, Norma Talmadge, and Mrs. Antonio Moreno, wife of one of Hollywood's best-known Valentino-type actors.

Lionel seemed to have at this time a fine disregard for the quality of the vehicles he appeared in, and he was distinctly not of the star firmament inhabited by such as Gloria Swanson, Milton Sills, Douglas Fairbanks, and Rudolph Valentino. His abilities were for sale to whoever offered him ready cash. When Hal Roach came along and offered him a sizable sum to appear in a half-hour comedy featurette, he accepted the offer, and later described his function in this small epic as that of allowing himself to be bopped on the head with a rubber hose. Soon Lionel was hiring himself out by the week at the rate of a thousand dollars per five-day shooting schedule. Hal Roach, among others traded on the Barrymore name and employed him in insignificant burlesque and slapstick three-reelers. Upon seeing some of these films his agent hurriedly took a train to the West Coast and warned his client that not even a Barrymore could survive such stuff.

Mixed in with these poorer films were a few of better "quality," such as *Children of the Whirlwind,* in which he was directed by Frank Lloyd. And, in *The Bells,* which appeared in 1926, Lionel's performance brought critical praise. As proof that his acting abilities were still keen, he organized a company to play *The Copperhead* in Los Angeles (at the Playhouse on Figueroa Street) and ran for eight weeks after some excellent notices. With him in this play was a young man whose name was Clark Gable, whom Lionel thought showed distinct promise.

Maury Small moved his offices to California in 1926 and proved significantly helpful to Lionel. Perhaps the most important thing he did for him was to get him under contract to MGM. This came about when Lionel was requested by George Hill for *The Barrier,* which he was about to direct for MGM. The Rex Beach novel from which the story was taken had been a best-seller and merited a handsome production, and Hill reached out for the best players he could find. Lionel struck him as the right man to play a sea captain whose pretty daughter (Marcelline Day) was a half-breed. Hill looked familiar to Lionel. It turned out that this important director had once carried

Billy Bitzer's camera for D. W. Griffith when Lionel had first worked in the movies.

The move to MGM was the most significant career change in Lionel's life. The studio, through an amalgamation of powerful movie interests, had become the most solid in Hollywood. It was run by the paternalistic L. B. Mayer (with whom Lionel formed an enduring friendship), and its productions were being supervised by the youthful, intelligent, and phenomenally successful Irving Thalberg. Proudly MGM termed itself "the home of the stars," and made good its claim by listing on its contract roster the popular Antonio Moreno; Ramon Novarro of *Ben Hur* fame; the famous man of many faces, Lon Chaney; the beautiful and mysterious Greta Garbo; and such younger and glamorous stars as Norma Shearer and Joan Crawford. Lionel could hardly be considered as having the same star ranking as these, but Thalberg considered his name valuable enough to be featured with those of Antonio Moreno and Greta Garbo in *The Temptress.*

This was only the second American film made by Garbo, her first having been *The Torrent,* an unimpressive movie which had nevertheless gained her some highly approving reviews. Lionel, while making *The Temptress* with her, at first worked under the direction of Mauritz Stiller, Garbo's companion and artistic mentor; but Thalberg, impatient with his arty and time-consuming methods, replaced Stiller with Fred Niblo, who had directed *Ben Hur*. All this boded well for Lionel's career, although Greta Garbo, playing a femme fatale, callously ruined his screen life. The movie was released at a moment when the "romance" between John Gilbert and Greta Garbo was being most luridly publicized on behalf of their forthcoming picture, *Flesh and the Devil.* The public made a mad rush to *The Temptress,* but Lionel was largely overlooked, because all eyes were on Miss Garbo. Besides, the picture had turned out to be just another routine Hollywood job.

Lionel was shunted into more of these routine MGM productions. He committed suicide over Aileen Pringle in *Body and Soul,* foolishly loved an unworthy tramp in *Women Love Diamonds,* and played an arch-fiend in *The Thirteenth Hour,* leading his pursuers through a maze of trap doors and secret panels before being cornered by an intelligent and righteous dog on a roof. Napoleon, the Wonder Dog, was the star of the picture.

It would be hard to find any other film star whose Hollywood career went through so many twists and turns as Lionel's. Any fans he might have had at this time could only have been thoroughly bewildered by what was happening to this actor who, only a half-dozen years before, had been one of the most celebrated of the stars of the theater, whose talents had been regarded as secondary only to those of his younger brother.

Lionel appears to have viewed his ups and down with equanimity. The casual manner in which silent-picture making proceeded appealed to his own nature. When called upon to do his job, he did it and did it well, and suffered little in the way of creative dissatisfaction because his artistic yearnings were focused on his music, his painting, and lately his etching. Hollywood had provided him the opportunity to escape the rigors of the family trade, stage work. He never spoke, as did John from time to time, of going back to the boards. Only once more did he stand behind the footlights, and this was in 1934 when, as part of the promotion of one of his films, he did a personal appearance tour with his famous soliloquy from *The Copperhead,* a speech which seems to have afforded him endless satisfaction.

He had grown heavy again, and had become increasingly lame from the knee he had injured many years before. Nearly fifty, and looking his years, he was no longer the leading man type, and usually played in support of stars of far lesser ability but of more appeal to movie fans. Among those he supported were John Gilbert, in a weird tale of the circus, *The Show,* and Gloria Swanson, who borrowed him from MGM for the first (silent) version of *Sadie Thompson.*

There were to be even more and more dizzying turns in Lionel's career, because sound was looming on the Hollywood horizon, and those first squawks quickly heralded a revolution in which Lionel participated. Actors accustomed to speaking lines of dialogue came into heavy demand, and Lionel was speedily borrowed by Warner Brothers to play the role of a millionaire in *The Lion and the Mouse,* billed (as were several others in 1928) as the first full-length dramatic talking feature. Not only did the film prove a box-office success, but the *New York Times* noted in its review that "Barrymore gave an excellent account of himself and overwhelmed the speaking attempts of the other principals." The crusty, middle-aged theatrical veteran was suddenly again one of the most wanted of actors. There never was any question that a Barrymore could talk, and exceedingly well.

MGM, which had lagged behind Warner's in adapting to sound, now attempted to make up for lost time. Lionel had been drafted to support a studio newcomer, William Haines, in a silent version of *Alias Jimmy Valentine,* and although it had been completely filmed, Thalberg ordered that it be dubbed with dialogue. This was a laborious undertaking but one to which Lionel was, of course, equal. Not so William Haines, whose acting training was rudimentary at best. Bosley Crowther, in *The Lion's Share,* told the story of how some jokester sneezed in the dead silence of the studio as Haines stood up to a microphone for the first time in his life and prepared to give voice. He nearly jumped from his skin when he heard the sneeze. The gruff but basically kindly Lionel helped steady the nerves of the young man, but when the film appeared Haines disappointed his fans and headed quickly toward his eclipse. Not so, Lionel. Audiences loved his rich, rolling tones.

Mayer and Thalberg decided that Lionel, valuable as he was as an actor on the talking screen, could prove even more valuable as a director while the studio went through its transition period from silence to sound. (Perhaps someone remembered Lionel had directed for the old Metro studio in New York some dozen years before.) Lionel was tried out on a two-reel short subject called *Confession,* which was made in a minimum of time and which delighted him when he viewed the finished product and discovered that it talked audibly and distinctly.

Thalberg, convinced that Lionel was exactly what they needed in this crucial hour, gave him the assignment to direct one of the studio's most important stars, Ruth Chatterton, in *Madame X,* a talking teary tale of a woman who killed to protect her son, a lawyer, and was defended by him in court. The movie that resulted was hardly a landmark in film art, but it was not inferior to other early efforts of the sound period, and one thing it did was to make L. B. Mayer shed a gallon of tears when he viewed it in the studio projection room. The public liked *Madame X* and, rather surprisingly, it was voted one of the best movies of 1929.

Lionel claimed that he advanced the technique of making sound pictures when he improvised the first movable "mike boom." At that time the camera was housed in a soundproof booth and the microphone was placed in a fixed position, so that it was up to the actors to adjust their positions in order to have their voices picked up. Lionel conceived an inspiration. "Just put the mike on a line attached to the pole," he said, "and move it over the heads of the actors." The idea was tried and found workable. Bosley Crowther had it, though, that it was Eddie Mannix, a studio executive, who first suggested such a contraption. If so, there is no record that he suggested it to Lionel.

The next directing assignment given Lionel was a ticklish one, involving nothing less than the overseeing of John Gilbert's first voice venture, *His Glorious Night*. To keep the record straight, it should be mentioned that Gilbert made his first attempt to breach the sound barrier in *Redemption*, which MGM had based on the very same Tolstoy play John Barrymore had acted so impressively on Broadway. The film was put on the shelf because the sound track revealed certain deficiencies either in the recording apparatus or in Gilbert's voice. Lionel could only prove that there had been nothing wrong with the recording apparatus. As a dashing captain in love with a princess, Gilbert's high-pitched voice made such dialogue as "I love you, I love you, I love you," sound even more ridiculous, and when the picture came out audiences all over the land were at first shocked and then hooted in derision. Gilbert's voice was not the only handicap that caused his swift decline from public favor. Flamboyant lovers such as he played were fast dying out on the screen.

Lionel, while directing, did not go in for riding pants, puttees, and the use of a megaphone. His dress had become careless—he wore loose-fitting suits, baggy at the knees—and he was in the habit of running his hand through his shock of rumpled hair. He would sit cross-legged on the floor, sometimes with his small Irish terrier near him. A man as impatient of stupidity as was his sister, Ethel, he never allowed himself to raise his voice to his actors, no matter how foggy they were in their unaccustomed lines or amiss in their interpretations.

If something became too much for him to bear he curbed his temper, would excuse himself, walk off the set, and in the privacy of another room would deliver himself profoundly of the exclamation, "My God, my God!" This would seem to refresh him, and composed, he would return to the set. He converted his dressing room into a combination office and sketching studio, and spent many hours there. He took his directing responsibilities with great seriousness, and was in the habit of calling up studio officials at all hours of the night if some problem prevented him from sleeping.

Because it was known that he composed, MGM entrusted him with the studio's first "all-color feature sound musical," *The Rogue Song*, taken from Lehar's *Gypsy Love*. Lawrence Tibbett made his film debut in this and gave vent to such robust sounds that the relatively primitive recording apparatus then in use was not up to the demands made upon it. Disaster almost came to Lionel when he was borrowed by Columbia to direct Barbara Stanwyck in *Ten Cents a Dance*. The reels were sent out in the wrong order, and the picture, when viewed out of sequence, made so little sense that it was thought that Lionel had ineptly squandered hundreds of thousands of dollars for Columbia. Luckily the reel-switching was discovered and the matter corrected before the film was scrapped.

Although a hit with the public, *Ten Cents a Dance* proved to be the last movie directed by Lionel, even though MGM scheduled him for another, *Never the Twain Shall Meet*. Lionel stayed long enough on the preproduction phases to helpfully discover an important star for MGM. He needed a certain type of actor for one of the roles and remembered the young man, Clark Gable, who had played with him four years before in his Los Angeles version of *The Copperhead*. Gable was still on the stage and conveniently happened to be appearing locally in *The Last Mile*. Lionel got hold of him at a matinee and rushed him back to the Metro lot for a screen test. One of the more minor mysteries of Hollywood is why Lionel had Gable take the test made up as an Indian warrior.

"Lionel was fidgety as a cat," Gable remembered. "He insisted on supervising the make-up job in his own office. As an Indian warrior, of course, I wore a minimum of clothing. When Lionel started walking me to the stage out on the lot where the test was to be made I created the sensation of all time. Guys were whistling at me, and the girls coming out of the commissary were yoo-hooing. I was never so embarrassed in my life. I whispered to Lionel, 'Let me go back to the dressing room and get a top coat.' 'The hell with all of them,' Lionel said. 'Haven't they ever seen feathers before?' "

Gable was not signed for the film Lionel wanted him for, and Lionel himself deserted the picture when he happened to come across the script of *A Free Soul*, scheduled by Thalberg for Norma Shearer. Lionel's sharp eyes detected in the part of a drunken criminal lawyer a chance for some bravura performing of the kind he could do best. In the final scenes the lawyer was called upon to defend his own daughter, and, after a magnificent charge to the jury, drop dead on the courtroom floor! Thalberg, who habitually looked with favor on any Barrymore request, gave Lionel the role, and the fifty-three-year-old actor seized his chance. Nor was Clark Gable forgotten. He was given a relatively small role in the film, but it was an attention-getter in that it permitted him to slam the great Norma Shearer into a chair.

The extended scene in which Lionel was to address the jury was planned by Clarence Brown, the director, to be shot in one lengthy take of several minutes. Lionel put everything he had into it, so much in fact that when he finished he told Brown he not only was too exhausted for another take but doubted that he could put as much steam into it again. Lionel then learned that Brown had prepared for exactly such a contingency. He had stationed three cameras to pick up the scene from close and far vantage points.

When the rushes were viewed the studio executives saw that Lionel had walked off with the picture and ordered that his performance be toned down to key in more with the other actors. But since there were no alternative takes of the big scene, the film had to be released as it was. It turned out to be a big box-office success for MGM, and it won Lionel an Academy Award nomination. At the awards ceremony George Arliss made the announcement that Lionel Barrymore had won the Oscar for "the best performance of the year by a male actor." Lionel, limping slightly, went up to the stage, and true to his reputation for taciturnity, merely mumbled to the stellar assembly, "Thank you." On the same stage with him, and winner of the award for the best female performance, was Marie Dressler. The two veterans posed together, genuinely pleased to be sharing the limelight.

There was now no question that Lionel had entered the company of the movie greats. MGM could proudly list him on their honor roll of stars, and from 1931 on, no matter how awesomely important or popular the personality he played with, he was either the star or the co-star. But it is very doubtful that his winning of an Academy Award and his promotion to full star status gave him as much satisfaction as another and less publicized honor that came to him in the same year. He was elected to the American Society of Etchers, and at the society's annual exhibit in 1932, in New York, Lionel's etchings were first shown publicly. According to his own lights, this for him represented something of a success.

O DOLORES! / *chapter XVIII*

FIRMLY SEPARATED from Michael, John Barrymore in June of 1925 made his permanent move to Hollywood, accompanied by an English valet whose name was Blaney and a monkey whose name was Clementine. These three set up quarters in a four-room upper suite of a detached bungalow on the grounds of the Ambassador Hotel in Los Angeles. The cost of his sojourn there was borne by Warner Brothers, who had also arranged to provide him his meals and a chauffeured automobile. The contract drawn up for the three pictures he had agreed to make was an impressive one. It provided him in excess of $75,000 for each picture, and established an exorbitant rate of pay for any overtime work that might be necessary. He was granted script approval and co-star approval, and it was also stipulated that publicity done in his behalf must be in keeping with his standing, reputation, and prestige.

The latter was undoubtedly high. Introduced at an official function shortly after his arrival as "America's foremost actor," he lifted his left eyebrow when called upon to say something to the audience, and remarked: "I like to be introduced as America's foremost actor. It obviates the necessity of further effort."

It has never been fully explained why John Barrymore went with

Warner Brothers, at a time when that firm was fairly low on the status totem pole in Hollywood, and when its biggest money-making star was Rin-Tin-Tin, America's foremost dog. The answer probably lies in the fact that Warner's was more persuasive than other studios: they offered more money. Warner's had two reasons for wanting Barrymore. On the one hand, they hoped to enter him in the Great Lover derby, then being led by Rudolph Valentino and John Gilbert. On the other hand, Warner's, a firm in the process of expansion, was aggressively lining up theater showcases for its products, and John Barrymore's name would lend the studio some badly needed prestige. There is no other way to account for their coddling of him. John's last previous appearance in pictures had been in Warner's *Beau Brummell,* two years before, which the *New York Times* had regarded as "one of those artistic celluloid efforts that come along none too frequently." But in spite of John's admittedly good performance, the film was weak and on the dull side. It did well enough in the big cities but not elsewhere.

Warner's hoped to employ John's profile, on his return to Hollywood, in *Don Juan,* but John had other ideas. He would do *Don Juan,* he said, but only after he was allowed to make a film of *Moby Dick,* a novel he admired greatly. When asked about the possibilities for love interest in the story, he said that he might manage to fall in love with the whale. A compromise was agreed on. John would do *Moby Dick* (retitled *The Sea Beast*), and Warner's would hire a screen writer able to provide the love interest. A lady writer, Bess Meredyth, was chosen for the task, and John appointed himself her artistic adviser.

At this time he was also advising, on more intimate terms, one of the loveliest of Hollywood's young beauties, Mary Astor, whom he had picked (from a photograph in a fan magazine) to play opposite him in *Beau Brummell.* He requested her, too, for *The Sea Beast,* but Miss Astor by this time had a heavy schedule of films to make and was unavailable. She would not be free until it was time to make *Don Juan,* and was instead contracted for that picture. Meanwhile Warner's engaged one of their young contract actresses, Priscilla Bonner, to spark Captain Ahab's passion in *The Sea Beast.* Miss Bonner never made it to the starting gate.

The unobtrusive romance between John Barrymore and Mary Astor had flowered under the very eyes of her watchful parents. The exquisitely pretty girl was seventeen when chosen for *Beau Brummell,* and she met John for the first time at a preliminary test designed to show how they would look together. Before the afternoon was over, Mary had fallen in love with John, and he with her. "I am sure," she wrote many years later in her memoir, *My Story,* "he was even more startled than I."

John was forty-three at the time, but, according to Miss Astor, he told her, "It seems so long ago that I was seventeen. I'm forty now." He was assured by the girl that the advanced age mentioned by him did not strike her as so awfully old.

As was his habit with those he loved, John was helpful to Mary, giving her hints and tips on how to improve her acting. He mentioned how helpful Margaret Carrington had been to him during preparations for his *Hamlet.* He cultivated Mary's parents, came to dinners at their apartment, and suggested to them that he teach Mary some of Mrs. Carrington's methods. They agreed and sat respectfully in the dining room while John and Mary were together in the living room. He finally insisted that they must work alone because Mary was being made self-conscious by her parents' nearness. Every Sunday he would send his car for Mary and her mother, they would be delivered to his hotel suite, and while the mother sat on the veranda in sunlight, John and Mary had the interior to themselves.

A year and a half of separation intervened while John toured with *Hamlet* and produced the play in London. When he returned the friendship was resumed, first in New York, then in Hollywood. Mary was now living in a house purchased by her father from Henry Hotchener, a devout theosophist who had dabbled in real estate during the Hollywood boom and who was responsible for the houses of Moorish design that sprouted on Temple Hill Drive. Hotchener and his wife, Helios, also a theosophist, a student of East Indian philosophy, and a firm believer in astrology, became friendly with Mary's father, Otto Langhanke. John met the Hotcheners in the house on Temple Hill Drive, reacted with instant favor to their mystical proclivities, and became good friends with them. He eventually asked Henry Hotchener to become his business manager, a task to which

Hotchener devoted himself for more than ten years. Helios was useful to John for her astrological forecasts. He would not begin work on a picture or take any important step without first finding out how Mrs. Hotchener's charts viewed the matter.

One day a girl in her early twenties was about to enter a car preparatory to leaving the grounds of the Warners' rather ramshackle Sunset Boulevard studio. She looked up and saw John Barrymore standing with Jack L. Warner on a balcony above her. A studio assistant beckoned to her to wait and then told her to return to the studio the next morning, as Mr. Warner and Mr. Barrymore wanted to see her. This was the first intimation Dolores Costello had that the eyes of John Barrymore had fallen upon her. In his own words, those eyes had fallen "upon the most preposterously lovely creature in all the world." And that one look was enough to banish from his heart all vestiges of feeling for Mary Astor.

"That is the girl!" he said to Jack L. Warner when he pointed her out. She was to be his leading lady in *The Sea Beast,* no arguments, that was all there was to it. She was exactly right, perfect, exactly the girl the picture needed.

Dolores Costello had been in Hollywood for only a few months. She had come there with her sister Helene, her mother, and her father, an aging and all but forgotten cleft-chinned hero of the early days of movies, now somewhat besotted and given to displays of ungovernable temper. Dolores was the older of the girls by two years; in their early childhoods both had played small roles in their father's pictures. Dolores had left school early, had studied "aesthetic" dancing, modeled for the magazine illustrations of James Montgomery Flagg, and had obtained a job in the chorus of George White's *Scandals,* getting her sister a job in the show, too. When the *Scandals* went on tour, the mother went along as chaperone. In Chicago they were seen by a Warner's talent scout, and both received invitations to take screen tests at a Chicago studio. The girls were brought to Hollywood as a result of the tests, but Dolores had been so nervous and ill at ease before the camera that her sour expression was first thought to be suited only for vampire roles.

Actually she was a girl of alternately sober and sunny disposition. She had fine hair of a reddish-gold coloring, soulful gray-blue eyes, and a shining complexion that needed little artificial coloring. Flagg had described her as "very slender, but with no bones showing anywhere." When John first saw her she had played two small parts in films, one in *Bobbed Hair* for Warner's, the other in an Edmund Lowe picture at Fox. Her contract with Warner Brothers gave her a weekly salary of seventy-five dollars, and this was what she received as John Barrymore's co-star in *The Sea Beast*.

The first thing John asked her was: "Miss Costello, how old are you?" With the next, her breath was taken away when he asked her how she would like to play opposite him in his new picture. "I think you've made a mistake," Dolores told him. "Don't you want the other one?" She meant her sister, Helene, who was having what was to be a short-lived Hollywood success. Dolores was at first conscience-stricken about having taken so important a role away from Priscilla Bonner, but she was told this attitude was foolish in a quixotic place like Hollywood. Priscilla Bonner, outraged, instituted suit against Warner Brothers for ditching her, received some recompense, and then headed for obscurity.

Dolores was slow in responding to John's passion, but would seem to have melted somewhat when John insisted on perfectionism in the love scenes he played with her. The takes were done over and over, and rumor had it, undoubtedly spread by the publicity department, that Dolores had fainted during one of them. John's idealization of her caused him to view her as a kind of seraphic angel come to earth in beautifully luscious form, and upon coming across her on the set with a particularly unworldly, if not downright heavenly, look on her face, he asked her what she was thinking of. "Mr. Barrymore," she told him, "I can't make up my mind whether to have a hot dog or a hamburger for lunch."

At his look of consternation she gave a mischievous laugh, and John swore afterward that she was laughing at the gray that was now well mixed with the brown of his hair. So possessive and jealous did John grow toward her that, before she had declared her love for him, he had the director keep her out of sight, either in her dressing room or on the sidelines, while he performed his scenes.

The relative slowness with which Dolores responded to him was due to what she later described as her "disgust with all actors, from having been brought up with one." On the other hand, after falling in love with John, Dolores felt she was able to tolerate much in him that would have been impossible for her if she had *not* been brought up by an actor.

When John came to call upon her at her home an almost immediate crisis developed in the Costello family. Her mother was all for the courtship, although she insisted upon complete chaperonage of the couple. So was her sister, Helene who had had one divorce already and was currently being wooed by a middle-aged leading man, Lowell Sherman, whom she later married (and divorced). But Father Maurice objected on the grounds that (1) John was still married, (2) the handsome swain was old enough to be Dolores's father (and was, in fact, six months older than her mother), and (3) was untrustworthy in general for so sweet and inexperienced a girl as Dolores. In the household battle that developed, Maurice said that he would leave the home for good if John were permitted to call. John called, Maurice called him a scoundrel and asked him to leave the premises at once; Mrs. Costello thereupon smartly slapped her husband's face, and *he* left the premises, never to return.

In a divorce suit he instituted later, Maurice testified: "When my daughters were shoved into success, I attempted to guide and advise them from years of experience. My suggestions were met with scorn and rebuffs from my wife and both my daughters. They gave me to understand I counted for nothing." He was granted his divorce. In his declining years, when he was broken in health and poverty-stricken, John and Dolores were extremely kind to him and saw that he had a good home to live in.

Meanwhile, back at the set . . . there was trouble with the whale, which had been conceived and spawned in the Warner Brothers' property department. This monster, which cost $15,000 to design and whelp, was to have been manipulated from its interior, in the waters of San Pedro bay, by two trained whale mechanics. When it was launched, the two occupants were fortunately not inside, for the whale sank at once into the bay and has, presumably, remained there since.

Miniatures were used instead, and the reviews that greeted the finished picture showed that no one was fooled. On the other hand,

John was given much credit for the energy and virility he displayed as Ahab. The *New York Times* noted that in the first part of the picture his face was "classical and pale, his forehead . . . high, his nose as straight as a die. He looks as if he had ought to have elected to be a musician or a painter." The second part was preferred by the critic, because his make-up was better. His hair was wet most of the time, as befitted the grim master of a whaler with a crew made up of "half-mad yellow, white, and black scum," and was long and unkempt. His eyes were blurred, and although there was no sound track, it was plain that he addressed his men in snarls.

The picture turned out to be popular, mainly because of the steamy love scenes between John and Dolores. These were not originally planned to stand out to any degree, but the director, failing to find single takes that pleased him, resorted to the expedient of pasting several takes of the same scene together and running them as one long scene, which when unveiled in 1926 was thought to rival the passionate John Gilbert-Greta Garbo embraces.

A Warner's publicist explained the many divergences between the movie and the novel in the Preface to a popular edition of *Moby Dick,* with illustrations from the film:

> There is an unreasonably cruel fate haunting the unfortunate Captain Ahab in *Moby Dick.* Apparently an infatuation with the relentless had seized upon Melville. In all justice, Ahab had suffered enough to be granted expiation and its rewards, but Melville killed him, and with him a generous source of goodness and greatness. Upon finishing the book, therefore, one feels like having been a witness to a horrible persecution, and that Ahab was heartlessly cold-decked. Though a license, it is a relief and a satisfaction that the picture version allows Ahab to live—with a mind restored, and with some of earth's possessions and happiness. There is in this interpretation a kind of justice which satisfies rudimentary humaneness and compassion.

Thus, John's attempt to make a great sea classic! Four years later he did a remake of the picture with a sound track, but aside from the agonizing shriek he gave when his leg was amputated, there was little to distinguish that version either. It had a stronger whale but weaker love scenes.

Immediately after *The Sea Beast* he turned his attention to *Don*

Juan, and attempted to have Mary Astor supplanted by Dolores Costello. The attempt failed, as Warner's was still embroiled in the suit brought by Priscilla Bonner. Miss Astor, who had heard rumors of a Barrymore-Costello attachment, had her worst fears realized when she saw two camp chairs placed just out of camera range, upon which sat John and Dolores greatly absorbed in each other. If she had any doubts about the ending of her romance they were dispelled when she attended the premiere of *The Sea Beast* and witnessed the smoldering love scenes. In New York Michael Strange saw the film and exclaimed: "That's not acting. He's in love with the girl."

In *Don Juan* Mary Astor represented the virginal love interest, while several other beauties were recruited for the Don's amorous dalliances, among them Estelle Taylor (the wife of Jack Dempsey), Myrna Loy, June Marlowe, and Phyllis Haver. A Warner's press agent, going through the completed footage, calculated that John delivered or received a total of 191 kisses during the course of the picture. John, as though determined to hold his own with Douglas Fairbanks and Milton Sills, climbed steep walls, leaped on to balconies, swam the torrents of the Tiber, and dueled to the death (of his opponent). In the end he headed toward a sunset, riding a white charger and clasping the pliant Mary Astor in his arms. The film was in two parts, in the first of which John played the father of Don Juan, and in the later section the irresistible Don himself.

After completing the film, and before taking on his next chore for Warner's, *Manon Lescaut* (retitled *When a Man Loves*), John hired an 80-foot motor yacht, *The Gypsy,* from Hal Roach, and sailed off on a cruise to the southern tip of Baja California. He took with him a captain and a crew of five, Blaney, his valet, and Clementine, his monkey, and waved good-by to Dolores from the Wilmington, California, yacht basin on December 26, 1925. The purpose of this voyage, according to Gene Fowler, was "to take an invoice of himself and his destiny." According to Dolores Costello's later recollections, John had wanted to take her along on the three-week voyage, and she was "dying to go," but her mother said No. "Jack," she added, "was terrified of my mother." Dolores had exacted from John a pledge from him to stop drinking, and presumably the trip was to help him in his new resolution of abstinence.

In *Good Night, Sweet Prince* there is a large section devoted to the "sea log" John kept on this trip, and to which he added when he and Dolores went off on a honeymoon trip nearly three years later. The log, which has much charm, a keen and original sense of observation, and shows many of the yearnings John Barrymore had at this time, found its way into the hands of Henry Hotchener, after seemingly disappearing, and was sold to Fowler after Barrymore's death by Hotchener for twenty thousand dollars. It was Dolores Costello's claim, in 1963, that the log had been kept by John as a kind of running letter to her, and that it remained in her possession for many years but eventually disappeared, and that it was very definitely her property.

A reading of the entries in the log, in this light, does tend to substantiate her claim. The entries seem written to amuse *someone,* and since all the entries have the air of being written in a state of euphoric love, and contain many references to "Winkie," as he called Dolores, and to "small cat" and "Wink" as he also called Dolores, and "our star," it can be safely concluded that the log *was* kept for Dolores's edification and amusement and was part of his continuing courtship of her. He proudly notes his daily success at remaining abstinent, and even when faced by the heady temptation of a glorious Mexican bar, allows himself only one small draught of beer. He attempts to justify his Hollywood existence; he referred to "the pathetic jack-ass years of absurdity in Europe," of his trying to make a life with Michael, and the equal absurdity of her trying to make a life with him. If properly used, he thought, "this West of hicks and sunsets," might provide him with a spiritual bath that would allow him to remain true to himself from then on! Not much proof that he was gaining the insight into his condition that he needed.

The opening of *Don Juan* in New York on August 5, 1926, was accompanied by the first Vitaphone short subjects (in which pictures were combined with recorded sound); and the feature film itself contained the first recorded musical score integrated with the action. Music to accompany motion pictures was, of course, not new to audiences, since everything from Wurlitzer organs to full symphony orchestras had been called into "live" service previously. Yet, Mordaunt Hall of the *Times* was moved enough to report to his readers that "a marvelous device known as the Vitaphone, which synchronizes sound with motion pictures, stirred a distinguished audience in Warner's Theatre to unusual enthusiasm at its initial presentation." The review of *Don Juan* contained restrained enthusiasm at best, and as it turned out, most of the other reviews were unfavorable, and some downright abusive.

How John Barrymore's new Hollywood career was striking his more intellectual contemporaries can be gathered from some comments made by Stark Young in *The New Republic*.

> Of these moving pictures, people, looking at them and wondering afterward, can only observe that they are rotten, vulgar, empty, in bad taste, dishonest, noisome with a silly and unwholesome exhibitionism, and odious with a kind of stale and degenerate studio adolescence. Their appeal is cheap, cynical and specious. The only possible virtue in Mr. Barrymore's progress is a certain advance in athletics; he is more agile, he leaps, rides and hops to a better showing, promoted by the fine air of California and the exercise imminent to such a clime. Artistically, the only thing we could say about Mr. Barrymore's performances is that he brings to them remnants of his tricks and mannerisms that stiffen them slightly and perhaps convey the sense of acting to a public that has seen but little of it.

In the "old" *Life*, Robert E. Sherwood noted that *Don Juan* had been as liberally panned by the United Brotherhood of Movie Critics as had any picture in his memory. Yet he found it necessary to confess that he enjoyed it. "The backgrounds are awful, and the costumes grotesque in their inaccuracy. Mr. Barrymore himself is almost as bad, at times, as he was in *The Sea Beast*; the story is dragged out and frequently confused. But the fact remains that *Don Juan* engaged my humble interest and provided me with considerable entertainment." He thought John Barrymore his old self when playing the father of Don Juan. But playing the title role, John became "the movie Barrymore, with a few flashes of brilliance and a great many glints of supreme silliness."

Critical enthusiasm could not have been increased by the decorations outside the Warner Theater. One gigantic cardboard display showed John kissing a girl in the clouds. There was a set of picture displays on which blue and red lights flashed alternately; when the blue was turned on, several naked female figures were revealed which had been previously invisible. In the lobby stood a full-length painting of John, flanked by portraits of nymphs half his size. The male ushers were dressed in high ruffed collars and the females in long, bell-skirted gowns, designed to make the customer feel he was at once in the fifteenth century.

The film now has an antique charm, and John Barrymore appears to have spoofed it all the way through. The accompanying Vitaphone score is faded and scratchy, and one wonders why a Wurlitzer wouldn't have been preferable.

But each time to its own wonders. Hollywood went all out when *Don Juan* and Vitaphone were unveiled in Los Angeles on October 27, 1926. *Variety* printed a special Vitaphone edition, with contents that would seem to have substantiated the charge that the movie capital was a fatuous dreamland. "Well, folks," ran the lead story, "they went and did it at Grauman's Chinese tonight! They put on something which Hollywood has been hearing about but never had the chance to hear. It was nothing more than that uncanny device, the Vitaphone . . . It was presented in conjunction with John Barrymore's sensational cinema, *Don Juan*. . . ."

John's nautical enthusiasm led him to purchase a yacht in 1926, the 93-foot gaff-rigged schooner, *The Mariner,* which was four years old at the time he bought it and reputed to be one of the fastest racing yachts on the West Coast. He put in a diesel auxiliary, had three staterooms built, and redesigned the galley. He planned to take Dolores off on a cruise, a voyage she was more than willing to make, but Mrs. Costello wouldn't have it. She very wisely was aware of the kind of publicity that would result for her daughter if she were to sail off alone with the still-married John Barrymore. Eventually John extended a cruising invitation to Mrs. Costello, too, and *The Mariner* sailed from San Pedro harbor (opposite Catalina) in June of 1926, handled by Otto Matthias, who was to be in John's employ for nearly ten years.

The cruise lasted only three days. Mrs. Costello came down with a violent attack of seasickness almost at once, and so miserable was she that John heeded the pleas of Dolores to turn back. He did not stay ashore long, having decided to enter *The Mariner* in the annual yacht race to Honolulu. His boat was becalmed en route and arrived in port hopelessly last and days late. Otto was put in charge of getting the boat back, and John sailed home on a steamship.

While engaged in making *When a Man Loves,* the last of the three he had contracted to do for Warner's, John decided to become one of the independent stars under the aegis of United Artists, the home of Charles Chaplin, Mary Pickford, and Douglas Fairbanks, then a company that represented considerably more in the way of prestige than Warner's. Part of the lure, too, was the chance to share in the profits made by a picture. As it turned out, he made only two pictures in two years for United Artists, and although he received $100,000 for each, the Warner Brothers contract had been much more lucrative, since it also included his maintenance, which was expensive. When he made a third film for United Artists, he was upped to $150,000, but the fact that there were no profits for him to share in was indicative that John was not making "hits" during this period.

When a Man Loves was not regarded highly, and John now thought it time for Dolores to leave Warner's too, rather than renew her contract with that studio. He advised the president of United Artists of her availability, and learned to his surprise that such actions were regarded as unethical in Hollywood, where stars were regarded as important financial properties. He did not succeed in obtaining Dolores as his leading lady in the three films made for United Artists. The first of these was *The Beloved Rogue,* in which John cavorted as François Villon; the next was *The Tempest,* a well-photographed tale of the Russian Revolution; and his last for United Artists was *Eternal Love,* a dreadful tale of Swiss lovers united in death, as Spencer Berger described it, "by a sympathetic avalanche." This last, directed by Ernst Lubitsch, was done without benefit of sound, and appeared when the sound revolution was well advanced. John was happy enough to leave United Artists and head back to Warner's for his first talking film.

In June of 1927 John Drew, the still-active uncle of the Barrymores, became seriously ill in Portland, Oregon, while on a "farewell tour" with a revival of *Trelawney of the Wells.* When the illness took a turn for the worse the aging actor was moved to a hospital in San

Francisco, where John and Lionel paid him a visit. Lionel, in the midst of filming *Sadie Thompson* at the time, soon returned to Los Angeles, heartened by signs of rallying on Drew's part. John, however, remained in San Francisco, spent many hours at his uncle's bedside, and was with the seventy-six-year-old man when he died in the early morning hours of July 9. Family members were unhappy that Lionel had not followed John's example in staying with the patriarchal actor, but Lionel was delaying a picture, and John was not.

The death of his uncle may have had a sobering effect on John, for his mood turned serious during the next several months. He began to dream of doing *Hamlet* in Hollywood Bowl, and he bought himself a house high above Beverly Hills on Tower Road. Although his adoration of Dolores remained undiminished, he had not bothered to ask Michael for a divorce. Perhaps, as Gene Fowler has suggested, because of his fear that marriage with Dolores might shatter his romance. When Maurice Costello's divorce case came to court a mild furor resulted in the newspapers, and John was pressed for a statement by the reporters, who were particularly interested in Costello's objections to his daughter's suitor.

"It is ridiculous to be prejudiced against a man because he is married," John was reported as saying. "The divorce courts are made to take care of trivialities like that. As for the difference in our ages, an actor is no older than he admits." John usually admitted to being only one year younger than his age.

Although John was still legally tied to Michael, Dolores, when she went off on a vacation to Havana with her mother and sister in March of 1928, wore an engagement ring. He had extracted from her a promise to marry him; she, in return, had extracted a promise from him to refrain from drinking for six months, at which time they would marry. On the return trip from Havana, aboard the S.S. *California*, the Costellos ran into Mary Astor, who was on her honeymoon. Mary saw the ring on Dolores's finger and inquired as to its meaning. Dolores told her she had bought it for herself. Then a strange conversation took place, in which Mary told Dolores of her own desperate involvement with John. "It made me sick to hear of it," Dolores recalled later. "I couldn't imagine why Mary found it necessary to tell me all those things." Back home she questioned John about Mary Astor's revelations. "Jack was a gentleman," she said, years later. "He didn't admit a thing, said she was making it all up." The incident demonstrated, however, the intense feelings John could rouse in those who loved him and the long-lasting effects of those feelings.

A Hollywood gossip columnist who "exposed" John's secret romance with Dolores precipitated the divorce arrangements with Michael, about which John had been laggardly. Michael claimed that she had asked John for a divorce some months before, and that he had not appeared anxious for one. Toward the end of June, 1928, John took the train to New York and arranged matters formally with Michael, meanwhile writing his old friend, Ned Sheldon, that he planned to visit him. Sheldon lived in an East Eighty-fourth Street apartment, very near where Michael had rented a brownstone. He was all but immobilized, and his ophthalmic nerve was beginning to be affected, a condition which would result in blindness in a few years.

In this letter John revealed that he was concentrating on plans for his production of *Hamlet* in Hollywood Bowl, a production he assured Ned would take place in September of 1928. Following this, he planned to give the play also at the Greek Theatre in Berkeley. "These sylvan interludes," he told Ned, "might be the precursor of better things."

But hardly had he mailed the letter when he signed a new contract with Warner Brothers—now riding high because of its pioneering of the talkies—for a million dollars. Under the terms of the contract he would owe them five pictures to be produced within two years. A talking John Barrymore was obviously worth a great deal more than a silent one.

When Michael saw John, after an interval of three years, she said, "My God, you've gone gray!" It was agreed between them that she would obtain the divorce quietly out of the city, and that the terms of the separation agreement made earlier would continue to provide fifteen hundred dollars monthly for Diana's support. There were additional monies that John was required to pay, for insurance policies, for one thing, but on the whole he was let off lightly, considering he was a man about to earn a half million dollars yearly, and in 1928 relatively lightly taxed dollars.

John's marriage to Dolores took place on November 24, 1928, and somewhere between the divorce and remarriage the plans for *Hamlet* disappeared, at least temporarily. Gene Fowler gave the reason as a fit of pettish jealousy over Dolores's smiling at someone, which sent John raging away on a yacht trip, but since six weeks of location filming on *Eternal Love* occurred during August and September, the dumping of *Hamlet* can be ascribed, too, to his anxiousness to start working on his Warner's contract, and to finish up as quickly as possible the last United Artists' picture—his last mute appearance on the screen. The site of the marriage was Mrs. Costello's home in Beverly Hills, but before the ceremony was performed another weird incident occurred, made much of by the newspapers.

"A mysterious woman," ran one of the accounts, "heavily veiled and expensively gowned, appeared in the marriage license bureau, and threatened to wreck John Barrymore's romance with the beautiful Dolores Costello. The woman did not reveal her name, but appeared excited when she ordered the County Clerk under no circumstances to issue a license for the marriage." The woman said she knew for a fact that there was no final divorce between John and Michael.

Hollywood braced itself for a new sensation: Was the devil-may-care John Barrymore about to flout all moral and legal law to have his beloved Dolores? Reporters came to Dolores for a statement. "Mr. Barrymore has asked me to marry him," she said simply. "For that reason I believed, and still believe, that he is legally free to marry." Her statement did, however, contain that tantalizing note of doubt. John merely said: "Even in this superb climate there are crazy people."

The marriage went ahead as scheduled. Meanwhile word was flashed to news agencies in Europe to find Michael, who was vacationing in the south of France, and get her statement on the subject.

In Europe, Michael revealed that a divorce actually had taken place and had been granted to her under the name of Mrs. John Blythe. The newshounds went quickly to work and ferreted out such details as could be discovered. The divorce, it was learned, had been obtained by Michael in Kingston, New York, on August 18, 1928. The grounds, in keeping with the New York State divorce laws, included adultery; testimony had been given, and the court papers then sealed. This did not stop the New York *Daily News* from finding out much of what it wanted to know.

On November 29, five days after the wedding, the paper revealed that it had come into possession of "the essential facts as to Michael Strange's sensational testimony."

"The screen idol's heavy lovemaking with her rival," the *News* story went on, "Mrs. Barrymore testified, was conducted in a beautiful thatched cottage, among the roses of the gorgeous gardens of the Ambassador. It was there that John was frequently secluded in his love idyl with a woman whom his wife elected to describe in her court statements merely 'as the woman whose name I do not know.'" These thatched cottages among the roses, the *News* said, rented for about fifty dollars a day. The support for Michael's allegations came from two documents, said the *News*, one from a man identified "as a prominent real estate operator." If the *News* story be given any weight, it would appear that Michael found the means to keep John regular in his support payments for Diana.

Dolores, during the ceremony (performed by a Unitarian minister, although both belonged to the Catholic faith), wore a wedding gown of cream lace over a bisque slip—as *Photoplay* reported to its waiting readers—and at her shoulder a diamond barpin, given to her as a wedding present by John. The pin held a spray of lilies of the valley to her shoulder. After the wedding they took up quarters at John's Tower Road residence, which he had enlarged from the original five rooms to include a "marriage house" of six more rooms connected to the older part of the house by a pergola. This was only the beginning of the additions he made to a house which was to become one of the most wondrous in Hollywood. Dolores was at work on a picture for Warner's and John had returned to the studio to prepare his first talkie, based on the novel *General Crack*. They were both more concerned, though, with the cruise they planned to take on *The Mariner*, whose hull showed signs of dry rot, and which John was having repaired and refitted.

John and Dolores, early in January of 1929, went off on a long

269

cruise on the repaired *Mariner*, a voyage during which Dolores proved her hardiness and handiness with shotgun and deep-sea fishing rod. The honeymooning couple visited Cocos Island south-west of Costa Rica, and ventured as far as the Galapagos, off Ecuador. By the time they arrived in mid-March, work was well advanced on further additions to the house(s) on Tower Road.

During the next few years "the House that Jack Built" became a fabled place. Over the years John had acquired, and had stored in various places, an enormous variety of objects, and these found their way into the Tower Road house, which originally had been built by King Vidor on the crest of a spur of one of the Hollywood mountains. The view overlooked miles of California and the Pacific, although today the view is occasionally limited by smog. The ap-proaching roads were so winding and steep that Jack sometimes found it necessary to include road maps with invitations to people who were visiting the place for the first time. Entering the gate one first beheld a group of red-tiled roofs, saw the blue waters of two swimming pools, and a trout pond, in which John would some-times fish if Dolores was in the mood for having fresh trout for supper.

One of John's additions to the property was the trophy room. Inside were stuffed fish, a stuffed crocodile that Dolores had shot in the Galapagos, part of the vertebrae of a whale, the skin and skeleton of a 560-pound marlin swordfish, the stuffed remains of a giant tortoise. The place of honor was held by the only dinosaur egg in existence (up to then) outside the Museum of Natural History in New York. John Roy Chapman presented it to John shortly after his 1925 expedition into the Gobi Desert.

Another room held John's gun collection. Collecting firearms had been his hobby since youth, and he had accumulated such items as a 1914 Harpers Ferry Flint Lock Rifle, an 1891 Springfield, several Remingtons, Winchesters, and Savages, and sets of dueling pistols. In this room were also kept antique swords, his *Hamlet* dagger, several stilettos, and an ancient crossbow.

While on his honeymoon trip with Dolores he began his bird collection, and built an aviary to house them. Some of his birds were kept in special cages, others had the freedom of the aviary.

John's favorite was Maloney, a king vulture from South Africa. They held long clucking conversations together, and the biggest problem in keeping Maloney happy was finding meat sufficiently decayed to appeal to his taste.

John was a bibliophile of some standing, and his library contained first editions of *Moby Dick* and *Alice in Wonderland*. He had a 1572 edition of three volumes of Cicero, with fragments of early manuscripts used in the bindings, a first edition of Hakluyt's *Voyages*, an atlas dating from the year 1542, and hundreds of other rare items. The literature he collected included much lore on pirates, the sea, bird culture, and hunting and fishing.

On the five acres were also a skeet range, a bowling green, two garden houses, a wine cellar, quarters for several domestics, greens keepers, and Nishi, his Japanese gardener, and a sun and moon dial which John imported from England for a reputed $15,000. In the music room, was a very fine Meissen chandelier, which John bought from an Austrian archduke at an exorbitant price.

There was a bar, naturally. This was an "English tavern room," which was furnished with a frontier bar he came across while on an Alaskan trip with Dolores, and which he sentimentally had shipped to Tower Road. One of the ornaments of the room was a giant brown cuspidor from a Virginia City, Nevada, hotel. The bar was a popular room, but family life was lived mostly on the patio, which surrounded one of the pools. It was on this patio that John and Dolores ate many of their lunches and dinners, served on a simple card table with rather uncertain legs.

In this unorthodox and baronial abode two children were born to Dolores and John. The first was a girl, born on April 8, 1930, and christened Dolores Ethel Mae Barrymore. Only a week earlier the new steel-hulled yacht that John had had built for a sum in excess of a quarter of a million dollars was launched and taken for its trial run. In honor of the forthcoming child the name *Infanta* had been suggested by Dolores for the yacht, which was designed along the sleek lines of a man-of-war and traveled at a speed of fourteen knots. The cabins were luxurious, and a special one had been fitted for the baby. The second child, a son, was born on June 4, 1932, and named John Blythe Barrymore, Jr. The two children spent their babyhoods either in the wondrous home or on the wondrous yacht, and both home and yacht contributed to John Barrymore's growing legend.

As for the house, Dolores always said about it that it was hard to live in and hard to run.

Was John happy with his Dolores, now that he had married his dream girl, put her into a dream house, had two dream children with her, and built a dream boat? "Well," said Dolores, "he was awfully happy just fishing and cleaning guns." But she also knew him to be a superstitious, frightened man, fearful that his mind would give way like his father's, afraid to start on a picture unless the astrological signs were right. "Actually," she said, "he was terrified. His insecurity stemmed from his mother's death and later from his grandmother's. Where would he be next, he seemed to be asking. What would he be thrown into?"

And, contrary to the impression given by Fowler in *Good Night, Sweet Prince,* Dolores's version was that John loved what Dolores had, a warm family life with her mother and sister. John was relatively remote from his own family. He was loyal to them, and they to him, but the austerity of their relationship gave him little of the family warmth he needed. When Dolores's mother died, it was a loss for John as well as his wife. His attempt to establish a family identity of his own had its pathetic side. This attempt would take the form of wearing the blazer from his English school at Wimbledon, and he liked to wear with it his Garrick Club tie. For his new boat, the *Infanta,* he designed a flag with a family crest that he invented—a crowned cocatrice of gold on a blue background. It amused Dolores because her family already had its crest.

His dissatisfactions, and they were many, stemmed partially from his disrespect for acting and particularly from his disrespect for men as actors. At the age of forty-seven he spoke proudly of the freehand drawing award he had won in England at the age of seventeen. "His very acting career that had made him so successful seemed to turn him inside out," Dolores said.

"And he had a diabolical side. His jealousy was dreadful to behold." He and Dolores seldom went out, mainly because of a jealous possessiveness that was close to being pathological in its intensity.

One evening they did go to a party attended by many of the Hollywood greats. Dolores made the mistake of accepting an invitation to dance with David O. Selznick. John swept her home early and kept her up until past three in the morning with an interrogation that drove her to distraction. "What did he say?" he kept asking. "WHAT DID HE SAY TO YOU?"

John accused Dolores of planning an affair. He knew for a fact that *no* woman, no matter how sacred her vows, could be faithful to a man. He had had the proof all his life, beginning at the age of fourteen, that women were flagrantly, bestially unfaithful.

High up on lonely Tower Road, John barred room after room of the lavish house so that some secret lover could not enter to ravish his Dolores.

And in his moodiness, his insatiable need for reassurance, his search for the *real* John Barrymore, for the woman who would always be true and love not the handsome actor but the lonely little boy inside, he drank, not always, but often. And yet, when he was sober there was no one, Dolores said, more sober and proper than her husband.

Dolores was sickened by this behavior, and yet tried to reason with him and comfort him. "What is wrong with you?" she pleaded. "I want to be your friend. Didn't you ever have a woman who was a *friend?*" In answer John raged all the more, just as he had with Michael Strange, as he had with his first wife, Katherine. These marriages, he claimed, had been ruined by their infidelities, and yet, underneath it all, he was tormented by the inability of his marriages to last, by the feeling he lost for his partners after a time and could never manage to reclaim.

THE ROYAL WAY / *chapter XIX*

ETHEL, during the 1920s, gave no thought to deserting the stage for Hollywood, even though she wondered in 1923, in a magazine: "What I am going to do next only God knows, and He has not given me an inkling. My mind is filled, as always, with big plans, big dreams, and big hopes. I still feel as if I were just beginning . . ." One big thing that she did was to appear in *The School for Scandal*, presented by The Players as the club's annual revival, for 1923, of a classic. The Players turned the benefit production into a celebration of John Drew's fiftieth anniversary on the stage. In the cast were such fine performers as Walter Hampden, Francis Wilson, and Grant Mitchell, but it was Ethel who commanded the most attention as a gorgeously gowned and fantastically hatted Lady Teazle. The one week of performances put Ethel once again on the pinnacle from which she had slightly slipped in the ill-fated productions of *Romeo and Juliet* and *Rose Bernd*. And while it was true that *The Laughing Lady* had re-established her popularity with the public, the critics had not been altogether happy with her because of the slender nature of the vehicle. As Lady Teazle to John Drew's Sir Peter she showed herself in full command of the classic style and spirit in acting.

"One extremely pleasant thing about the Barrymores," commented Dorothy Parker, "is that every one of them will be fairly certain to know what the play is about before the curtain goes up. Ethel's Lady Teazle is the best of our times."

Accolades such as this did not stop Ethel from taking *The Twelve Pound Look* out again on the summer vaudeville circuits. She was still able to charm newer generations of playgoers with Barrie's old one-acter; and it remained a tried and true money earner for her for thirty years.

Her Lady Teazle was to be repeated often, too, although it is doubtful that she ever again aroused quite the emotion of the evening she came before the curtain after the first performance for The Players and faced round after round of applause. The velvet curtain closed and swung open again, and the audience would not rest until Ethel and John Drew stood alone together on the stage. A lady with tear-filled eyes, seated next to Otis Skinner in the audience, turned to that actor and said: "There stands the aristocracy of the theater." Otis Skinner could only nod his agreement.

But the aristocracy of the theater must face its hard times, just as any other members, and the next play she was in, *A Royal Fandango,* written for her by Zoë Akins, was crushed by the critics and closed after a poor run. The play was not a total loss, though, for it marked the debut of a new young actor, who had only a few lines to say but was dreadfully nervous about the task. His name was Spencer Tracy, and Ethel said to him just before he made his entrance, "Relax. That's all you have to do. Just relax. It'll all be the same in a hundred years."

Ethel traveled to England in 1924, after the closing of *A Royal Fandango,* and if musty gossip can be believed, the trip was made necessary by a crush, a veritable passion she had conceived for Henry Daniell, an English actor who had appeared with her. But passion or lovesickness did not prevent her from looking up her old friends in England, among them Winston Churchill.

In New York, with no new play at hand, Arthur Hopkins suggested that he star her in a revival of *The Second Mrs. Tanqueray,* the Pinero warhorse that had first been presented thirty years before. Ethel agreed, and she made of the play a *succès d'estime,* and a moderate commercial success besides. Walter Hampden was an actor of note by this time—he had played a servant in *The School for*

Scandal—and opened a repertory theater for the playing of the classics. Ethel appeared as Ophelia with him in *Hamlet,* and as Portia in *The Merchant of Venice.* She did not play these roles for long, but she made favorable impressions in each.

How did she justify a forty-six-year-old woman playing so youthful a role as Ophelia? "She is often played by little flibbertygibbets," she said, "chosen apparently for both their youth and their imbecility. So that, when Ophelia does go mad the shock which Shakespeare meant audiences to feel is no shock at all." To get all the subtle, tragic, and beautifully poetic nuances from the character, it was necessary, she implied, that she be played by a mature actress—as had been done often enough in the past.

As Portia she broke with long-established tradition when it came time for her to make the speech that begins, "The quality of mercy is not strained . . ." The audiences, waiting for Ethel's version of fire and brimstone, were astounded when she delivered the speech quietly, developed her plea with legalistic matter-of-factness, and ended as though charging a dubious jury.

Ethel's acting possessed naturally the kind of eloquence that, in years to come, was to be regarded as more characteristic of the old school. Ethel's avowed purpose was to make her audience feel and understand. A French actor saw her do *The Second Mrs. Tanqueray* and suggested that she bring the play for a season to Paris. "But, my French isn't good enough," Ethel said. "What I meant is," the actor said, "that if you play it in English the audience will have no difficulty in understanding you."

The secret of this eloquence was once hinted at by Ethel herself. "Always," she said in a moment of self-revelation, "I have tried to leave my authors alone. You don't have to be bewildered by Shakespeare. There he is. Leave him alone. Say what he says and thank God that he has given you a trumpet through which to blow so sweetly. You don't have to be bewildered by Ibsen. There he is. Leave him alone, and he will tell a woman's life in three hours. Thank your gods for those three hours, because if you are true to yourself the very saying of them will make you an artist. That at least is what I feel about my own work. I sing my lesson and have done. I want no mystery, no green lights, no Czechoslovakian producers, or early Metro-Goldwyn wind machines. I want to speak, and feel what I am speaking, and that is all I know."

But conscious craft entered her performances, too, as when in *The Constant Wife* she would begin to cry, on cue, in the last act, then stop on cue and resume her bright, gay tone. Max Reinhardt, the European impresario, saw her do this and asked her afterward if she was able to shed tears at the same moment every night. He knew the self-training required to be able to do this. Not so even the friendliest of drama critics. Percy Hammond irked Ethel by reporting "Miss Barrymore indulged in a few vaudeville tricks in the last act."

This, her greatest hit of the twenties, came along in 1926. The play, by W. Somerset Maugham, opened in Cleveland before coming to New York and gave Ethel her worst case of stage fright, a disease she caught chronically through the years. Large gaps in her memory opened as she performed the role of Constance Middleton. George Cukor, new to directing, hid in the fireplace and prompted her. As the evening proceeded, pages containing her lines were scattered in several places on the stage so that she could stroll about and look at them. Maugham, who was present, suffered agonies watching Ethel struggle through the performance. He went on stage after the curtain was lowered for the last time, there to be greeted effusively by Ethel. "She flung her arms around my neck," he reported afterward, "kissed me on both cheeks, and said, 'Darling, I've ruined your play, but don't worry, it'll run for two years.'" And it did.

The Cleveland newspapers made that first night of Ethel's into what they chose to regard as an insult to the city's civic pride. Cleveland, they said, at least deserved the consideration of a star's knowing her lines. She did know them, Ethel always claimed afterward, and to prove it she was letter-perfect on the second night, disdaining her prompters and the pages strewn about the stage.

In New York, when it opened November 30, 1926, the play was greeted as a comedy of endless delight written by an older hand who could still teach that young upstart, Noel Coward, a thing or two. The newspapers noted that for Ethel it represented a return to Maugham after almost twenty years, a return to the Frohman management (but only for the duration of the run), and a return to contemporary drama after her bouts with Shakespeare in repertory.

Including her usual touring, the play gave her her livelihood for better than two years and contributed substantially to Maugham's prosperity.

Maugham, looking back over his own career in 1940, said: "I think I can honestly say that the one single performance that satisfied me most was that of Ethel Barrymore in *The Constant Wife*. There was always that extra way she put over a single word, and she always exhibited a wonderful command over audiences."

Her brother John once attended one of Ethel's performances and noticed that not a single cough came from the audience. He mentioned this eerie occurrence to Ethel, and she told him: "But I don't let them cough."

"You don't?" John said. "And how is that done?"

"I just turn on something inside myself," she said, "and they don't dare cough."

She was never quite sure whether it was by voice or look that she was able to keep her audiences from coughing, but she always did manage to convey to them that they must not cough. George Cukor once said about Ethel that she did not suffer fools gladly. Nor did she suffer coughers.

Still the most celebrated of American actresses as the twenties headed toward the stock market disaster, Ethel lived well but not always wisely. The salaries she earned were dissipated with regal lavishness. There were no investments made of her earnings, no use of capital to build more capital. She lived much the way her rich friends lived, but, unlike them, she lived off her earnings and not capital. If she saw a Steinway and wanted it she would buy that Steinway and have it shipped to her Mamaroneck house or to the town house on East Fifty-fifth Street she kept for a winter residence.

Her two boys went to a series of good and expensive schools: Portsmouth Priory in Rhode Island, the Fay School in Southboro, Massachusetts, St. Bernard's in New York, and Canterbury in Connecticut. Sammie Colt, the older of the two, went on to Andover and to Brown. The junior Ethel, or "Sister" as she was called in the family, after finishing at the convent school, which had moved its boarding pupils to a new and larger building at Moylan, Pennsylvania, was placed in a private school of the "finishing" type in

Verona, Italy, where she learned Italian and French, studied art and singing, visited museums, and traveled under supervision to the cultural centers of Italy and France.

When Ethel traveled abroad for a summer it was done in grand style, and involved renting a house near London for herself and the three children and hiring a domestic staff. She was inclined toward highhandedness in filing her income tax returns, a habit that later caused her some distress. But it was not as though she was a hoarder of money. If the boys ran up bills in the stores where she had charge accounts, they were paid without question. And there was the faithful family retainer, Georgie Drew Mendum, to look after, too. Georgie was a few years older than Ethel, a first cousin, and an actress who played character parts in Ethel's plays whenever a part was suitable for her. She could play comedy skillfully, and as the years went on became "like a little bird," according to Ethel's daughter. She received Ethel's hand-me-down clothes, and preferred the longer dresses, which she wore ankle length at a time when skirts were greatly higher. She always wore black stockings, and was something of a character. She had a hotel room in the Times Square area, but mainly lived at Mamaroneck with Ethel, where she served as a kind of female major domo.

Ethel, when she worked, wanted familiar faces around her. Georgie Mendum's was perhaps the most familiar of those faces, but there was also Anita Rothe (the wife of her first stage manager, James Kearney), another actress she employed as often as possible and who was familarly known as Schotzie. A third close and constant friend was Mrs. Jacques Gordon, whose first name was Ruth, and who was consequently often confused with the actress Ruth Gordon (also a friend of Ethel's). Mrs. Gordon was the wife of a concert violinist, met Ethel in the mid-1920s, and was her frequent companion for more than twenty years.

"Oh, you have no idea what a great woman she was," Mrs. Gordon felt moved to say about Ethel in 1962. "She was a great woman in the true meaning of greatness, that isolation of the great who live on peaks. And the great have no friends; they merely know a lot of people."

But Ethel carried on many friendships over the years, and they were good ones, if not always intimate. In the twenties her favorite city was Washington, for there she knew Evalyn Walsh MacLean, owner of the Hope diamond, rather a diamond in the rough herself as a person, and an indefatigable hostess. Cissie Patterson, who ran the Washington *Times-Herald,* was a good friend, as was Alice Longworth, with whom Ethel had attended parties as a teen-ager and who had become distinctly a grand lady.

In New York Ethel lunched often at the Algonquin, where the Round Table prized her presence. In that circle was Herbert Bayard Swope, editor of the New York *World,* active in politics and literary circles, and the owner of an estate at Sands Point, Long Island. Herbert and Margaret Swope held regular Sunday lunches, to which were invited large groups of "interesting" people. Swope knew "everyone," and Ethel loved going to his luncheons, sometimes contriving to have her children invited too.

As for the men in her life, her daughter Ethel Colt had it that her mother, after her divorce, was almost nunlike in her conduct. "She was very Victorian in that sense. Her leading man in a play would become her temporary escort. There was always a lot of gossip, but I never saw the slightest romantic interest on her part in any of these men."

Mrs. Gordon saw differently. She thought there might well have been affairs on occasion with one or another of her leading men. "If such romances occurred," Mrs. Gordon said, "they seldom lasted more than a few weeks, for, if not Ethel, sooner or later the man in question would rebel, and the reason for this was that Ethel in her relationships with men was ready to give herself for twenty-four hours a day, seven days out of each week, and there wasn't a man alive who could take it. For this reason, her relationships with the men she cared about—and they were really very few—caused her great unhappiness. Somehow a change would come over her, and a possessiveness in her personality would emerge, and with it an unusual sort of touchiness."

And once, Ethel, letting her hair down, told Mrs. Gordon: "It's not the church affiliation that prevents me from marrying again. The plain truth of the matter is that I've never met the man I would want to be married to."

It was now that Ethel reached the delicate age—that period when a glamorous and beautiful actress discovers that the parts she must play are the parts of mature women, and when the men she is attracted to, or who are attracted to her, are a little too young. She could look marvelous, indeed, on the stage, but in the hard light of the dressing room the truth had to be faced. A woman of fifty, no matter how beautiful she is, is still a woman of fifty. And who was there to talk to about this in what, for Ethel, was her period of change? Her life was magnified enough as it was, enough to make her more than normally shy, to take to cabs rather than walk through streets filled with people who would recognize her instantly. Ethel, who had traveled by hansom cab during the fullest flush of her youth, now took taxis everywhere as a way of shielding herself from the gaze of strangers.

Was it true that now and then she shared the notorious habit of her brother, John? One drink was worth a thousand rumors in Ethel's case, and it took her fifteen years before she was finally able to scotch them.

In 1927 a play called *The Royal Family* made a hit on Broadway. It was written by Edna Ferber and George S. Kaufman, and it dealt with a family of actors called the Cavendishes, whom everyone assumed represented the temperamental, talented, and flamboyant Barrymores. The Julia Cavendish of the play was regarded as a thinly veiled portrait of Ethel, and Anthony Cavendish was clearly John. When asked to be present for an occasion on a certain future date, Julia Cavendish remarked haughtily that "on that night I expect to have laryngitis!"

"All that eating and eating done by the Cavendishes in the play," the nettled Ethel commented. "As everyone knows, eating was never the Barrymores' besetting sin!"

Both Edna Ferber and George S. Kaufman piously disclaimed any resemblance between Ethel and the Julia Cavendish of their play, but they did admit that Anthony Cavendish bore some resemblance to John Barrymore. "We only used bits of him, though," Edna Ferber said. "He was, of course, much too improbable to copy from life."

In an unpublished manuscript written by Ethel at this time, she vented some of her feelings about the image held by the public of such as herself. "The legend has it that we artists are wild, careless, touseled, and immoral. We live en famille and such a famille! An organization of idiots, chaotic, arty, self-conscious, thinking theater, breathing theater, smelling theater. To those half-baked intelligences a theatrical family is only a theatrical family, not an association of normal, healthy, human beings."

It was something of a small miracle that Ethel, who, if she merely wandered into a store to buy a pair of gloves, would be surrounded by the admiring and the curious, could still regard herself as a normal human being, not to mention her younger brother, who created gossipy headlines every hour on the hour!

"An artist, a theatrical artist," she insisted, "must be a human being first, and an artist second. When you applaud it is not only our art but our life, for we are what we have been, not only on the stage, but off it. When I'm not in the theater I don't think of the theater. Of course if I'm doing a new play, if I'm trying to interpret a character who fascinates me, for a few days I become that character. But otherwise, in the normal run of existence, the theater is the theater and life is life, and never do the twain meet except between the hours of eight and eleven. I seem by accident to have hit upon the secret of the whole thing—the loneliness of all those who are trying to create. You can't escape it. You are alone, bitterly and inevitably alone."

Perhaps, after writing the above, she felt she had exposed too much of herself, and the pages, of which the above quotation are a part, were never published.

George S. Kaufman was given his comeuppance by Ethel many years after *The Royal Family* had closed and was all but forgotten. During the Bundles for Britain campaign of the World War II years, Kaufman conceived the idea of having three famous Ethels perform a skit at a gigantic benefit to be given at Radio City Music Hall. The three were to be Ethel Merman, Ethel Waters, and Ethel Barrymore. Fired up with this notion, he telephoned the last-named Ethel and told her about it. "The second Sunday in February did you say?" Ethel asked. "Oh, I'm sorry, but on that night I expect to have laryngitis." It took Kaufman awhile before he was able to figure out why her reply had such a familiar ring.

Ethel could be equally cutting toward herself. After a matinee her stage manager, Eddie McHugh (who followed James Kearney in that capacity), knocked on her dressing room door to say that there was a lady calling who had gone to school with her. "Very well," Ethel groaned, "wheel her in."

A new honor came Ethel's way late in 1928, when the Shuberts named the new theater they had built on West Forty-seventh Street *The Ethel Barrymore.* The Shuberts managed, also, to lure Ethel to their management with *The Kingdom of God,* the work of the Spanish author, G. Martinez Sierra, who had brought his own company of Spanish players to New York two years before.

Ethel dedicated and inaugurated the playhouse on December 17, 1928, received a lifetime key to her own special dressing room, and caused Heywood Broun to say that her performance was the "most moving piece of acting I have ever seen in a theater." The critics argued among themselves, though, as to whether or not *The Kingdom of God* was or was not a play. Such plot as could be discerned in it related three episodes from the life of a Spanish nun.

> For no reason at all [carped Whitney Bolton of the Telegraph] a Spanish girl of nineteen, gently born and exquisitely nurtured, abandons her comfortable existence to take up the rigors of the Sisterhood. We see her at nineteen as a probationer in an asylum for ancient and penniless men. We see her again in the second act, at twenty-nine, in a maternity home for girls who could not master a simple negative. We take our last look at Sister Garcia in the sparse, unhappy room of an orphanage; she is seventy, her back has been bent with godly deeds, and a stick is her prop against evil and a fall downstairs. That is all there is to it.

In spite of her personal triumph, the play did not manage to run through the whole season. It was taken off in the spring of 1929 and replaced with *The Love Duel,* which was regarded as empty claptrap. Ethel took both plays on tour the next season, visited John while playing Los Angeles, and stayed with him at his new home on Tower Road.

One evening the family sat together having dinner on John's patio.

Lionel was there, as was their cousin, Georgie Mendum. Ethel chose the occasion to deliver something of a sermon to her brothers on their desertion of the stage for the Hollywood trash they were presently engaged in fostering. In the midst of her dissertation she looked at her watch and called, "Georgie! We'll be late for the theater."

John attempted to keep the two ladies a moment longer to sip some brandy, but Ethel insisted on leaving at once, and the two brothers escorted her and their cousin to the car. John said during the walk: "Lionel, how tragic it is that you and I have become bums, that we have given up the fabulous stage for the unspeakably low labor of the movies. Here are these two ladies, going to work, carrying on the family tradition. They'll recite lines they've been saying for weeks, and have a magnificent evening. Meanwhile, you and I will be forced to sit in a patio under the stars and sip aged brandy."

"We must try not to be envious," Lionel cautioned him.

"You may both go to hell!" Ethel said, getting grandly into the car.

It was not too long before Ethel was to join her brothers for a session under the stars and before the camera, but first she made another effort to win over Broadway, this with a play that she commissioned herself. She had become enchanted with Julia Peterkin's novel about Gullah Negroes, *Scarlet Sister Mary,* and arranged for Daniel Reed to adapt it. While casting it, one of the aspirants for a role in the play turned out to be her own daughter, Ethel Colt.

Ethel had gone to England for the summer of 1930, had gathered up Sister from her school in Verona, and had the boys come over too. It had earlier been decided that Sister would make her social debut at the Colony Club in the fall, but, no, Sister had become bitten by the acting bug and asked her mother for the role of Serafine. John Colt—Jackie—who was sixteen, asked for a part, too, and Ethel put both her daughter and son in the cast. Not that anyone recognized them, for the entire play was done in blackface, to the amazement of the critics and the audience. "The game," as John Anderson commented, "was not worth the lamp-blacking," and he saw no reason why Ethel should have sacrificed her beauty in order to prove her faith in the theater.

"God," the younger Ethel remembered some years later, "we weren't able to get ourselves clean for six months," which is to say, several months after the play folded.

Ethel, after *Scarlet Sister Mary,* couldn't find a play she wanted to do, although several scripts were sent to her. Too many of these, she said, were "dirty-word scripts," and one offended her so much that she returned it with a notation on the envelope: "Opened by mistake." There was nothing to do, then, but to form a company and take *A School for Scandal* on a tour of the road. Her daughter did not go with her because she had been tapped by George White to appear with Rudy Vallee in his *Scandals,* a disastrous experience for the girl, who had never so much as heard a word of advice about acting from her mother, and whose singing voice, while excellent, had not been tested professionally before.

Anne Seymour, related distantly to the family through the Rankins, took McKee Rankin's promptbook for *A School for Scandal* to Ethel and was asked if she would like to play Maria on the tour, which was to open in Denver before proceeding to the West Coast. Anne, a budding actress, liked the idea immensely, and was to spend thirty weeks with the great lady of the theater. "I was terrified of her," Anne remembered. Ethel did the directing herself, using Georgie Mendum to supply her with her own cues. But she did little rehearsing for her own part of Lady Teazle, and in Denver, in July of 1931, Ethel went through a horrendous and puzzling experience.

"On her entrance," Anne Seymour recalled, "Miss Barrymore went down on one knee and found she couldn't get up. When she did, she staggered as she walked across the stage. The cues she received made little impression on her. Backstage, between the acts, she was in an absolute panic. 'I've lost my mind,' she told us. 'I can't remember anything.' "

The performance was not only reviewed in Denver as "the worst of Ethel Barrymore's career," but the reviews were thought newsworthy enough to be put on the wire services. All over the country heads nodded knowledgeably. Ethel, it was plain, shared the Barrymore weakness, a weakness more than hinted at by the Denver critics. The Denver *Post* said: "Miss Barrymore first amazed and then utterly shocked her hosts of Denver friends by a bizarre and unorthodox portrayal. She took the unusual liberty of making the historic Lady Teazle a more-than-slightly tipsy character."

The members of the cast might have been willing to accept drunkenness as the explanation of the strange performance except that those with her during that day and evening had not seen her sip anything that resembled an alcoholic drink.

Ethel herself the next morning wrote out an explanation of the happening and sent it to the Denver newspapers. A curtain of darkness had seemed to hover over her throughout the play, she related, and her mishap while attempting an old-fashioned curtsy had been caused by a strained ligament in her left leg. "I was in a daze," she went on, "but at the time I thought I could carry through the play." Other factors were the long, hard train trip from New York, the unexpected heat wave in Denver, the strain of rehearsal and getting the sets up, the high altitude, the accident to her leg during rehearsals. "I am simply reciting the facts of the case and they're absolutely true," she ended.

The house was packed for the next performance, and everything proceeded normally. But on the last night of the week-long engagement Ethel fainted on stage and could not be revived in time for the last act. The play had to be finished without her. Something was very clearly wrong with Ethel. On the arrival of the company in Santa Barbara Ethel was met by Lionel, and was persuaded by him to cancel the tour for a week. The company was instructed to proceed to San Francisco, where Ethel would join them in a week's time, and Lionel delivered his sister to John and Dolores, who had already planned to take her off for a cruise on his new yacht, the *Infanta*.

John told Dolores to take Ethel to her cabin and see that she got to sleep. Meanwhile he commandeered Ethel's luggage and went through it piece by piece. Dolores came back to report that Ethel was sleeping soundly and found John with a look of puzzzlement on his face. "Winkie," he told Dolores, "I'm an old, practiced hand at secreting the stuff, but if Ethel is doing it she's better at it than I am. The only thing I've been able to find is this." He showed

Dolores several bottles of an ordinary drugstore potion called Bromidia, a preparation for calming the nerves.

The explanation then came out. Ethel had been drinking the bromide for its calming effect and had suffered unforeseen effects as well. The stuff was tossed overboard, and during a sea voyage to Santa Cruz Island and back to San Pedro she took on a bloom of health, and on arrival in San Francisco was her radiant self again.

Valiantly she went on with her touring during a time of national depression that found theater audiences dwindling. It is not known just how John and Lionel conspired to get Ethel into a motion picture in order to resuscitate her failing financial fortunes, but manage it they did, and Irving Thalberg of MGM obligingly conceived the notion that the three Barrymores in one movie might be one of the outstanding box-office draws of all time. Picking up the telephone, he called her in New York. Would Ethel accept the role of the Empress in *Rasputin and the Empress?* Ethel, in vaudeville at the time with *The Twelve Pound Look,* would be delighted. But the film, she specified, must be finished in time for her to meet a commitment for a fall stage production in New York. The salary for her first appearance in a talking picture, and of her first acting job together with her two brothers, was reputed to be $100,000, but, as a subsequent tax action by the government showed, came to something less than that. Nevertheless, the film work helped postpone the financial reckoning for Ethel that was soon to be due.

BARRYMORES RAMPANT

chapter XX

FOR A TIME it was stylish at Metro-Goldwyn-Mayer to use Barrymores in tandem, this after Lionel became an Academy Award winner, and after John left Warner Brothers in 1931 and wandered over to the Metro lot on a nonexclusive contract. Irving Thalberg had great respect for the Barrymore name, and he also saw the box-office possibilities (and the publicity values) in pairing the brothers. The vehicle he chose was *Arsene Lupin,* a light mystery yarn. *Time* magazine regarded the appearance of two Barrymores in a single picture as a noteworthy event and awarded them its cover for the issue of March 7, 1932. Inside, an anonymous writer commented: "The appearance of both in the same picture indicated that it is now merely sentimental to regard the Barrymores as the royal family of the stage and it italicized the dispute whether histrionically the cinema is a more important medium than the theater." We may be sure that if Ethel happened to read the statement she gave a pronounced sniff.

When he paid his first visit to Thalberg's office John was asked if he owned a dress suit. The question had two barbs, one having to do with the fact that John had attended a much publicized motion picture premiere wearing his well-worn carpet slippers. The other referred to John's lessening appeal to the broad movie public through some less than glamorous roles he had recently undertaken at

Warner's. "If you don't own one, get one," Thalberg said, "because at MGM you're only going to appear in full dress."

At Warner's John had been allowed to select his vehicles and to exercise his editorial judgment on the scripts. His judgment as far as the more literate values were concerned was probably better than that of the studio executives, but when it came to guessing what the public wanted from him he was less than accurate. He had returned to Warner's after a sojourn at United Artists and had agreed to make five talking features. The first was adapted from a novel, *General Crack*, which in written form was a colorful tale of a soldier of fortune in the service of the Emperor of Austria. John took full advantage of his script approval clause to interlard his copy of the novel with notes such as, "All these lines should be acrid and amusing." In spite of the admonition, addressed to the script writers, he did little more than swagger about in the film, showing the audience only his left profile, which he had come more and more to favor.

With him in the film was Lowell Sherman. The brothers-in-law did not get on at all, and Sherman had gone so far as to forbid his wife to visit her sister's household. There was a story that he had once twitted John when he was about to deliver a reading of a *Hamlet* soliloquy at a charity party, and had actually shouted "The hell with Hamlet!" The story then went that John had chased his brother-in-law around the garden. Another had to do with John's having become annoyed at a telegram sent by Lowell on the occasion of his and Dolores's first wedding anniversary. "Congratulations on the first year of the run," Sherman had wired. "If anything happens, remember there is always vaudeville." Sherman was also supposed to have been behind Helene's getting after Dolores to do something about John's drinking. On the set John exacted his own form of revenge. Having approval over all costumes in the picture too, he insisted on Sherman's submitting all his items of apparel to him.

The public showed itself unready for his sudden change of pace in *The Man from Blankley's*, his second talkie. Here he played a mild-mannered English nobleman whose hobby is collecting beetles. Having become disoriented from too much wine, the beetle collector wanders into the wrong house, is mistaken as a hired dinner guest from Blankley's, an employment agency, and regales his hostess with an enthusiastic description of the home life and personal habits of his favorite Egyptian scarab. "The role of Lord Strathpeffer," Spencer Berger wrote some years later, "remains a monument to Barrymore's genius for satire." But he also noticed that *Photoplay* had gauged the reaction of audiences better than the impressed critics. ("This is John's little joke, and we refuse to take it seriously," said *Photoplay*.)

John next decided that his Captain Ahab of *The Sea Beast* had been frustrated by his inability to talk, so he made a sound version of that picture, calling it *Moby Dick* this time. Dolores Costello stayed at home up on Tower Road while Joan Bennett took her place as the love interest.

It was during this period that he recited a soliloquy from *Richard III* in a Warner Brothers compendium called *Show of Shows,* which was supposed to dramatize the wonders of the new medium of sound. The Barrymore segment today still offers graphic evidence of his extraordinary power in the role. Slightly overdone when compared with more modern standards of performance, the sample of the Barrymore interpretation has nevertheless a marvelous fascination.

John then donned a long beard, encased his remarkable nose in putty, and put glass covers over his eyes for *Svengali,* a still remarkable characterization (when it shows up on late television), although the movie was hampered by the performance of Marian Marsh, the studio's choice for the docile Trilby. Miss Marsh seemed to play her role in a state of perpetual shock. For some strange reason John reworked the same theme in his last Warner's commitment, *The Mad Genius,* after which he said good-by to the Warner Brothers' lot, which had moved to the former First National quarters in Burbank, and joined Lionel at the MGM studios in Culver City. He began work at a per picture salary of $150,000, a not inconsiderable sum as star salaries went in those early Depression days, and perhaps not justified by a strict box-office yardstick. John had distinctly lost his drawing power, while his elder brother, much like the tortoise overtaking the hare, was demonstrating a growing hold over audiences.

How account for the lapse of John's popularity? Spencer Berger's theory, which holds a good deal of water, was that "so much of his playing was a reflection of his own magnificently bizarre mind that he could not always furnish audiences with the happy comfort of identification. Used to dreaming sweet dreams with Crawford or Shearer, many filmgoers felt a wall between themselves and Barrymore's art." Plainly, then, John was ahead of his time, but his name alone still represented enormous prestige, and it was for this prestige that his earnings during a period of declining popularity for him came close to half a million dollars per year.

Arsene Lupin re-established his popularity to a degree. He and Lionel were given parts of equal importance, with Lionel as a hobbling, growling chief of detectives trying to snare the subtle, dexterous thief, played by John, who carried the proud name of the Duke of Charmerace and who prowled around as the notorious Arsene Lupin. True to Thalberg's dictate, John appeared in white tie and tails, and exchanged amorous banter with Karen Morley, who was supposed to be spying for Lionel and fell in love with the quarry. The plot of the picture may have been creaky, and the pace slow, but, as *Time* put it, "The pleasure consists in seeing both Barrymore brothers at the same time."

Following this the brothers were placed with Greta Garbo, Joan Crawford, and Wallace Beery in MGM's all-star cast version of *Grand Hotel*. Prior to this Lionel had acted (for the second time) with Garbo in *Mata Hari,* in which he found her aloof but unpretentious. Her wraithlike appearances and disappearances from the set were caused less by her mysterious desire to be alone, he discovered, than from simple shyness. After a time she began to react to Lionel's humor, and also to John's when all three were together in *Grand Hotel.*

This film, with its many stars, represented an attempt on the part of MGM to counteract the effects the Depression was having on the film industry. The more stars in a movie, was the theory, the more people who would pay to see it. Garbo had expected John to be self-important, but on meeting him and getting to know him she was surprised to find that he possessed an essential shyness not unlike her own. When together on the set they talked mainly about acting and other actors.

Garbo mentioned an actor she thought particularly good. "There are no good actors," John told her. "There are only bad ones who try to make themselves and others think they are good. Some can bring it off; others can't."

John was able to sense when she felt uncertain about her work in a scene. He once whispered to her just before a take, "You're the most enchanting person in the world." In the scene he subordinated his own acting to hers, and Garbo, aware of this, caused a sensation on the set when the scene was over by throwing her arms around John, kissing him, and exclaiming what a great artist he was.

When asked his opinion of Garbo by a reporter, John said: "She is a great lady and a great actress—and, the rest is silence."

While *Grand Hotel* was being made it was publicized as "the battle of the stars," and the apocryphal stories from the set told of how Garbo snubbed everyone with careful impartiality and of how John complained irritably about the lighting. Actually, on the very first day of shooting, John arrived early to greet Garbo, whom he had never met, and Garbo waited at the entrance to greet him and pay him the honor to which she thought him entitled by accompanying him to the set. A half hour went by before the situation was straightened out and they were presented to each other. Several months later some articles purportedly written by John (but done by a "ghost") appeared in a magazine, and in one of them was a reference to the lighting matter. John's version was that he was in total ignorance about such abstruse subjects as lighting, and that Bill Daniels, the photographer, had asked him how he preferred to be lighted. "I know how I want to look," he said he had told Daniels. "I'm fifty years old and I want to look like Jackie Cooper's grandson."

Gossip appointed Lionel as the peacemaker among the stars, and he was said to be the harmonizing influence on the set. Joan Crawford was particularly grateful for his attentions. Playing the role of a gaudy little stenographer, and attempting to compete with some of the best acting talents of her time, she was reassured by Lionel about her abilities. "Every single day Mr. Lionel Barrymore would say something nice to me," she confided to a friend. "He'd say, 'How are you, baby? I never saw you look so beautiful,' or he'd tell me that I had acted better than any other day that week. I know he didn't mean it, but it was nice to hear."

Lionel's interpretation of Kringelein, a pitiful clerk dying of heart disease and in quest of some gaiety before passing away, won him even more acclaim than he had received for *A Free Soul,* and many thought him the best of the glittering stars in the picture. His scene toward the end with Flaemmschen (Joan Crawford's role) was highly affecting, and there is a story behind how it became so. Lionel, as the clerk, timidly asks the stenographer, whose morals are on the loose side, if she will accompany him to Paris. When Lionel spoke the lines, Joan Crawford was so touched by his manner that she burst into genuine tears. Although tears were not called for in the script, the director hastily ordered the scene to be shot, and it became one of the film's best moments. For Lionel it was all in the day's work. No sooner were the lights dimmed when he was profanely searching for the mustache he had pasted on as part of his make-up. It had a way of constantly dropping from his lip and getting lost.

Garbo and John Barrymore also came in for plaudits when the premiere of the picture was held early in 1932. Garbo played a sad and weary Russian ballerina disconsolate over the loss of her lover. So disconsolate is she that it seems her career will soon go to pot. But at the Grand Hotel in Berlin she meets a charming baron, played by John Barrymore. Richard Watts, Jr., said of John's performance: "In the more conventional role of the unscrupulous baron he succeeds in being so charming and engaging a hero that he makes one forget that his part really is merely that of a conventional leading man. Here is Barrymore magic to an almost miraculous extent." Watts ended by saying that it was the acting that made *Grand Hotel* so triumphant a film.

John and Lionel were separated, but only temporarily, after finishing *Grand Hotel.* Lionel remained at MGM to make *Washington Masquerade* (in which he created another notable portrait as a congressman), while John went over to RKO to work for David O. Selznick in *Bill of Divorcement,* based upon the famous Clemence Dane play about an escaped mental patient who returns home to find his wife about to divorce him. The other key role, that of the father's grown daughter, was played by a newcomer to films, Katharine Hepburn. She, dripping sensitivity and understanding, gets her mother off the premises, and on learning of her father's hereditary condition and that she may well have the same taint, breaks off with her fiancé. At the end, daughter and father are seated together at the piano while she attempts to help him finish a long-abandoned piano sonata. The movie was immediately regarded as "historic" because it introduced an actress of uncommon talent and because John was said to give his greatest performance in it. On re-examination the film shows John giving a less than accurate portrait of a mental case, and being very careful again to show only his left profile. George Cukor, who was to become one of the most important of Hollywood's directors, put the stars through their paces in a style aimed at evoking pailfuls of tears from the women in the audience.

One widely circulated report emanating from the set was that John and Miss Hepburn got along badly. She was said to have remarked at the finish of the picture, "Thank God, I don't have to act any more with you." John was then said to have replied, "I didn't know you ever had, my dear."

According to George Cukor's vivid memory, the two got on very well, and the only real conflict between the two temperamental personalities came when "John made a pass at her and she promptly rejected it. After that, all went smoothly, and they were most considerate of each other during their scenes together."

In early June of 1932 the three Barrymores came together for *Rasputin and the Empress,* and the publicity mill now ground out tidbits to feed the Barrymore legend at an accelerated pace. The first item transmitted over the wires was that by virtue of being in the same picture together they, in the view of the film colony, had become "the royal family of Hollywood." Lionel, asked to comment on the prospect of three Barrymores acting together, remarked, "What poor, unsuspecting maniac of a director is going to take on that job?" He had not made the remark seriously but it was immediately flashed from coast to coast as a warning of what was to come.

When Ethel entrained for Hollywood she was advised by John to get off the train at Pasadena; otherwise she would run into a flock of reporters sent to cover her arrival. Some unkind remarks were made to the effect that John wasn't anxious for his sister to seize the major share of the publicity, and for that reason had advised his sister as he did, but this is highly unlikely. What is more likely is that he knew his sister was having difficult times and that she would look less than her best after a long train journey. At any rate, when John got to the Pasadena station he found several MGM executives there to greet Ethel and a large group of reporters attracted by the unusual gathering. As Ethel stepped off the train, John whispered in her ear, "Get Bill Daniels."

"Who is Bill Daniels?" Ethel asked.

"Garbo's photographer," John told her. "He'll make you look younger than Mona Lisa."

Ethel remembered this and astonished Thalberg at her first meeting with him by requesting the famous photographer. The request was granted.

At the station a reporter asked Ethel if she was worried about appearing with such expert scene stealers as her brothers. John answered for her: "You need not worry about Mrs. Colt. Our sister will be standing right before the camera, in front of us." Whether John was having his little joke, or whether he had by now a sensitive knowledge of the ways of movie publicity, he did his bit to fan the story of a feud among the Barrymores, and without benefit of a press agent. He had never hired one, nor had Lionel or Ethel. But it was obvious they needed no press agent for this film.

With Ethel on this trip west were her now fully grown children, Sammy, Jackie, and Ethel. Her Hollywood agent took the liberty of renting one of the largest Beverly Hills homes for her, complete with tennis court and swimming pool. Ethel, who went to work immediately with her customary energy, hardly so much as glimpsed these luxuries, but she had the satisfaction of knowing that her children—twenty-two, twenty, and eighteen, respectively—were enjoying their western vacation thoroughly. On her income tax report for 1932 Ethel put down receipts of $57,500 as the fee for her movie work, and against that reported expenses during the making of the movie as more than $60,000! Presumably this not only included the rental of the establishment in Beverly Hills, and expenses incurred in supporting her family, but the maintenance of her house and employees in Mamaroneck. As George Cukor put it, "All three Barrymores were slapdash about the way they spent their money."

When interviewed in the library of the Beverly Hills house, Ethel was very grand as befitted the queen of the theater who was about to play for the movie-struck masses the tragic queen of all the Russias. "I am happy to be making a picture," she said, "and I am especially glad to be in California with Jack and Lionel, and my charming young niece and my new nephew, besides my own children. I fully expect to see the gardens of this place, and the swimming pool, simply alive with Barrymores of all ages and denominations at all times."

She also gave her comments about her brothers' acting abilities: Lionel she regarded as the best living actor of his type, and John she loved most "when he isn't profiling himself through a role—handsome though his profile may be!"

The loyalty of the Barrymores to each other thus commented upon, newspaper readers were then warned to be on the lookout for a battle royal when shooting of the film began.

Public interest in the filming was further heightened by the nature of the story itself, which would unfold the wicked doings of the Russian monk Rasputin (who would be played by Lionel), his hypnotic influence over the Czarina (Ethel) and her sickly son, and the fate he met at the hands of Prince Paul, played by John and identified by him soon enough to an interviewer as a combination of Grand Duke Alexander and Prince Youssoupoff. He had known both personally, he said, and they used to quaff each other's health. Ethel, on the other hand, had met the Czarina at the time of Queen Victoria's funeral in London, and the two young women were supposed to have been look-alikes. She thought the Russian nobility were treated outrageously in the script and backed up her objections by telling Brabin, "You forget, I knew her Majesty personally!" She also informed some of the MGM powers that the Russian Czar and the reigning English family were related, and that embarrassment might result if the Czar and Czarina were too boldly caricatured. Bernard Hyman, supervisor of the production, might well have listened to Ethel's warning, but he didn't. She already had a reputation for imperiousness when she had calmly asked Thalberg for Bill Daniels as the cameraman and had gotten him.

Lionel, the only Barrymore who had never known any members of the Russian nobility, made up for his lack of personal acquaintance with genuine Romanoffs by reading everything he could find about them. Soon enough he was as much of an authority as Ethel (who, her brothers said, had read everything on and about everything), and one thing he did immediately was to correct the description in the script of his wardrobe. The script had Rasputin wearing sandals. Lionel changed this to boots. He quoted scholarly authority, too.

Ethel, who had a play to do for Arthur Hopkins in the fall, was adamant about remaining in California only the agreed eight weeks, and something close to panic developed at MGM when the script, one of a half-dozen versions, was found unsatisfactory. "When do we start?" Ethel asked impatiently after three days of inactivity. When she heard the script was still being worked into shape, she suggested that Charles MacArthur be put to work on it. Charles was married, after all, to Ethel's good friend and colleague, Helen Hayes. MacArthur was prevailed on to step in and make script changes, and Ethel gave him a quick filling in on recent Russian history as she saw it. The research department at MGM filled him in on the rest.

MacArthur barely managed to stay ahead of the actors, as his changes were delivered and then suggestions delivered to him for further revisions. Charles Brabin, who had once been dropped as the director of *Ben Hur,* was now dropped again for being too slow. A tight schedule had to be kept, not only to hold costs in line with Depression rigors, but to accommodate Ethel's timetable. The new director brought in was Richard Boleslavsky, an émigré Pole who had written a best-selling book, *Way of a Lancer,* and was reputed to know something about Czarist Russians. Boleslavsky was employed on the lot at the time as a writer. Ethel happened to notice him, recalled that he had once worked with the Moscow Art Theater, and mentioned this fact to Thalberg, who assumed it was a hint and had him on the set the next day.

When publicity about the Barrymores feuding with each other

built up to such a degree that people in Hollywood began referring to the picture as "disputin' and the Empress," the Barrymores one and all denied any such nonsense. Ethel said she hadn't been near a movie studio for fifteen years and naturally needed help in adjusting to the new sound technique, help freely supplied by her brothers. But she was not happy about the way she looked in the rushes. "I look like Tallulah's burlesque of me," she said of her broad gestures, and would watch rushes no more. Nor was she the least interested in seeing the picture when it was released. Although in the habit of seeing her brothers' movies, she had no time for this one.

Perhaps it was the Barrymore sense of humor and a certain amount of impishness that made each of the three contribute to the myth of their rivalry. A studio photographer saw John and Ethel sitting together without speaking and suggested that a nice photograph might result if John would tell his sister something.

"Tell her something!" John said. "I should say not. But I will *ask* her something."

On another occasion Ethel came out of her dressing room wearing her expensive jeweled white Czarina costume and was handed the most convenient chair. "John used that chair yesterday!" she said in regal tones. "Take the offensive thing away!" Only when the remark—evidently relayed by someone on the set—appeared in the columns did she explain she had meant it as a joke.

Lionel admitted to only one moment when he thought John was being a little too playful about detracting from his, Lionel's, performance in a scene they shared. Lionel had the words; John was to listen. But John did his listening with a good deal of activity. He kept touching Lionel's arm, at exactly the instant when his timing would be upset. Lionel went to Boleslavsky and suggested that his younger brother be kept in line. Boleslavsky appealed to John, who grinned, and cooperated from then on.

Lionel had by far the best part of the three, and he saw to it that he stole the show. John didn't have much to do beyond appear handsome, dependable, and loyal to the crown. Ethel was mainly seen looking stately and distressed, and seldom did her magnificent voice burst forth in its full range. But Lionel—he wore a beard, high

Russian boots, a tunic, and had a huge good time showing what an orgiastic beast he was, even at one point lasciviously attacking a young princess of the court (played fearfully by Diana Wynyard). The best moments in the film came when the prince played by John was called upon to kill the mad monk. The struggle went on and on, and probably a more protracted dispatching of the villain by the hero has never since been seen on the screen. At times it seemed that John despaired of ever being able to kill his brother.

The murder occurred in the cellar of the prince's palace, where John, secreted in the pantry, had been feeding Lionel poisoned cakes. The dissolute Lionel pawed at some pretty female companions and ate the cakes with huge relish, but with no immediate poisonous effects, and upon discovering that his revels were being held in the prince's home went after John with a gun, fired one shot, after which the poison began to take its belated effect. John, eager to have done with the nasty job, tried to hurry it along by pushing Lionel into the fireplace. Lionel writhed from his grasp, and John took up a poker and gave him a whack across the nose. Bending over the writhing Lionel on the floor, John departed from the script and muttered: "*There*, you son of a bitch." Lionel murmured back promptly, "Whoever calls his brother a son of a bitch is speaking autobiographically." But Lionel still refused to die. After mashing him some more John finally dragged him outside in the snow and pushed his head into an ice-filled stream, drowning him.

While Lionel met his end horribly, Ethel met hers with more dignity, dying before a firing squad, her executioners a motley group of revolutionaries.

Rasputin and the Empress was still short several of its scenes by the time Ethel was due to leave Hollywood, and there was no persuading her to stay. Off she went, dropping pithy quotes along the route of her train journey to New York. Later she claimed to have been misquoted when a Chicago newspaperwoman reported her as saying about the film acting of her brothers: "My two brothers are nothing more than overpublicized and overpaid factory hands." Sidney Skolsky, reaching her in New York in behalf of his Hollywood column, asked her to explain the remark, and she amended it to: "My two brothers have become an institution in Hollywood." At least that was what she had *meant* to say.

She did not, however, take back for some time another of her remarks about Hollywood. Asked to give her impression of the place, she said: "The people are unreal. The flowers are unreal. They don't smell. The fruit is unreal. It doesn't taste of anything. The whole place is a set, a glaring, gaudy, nightmarish set, built up in the desert."

When the movie was released the reviews reflected a wide-ranging variety of opinion. There were critics who said that the Barrymore acting, en masse, was superb. Other critics complained that the Barrymore acting was not up to their norm. The movie was said to be splendidly conceived in terms of its pageantry and crowd scenes, and it was also said to be a skimpy production, clearly showing MGM in an economy-minded mood. The movie was a better than average product of its period, handsome in its details, less static, less talky than the theatrically influenced films that came from the studios in the early thirties, but certainly warranting the attacks it received from many quarters for its historical inaccuracies. Alexander Bakshy complained in *The New Republic,* for instance, that Ethel's portrait of the Czarina was an extremely prettified version of the lady's true character. And Rasputin, he said, was a far more powerful and magnetic personality than the man portrayed by Lionel. Another critic suggested that Charles MacArthur be given an Academy Award for "the best original screenplay of the year."

But MGM was to run into some costly trouble, less for the film's inaccuracies than for its accuracies. Richard Watts, Jr., who was then the motion picture critic for the New York *Herald Tribune,* wrote: "It achieves one feat which is not inconsiderable. It manages to libel even the despised Rasputin."

Mr. Watts was proved prophetic about the possibility of libel actions against MGM. Fanny Holtzman, a New York lawyer specializing in libel cases, soon enough represented Prince Felix and Princess Irina Youssoupoff in an action against the film company. The Youssoupoffs hardly lacked justification, for large on the screen were the following words as a preface to the film, composed by its producer, Bernie Hyman: "This concerns the destruction of an empire, brought about by the mad ambition of one man. A few of the characters are still alive. The rest met death by violence."

What the Youssoupoffs were concerned about was not only violence but violation, and this came out in the trial held in London early in 1934. The plaintiff contended that the pretty young princess seized and raped by Lionel, the mad monk, could only have been the girl later married by Prince Youssoupoff, clearly identified by John Barrymore, by the way, as partial model for his own portrayal. Ergo, the reputation of the prince's wife had been besmirched. Award by the jury: $125,000 in damages. MGM was further on the spot, because suits were now pending against all the theaters showing the picture. A settlement was made by MGM.

The exact amount of this settlement MGM never chose to reveal. "However," wrote Bosley Crowther in *The Lion's Share,* "it was generally reported at the time that $750,000 was paid to the Princess and the company absorbed some $380,000 in 'costs.'" Ethel, upon hearing about this, said scornfully that it was the company's own fault. She had warned them about doing "some parts of the story," and she said that it was after she had left Hollywood that MGM had gone ahead and done them.

One long-lasting Hollywood precaution did come out of the Rasputin affair. The studios made sure to preface each of their films with a foreword along the following lines: "The events and characters in this film are fictional and any resemblance to characters living or dead is purely coincidental."

Ethel was never to appear with her brothers again, either on the stage or in films, but Lionel and John were together on two other occasions during the following year.

In *Night Flight,* made for MGM, John and Lionel ran an airline that flew over the dangerous Andes and shared their star billing with Clark Gable and Myrna Loy. In *Dinner at Eight* John was an aging actor invited to the elegant dinner party given by Billie Burke as the wife of Lionel, who played the owner of a shipping firm. John played a man who would not face up to the realities of his alcoholic addiction and the loss of his fame. Some thought the role tailored around his own personality, but it could as easily have been Maurice Costello who served as the model. It was another of those all-star

MGM casts: Marie Dressler, Jean Harlow, Wallace Berry, Lee Tracy, and Edmund Lowe attended the dinner party, too. Young Madge Evans was a pretty society girl enamored of the ham actor.

The scenes in which John bullied a bellhop into searching for bootleg whisky he could not pay for had, as might have been expected, a certain amount of realism in the playing. George Cukor, the director, claimed that the performance was modeled on John's father, and he also said that John himself was on the wagon at this time, although that wagon became harder and harder for him to stay on.

Cukor had come fresh from directing the film version of *The Royal Family*, with Fredric March playing the role fashioned blatantly upon the mannerisms of John Barrymore. And it might be mentioned that *Dinner at Eight* had been written for Broadway by the same playwrights, Edna Ferber and George S. Kaufman, who had pilloried the Barrymores in *The Royal Family*. Unlike their sister, neither of the Barrymore brothers was inclined to hold a grudge.

Fredric March had played the Barrymore role in a stage production of *The Royal Family*. Originally scheduled for the role in the New York stage version, other commitments had interfered, and he did not take it up until a company was formed to tour the West Coast. "I made no bones about making it a virtual impersonation of John," he said later. "I got into it the quick walk, the sudden turns, the view of his left profile, but one night in San Francisco I became a little nervous when I was informed that the original, John Barrymore himself, was out front. I had heard of his athletic prowess. However, I carried on. Then I was told he was coming backstage to see me. I waited in my dressing room, and in he walked, a much smaller man than I had thought he would be. He walked around me at first and sort of looked me over. Then he burst out, 'Christ, you were great! Come on, now, why the hell are you doing it?' He couldn't have been friendlier, though, although his language was more colorful in its profanity than I had thought so literate a theater and film star would possess. 'You know something,' he said. 'Chaplin loves to do an imitation of me. God, you should see it.' I did see that Chaplin imitation later on, and it was marvelous to behold, but I'm afraid it was a little too indelicate to describe accurately for posterity. No one, Chaplin told me, laughed harder at it than Barrymore."

Fredric March was free in admitting his gratefulness for the chance to imitate Barrymore, for through it he was able to gain his admittance to screen stardom. When he was a star himself, John Barrymore came to him and asked him for an autographed photograph for his daughter, Diana, who had taken a fancy to March on the screen. "He couldn't have been more serious about the request," the amazed Fredric March said, "and behaved as though I was doing him an enormous favor."

When he co-starred with Lionel Barrymore later in *Road to Glory*, March found Lionel as modest about his acting ability and attainments as John. "In fact," said March, "they were both downright disrespectful about the craft of acting, as it applied to themselves."

THE AUTUMN
GARDENS

chapter XXI

"THE NEXT YEAR was a very bad and harrowing time," was the way
Ethel Barrymore spoke of it when asked to recall the time when the
banks closed their doors, when audiences brought scrip to the box
office to pay for their tickets. She was speaking of 1933, but the lean
times extended for many more months than twelve. She had rushed
back to the East after finishing her film work in *Rasputin and the
Empress* in August of 1932, eager to take to the Broadway stage
again in *Encore* and to renew her association with Arthur Hopkins
and Robert Edmond Jones. But it was late October before rehearsals
began, and the play was too weak a vehicle to take to New York,
where it was scheduled, but did not open. Ethel always maintained
that it was a very funny play. It told the story of an opera singer who
kept getting younger and younger, marrying again and again until, on
her last wedding march, she appeared in a white organdy dress with
a blue sash. She was surrounded by four leading men, and such good
comedy talents as Josephine Hull, and Georgie Drew Mendum, but
either the play was not as funny as Ethel thought it was or the times
were not right for it.

Hopkins gave up on the play after a brief tour which reached as
far as Chicago (where the banks closed), and Ethel decided she
would become her own production manager and tour the vehicle
under a new title, *An Amazing Career*. A new opening was sched-

uled for Springfield, Massachusetts, on March 15, 1933, and that
was the last that was heard of *An Amazing Career*. Now, with the
house in Mamaroneck to maintain, and a town house on East Thirty-
sixth Street in Manhattan that she rented for the winter months,
Ethel discovered that funds were a problem. Regretfully, living in
Manhattan had to be given up for lack of money to pay rent. Ethel
retreated with Sammy, Sister, and Jackie to Mamaroneck. One cold
night the lights in the big house went off. The first lady of the
American theater was forced to sit in the dark because she had failed
to meet her bills for electricity.

To make matters worse, the Bureau of Internal Revenue chose
this time to persistently press claims against Ethel for nonpayment
of some of her taxes during the 1921–1929 period when times had
been rosy and prosperous for Ethel as well as most everyone else.
Ethel never lost her majesty during these trying periods. She had
managed before and she would manage again. Mrs. Jacques Gordon,
one of her closest companions, never heard Ethel talking about
money, even when things were roughest. Mrs. Gordon was more
likely to learn of bare cupboards from the younger Ethel, who had
a keen sense of practicalities and didn't believe in acting like royalty
when there was no economic basis for it.

The public learned of Ethel's neediness when a court petition to
make use of the annual income from her youngest son's $50,000
trust fund was reported to the newspapers. Sammy Colt, now
twenty-three, was already receiving a small and handy income; Sister
was due to receive hers when she reached her twenty-first birthday
in April. These yearly sums of $2500 were necessary, Ethel said,
for the protection of her children. One thing is certain: Ethel would
not have stooped to beg the courts for money if it was only herself
involved. But a kind of wild protectiveness came over her when she
felt her children were threatened.

"The real greatness of this woman showed during the Depression,"
Mrs. Gordon said. "She had seemingly lost her audiences, her enormous income, virtually her way of life. And yet you never noticed a
change in Ethel's manner. She smoked her cigarettes, listened to
the radio—she was an avid radio fan—loved to listen to the ball games

and talk about them, attended concerts as before. She was mad for Toscanini, and knowing this my husband and I once got tickets for her, too, when we attended a series of Beethoven concerts he gave at Carnegie Hall with the Philharmonic. The best seats we could obtain were in the second tier boxes. We went up with her, and Ethel noticed that the seats were in the *second* tier, not the first. Someone came into the box she didn't know and sat in one of the chairs. Ethel became nervous, tense, fidgeted with a necklace she wore, then suddenly got up and said, 'I can't stand this,' and went home. She just couldn't be happy sitting in a second tier box!"

Ethel's daughter still has vivid memories of this period in her mother's life. "No one," said Mrs. Miglietta in 1962, "has to tell a great star when she's through. She hears the sound of silence, and no sound is so terrible to her as silence. For Mother, it was as though her life's work had gone out of the window. A whole year, two years to go through without stepping on the stage of the theater that is named for you! You know fear and terror. The end has begun, and in silence. That big financial scale you're living on is no longer possible, and the maids must go, and your beloved chauffeur can't be paid. And suddenly you're not invited to places, and parties."

Cornelia Otis Skinner, who knew Ethel well, said: "Ethel's performances, even during her leanest years, were invariably good, but somehow that magic spark was missing. It seemed as though she not only struggled against odds of inadequate scripts, but against some kind of spiritual weariness. What caused this we will never know. This lady was both gallant and reticent."

How remarkable that she had retained her place this long, when newer and younger stars, such as Katharine Cornell, Helen Hayes, Tallulah Bankhead, and Gertrude Lawrence were her competition. Where, it might have been asked, were Ethel's contemporaries, great stars such as Maude Adams, Annie Russell, Elsie Ferguson, Julia Marlowe? Gone, all of them. Dead or retired. Gone were Hattie Williams, Marie Doro, Clara Bloodgood. They had been great Frohman ladies, too. The winsome Ethel, still beautiful, had reached her mid-fifties, and rather than occupy a box in the second tier she would stay at home.

Where had her money gone? The agents from the Bureau of

Internal Revenue scrutinized her books and found evidence of royal squandering. Not jewels, but keeping on the payroll maids, cooks, gardeners, a chauffeur, no matter how her income had fluctuated from year to year. The houses she rented had to be furnished well, and one year she took to keeping a Siamese cat, and when the cat had kittens she took with her on tour that whole feline family and rented hotel suites large enough to keep the cats in a separate room. There were some missing funds. Where were they, the agents wanted to know. Ethel dismissed the matter like a lioness brushing off gnats. One of her company managers had absconded with a sum of money. She hadn't been able to do much about it. The man and the money had simply disappeared.

"She was an easy touch," said her daughter.

And a poor drinker. For this was the time in her life that Ethel now and then turned for consolation to the bottle. Mrs. Jacques Gordon guides us over these shoals. "We took a house in Connecticut in 1933," she said, "my husband and I, and Ethel once came to visit us there. She seemed strange to me in her manner, and my husband noticed it too and said to me privately, 'She's drinking.' 'You're crazy,' I told him, for I had never seen her do more than sip at something placed in her hand at a party. But we noticed how frequently she went upstairs to her room. I decided to search the room and finally I found the brandy bottle she had hidden. There might have been two or three other periods during the next few years when she would take to the brandy bottle, but never for more than a month or two. She would decide not to drink, and she wouldn't for a long time until one of those dreadful periods of discouragement would hit her."

Ethel's whole personality would change under the influence of brandy, said Mrs. Gordon, and it would take no more than a drink or two to effect the change. "She'd grow unusually sensitive to anything someone might say, and want to pick a quarrel over it. It was a curious thing. Ethel always knew she shouldn't drink, and once she told me, 'No one in my family should drink, because it's poison to us.' How vividly she illustrated that to me one evening when we went together to a New Year's Eve party given by one of her grand friends. Her host handed her a glass of champagne, and she took it, because it was the occasion of a toast to her. When the toast was made she took a sip of the champagne. I drank my glass, but Ethel held on to hers, and when mine was empty she handed me her almost full glass and said: 'Let's swap.' The rest of the evening she held on to the empty glass. Presently we left. Waiting for the elevator in the hall of the apartment house, I looked at her and cried out, 'My God, what is that?' For Ethel's neck and the upper part of her bosom were one terrible blotch of blood red. 'You're the witness, Ruth,' Ethel said, 'you know how much champagne I drank tonight. That's what one sip will do.'

"She claimed that all the Barrymores broke out that way after one sip of something alcoholic. Then how did she manage to drink later on? Their systems adjusted to it somehow if they kept on drinking. It was that first drink that would cause the mass of eruption. Ethel finally, it must have been in the late thirties, made a stern vow to herself that she would never again in all her life touch a drink that contained alcohol, and there are many who can attest to her keeping that vow, even at a time when it was rumored on Broadway that she was as unreliable as, say, Laurette Taylor."

In July of 1933 Ethel took her old reliable little vehicle, *The Twelve Pound Look,* to the Capitol Theatre in New York for a five-a-day vaudeville appearance. She shared billing with *Storm at Daybreak,* an MGM movie starring Kay Francis and Nils Asther. Georgie Drew Mendum was in the cast with her, as was her stage manager, Eddie McHugh. Ethel came on following a short subject which showed kangaroos holding a track meet and after orchestra leader Phil Spitalny had rendered his orchestration of the "St. Louis Blues." Notwithstanding, Ethel held forth with skill and distinction. A reporter sent to cover the event wrote for the New York *World* later: "You admire her for it. You admire her in spite of this, of that, and of the other thing."

While making her appearance in New York summer vaudeville she took rooms at a hotel on upper Broadway, a hotel which can be said to have lacked the distinction which Ethel formerly would have regarded as customary. Not in the least disturbed, Ethel had some furniture brought in from the Mamaroneck house, and from her top floor windows was able to have a nice view of the Hudson

River at sunset. Lacking her usual maid service, she depended on her faithful retainer Schotzie, who would come in, fix her meals, and buy her the cigarettes she now smoked constantly and with little damage to her marvelous voice. (Jean Muir, the actress, met her at a party, and Ethel approved of her neither smoking nor drinking. "They're both bad for an actress's voice," she grandly told the young star, and immediately lit a cigarette.)

"She lived at that hotel like a queen," said the admiring Mrs. Gordon, "and never once apologized for it."

But following the vaudeville appearance, long months of inactivity stretched before Ethel. If the theater was bad, vaudeville appeared all but dead, and it began to look as though she should have made her peace with the movies long ago. Ethel proudly refused to bow. The theater was her life. Now her son Sammy was making a bid (one to be short-lived) to follow the Drew-Barrymore tradition. He had joined Eva Le Gallienne's Civic Repertory Theatre and after its demise during the early years of the Depression went with her on tour in productions of *Romeo and Juliet* and *Alice in Wonderland*.

When the latter play opened in Philadelphia, Ethel went there to see her son, and on December 1, 1933, Ethel made the headlines again. Miss Le Gallienne had, the previous spring, made an engagement to speak at the annual meeting of the Philadelphia Lecture Assembly. The evening came, and Miss Le Gallienne failed to appear. The clubwomen, from prominent Philadelphia families, were much wroth, and bitter remarks were made from the speaker's platform concerning her absence. The following afternoon Eva Le Gallienne came before the group to apologize over a mix-up in dates on her calendar, gave her talk on her new plans for forming a national theater repertory company, and introduced Ethel Barrymore as "an added attraction."

Ethel, as it turned out, had not liked the tone of the proceedings, not at all. In fact, she thought some remarks by the speaker introducing Miss Le Gallienne somewhat cavalier, even though the actress had made a few tart remarks herself about the Assembly's lack of faith in her.

Ethel rose to speak, and what she said made the good ladies of Philadelphia gasp in astonishment.

"I don't know why we bother to speak to you," Ethel said, her great eyes blazing. "Miss Le Gallienne and I do you an honor to be here at all. You don't know anything. You don't understand anything. You don't appreciate anything, and you never will. I have given thirty-five years of my life to the theater. I don't know why we do it. We get no thanks. I think Miss Le Gallienne has done you a great honor. I don't know why. I don't know why anyone should honor you. You do not come to see my plays. You should be happy to come here for two or three times in order to hear Miss Le Gallienne once!"

The fire died from Ethel's eyes for a moment. "My grandmother had a theater here in Philadelphia," she said, more softly, "when people here in Philadelphia still had manners. But then, you wouldn't know anything about that. It doesn't matter." Her voice died away. She took her seat. The three hundred ladies of the Lecture Assembly cast their cold eyes on her.

After the meeting Mrs. Houston DeCoursey fumed, "It was the most atrociously impolite thing I ever heard." The chairlady, when asked by a reporter to comment, said: "This is the greatest insult a Philadelphia audience ever had." Mrs. Waters was evidently unaware of the spate of jokes about Philadelphia so frequently recounted by actors. "I can't imagine," said one of the ladies, "how we ever came to consider Ethel Barrymore an actress." Ethel had encountered that very problem on her first starring appearance in Philadelphia, in *Captain Jinks of the Horse Marines*.

The newspapers not only carried quietly gleeful accounts of the big Philadelphia fuss about Ethel, but queried other actors on their views of the matter. In Hollywood Fredric March said: "I am sure Miss Barrymore was right. She always is, and she is to be congratulated on coming to the aid of a fellow actor."

Wynne Gibson said: "An actress who agrees to give a lecture to a woman's organization on the theater deserves anything that happens to her."

The mortified Miss Le Gallienne said that she had neither planned nor expected Ethel to rise so thunderously to her defense, and she chose to forget "the tempest in a tea cup."

And the upshot of it was that Ethel now had a reputation for arrogance, in addition to this and that and the other thing. She decided she would go to England and present *The Twelve Pound Look* at the Palladium in London. There she met more disaster, for the London vaudeville audiences failed to appreciate a lady who was willing to work for twelve pounds a month at a time when hundreds of thousands of men couldn't find jobs. One English critic, Hannen Swaffer, delivered a scorching attack on the creaky stage vehicle she brought to England, and when her engagement at the Palladium was terminated he wrote even more nastily that she had been removed to "make way for a dog act." Ethel took this in stride. All right, they didn't like the play, the English thought it was old-fashioned. "I don't know what they didn't say about it," she wrote afterward in reasonably good humor. But it was obvious that *The Twelve Pound Look* could no longer be depended upon as a stopgap for her.

In May, 1934, she came home on the *Berengaria,* her most pleasant memory of the trip to England a visit with her old friend Winston Churchill at his Chartwell estate. Winston was out of power, too, and Ethel took some gloomy satisfaction in the fact that his, like her own, was a voice in the wilderness crying out against evil times. After a quiet summer of retrenchment at Mamaroneck, she appeared as the Duchess of Parma with Eva Le Gallienne, her good friend, in Rostand's *L'Aiglon* with the Civic Repertory Theatre company at the Broadhurst. Ethel's daughter appeared in the play, too, as a ballet dancer, a part for which she had trained by taking ballet lessons. Ethel was pained that everyone took it for granted that Sister should be able to make her entrance *en pointe.*

And now there were no more plays, none at all, the idleness broken only with occasional visits during the warm months to Alexander Woollcott's island farm, Neshobe, on Lake Bomoseen, Vermont (Woollcott had gotten back into her good graces through his appreciation of her work in *The Kingdom of God*), and to Katharine Cornell's place on Martha's Vineyard. And she was always more than welcome at the Sands Point estate of Margaret and Herbert Swope.

But for the most part life took on a bitter cast for the great lady, as unemployed now as any coal miner. What seemed to her like ridiculous suits for money, for unpaid bills, plagued her endlessly, and she would deal with these matters with outward good humor, and sometimes private rage. The government claim against her had grown to nearly one hundred thousand dollars, and if she had been a collector of jewels these could have been attached. But how seize a collection of old prize fight pictures in the billiard room in the Mamaroneck house, or the beautiful plum trees she had nurtured over the years? New York State claimed taxes amounting to fifteen hundred dollars and threatened to take the amount out of the Taylor's Point property, "What about it?" she was asked by a reporter. "I don't know anything about it," she replied.

"How did you handle all that?" Adela Rogers St. Johns asked her later. Had she some rule, some philosophy she had worked out?

"I don't think in those terms exactly," Ethel said. "You must learn above all not to waste your soul and your energy, your brain and strength, on all the little things. You must learn day by day, year by year, to broaden your horizon. The more things you love, the more you are interested in, the more you enjoy, the more you are indignant about—the more you have left when anything happens."

She thought about it and found she had more to say. "I suppose the greatest thing in the world is loving people, wanting to destroy the sin and not the sinner. And not to forget that when life knocks you to your knees, which it always does and always will—well, that's the best position in which to pray, isn't it? On your knees."

It was on her knees that Ethel began to recoup her strength, little by little, but it was not easy, and it was very slow.

Alexander Woollcott may have helped at a critical point. Having broadened his own horizons beyond that of drama critic, he had taken to radio and had become a host and a "personality" known to millions. Presiding over a mammoth holiday radio show, which was supposed to dazzle the nation's listeners, he brought on Ethel as a guest. "There are certain sounds," he said into the microphone that carried his voice to millions, "that seem to me characteristically American. One of them is the soughing wind in the pine forests. Another is the voice of Ethel Barrymore."

Ethel then stepped to the microphone to make her debut in a new medium, radio. She gave some readings from *The Kingdom of God*.

This led to other occasional radio appearances on the Radio Theatre of the Air and as a comedienne on Ben Bernie's popular program. In the winter of 1935–1936 she went out on the road briefly in *The Constant Wife* and came home little the richer for it. The stage, she decided, was entering a phase of atrophy, and it was time for her to make her retirement. She chose to make her announcement in an odd way. On Ben Bernie's program during the summer of 1936 the guests, of whom she was one, were playing a silly game of Knock-Knock. When it was Ethel's turn she said that first she had an announcement to make. "This is my last public appearance," she said. Further, she would now devote her life to teaching others the art of acting. That was all, and turning to Bernie she proceeded to play the game. "Knock, knock," she said.

"Who's there?" Ben Bernie asked.

"Saul."

"Saul who?"

"Saul there is—there isn't any more."

That was the way she had chosen to end, not with a bang but with a pun.

Ben Bernie's hook-up was nationwide, and millions had heard this renowned Barrymore declare that she was available to help the young. She clarified her announcement for reporters who called the station immediately wanting to know more. "I hope," she said graciously, "that any and all young people who want help or encouragement in the line of speech, dramatics, radio or public presentation will call on me. I'll be so happy to help them."

When a staff writer for the New York *World-Telegram* came to see her at Mamaroneck in August, she received him on the wide enclosed porch, smiled, served and drank iced tea, said she really was through with the stage, that there would be no annual series of farewell tours à la old Mrs. John Drew, and that all she wished was "to leave them smiling." She was a little vague about just how she would do her teaching of the young, but she thought her school would probably get under way in October. "There will have to be a number of courses," she thought. "Fencing for one—if actors are going to play Shakespeare they must be at home in Shakespeare—and dancing, and languages. There are four little theaters in Mamaroneck, and we will put on plays with an audience, because not even a rehearsal is any good unless it's on a stage."

Then came the deluge of letters. The Mamaroneck postman was one day bowed down by the weight of hundreds of letters addressed to Miss Barrymore. The avalanche of mail increased. Some of the letter writers begged merely for advice, others for personal coaching. A few said they would be glad to take her course if she would guarantee them a place in a Broadway hit.

Behind the postmen came literally hundreds of young men and women. They came right to Ethel's porch steps and said they were ready to be molded into the shapes she thought most desirable for them. A boy walked all the way to Mamaroneck from Boston, and Ethel thought he deserved a private audience.

It turned out that what he really wanted to do was to write popular songs and he had thought Ethel would be able to give him the professional touch he needed.

Gilbert Miller, noticing the sudden rash of newspaper articles about Ethel's plans for active retirement, let it be known that she need not retire if she did not wish to. In fact he had a play called *Promise* that would be absolutely right for her to make an emergence from retirement. The play was sent to Ethel. She declined.

The Studio of Acting, a theatrical school with an impressive advisory board and a roster of fifty pupils, next contacted Ethel and, in the person of Leighton Rollins, the managing director, offered her an honored place on the school's faculty. This she decided to accept. It would make it so much easier for her to function as a teacher, and she explained a little apologetically that "these people with their studio have what I suppose you'd call a working plant. It's all organized. And I was so overwhelmed in Mamaroneck."

The first classes she was scheduled to teach were to take place on October 29, 1936. She would direct a studio production of *Captain Jinks of the Horse Marines.*

She never gave that first class. Instead, when October rolled around she was embarked on a twenty-six-week series of radio programs of her own on the NBC-WJZ network. The idea of the series was that each Wednesday evening she would revive plays in which she had acted on Broadway. Bayer's Aspirin sponsored the thirty-minute program and agreed that Ethel would act her old roles in the chronological order of her appearance in them. She naturally began with *Captain Jinks,* which suffered from age and from being constricted to thirty minutes less commercial. Ethel, fifty-seven years old, allowed no audience to watch her as she played the role of Madame Trentoni once again. "There's no such thing as an old lady's voice," she told an interviewer. "It doesn't have to be. If you've got artistry enough in the first place and physical fitness enough in the second place your voice can be exactly the same at a hundred as it was at twenty."

The radio series, while not enormously popular, enabled Ethel to make at least a slight recovery from her financial difficulties. She moved into town again, staying at the Elysée Hotel in a large suite that had been done over for Tallulah Bankhead a few years before. The management let out the suite at a reasonable rental to Ethel, and there were times when they discreetly overlooked lapses in rent-paying. Ethel began to emerge from her shell. She missed not a game of the 1936 World Series, went to the prize fights as before, attended the Philharmonic symphony concerts, and was an avid fan of *Gang-Busters* on the radio. She announced that she was writing her memoirs, a task that took her more than fifteen years to complete, even though she didn't believe in worrying about dates and strict matters of chronology.

In 1937 she made a settlement of her tax difficulties with the Bureau of Internal Revenue for $7,500, a sum the bureau was quite pleased to receive for reasons which were included in the report the agents wrote when they closed the file on her case. "It is generally known," the astute gentleman of the Revenue Service wrote, "that her popularity has been on the decline for the past several years. At the present time there is practically no demand for her services. And she has no future on the stage." These agents of kind heart actually wondered in the report if they should be so cruel as to take the seventy-five hundred dollars from her, but, they said, "If the money is not accepted she would in all probability squander that in the same manner as she has vastly greater amounts in the past."

With the matter settled, Ethel returned to the stage again.

The occasion was the Theatre Guild's production of Sidney

Howard's *The Ghost of Yankee Doodle*, meant as Howard's contribution to solving the problems presented by the dangerous growth of fascism in the world. The play was full of melancholy brooding and it also had some comedy, as it showed a wealthy family of American liberals attempting to adjust to the war spirit of the times. Ethel's role was that of a gracious lady who presided over the family squabbles, and while the play was not very good nor much of a success, there was not a critic who did not have something of a rave for her.

Brooks Atkinson joined the Barrymore admirers by saying, "Miss Barrymore presides over the most attractive role with the patrician tossing of the head, the flashing eyes, and the quiet grace of the celebrated Barrymore style." John Mason Brown thought her more than enough to make a visit to the Guild Theatre "rewarding, if not compulsory." John Anderson thought her performance "brilliantly sustained." The old Barrymore magic was working again.

From behind the scenes comes a little portrait of Ethel in action at this time, provided by her nephew, John Drew Devereaux, the grandson of John Drew. He had became an actor and took the part of her son in the play.

"It was the first time I had ever seen the workings of Aunt Ethel at close range," he said. "It was very exciting and also terrifying. What was exciting about it was that she seemed to have, as I suppose all great stage stars do, at least five different points of concentration. She could be playing a scene with you and seemingly looking right into the innermost depths of your eyes, but if somebody moved over on the other side of the stage she would notice it immediately. They say that eyes can flash, but I've only known two people who had that sort of eyes—my mother (Louise Drew) and Aunt Ethel. They could both, as we used to say, quell you with a look. They'd just look at you and all of a sudden fifteen hundred watts would blaze out at you. Most people, when this happened, just stopped what they were doing, or at least they stopped talking.

"The most terrifying thing that happened during the run took place on opening night in New York. The amusing lines were sprinkled throughout the play and I happened to have one of them. Well, during that opening night one of the members of the cast, a girl—Barbara Robbins, I think it was—stepped on my laugh, and I remember that all of a sudden everything seemed to stop in time. The rest of the world was going on, but in this fifteen-foot circle everything came to a screeching halt. Aunt Ethel took about two or three steps down toward the apron, turned around, looked at the girl and said: 'Don't you ever do that again!' then stepped back and went right on with the scene. The poor girl was absolutely appalled. I couldn't help remembering a story my mother had once told me about how Ethel had dealt with some people in a stage box who had come in late and were chattering away and rustling programs. She had with her in that play a marvelous old character actor, Charles Cherry, who was a little hard of hearing. It got so that Ethel couldn't stand it any more, so she stepped down to the apron, made a sort of deprecatory gesture to the audience and looked up at the box. 'Excuse me,' she said. 'I can hear every word you're saying, but Mr. Cherry is slightly hard of hearing. I wonder if you would speak up for him?' She stepped back, went on with the play, and you can be sure those people were the very models of silent attentiveness.

"But to get back to this moment on opening night: You see, Aunt Ethel insisted upon a rigid adherence to stage etiquette. She of course thought that the squelch had been done on purpose by the young actress, and as far as I know she never spoke to her again during the run of the play. She felt it was an absolutely unforgivable breach of stage behavior. I went several times to her dressing room saying such things as 'Aunt Ethel, I know she didn't do it deliberately,' and 'If anyone were going to do such a thing to me they certainly would not do it when you were right there on the stage watching . . .' But Aunt Ethel would not relent. She had formed her conclusions and stuck to them."

Another thing she insisted upon was that no one, no stagehand or member of the cast, was to be allowed in the wings when she performed. The one exception to this rule was her stage manager, Eddie McHugh. If anyone else happened to be there and she looked up and saw the offending person, Eddie McHugh was informed about it and requested to deliver the appropriate rebuke.

After that opening night, family members and close friends repaired to Ethel's quarters at the Elysée Hotel, bringing with them the apples that had been sent to the dressing room and that could now be eaten on the assumption that the performances (of Ethel and John Drew Devereaux) were worthy of the honor. Now there was no more talk of retirement. *The Ghost of Yankee Doodle* did not stay beyond its subscription season, but Ethel made it plain that her faith in the theater had revived and that she was ready for suitable roles.

As it turned out, Lionel helped bring one to her. In England making a movie he had seen a play called *Whiteoaks,* based on the Mazo de la Roche *Jalna* novels, he had been impressed by the character of the grandmother, a 102-year-old woman. Ethel happened to notice in a newspaper that Lionel was in New York on his way to Hollywood and called him up to ask politely, "May I come to see you?"

"No," Lionel said. "I'll come to see you." He came to see Ethel and told her about the play and the part of the old grandmother.

Not much time passed before Victor Payne-Jennings, a London manager, called up Ethel, told her he wanted to produce *Whiteoaks* in New York, and asked her how she felt about playing a woman more than a hundred years old.

"I'd be perfectly delighted to play her," the fifty-nine-year-old Ethel responded. "That's just what I feel."

When the play opened at the Hudson (she had opened the theater in *Cousin Kate* thirty-five years before) in March of 1938, several of the critics had commented on Lionel's extraordinary resemblance to Ethel when he had disguised himself as an old woman in a movie called *The Devil Doll* a few years back. "One thing is certain," John Mason Brown said. "Miss Barrymore cannot and does not look like Miss Barrymore in her latest vehicle." John Anderson wrote: "She thwacked her progeny with her walking stick and tossed her fortune about, laughing at their discomfort, tippling port . . . This Mrs. Methuselah is a careful portrait of the sere and yellow leaf, a woman with one foot in the grave and the other on the second act." In other words, Ethel had come to peace with herself and was doing exactly what a great actress should be doing when her beauty has mellowed —she was playing a character.

S. J. Woolf of the *New York Times,* calling on her in her dressing room between the second and third acts (by which time Gran

Whiteoaks had expired, leaving her fortune to a weakling grandson), was surprised to find a tall, lithe woman puffing a cigarette instead of the limping harridan he had seen on the stage. He was further surprised when Ethel took her curtain call in character, but without lining her face.

"I don't use much make-up," she explained. "I whiten my own teeth to a pure white to make them look false. For the rest, I depend upon facial expression. Acting, after all, is like the other arts. Its purpose is to create an impression, to get over the footlights the feeling of age or youth, of good or evil, of happiness or sorrow."

The critics were hardly more than lukewarm in their appraisal of the play, but Ethel's impersonation was striking enough to keep it on Broadway for the remainder of the season. Then she took the play into summer stock (summer theaters were beginning to shed their amateur status and to attract established stars) and after that on a forty-four-week tour of the country, some of which she did by car and some by train. She arranged with Actors' Equity to pay off in installments the debts to actors she had incurred when she had taken *Encore* over from Arthur Hopkins in 1933. She was solvent again, and it must be said that she did not exactly husband her resources. The watchful Bureau of Internal Revenue of course made sure to claim every last cent of its tithes from her income. In fact, after the government had declared her through as an actress and not of much account as a taxpayer, she proceeded to pay many hundreds of thousands of dollars in taxes during the remainder of her career!

On Tuesday, August 15, 1939, she reached the age of sixty, and naturally it was the time for the newspapers to remind her of that fact, and to get her to appraise the stage from the vantage point of her long experience. "The stage hasn't changed," she said, in reply to a question, "since I first began to act. There are still good plays and bad plays, good actors and bad actors. But there is one thing that grates on me, probably because of the way in which I was brought up: some of the language that goes on today. When I was young I was taught there was such a thing as good taste. I don't think bad taste is any more excusable on the stage than in the living room. However, I have noticed that this trend is not confined to the theater."

She regretted the passing of old-fashioned vaudeville, saw hope in the growth of little theaters around the country. She explained that by vaudeville she meant "those marvelous shows when great actors and actresses did not hesitate to appear on a bill with comic acrobats and trained seals.

"Now I'll tell you something few people know," she said. "I have always had a hankering to be a sculptor. Perhaps some day or other, when I am too old to play the part of a hundred-year-old woman, I'll get myself a hunk of clay and some modeling tools and try my hand at it." (She never did.)

She had some seasoned remarks to make on acting. "Thinking, thinking—that is what acting is all about. It is the only thing in acting. The thought running through the person's mind is what the actor has to capture. You pounce on that thought; you reach out and grasp it and never let it go. If you can't do that you had better stay at home. You aren't an actor. At rehearsals one must do a great deal of that kind of thinking. But the real time for thinking is at the performance. Most of all at the performance, because the actor's thought has to grip the audience. It's this that does it." She tapped her forehead with a forefinger. "Years of experience at acting give a player the ability to call on his thought and be sure of it. It's like a good serve at tennis. But when you have done your thinking all through a play, leave it behind you in the theater. Don't take it home with you. I don't like to hear people talk about living their parts all day long. It smacks to me of the good old amateur."

A few weeks later Ethel turned on her radio one morning and heard the voice of an old English gentleman, Neville Chamberlain, announcing that England was at war. "Once more," she said with a sigh, then buried herself in work again. This time it was another old woman she played, only ninety-seven, not a matriarch but a woman of the South African soil, whose mind wandered and whose ears heard ghosts. The play was called *Farm of Three Echoes*, and John Mason Brown said about it that in any other hands but Ethel's the "South African melodrama would have been shown up as the arrant, often boring, hokum piled on hokum that it is." But Ethel acted with such relish, used her "magical voice with such effect," brought such energy and distinction to her characterization that Brown hated to see her leave the stage at all. Otherwise, he said, Noel Langley, the author, had "hit below the veldt." A psychiatrist wrote Ethel that her performance was "the most magnificent portrayal of senility he had ever seen." She was delighted to hear it.

But she was still waiting for a play. She trudged on gamely through these minor efforts, but instead of playing *Farm of Three Echoes* during the summer of 1940 in the little playhouses of the eastern tour, for which she had been booked by her agent and friend, Johnson Briscoe, she decided to bring her Lady Teazle out of mothballs. Day Tuttle, who ran the Mt. Kisco (N. Y.) playhouse, had requested her for a week. No, she said, she would tour the play for the entire summer. She did the direction herself, again under the name of E. M. Blythe, with the assistance of Eddie McHugh, and had herself a royal time, playing in Mt. Kisco, in White Plains and Westport, and journeying as far north as Skowhegan, Maine.

During the previous spring a play by Emlyn Williams, *The Corn Is Green,* had been submitted to her by one of several producers who tried to cast the central role of Miss Moffat, a Welsh schoolteacher, without success. The play had been a great hit in London, but at that time it was thought that British plays did not travel well to Broadway. Dame Sybil Thorndyke had played the role in London but couldn't come to New York because of travel restrictions. Helen Hayes had been offered the play, but she had had misgivings about taking on the role. There were other prominent actresses who were approached, and who said No to doing it. Ethel would have been considered sooner, but she had had such a long string of flops or at best semi-successes (from the producer's viewpoint) that she was not regarded as the best of all possible risks in a theater now less financially healthy than ever before. When the script was first given to her to read, Ethel was forced to say that she had a previous commitment, one she was loyal to, to Vincent Sheean's play, *International Incident,* and she sent back *The Corn Is Green. International Incident* was regarded as a trifle and lasted only fifteen performances. At the end of the summer Herman Shumlin, who had taken over the rights to *The Corn Is Green,* approached Ethel and talked about the play with her at the Colony Club, of which Ethel was a long-time member. They reached an agreement. She would receive a thousand dollars a week against seven and a half per cent of the gross receipts, an arrangement which turned out to be very advantageous to Ethel. It was also specified that Eddie McHugh would be her stage manager.

Ethel rather startled Shumlin when she gave him her opinion of how the play should be directed, telling him, "It's a simple play about a simple Englishwoman with a gift for teaching, who gets a wonderful chance."

The play turned out to be a wonderful chance for Ethel, too, as soon became apparent when the play tried out in Baltimore, Washington, and Philadelphia. The reception was warm, the receipts gratifying. Opening night in New York at the National Theatre was on November 26, 1940. An incident occurred just as Ethel was scheduled to make her first entrance. McHugh, the stage manager, happened to pick up a chair before the curtain rose and replace it in the position it was supposed to be in. It was against union rules for anyone but a stagehand to touch a prop, something that an electrician who walked by realized. He immediately reported it to the stagehands' union delegate, who said that the curtain could not be raised until the matter was dealt with properly. Ethel's topaz eyes blazed with anger, and she delivered another famous slap, this time to the delegate's face. That was the end of that. The curtain rose on schedule, and Ethel made her appearance wearing shirtwaist and skirt, a straw hat, and astride a bicycle. The theater rocked with applause, and one of the greatest hits of the American theater, the biggest hit of that 1940–1941 theater season, was under way.

Among those who rejoiced was Alexander Woollcott. He wrote to a friend: "Ethel has passed through the valley and has come out on the other side—serene, genial and more beautiful, I think, than ever."

Ethel could now bask in a set of reviews it was almost worth a lifetime of effort to receive. John Mason Brown reported to readers of the New York *Post* the day after the opening: "The bravos which filled the theater at the final curtain were deafening and prolonged. There was every reason for them because Ethel Barrymore gives the finest, most thoughtful and concentrated performance she has given in many years." Brooks Atkinson found her magnificent and at the peak of her talents. Richards Watts, Jr., thought her performance rarely beautiful, "a characterization of greatness and true nobility."

Miss Moffat, as played by Ethel in the opening scenes, was truculent and aggressive; as the play progressed she showed her inner core of grace and perception. And by the time the curtain had fallen she had vividly illuminated the story of how, as Brooks Atkinson put it, "by faith, resolution and generosity, she passes the flame of enlightenment on to a hand that will carry it further." It was a story that was supposedly autobiographical, at least in part, for Emlyn Williams had encountered at age twelve just such a woman as Miss Moffat who had helped him escape a coal miner's life. But the *real* Miss Moffat for many thousands of playgoers was Ethel Barrymore.

"Well, the news is," wrote John Anderson, "that Miss Barrymore has found an author, if you can still call it news when the whole country must know by now the blissful fact of her stardom. She *couldn't* quit; she must have known she had to do this."

There was no dearth now of pleasant happenings for Ethel. In February, 1941, the NBC network devoted a half-hour to celebrating the fortieth anniversary of Ethel's stardom, from *Captain Jinks* to *The Corn Is Green*. Tributes were spoken by Arthur Hopkins and Herman Shumlin, by Helen Hayes and Louis B. Mayer, by Alexander Woollcott and the brothers Barrymore. In fact, something of note occurred when it was realized this was the first occasion on which all three Barrymores shared a radio program. Lionel had hoped to tell Ethel over the radio: "We bought a big red apple for you, but John drank it." The line was cut from the script. He contented himself with wheezing: "The corn is green. How green is the corn? I don't know, but I bet Jack will."

John recalled their first acting performance together in a barn in New Jersey when they were all kids. Then, soberly, he saluted his sister's "gaiety, charm and splendor. One has only to think of her to be invested with a God-given quality of humility."

The program was warm with sentimentality, moist with tears, some of them Ethel's. "Thank you all," she said in her deep, golden voice, "for this treasure you have stored for me, in my particular heaven."

There was more to come. In May she received the Barter Theater award "for the outstanding performance given by an American actress during the current theater season," the award being presented by Eleanor Roosevelt, first lady of the land, at an Astor Hotel luncheon. Mrs. Roosevelt said: "Miss Barrymore is one of the first people who made me love the theater." She contrasted the destruction of "things we have looked upon as culture and heritage" (referring to recent Nazi bombings of England) with America's task of preserving art and culture. Of this preservation Mrs. Roosevelt made of Ethel, then a Republican, a symbol.

Into the hot days of July she played on as Miss Moffat, setting on July 5 a new long-running New York record for herself of 258 performances, her best since *Déclassée*. She went on to a total of 461 on Broadway before beginning an active and extremely profitable countrywide tour in the play. During this tour, with her own country at war and with travel restricted, she did without her customary maid and insisted on doing all her own packing. So as not to take up any needed room on trains she went by car when gasoline was available, meanwhile giving up the use of her own car from Mamaroneck to New York.

Little of her renewed celebrity went to her head. Richard Maney, the press agent for the play, reported her as having said to him: "Now that I'm a hit again people I haven't seen or heard from in years are banging at my door. They're crawling out from under rocks and worming their way out of the woodwork."

Jack L. Warner was one of those who did not make a pilgrimage. He bought *The Corn Is Green* for his studio and promptly announced that Bette Davis would play the role. Nothing could have bothered Ethel less.

In Washington with the play, she was a house guest of Alice Longworth's. Among the group in the upstairs sitting room late one evening were a senator, a member of the cabinet, and a very young and slightly nervous Marine. As Ethel rose and said she was retiring for the night, the Marine jumped to his feet and asked if he could kiss the greatest actress in the world good night. Ethel turned in the doorway, opened her arms, took the boy to her and kissed him. Then she held him away from her and for a moment looked into his face. "God bless you," she said softly. Adela Rogers St. Johns, who was there, saw tears in everyone's eyes.

She was not always so gracious. Friendly as she was and fond as she was of Tallulah Bankhead, she had no words of praise for her performance in *The Skin of Our Teeth*. When asked what she thought of it, Ethel said merely, "Revolting!" Richard Maney said it was difficult indeed for him to get a kind word out of her for any other actress, especially when he had set up a newspaper spread for her to choose the ten greatest female acting performances she had seen during her lifetime. As *The Corn Is Green* ran on, a number of changes were necessitated in the cast, and previous photographic stills used for publicity became invalid. Maney went to Ethel and asked her if she would pose with some of the new players. She wouldn't go near one of those dreadful photographic studios, Ethel said.

"But, Miss Barrymore," Maney pleaded, "I'm in an awful position for requests for publicity stills. All I have left are singles of you."

"Oh," Ethel cried out, "you're in a *hell* of a fix, aren't you?"

Although it was years since she had sipped anything stronger than iced coffee, her reputation as a consumer of alcohol with a thirst equal to or greater than her brother Jack's still pursued her through the run of *The Corn Is Green*. Two ladies sat down together at a matinee and one twittered to the other: "Well, do you think she'll be sober today?" Behind them happened to be sitting Ethel's son, Jackie Colt. He leaned forward and very politely said to them: "I don't think you need worry. I just had lunch with her today, and I am her son." The two ladies almost ruined Ethel's performance, so madly did they applaud each time she opened her mouth.

Ethel was in the midst of touring with *The Corn Is Green* when she was approached by RKO to play Ma Mott in *None But the Lonely Heart,* and incidentally the mother of Cary Grant. Although Laurette Taylor had been the studio's first choice, Clifford Odets, the director and screenwriter, insisted on Ethel after seeing her play Miss Moffat in Los Angeles. He persuaded her to make a test, something she agreed to do reluctantly and only because she conceived a liking for Odets. When the test came out well, Cary Grant joined in the coaxing. Ethel said: impossible, she had to continue the tour of her play. RKO took care of that objection by simply putting the whole *Corn Is Green* troupe on salary for a six-week layoff period, paid Shumlin what he would have taken in if the tour had continued, and reimbursed theater managements for the cancellations they had to suffer.

Ethel's characterization of the elderly lady who ran a rummage shop in the seamy quarter of London was superb, but Odets did have a few troubles in dealing with her. For one thing, her carriage was so queenly that it was difficult to make her seem the down-at-heels old lady she was supposed to play. In some of her scenes she was supposed to be wearing a dilapidated hat. Odets saw her in one the costume department had provided and said it just wouldn't do. "It makes you look like a dowager countess," he complained.

More hats were tried, and each time she came out Odets said she still resembled a countess. He raged at the costume department and was told the hats had been purchased for seventy-five cents each in a rummage shop. Finally Odets tore at some of the ribbons of the last hat she was given, and stamped on it. The effect was slightly better, but he was still far from satisfied with his efforts to turn Ethel into a frump.

In the early scenes both Odets and Cary Grant noticed that Ethel was absolutely magnificent in the rehearsals of her scenes, but that she had a tendency, unknown to herself, to tighten up slightly during the camera take. Odets hit upon an expedient. He informed only Grant which was to be the rehearsal and which the "take," and then caught Ethel on film during what she had thought was a rehearsal of a scene. When she loosened up after a while, there was no longer any need for this subterfuge, for Ethel gained complete command of her film performance, one which Bosley Crowther thought glowed "with beauty and spiritual fire." *Time* magazine said: "Ethel Barrymore, with her grandeur of presence, her goose-pimpling voice and her magnificent eyes, calmly knocks you flat and forces you to believe everything you see. In fact, her return to the screen in itself would make *None But the Lonely Heart* an event."

The film, an unusual one for Hollywood of that period, with its dark, moody treatment of the slum people of London in the 1930s, was one of the most notable of that year, and time has not yet dimmed the throat-catching quality of Ethel's performance. Quite rightly she was given the Academy Award for the best performance by an actress in 1944. Being given the award was agreeable to her, Charles Brackett remembered, "but she was not particularly impressed." She was prouder of the fact that on her last scheduled day of working in the picture she finished at noon, and at one o'clock was on the train to resume her tour of *The Corn Is Green.*

But she now took a kindlier attitude about working in Hollywood. Movies, she thought, could be "just like the stage—as subtle, and about things that matter." In short, said Ethel, "I had a very happy time," and perhaps warmed by this, and by the sun itself, it was not long before she was in Southern California for good.

The Barrymore family in 1932, photographed in Ethel's rented Beverly Hills house. On the left side of the sofa is Irene Fenwick; seated are Lionel, Ethel and Dolores Costello Barrymore. Dolores holds Dolores Mae, and next to her John holds the infant John Barrymore, Jr. Standing behind the sofa are Ethel's three children, Sammie, Ethel and John Colt.

John Barrymore and Dolores Costello, his third wife, in the trophy room of their Tower Road home. Dolores complained that housekeeping wasn't easy in the palatial residence. The photograph was taken in 1930.

John had as much of a penchant for grotesque makeups and characterizations as did Lionel. Here he is seen in *Svengali*, made in 1931.

John gave one of his best screen performances in *Twentieth Century*, in which he played an egomaniac theatrical producer attempting to persuade Carole Lombard to star in his next production. The film was released in 1934.

John and Lionel appeared together in several talking pictures—among them *Grand Hotel*, an all-star film in which Greta Garbo also appeared.

The only occasion on which all three Barrymores acted together was in the 1932 MGM production, *Rasputin and the Empress*. Publicity built up a feud among them, but it was only that—publicity.

During the making of *Rasputin and the Empress*, the three famous Barrymores consented to be photographed on the ground of Ethel's rented house in Beverly Hills.

Ethel making her premature announcement of her retirement from acting on the Ben Bernie radio program in August of 1936.

Ethel had her ups and downs during the 1930s, and was still searching for a hit when she played this elderly lady on Broadway in 1939 in *Farm of Three Echoes*.

Here she co-stars with Dudley Digges in the Theatre Guild production of *Ghost of Yankee Doodle* (1937).

This photograph represents a rare dispensation from Greta Garbo, for she usually forbade the taking of photographs while working on the set. But because she got along so well with John Barrymore during the making of *Grand Hotel* she allowed this shot to be taken, and was even thoughtful enough to allow for proper coverage of John's left profile.

One of John's best screen characterizations was Mr. Topaze in a version of Marcel Pagnol's *Topaze* made by RKO in 1933. Seated with him here is Myrna Loy.

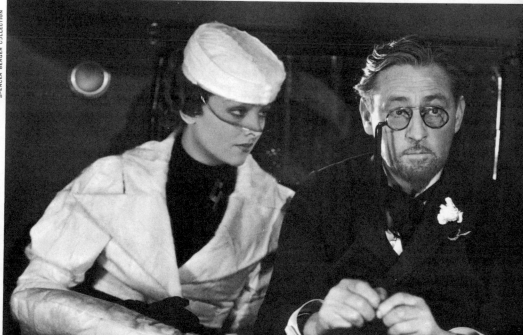

Diana Barrymore, John's daughter by Michael Strange, arrived in Hollywood in 1942 for her film debut. This picture shows John greeting her.

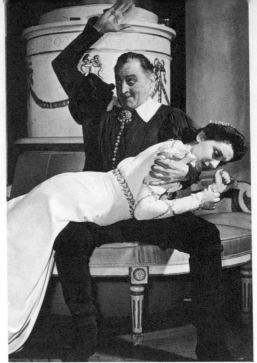

John's fourth wife was a young New York girl who called herself Elaine Barrie. She had stage ambitions and achieved them when she played with John in *My Dear Children* in 1939 and 1940.

John, with his fourth wife Elaine, and his mother- and father-in-law Edna and Louis Jacobs. The picture was snapped in March 1939, while they dined at El Morocco.

Lionel played Billy Bones in an excellent MGM version of *Treasure Island*, made in 1934.

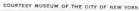

Through most of *The Devil Doll*, made in 1936, Lionel was dressed as a fragile old woman, but actually, in this good horror film, he was an escaped convict who possessed the secret for reducing human beings to one-foot dolls.

Each Christmas day for many years, beginning in 1933, Lionel was heard coast-to-coast on the radio as Scrooge in *A Christmas Carol*. Although unseen by his audience of millions, he nevertheless spoke the role in appropriate costume.

Confined to a wheelchair because of two bad hip injuries, Lionel won a new following as Dr. Gillespie in the long-lasting film series Dr. Kildare. In the above, he appears in *Secret of Dr. Kildare*, made in 1939.

In 1940 Ethel achieved one of her greatest triumphs as Miss Moffat, a Welsh schoolteacher, in *The Corn Is Green*. Her entrance riding a bicycle always brought down the house.

She was persuaded to play a frumpy English cockney woman, the mother of Cary Grant, in *None But the Lonely Heart,* adapted and directed by Clifford Odets. For this role, Ethel won an Academy Award as "the best motion picture actress of 1944."

part *FIVE*

EPILOGUE TO GREATNESS / *chapter XXII*

FOR MOST OF HIS ADULT LIFE John Barrymore was haunted by the memory of his father's collapse into insanity, and of all his fears and torments—well hidden, except to his wives—the fear of an insane end for himself was the strongest. Intimations of potential collapse came to him on October 30, 1933, when he was called to Universal Studios for a retake of a scene for the all-but-completed *Counsellor-at-Law,* in which he re-created the role of a successful self-made attorney that Paul Muni had played so brilliantly on Broadway. John knew well the lines required of him for the retake, but time and time again, as William Wyler, the director, patiently continued to take the scene, John stumbled over easy speeches and "blew up" a total of fifty-six successive attempts. Barrymore struggled, perspired, kept doggedly on in spite of the fear that he had begun to repeat his father's sorry pattern. He was not drunk, according to eye witnesses of these strange lapses, nor did it seem that fatigue explained his condition. The next day he came back and completed the scene in one take.

This was the beginning of the lapses of memory that plagued him for the remainder of his life. What caused this to happen to a mind that, so far as anyone was able to ascertain, was not diseased? Gene Fowler came up with something he termed the Korsakow Syndrome to describe the condition, "a toxemia, the result of a circulating poison that has a specific affinity for brain tissue." Dr. Harold Hyman, who treated John all through the nineteen thirties, said that doctors would today more simply ascribe John's memory troubles to "alcoholic wet-brain," resulting from the absorption of certain of alcohol's toxins by areas of the brain that affect the memory. Usually such a condition would occur in tandem with a serious liver ailment—an ailment John was later discovered to have, too.

The first of his serious illnesses had taken place about three and a half years before, when he had undergone treatments for a duodenal ulcer. In November, 1930, while cruising with Dolores on the *Infanta,* he sustained a severe gastric hemorrhage and collapsed from loss of blood. He managed to be dressed when he disembarked from the *Infanta* at the Long Beach wharf, and even though the press was out in force, kept the news of his illness from reaching the public. Soon headaches on the right side of his head developed and continued intermittently for ten years. The cause of his varied ailments was never less than clear; he was systematically poisoning himself by the amount of alcohol he consumed, the drinking that he was less and less able to tolerate.

And yet some of his most brilliant screen work was done under these conditions of physical duress. In *Counsellor-at-Law* he was "magnificent," according to the New York film critics, and the movie at this writing, though distinctly "stagy" in its screen technique, still holds its fascination. After completing the film he began an exchange of letters with George Bernard Shaw about the possibility of filming *The Devil's Disciple* for RKO in England. Shaw, although fully approving John in the role of Dick Dudgeon, was unhappy with the draft of the script submitted to him, and the project never came off.

In December, 1933, John made a test for a Technicolor version of *Hamlet* which David O. Selznick was eager to produce, with the financial assistance of John Hay Whitney. The director of the proposed film was to be Robert Edmond Jones, who came to Hollywood with his wife, Margaret Carrington, and who supervised the test. A copy of this test, 492 feet of film, is still to be found in the film archives of the Museum of Modern Art, and it reveals a somewhat portly John Barrymore in Hamlet costume, attempting to emulate the greatness he had achieved more than eight years before. During the making of the test he again suffered lapses of memory, but even in those speeches which he was able to recite without pause it was sadly evident that John was only a paunchy, thick-ankled ghost of his former gloriousness. The filmed *Hamlet* of John Barrymore was sensibly abandoned.

But even though Hollywood was keeping a wary eye on John's health and condition, he rose to new satiric heights in *Twentieth Century,* which Ben Hecht and Charles MacArthur adapted from the play they had written with Charles Mulholland. John was seen as a fantastic theatrical producer of maniacal ego who can save himself from financial disaster only by signing a famous actress— whom he had raised to stardom, loved, and alienated—to a contract. Most of the action of the film, as in the play, took place aboard the Twentieth Century Limited, bound from Chicago to New York. The role of producer Oscar Jaffe, played by John as a sustained, highly keyed caricature, was to be his last important roistering film characterization, although he made more than a dozen films afterward.

Carole Lombard, who was cast for the role of Lily Garland, the actress, was not yet the star of magnitude she later became, and on the first day of shooting was so stiff as to worry Howard Hawks, the director, and to fill John with a bilious, foreboding sense of depression. Hawks's recollection of what then happened was told in 1963 to James Silke, editor of a West Coast magazine, *Cinema.*

> We were rehearsing the first day [Hawks said] and John Barrymore began to hold his nose. I made him promise that he wouldn't say anything until three o'clock in the afternoon. I could see him getting very worried over her stiffness, which came from her trying to imagine a character and then act according to her imaginings. I took Miss Lombard for a walk around the stage and I said, "You've been working hard on the script." She said, "I'm glad it shows." And I said, "Yes, you know every word of it. How much do you get paid for the picture?" She told me. I said, "That's pretty good. What do you get paid for?" "Well, acting," she said.
> And I said, "What if I would tell you that you had earned

all your money and you don't owe a nickel, and you don't have to act any more?" She just stared at me and I said, "What would you do if a man said such a thing to you?" She said, "I'd kick him right in the ——." "Well, Barrymore said such a thing to you, why didn't you kick him?" She went "Whnnnnnah" —snarled, you know, with one of those Lombard gestures, and I told her that he said that to her when he said such and such a line. "Now we're going back in," I said, "and make this scene and you kick him, and you do any damn thing that comes into your mind that's natural, and quit acting. If you don't quit, I'm going to fire you this afternoon. You just be natural." "Are you serious?" she asked. I said, "I'm very serious." And she said, "All right."

We went back in and I said, "We're going to make this scene." Barrymore said, "We're not ready." I asked him who was running this, and he said, "You are, okay." We made about an eight page scene. She made a kick at him, and he jumped back and started reacting and they went right through the scene. He made his exit, and I said, "Cut and print it." Barrymore came back and said to Lombard, "That was marvelous— what've you been doing, kidding me?" She started to cry and ran off the stage. Barrymore asked me, "What's happened?" I said, "You've just seen a girl who is probably going to be a big star, and if we can just keep her from acting, we'll have a hell of a picture."

Howard Hawks turned out to be prophetic, and so did, for a change, *The Literary Digest,* which, in reviewing the film, said: "Carole Lombard outdoes herself in the role of a temperamental actress." The film was successful with the critics and the public, and brought new luster to John's name. And certainly not to be overlooked among the gallery of characterizations for the screen that John accumulated was the movie that had opened unobtrusively in New York a year earlier, and which starred John as a bearded, gentle French schoolteacher. This was *Topaze,* adapted from the Marcel Pagnol play. Mordaunt Hall of the *New York Times* called it "a production fired with far greater intelligence than most Hollywood offerings." Too bad that the film commanded so little attention from the public, for John's whimsical characterization had its enduring values, and he was every inch the screen artist.

If the period of his decline—from which he seemed to rally on occasion—can be dated, it must be put in May of 1934, when he was in so dazed and drunken a condition that he was unable to remember any of the words of his new script for an RKO film, *Hat, Coat, and Glove*. When he stopped the drinking and appeared supposedly sober on the set he was still not able to make his proper exits and entrances. The producer of the film suggested to Dolores, and to Henry Hotchener, that John be made to take a lengthy rest, and replaced John with Ricardo Cortez.

"He had been drinking steadily for two years," Dolores Costello remembered in 1963. "It hardly seemed that he drew a sober breath. Combined with the drinking was his habit of spending and squandering the immense amounts that he earned. And while he was doing this spending I tried to save, cutting down on the expenses it was left to me to handle. It was as though I knew how it would end."

A conflict began between Dolores and Henry Hotchener as to how to best handle John. By her account, there was never very much good feeling between herself and the Hotcheners, who she sometimes thought intrigued against her (according to their lights of what they deemed best for John's welfare) and against whom she developed a mistrust and an eventual enmity. Nor did she approve of his methods for what she termed Hotchener's "pacifying of Jack. When it was plain that he was exhausted from having made nine pictures in two years, when he was fast becoming an almost hopeless alcoholic, Hotchener took him to an osteopath!"

This was too much for Dolores and she faced Hotchener down in John's presence at the Tower Road home. "Tell him the truth!" she pleaded with Hotchener. "Jack can take the truth. He doesn't know he was fired!"

Upon which the neat man with round, bespectacled face and thin hair parted precisely in the middle, bowed to the will of John's wife and said with formality, and a sense of warning in his voice: "I turn him over to you, Dolores."

John now seemed aware of the truth of his situation for the first time and said: "I've been fired?" And, realizing that he now faced the end of his career in Hollywood, he begged Dolores, with whom he had been drunkenly quarreling for months, to help him resuscitate himself. The account given here varies considerably from the long and graphic account of John's decline in *Good Night, Sweet Prince,* but Fowler, it must be remembered, was drawing largely on Hotchener's recollections which, while often precise enough, came from a particular view of the situation. Fowler, it must be admitted, often shows a bias against the women in John's life, preferring to all but ignore them at times and to ascribe John's perennial search for an ideal mate and his frequent finding of these mates to "bus accidents." Colorful and vivid as the Fowler biography is, the book tends to omit John's extreme and neurotic dependency on his wives and to make the women more mean and possessive than they in reality were. John's own memory of his marriages was, in his later life, rather undependable, and he particularly seemed unable to recall his gargantuan rages and jealousies.

At any event, he placed himself in Dolores's hands at this extreme juncture, and Hotchener retreated tactfully from the scene, for the time being.

Dolores called up Dr. Samuel Hirschfeld, who had been treating John (and would have committed him if Dolores had agreed), and told him: "Jack's willing to be treated at a hospital." The doctor came over, and the two of them managed to get Barrymore into a car, and drove him to the Good Samaritan Hospital. He stayed there a period of slightly more than two weeks. Fowler describes a series of tests, physical and mental, that were made, but he does not describe certain occurrences at the hospital which caused grave concern among the doctors, particularly Dr. Hirschfeld, who viewed John not only as a grave alcoholic but as a risk to the nurses. The drying-out process involved small daily doses of liquor, but these did not pacify Barrymore. Particularly in the middle of the night he was given to making violent attacks on the nurses who attended him. It was suggested that Dolores take a room next to his, which she did, after sending the children off to a private school under the name of Blythe—for she now feared that the name of Barrymore would be too scandalous a one for the children to bear. Even with Dolores in the next room, John continued his attacks on the nurses. After a week in the hospital Dolores lost twenty pounds, and it was now suggested to her by Dr. Hirschfeld that she commit John to a mental institution. "I sometimes think it was my fault that all that happened afterward happened," she said. "I wouldn't put him away. I wouldn't do it."

Instead she developed the idea that a long cruise on the *Infanta* would help put John to rights, that by keeping him completely dry, by getting him back into good physical condition, she would be in a position to give him proper rest and care. The doctors reluctantly agreed that it was possible a long, nonalcoholic cruise would be of some benefit. The Barrymore family, including the children, a maid, and a nurse for John, left for Vancouver to board the *Infanta*. John had meanwhile managed to send a message to Hotchener to meet him at Vancouver. Dolores, on the other hand, suggested that Hotchener stay away and leave Jack in her care. "Give me three months," she said to him. Nevertheless, Hotchener appeared in Vancouver, another confrontation between him and Dolores took place, and again he was asked to stay away. The Barrymore family then went off on a long "therapeutic" cruise to Alaska, returning eventually to Vancouver, where an incident occurred that disheartened Dolores. During the last three days of the cruise John was not only completely rational again, but seemed well. True, he had ransacked Dolores's vanity case and had drunk her perfume, but eventually everything of an alcoholic nature had disappeared from the ship. In the harbor at Vancouver John suddenly went wild again. Perhaps imagining that his nurse and Dolores were attempting to keep him from going ashore, he attacked the nurse viciously. All she had said was, "Mr. Barrymore . . ." and got no further. With a blow he broke her nose, and Dolores, grabbing him and holding on, was barely able to keep him from injuring the woman further. "It was accidental," John later claimed.

But the nurse, who later instituted suit, did not regard it so, nor did Dolores, who packed herself and the children that night on a train bound for California. John, meanwhile, proceeded to California on the yacht, wiring the faithful Hotchener to meet him. When the outraged Dolores, the face-bandaged nurse, John and Hotchener, all met, John seemed in a state of panic. Later he told Hotchener that he suspected Dolores and Dr. Hirschfeld were conspiring to have him put away, and said they must secretly flee from California. The flight took place by air in late August, 1934, and before leaving

John telephoned Dolores and told her he was going east to do some radio work in New York. It was Dolores's feeling that the Hotcheners had virtually kidnaped John, and she wired Henry that she would hold him personally responsible for "anything untoward that may transpire."

His marriage to Dolores ended, in effect, with this weird flight. The disturbed man had lost the sympathy of even the tolerant and understanding Lionel, to whom Dolores went with the recital and her explanation of all that had happened. Lionel told her: "You're his last chance, Dolores. If he goes through with this, if he breaks up with you, I'll never see my brother again." It was not a word that he kept.

No part of John's life has been more chronicled in the public prints than the period that ensued after his precipitous leave-taking of Dolores. It makes for a strange, absurd, pathetic story, for the John Barrymore now met is a caricature of the earlier John Barrymore, flamboyant as *he* was. This was no case of "Out, brief candle!" but of a long, guttering, flickering consumption of incredible, if diseased, energies. And it must not be supposed that the fine intelligence possessed by John was lost, for, as Ethel Colt put it, "Even when he was a very sick man he managed to look at the wreck of his life with sardonic humor." There were many who were shocked, many who snickered and laughed, but John appreciated the joke, too.

In New York John's attorney advised, in view of a looming legal battle with Dolores, that he be examined by an authority on mental and nervous disorders—this in the event of an extradition procedure on the part of Dolores's lawyers. A neurologist, a faculty member of the Cornell University Medical School, and a consultant at Bellevue Hospital made the examination and found that John's mental status was "in every way normal except that there is some slight impairment of memory for recent events, which in my opinion is due to fatigue . . ." This strange report, ignoring any evidence of a nervous breakdown on the set in Hollywood, of violent attacks on women in the Good Samaritan Hospital and on his own boat, and ignoring the already pronounced effects on his system of the prolonged drinking, served a useful legal purpose and helped allay John's fears that he would be committed to an institution. But, like a child putting troublesome matters out of sight and therefore out of mind, he decided to embark at once for London with the Hotcheners, leaving his affairs to be handled and straightened out by Maurice Hotchner (his lawyer in New York, and the brother of Henry, although he spelled his name slightly differently) and a firm of attorneys in Los Angeles.

Dolores, however, took no legal action against him at this time. She stayed at the Tower Road home, and had the unpleasant task of dismissing most of the household help, except for a caretaker, Camomile, who packed John's trunks and shipped them to John in New York. He included John's Hamlet costume and promptbook. In London John stayed at Grosvenor House on Park Lane and made plans for film work. He signed a contract with Alexander Korda to do a movie version of *Hamlet* (without the precaution of making a test), but upon dressing himself in costume and examining himself in a mirror John decided to disqualify himself.

Now still in flight (presumably from facing too much reality) he sailed with the Hotcheners for India, the three of them having agreed that an ancient Hindu cure called the Ayurvedic Treatment would fix up all that ailed him. In October of 1934, before sailing, he made out his will, leaving his estate to his three children, and cutting out Dolores completely, having been rightly informed by Hotchener that she had a considerable amount in stocks and bonds accumulated from her own earnings (which had reached as high as $4,500 weekly) and from some $70,000 invested for her in a trust fund by John during his palmy earning years.

In November of 1934 John and the Hotcheners reached Bombay, where the actor underwent a cure to "control" his thirst. The Hindu doctor, Srinivasa Murti, wise beyond his time, suggested that John do something about controlling his cigarette chain-smoking as well, and put him on a spiritual and alimentary diet, included a liberal sprinkling of flower petals before a brass altar installed in his hotel suite, and brought in four more Hindu physicians to recite various incantations. John was given medication consisting of herbs, and massages and baths were prescribed frequently. (He had developed a skin condition which had forced him to cut down on his bathing.)

After six weeks of the cure, John seemed considerably improved in health, upon which he simply disappeared for an entire week.

His whereabouts during this week were a mystery until John, a few years later, began regaling such of his friends and drinking cronies as Gene Fowler, Charles MacArthur, Ben Hecht, and John Decker with tales of what had transpired during a lengthy visit to a brothel in Madras. Liking the place, he had rented it for a week, including the premises, the girls, and the madam. Returning to his hotel, he tried the cure again for another two days and disappeared again, presumably for a return visit to the brothel. In spite of an increasing appetite for prostitutes during the years that followed, John miraculously escaped contracting a venereal disease.

In January John and the Hotcheners set sail for London, where there were still contractual obligations to Korda. In midcourse, at Genoa, John decided to ignore these obligations and took ship for New York instead. He sailed up the Hudson on January 31, 1935. After writing a "farewell" letter to Dolores, which his lawyer advised him not to send, John dispatched Hotchener to California to look after his interests there. Dolores had meanwhile moved from the Tower Road home to a small house in Los Angeles, and Hotchener discovered that, without servants to look after it, the place was not in the best of condition. Dolores had taken with her enough furniture to furnish her new home, leaving behind all of John's conglomerate collection of possessions.

While Hotchener was away, John paid a visit to his not quite fourteen-year-old daughter Diana at her boarding school outside Baltimore. The reunion thrilled Diana, who was now enraptured by movie stars and the glamour of her father's name. After a chat together on the school grounds John talked the headmistress of the school into allowing Diana to have dinner with him in Baltimore. Permission was granted on condition that a schoolmate accompany her. On this evening Diana was introduced to the wonders of drinking cocktails by her father, was taken to a movie, discovered her father and the schoolmate kissing, and, during the ride in the car on the way back to the school had to sit uncomfortably by as John Barrymore pawed at her schoolmate. John had all but passed out by the time the school was reached, and the headmistress, taking charge of the situation, poured coffee into John and sent him back in the car to Baltimore. Michael Strange (now Mrs. Harrison Tweed) viewed newspaper pictures of her daughter and her former husband together in a night club, was incensed, and removed Diana from the school after the completion of the term.

In mid-February, 1935, newspaper reports said that John Barrymore had collapsed with influenza and had been taken to New York Hospital. This "collapse" was viewed with understandable suspicion by members of the press fraternity, but security in the hospital was tight, and it was not generally known that John was taking another "cure." He was hospitalized for nearly a month, and was visited there by several of his old friends, Jack Prescott and Al Woods among them. Michael Strange and her husband, Harrison Tweed, visited him too, having heard from Hotchener that John's condition was serious. (He had come close to literally drinking himself to death before entering the hospital, and one evening had showed almost no discernible pulse.) Perhaps fearing the end was near, Michael sent Diana to visit her father, and she brought with her several chattering, star-struck schoolmates. The sight of so many pleasant, virginal girls brought back much of the gay charm to John's manner. Kept from drinking, it was extraordinary how quickly he was able to recuperate.

During Diana's visit John invited her to take a cruise with him on the *Infanta*, which was moored at Miami. Michael doubtfully agreed to allow her daughter to take the cruise, on condition that her stepfather accompany her, and Tweed, a prominent lawyer, further stipulated that he be given the legal authority to take over the yacht should John's condition necessitate it while at sea. The yacht cruise, once John was deemed fit enough to leave the hospital, seemed like a good idea to everyone, and with Tweed aboard, and with the aid of the well-trained master, Otto Mathias, the boat could be counted upon to be kept "dry."

Meanwhile John had another visitor, a nineteen-year-old stranger whose name was Elaine Jacobs, but who called herself Elaine Barrie. She was a sophomore at Hunter College, was taking journalism courses, and had been assigned the task of interviewing a celebrity as part of her course requirements. She chose John Barrymore, having read in the papers that he was staying at New York Hospital, had sent him a letter requesting the interview, and he had been kind enough to grant it in a return letter. Miss Jacobs was not a beauty, but she was reasonably comely; she had large dark eyes and a trim figure; and when she entered his hospital room she was aglow with excitement and bore an armful of flowers. The first visit, or interview, was a great success, and she paid him several visits during his stay. John's claim was that the girl had talent and that his interest in her was professional. She claimed that he was planning to make her into a radio actress, and that she had always had theatrical ambitions. That was why she had changed her name to Barrie, in honor of the Barrymores. The romance that soon developed between them was one of the most tempestuous and ludicrous in the annals of theatrical romance, and the newspapers kept the country regaled for many months with step-by-step accounts of its progress.

Elaine was the daughter of Louis and Edna Jacobs, who lived in an apartment on Riverside Drive in Manhattan. Jacobs was a traveling salesman, and was away a good deal, but it has never been revealed exactly what he sold when he was traveling. He appears to have been a man thoroughly dominated by his wife and daughter, and when he returned from a trip to find John ensconced in his apartment he showed little surprise, and was remarkably agreeable about sharing his somewhat limited quarters with the fifty-three-year-old prince of the royal family.

John interrupted the pursuance of his affair with Elaine (who claimed in her memoirs, *All My Sins Remembered,* that she had been seduced by John in her own apartment) to fulfill his promise to Diana to take her cruising. He astonished everyone by getting drunk on the supposedly alcohol-proof boat, and the mystery was solved only when it was discovered that he had siphoned off a pint of alcohol from the engine cooling system.

On his return he resumed his courtship of Elaine, and during the next few weeks ran up bills amounting to nearly six thousand dollars for various items of feminine apparel—later revealed to be shopping sprees on which he had taken Elaine and Edna Jacobs. They demurred, but he insisted, Elaine chronicled in her book.

Elaine Barrie made her radio debut in May of 1935, supporting John in a scene from *Twentieth Century*. Not only did this debut receive a remarkable amount of publicity, but so did her setting off the next day on a cruise with John aboard the *Infanta* (then docked in Brooklyn). The destination was Havana. Mrs. Jacobs went along as friend and chaperone.

At this Dolores, who had avoided public comment on her separation from her husband, filed suit for divorce, charging John with intemperateness and ill temper, and also claiming nonsupport. When the *Infanta* reached Havana the reporters asked John about Dolores's suit. "It's news to me," he said airily. "My lawyers probably know all about it. But I find it strange that my wife claims nonsupport after I settled $85,000 on her three or four years ago. The only thing I can say, and that rather wistfully, is that she's not supporting me when she makes such charges."

Asked for the significance of Elaine's presence on the yacht, John replied that the girl was a "real artist," that he considered her a genuine find in her profession, which was radio. She would continue to act with him on radio programs, he said.

While in Havana, visiting the estranged (and third) husband of his sister-in-law, Helene Costello, he exhibited the degree of jealousy he was capable of when, in front of others, he viciously slapped Elaine's face. He had not liked the way one of the Cubans looked at her. But by way of apology, and as an "engagement" present, he bought her a canary diamond ring of nine carats. Elaine wore the ring on the return trip, and did not declare it at customs on arrival. The Customs Bureau took the position that the ring, purchased for $1800, would have to be forfeited unless $3200 in duties and penalties were paid on it. John paid.

Elaine's reason for not declaring the ring was given to the papers as follows: "We had been advised not to declare the ring because Mr. Barrymore was not yet divorced and it would not have looked well." By this time the two had quarreled and John had taken the ring back. "But it's mine and I expect to get it back shortly," she added, and she was right.

In August of 1935 John appeared ready to marry Elaine. In September he had a loud quarrel with the girl and her mother, and moved out of the apartment. As Fowler pointed out, instead of spending all the hot, humid summer in the Riverside Drive apartment he could have been in the cool, sumptuous quarters of his yacht, which was docked, at a huge cost, on the East River. He was living vastly beyond his earnings, and his money was going at a fearful rate, and looming now was the expensive divorce settlement with Dolores. Suddenly a new suit descended upon him, brought by Elaine and her mother, for the return of the diamond ring as well as for a robe (brought from India) that John had presented to Elaine. The suit was resolved out of court by John's payment of $3500, of which $2000 was a fee for their lawyer! The diamond and robe would be returned, after being placed for a year in escrow, if the two Jacobs ladies would refrain from giving interviews to the press. They had become national celebrities, made excellent copy for the yellow press (and for the more dignified press), and seemed to thoroughly enjoy the attention to which they had hitherto not been accustomed.

Next Dolores's suit against him was settled with a property agreement, one that was surprisingly light in view of the fact that John's earnings had been in excess of three hundred thousand dollars in 1933. He was allowed to keep the Tower Road house and property —virtually a gift to him from Dolores in view of the usual California practice to grant the wife in a divorce suit the place of domicile— and was to pay $850 a month for the support of his two children. Naturally Dolores received custody of those children. Free of his suits, one of which would have kept him from leaving New York, and the other which would have made it difficult to return west, he left for California by train on September 19, 1935—the signal for a great chase to begin. For the now lovelorn Elaine followed him on a wild cross-country pursuit that sent shock waves of derisive laughter over the entire nation. The headlines about this nationally advertised game of hide-and-seek swallowed up all other important news of the day. Yet John, with his habit of not reading newspapers, seemed unaware of the storm he was helping to cause.

Elaine almost caught up with John in Chicago, after taking a plane there. Reporters in Chicago were eager to help Elaine, and even booked for her the suite next to the one John was supposed to occupy for the remainder of his journey. But he had switched from a fast train to a slower one. In Kansas City Elaine gave up the chase and took to the radio, again helped by maliciously kind reporters. Over the countryside went her clarion call to John, wherever he was: "I address this appeal in an effort to reach John Barrymore, whom I love very deeply. I also address this to the kindly people of Kansas City and the entire Middle West, who have been so sympathetic and understanding. John, dear, I know you need me now— more than ever before. I realize that certain people are keeping you from me. When you were with me I was able to nurse you back to health. I want to help you and save you from those who would destroy you. Please, dear John, don't think I have deserted you. I am here in Kansas City waiting for your call. Please come to me. I am waiting."

The heart-rending appeal was ignored. John proceeded westward and Elaine retreated eastward. In Beverly Hills, John stayed with Lionel for a day, said the Elaine affair was off, then telephoned Elaine in New York the same night, effecting another in what was to be a series of reconciliations with her. Shortly after Dolores obtained her uncontested divorce decree in October, 1935, Elaine and Edna Jacobs arrived in California. The Jacobs' lawyer, Aaron Sapiro, soon became John's attorney and business manager, replacing Henry Hotchener.

John took up residence in a fashionable sanitarium in Santa Barbara, California, toward the end of 1935, and early in 1936 Irving Thalberg took the chance of casting him as Mercutio in a star-laden production of *Romeo and Juliet*. Elaine, who had added ambitions of movie stardom to her theatrical hopes, was put under contract at MGM, probably on the theory that had become prevalent, that she was "good for John." She conceived an intense dislike for John's Tower Road residence, and although invited to stay there, preferred to live in a Hollywood apartment on Franklin Avenue.

George Cukor, who directed *Romeo and Juliet*, found John on his return to moviemaking a somewhat changed man. "He was absolutely on the wagon," Cukor remembered in 1963, "but something had happened to him and he couldn't remember much of anything. He was very vain at the time, still very intelligent, remem-

345

bered incidents from the more distant past, but was rather helpless. He was on the defensive, actually, and he would say, 'Where do I go?' in a snappish way. Margaret Carrington was again brought out to Hollywood and we asked her to get him through. She was marvelous with him, behaved toward him like an older sister."

She once told John on the set, good-humoredly, "If drink would only kill the Barrymores then we could all have a peaceful life." But her kindness and goodness toward John helped him enormously, and although relatively minor in the film (Norma Shearer and Leslie Howard played the star-crossed lovers) he gave a performance that was universally regarded as brilliant. It was on the basis of this that Thalberg, as devoted a fan of the Barrymores as ever, decided to cast both John and Lionel in *Camille,* in which Greta Garbo and the young Robert Taylor were to star. John, however, became unavailable. He had entered a sanitarium run by James and Louise Kelley for the care and keeping of alcoholics.

The on-again, off-again "engagements" of John and Elaine continued throughout the better part of 1936. There was, as usual, much speculation in the press and among his more loyal friends as to the underlying causes of his love for Elaine and hers for him. There seems no doubt, now, that he had a need for her and a dependency upon her. As for Elaine Barrie Jacobs, she has recorded her own version of her participation in the swirling notoriety of John Barrymore's later life and career. She thoroughly disliked his associates, Hecht and MacArthur, Gene Fowler, and the painter John Decker, and they, it can safely be said, bore no liking or love for her. But there is a certain poignancy in her account of how she and her mother bought a bottle-capping machine, and considerably weakened the alcoholic content and recapped each bottle of beer that came into the menage he shared with them when he was not retreating to his now somewhat ramshackle quarters on Tower Road.

Not much more than a year after the interlocutory period of his divorce from Dolores ended, John eloped to Yuma, Arizona, with Elaine and married her. The date of this event was November 8, 1936. Ben Hecht and Charles MacArthur had, the day before, attempted to dissuade him from taking what they regarded as a foolhardy step, but John calmly turned aside their cogent arguments.

"Gentlemen," he told them, "you are talking to a man who is about to go over Niagara Falls in a barrel." Hardly two months passed before the newly married couple demonstrated their ability to keep newspaper readers amused and fascinated. At a New Year's Eve party at the Trocadero in Hollywood the two indulged in some noisy name-calling, in which John was clearly the aggressor. The upshot of this was that Elaine left him and announced that she would file a complaint for divorce. She was by now inhabiting a new home John had purchased in Benedict Canyon in Bel Air, and later reported in her reminiscences that John was in the habit of skulking jealously around the grounds during their period of separation.

John had obtained a new lawyer, Henry Huntingdon, to handle his affairs. While Huntingdon was obtaining a revocation of Aaron Sapiro's power of attorney the roof all but fell in on John, who was hit for nonpayment of several large bills that had been incurred during the early weeks of his marriage. So many debts were outstanding that, early in 1937, Huntingdon filed a petition of bankruptcy on behalf of John. Several of his friends—Fowler, Hecht, and MacArthur among them—attempted to stave off the selling of the *Infanta* to meet debts of more than $150,000, but in August of 1937 the yacht was sold, an event which all but broke John's heart, although he seldom set foot on the boat.

He had managed to finish another picture, *Maytime,* a movie version of the operetta, with Jeanette MacDonald and Nelson Eddy in the important roles, but his career seemed all but finished, due to his well-known physical condition and grotesque behavior. Yet he somehow managed to continue working, striving to clear his record of debts in between frequent visits to the Kelleys' sanitarium and occasional trips to a lonely desert house near La Quinta, California, where his health often seemed to improve. "Barrymore's performance as a dying man lasted several years," wrote Ben Hecht in *A Child of the Century.* Certainly rumors that the great actor was dying were current in the newspapers. Nevertheless, time after time John arose from what seemed a descent into the last dark valley and managed to astonish his friends and the avidly watching world. Replying to a query as to the possibility of John's imminent demise, Gene Fowler wrote to the King Features Syndicate: "The Barrymores never die.

347

It would be against family tradition to do anything so common-place."

Elaine filed suit for divorce in February, 1937, and added to John's woes by asking for $2500 a month alimony, or almost four times the sum John was already paying Dolores for the support of his two children. In addition, he still sent a considerable sum each month for the support of Diana. He wrote his daughter a letter, asking for surcease from this financial burden, which he had carried continuously since his separation from Michael twelve years before, but she did not deign to reply. No wonder John tottered through four more pictures in 1937. These were such sorry items as *Bulldog Drummond Comes Back*, *Bulldog Drummond's Revenge*, *Nightclub Scandal*, and a better than average comedy with Carole Lombard, *True Confession*.

John's memory for lines had all but disappeared, and a studio practice of writing his speeches on placards and blackboards was instituted for him, these being held just out of camera range. A studio assistant was assigned to hold these aids. One day John asked the fellow to hold his blackboard higher. The request was complied with. "Higher," John said. The man stretched to his fullest height and held the board above his head. "Higher," John called. A ladder was procured, and the assistant climbed up and held the blackboard several feet above John's head. "Higher!" John shouted. Upon which, the director canceled the shooting of the scene for the day.

Garson Kanin, who directed John later in *The Great Man Votes*, told Spencer Berger about the blackboard procedure used during the making of that movie. "There were three blackboards of varying size," he said, "depending on the length of the speech." During one very short scene a character came in and said to John, "Are you Gregory Vance?" John's reply was to be simply, "Yes." When Garson Kanin saw the blackboard man write "Yes" on the blackboard he felt he had had enough and asked John, "You don't have to have *that* on the board, do you?"

"Why not?" John replied.

"What else could you possibly say?" Kanin asked him.

John considered this for a moment before answering. "No," he said.

The following headlines from the Los Angeles *Times* indicate the love tribulations of John and Elaine through several months during 1937:

RECONCILIATION RUMORED (Feb. 17)

ELAINE DROPS ALIMONY PLEA (Mar. 2)

SAYS SHE'S IN LOVE WITH JOHN (Mar. 25)

RECONCILIATION PROSPECTS NOW DIM (Apr. 16)

ELAINE GRANTED DIVORCE (Apr. 24)

JOHN, ELAINE MAKE UP, PLAN TO REMARRY (June 23)

DIVORCE SUIT DISMISSED (Aug. 11)

In 1963 Elaine commented to Helen Dudar of the New York *Post* on the furor she caused in the newspapers. "The thing I deeply resented," she said, "was the fact that I was presented as much more deliberate and much more sophisticated than I was. I was a very young girl, very emotional, very impulsive. On the surface all it looked like to the average person was a girl attached to a much older man. They couldn't imagine that there could be any real emotional relationship between two people like that. Well, there was . . ."

During 1938 John was domiciled more or less peacefully with Elaine and Mrs. Jacobs, who obtained a divorce from the stoical Louis Jacobs. During the year John acted in six movies. In one of these, *Hold That Co-Ed*, his young wife appeared in a small role, but landed on the cutting room floor. He was working incessantly to pay off his debts, now augmented by some California state income tax liens slapped on him. He took to doing more radio broadcasts. Early in 1939 he returned to the stage he had left fourteen years before, urged by the theatrically ambitious Elaine, who hoped eventually to appear on Broadway as Lady Macbeth, but who was willing to settle for something lesser first.

John had been in sporadic contact with the blind, bedridden, and still devoted Ned Sheldon. While doing some radio work in New York he visited Sheldon and spoke to him about doing a proposed

349

Macbeth with Elaine, and read aloud to him portions of a play called *My Dear Children.* Sheldon advised John against doing *Macbeth,* reasoning as follows: *Macbeth* had never been a popular play in New York, no matter who had essayed it; no actor had ever made a great personal success in the role of Macbeth; there was great danger involved in Elaine's making her first New York appearance in so exacting a part as Lady Macbeth. As for the script of *My Dear Children,* Sheldon frankly let John know that he thought it claptrap. Writing to John afterward, he strongly advised him to seek "disinterested and sympathetic advice." He stressed that the advice of such of his friends as Ben Hecht, Charles MacArthur, Arthur Hopkins, and Robert E. Sherwood, would be extremely valuable.

"What about Shaw's *Caesar and Cleopatra?*" Sheldon wrote. "A superb play with two magnificent parts . . ."

John did seek the advice of Charles MacArthur on *My Dear Children,* this time asking him not how good but how bad he thought the comedy written by Catherine Turney and Jerry Horwin, one that had been passed around among Broadway producers for years without success. It had eventually reached the hands of Elaine, who was searching for a vehicle with which to make her Broadway debut in company with her famous husband. She found it captivating and gave it to John to read. Not that she thought it a great play, but as she blandly explained (this according to the late Charles MacArthur's recollection), it would serve to introduce her to New York and pave the way for a production of *Macbeth* later in the season. MacArthur warned John of public lynchings if the play were ever produced.

In New York the producing firm of Aldrich and Myers was approached by William Morris, agent for the Barrymores. With the prospect of John Barrymore as the star, the producers read the play again and found it more to their taste. It was the story of an aging actor, Allan Manville, who while a guest in the Swiss villa of a friend is suddenly confronted by three adult daughters, whom he had conceived but afterward been aware of only vaguely. John would play the old actor, and Elaine one of the three daughters.

Otto Preminger was engaged as director and co-producer, rehearsals were scheduled, and the first performance given on the Princeton campus, in the McCarter Theater, on March 24, 1939. From that day forward the play had a long, colorful, and checkered history, for John had served notice that he did not intend to be held to the lines written by the authors or the revisions made during rehearsals. In fact, that first night when prompted from the wings by the stage manager, he called out, "Just a little louder, darling, I couldn't hear you."

In Washington a society first-night audience turned out to see the stage resurgence of John Barrymore, but he had lost his voice to laryngitis, and the box office had to refund the ticket money.

After a period of recuperation for John in New York, the road tour of *My Dear Children* resumed in April of 1939, John now accompanied by a husky young male nurse, Karl Steuver. Storm clouds again gathered over the relationship between John and his fourth wife, and in St. Louis Elaine flounced out of the show. Otto Preminger was sent for and was informed by the irate Edna Jacobs that she intended to tell the press—which gathered everywhere the train bearing the acting company paused—that John had been attempting to rape her for several weeks. "Why would you tell them that?" Preminger asked her. "Because he's trying to ruin my daughter," said the overwrought mother. Matters were fixed up by an agreement to pay Elaine the $500 dollar weekly salary due her during her run-of-the-play contract, and she returned to Hollywood. She was replaced by a young actress, Doris Dudley. The newspapers speculated that the reason for Elaine's leaving the play was that John had spanked her too hard on the stage, so hard that he had split her skirt.

In Omaha, Nebraska, where Doris Dudley joined the company, John gave a performance liberally sprinkled with ad-lib obscenities, shocking the ladies of the Omaha Drama League to such a degree that they left in a body before his curtain call. Also in the cast and performing in her home town was Dorothy McGuire, who left the play and returned to New York while the company was still on the road. She told Otto Preminger why she was leaving. "I like this profession," she said, "and I had a great admiration for John Barrymore when we started, but I cannot watch this man making a fool of himself."

After the first Omaha performance John noticed Preminger glowering. "The herr professor is mad?" he said to Preminger. "You didn't like the performance?"

"I found it beneath human dignity," Preminger said.

"Come tomorrow," John said softly.

The following night John gave a line-perfect and position-perfect performance. "John," said Preminger, "why don't you do this every night?"

"Bored, dear boy," John said. "Bored."

Early in May John filed suit against Elaine for a separation, and demanded an accounting from mother, daughter, and their new financial adviser, David Fisher, for funds amounting to more than a quarter of a million dollars. At the same time he telephoned Henry Hotchener in California and asked that his former manager take over his affairs again. Hotchener responded to John's call, looked into the actor's financial situation, and found his affairs as tangled as ever. The week following his suit for separation Elaine filed another suit for divorce. This time John decided to contest the divorce action. Troubles meanwhile had hit the show. Business had dropped off, following newspaper reports of John's off-color antics, and by the time Des Moines, Iowa, was reached the producers considered canceling the rest of the bookings. They were strengthened in this determination by an offer of a large sum from RKO to release John for a movie the studio had in mind for him.

John made the decision. The RKO people would be held off for a week to await the results of an opening of *My Dear Children* in Chicago. To help get it open the company manager, Captain Pierce Power-Waters put up fifteen hundred dollars of his own money. John then, beginning the night of May 8, 1939, proceeded to make theatrical history in Chicago, for *My Dear Children* ran there for the almost incredible total of thirty-four weeks. It was felt generally that playgoers flocked to the Selwyn Theatre to see John make a spectacle of himself. He was as much at home in the play, said one unkind reporter, as "a bat in a belfry." The playgoers went to see the spectacle of John belching, ad-libbing, and, hopefully, being drunk on stage.

During some performances John was so tired that he would play the whole evening sitting down, forcing the cast to adjust to him accordingly. On one of these occasions after the curtain calls he was found collapsed on the stage. Rumors sprang up every few days that he had dropped dead. When one of these rumors was broadcast on the radio, Captain Power-Waters, who had become John's financial watchdog, checked into it by telephone and was relieved when he heard the Barrymore voice. "Then you're not dead?" he asked. "No," John said, "but I wish I were." About a month after the show had started playing to capacity in Chicago John did have a heart attack and was put in an oxygen tent several hours of each day. Elaine flew to Chicago, but John refused to see her. When the show reopened he gave the same uproarious performance, knowing what the audience had come to see, and making sure that they got it. If brought a glass of water he would gulp it down, give a shudder, and gasp, "Not enough gin in it!"

"Barrymore will lurch, his knees will sag," reported John Chapman sent from New York to witness John's Chicago cavorting, "he will mouth a phrase while his eyes roll glassily. He will burp, collapse in a chair. He will open his lips and no words will come out. He will point a vaguely waggling finger. Then comes something that is important to the show—a line that must be gotten over with force, a bit of business that must be done with precision, a chance to fling an ad-lib line at the audience. Whereupon, Barrymore leaps like a whippet, in complete command of himself, the stage and the audience, something no alcoholic can do. He has just been having fun pretending to be jingled. The customers, he confided to me, have a right to their innocent amusement."

John did not neglect his carousing in Chicago, but "a little liquor went a long way at this stage." Ashton Stevens, the critic and old friend of John's from his San Francisco days, wrote in a letter to Gene Fowler. What would have been moderate drinking for someone else became active alcoholism for John, who in long night-club parties following his performances would regale listeners with off-color raconteuring. During one period of his Chicago residence he

353

took quarters in a Negro brothel, at another time lived in a small house, attended by Karl Steuver, on the outskirts of the city. He was alternately well and ill.

His daughter, Diana, coincidentally came to Chicago in a touring company of *Outward Bound*, appearing with the renowned but also unpredictable Laurette Taylor. Diana had become seized with stage ambitions, and found the name Barrymore very useful in obtaining parts. Only eighteen and already a well-publicized debutante in New York, she had achieved an outward aspect of callow sophistication, or what Stevens called "an infantile worldliness." John welcomed his daughter with open arms, allowed her to share his dressing room—her theater was right next to his and used the same stage entrance, and took her out for occasional night-club expeditions. One night her sophistication got on her father's nerves, and he growled at her, "Oh, stop trying to be a Barrymore and be yourself."

But in her honor he held a special matinee performance for her of his play, and embarrassed Diana with one of his ad-libs, put in especially for her benefit. During a bedroom scene John said: "That couch reminds me forcibly of my little daughter. How regularly she wet the sheets! I was kept as busy as the Sorcerer's Apprentice."

During the Chicago engagement John's contract called for him to be paid ten per cent of each week's gross receipts. The money he received was handled for him by Captain Power-Waters (Hotchener's services had again been terminated by John), and the way it was doled out can be seen from the following itemized list of John's expenses. It will be noticed that Elaine's takings from the show were coming partly from John's share. The list represents a typical week's disbursements.

Elaine Barry salary	$ 250.00
Dolores Costello (for support of two children)	200.00
John Barrymore (spending money)	125.00
Dr. Thomas (a heart specialist who attended John)	100.00
Nurse (Karl Steuver)	56.00
Entertaining Diana Blythe Barrymore	25.00
Rent	125.00

House (incidental expenses)................ 28.72
Legal expenses............................ 125.00
Chicago lawyer (for money out of pocket)...... 19.64
Total $1029.36

The total sum due him for receipts that week came to $1,068.46, leaving a net of $39.10 to take care of the various suits and claims made against him constantly. Because Elaine or her manager had been accustomed to paying his bills while with him, John was not prepared for the consequences when she no longer made these payments. Dolores suddenly complained about nonpayment of the maintenance due her for the children. A St. Louis hotel bill John had mistakenly paid with a check from an overdrawn bank account suddenly rose up to haunt him. Maurice Hotchner in New York presented him with a bill for over ten thousand dollars for services rendered. There was seemingly no end to what John owed, and he learned to his sorrow that the house in Bel Air he had purchased and thought he owned had been signed over to Elaine.

One reason the show was kept running in Chicago and the road for so long—*My Dear Children* proceeded to Pittsburgh after the Chicago closing—may have been due to the desire of the producers to allow Elaine's contract to lapse before going on to Broadway. Her contract expired at the end of 1939. If before that date the show had opened on Broadway, Elaine would have been entitled to twenty-five per cent of the net profits. Once in New York, John's income would be enlarged to approximately four thousand dollars weekly if the show played to capacity, and this must account for his desire to face Broadway and its critics in so zany a farce.

Ned Sheldon, horrified by the thought of his friend's coming to New York in *My Dear Children*, wrote John and suggested that he return to Hollywood to do a few more pictures. But John, although nervous about coming to New York, was also anxious to be back in the city where he had achieved his greatest success and fame. In Pittsburgh, during a moment in the play when as the aging roué, Allan Manville, he recited the "To be or not to be" soliloquy from *Hamlet,* John caused a hush to fall over the audience as he gave a quiet, serious reading. Suddenly a member of the audience shouted,

"Louder!" John paused good-naturedly to reply, "I'm just trying to remember it, Gus."

John opened in New York with *My Dear Children* on January 31, 1940. The occasion was memorable less for the performance than for some events that surrounded it. Ethel and Diana helped look after John, with the assistance of his old friend, Jack Prescott, keeping him away from reporters and photographers in a house in Bayside, Long Island, until he was due to make his appearance. There were reports that Elaine Barrymore was in New York, hoping to effect a reunion with her husband, and this may have accounted for so much protective activity. Elaine did enter the Belasco Theatre shortly after the first act had begun.

Spencer Berger was in that first night audience and described it to Gene Fowler as "an unbelievably baleful performance." John had evidently decided that he would not cut up as he had done on the road. Without the ad-libs the show was very close to being a bore, although some of the critics, prepared for the worst and thinking they had seen it, deplored John's making such "a foolish show of himself." Brooks Atkinson, in a kindly mood, wrote: "If Mr. Barrymore were a ham, this trashy story, and his appearance in it, might be a pathetic ordeal for his old admirers. But he is a wit. He plays it with an alert sense of mischief. Although he has recklessly played the fool for a number of years, he is nobody's fool in *My Dear Children,* but a superbly gifted actor on a tired holiday."

He had had to make his way into the theater, Atkinson reported, through a street that was packed with a gaping mob. "Theatergoers jostled one another in the lobby and squeezed by the ticket taker as if they were going to a notorious peepshow. There was something a little horrible about the mood of that audience. But the important thing was that he owned the stage he trod on."

Although the audience had not received quite what it had bargained for, the applause at the final curtain was thunderous, mainly, Spencer Berger thought, as a demonstration of affection for John. Now one of the most garishly strange of all events in John's career occurred. As he was about to make a curtain speech, as the audience began drifting from seats to exits, an unemployed actor dressed in

356

costume of green tights leaped to the stage and informed John that he was "Hamlet's ghost."

"I've always wanted to play *Hamlet* with you, Mr. Barrymore," he said. The startled John put his arm around the man's shoulders and talked him out of his idea. It was assumed by everyone present, and even by Otto Preminger, that this was some planned publicity gag (an idea of the producers, Otto Preminger angrily thought at first), but it wasn't. The curtain came down and when it rose again the man in green tights, Bert Freeman by name, had been hustled off stage. John made his curtain speech to a house nearly empty, but he was still adamant about this being "the happiest evening of my life."

Now it was time for the next episode in the evening's series of incidents. Elaine went backstage and attempted to force her way into John's dressing room. As Diana described her as she saw her upon opening the door of John's dressing room a crack, "There she stood in a gold mesh dress, sloe-eyed and sexy." Diana tried to shoo her off, but Elaine kept pounding on the door until at last John agreed to see her. He spoke to Elaine alone in his dressing room, but then a group of his well-wishers, including Diana, and her half brother, Robin, entered in a phalanx and rushed John Barrymore off, refusing to tell Elaine where they were bound for.

Their destination was a fashionable night club, The Monte Carlo, where a party was being held for John. Elaine managed to find her way to the right place. She barged over to John's table, was soon whispering to him, and put the protective Diana to rout.

"Look, Miss Jacobs," Diana said angrily, "this is my father. We are Barrymores and you have nothing in common with us. Please go." She turned to her father and said, "Daddy, either this woman leaves or I do."

"Well," said her father, settling the matter, "you leave, Diana."

It was four o'clock in the morning when John left with Elaine. "Tonight," he told a friend, "for a change I shall sleep with my wife."

After three New York performances John, suffering from nervous exhaustion, was in the hospital again, this time Mount Sinai Hospital on upper Fifth Avenue. A week later John was back in the play—suspended during his illness—and now Elaine was with him, replacing Doris Dudley. *My Dear Children* was a smash success in New York; it ran for four months, and would have run much longer if John had not suddenly tired of the nightly grind. He had received an offer from 20th Century-Fox to play what was virtually himself in a movie, *The Great Profile*. In the summer of 1940 he was back in California again. The play in which he appeared for more than a year had earned, by the time he left it, some $660,000. John had managed to keep for himself out of his share approximately $5,000, all that he possessed when he returned to California. But he had also accumulated $110,000 in new debts, about fifty per cent of which represented fees for attorneys, and sums owed his various business managers. He had been cleared of bankruptcy in November of 1939, and now new bankruptcy proceedings loomed for him.

Some of his debts were honorable ones, but he was also preyed upon, as Gene Fowler pointed out in *Good Night, Sweet Prince*, by a collection of what Fowler called "fair weather leeches and foul weather bleeders." The fetid crew, said Fowler, crawled over him with duns and writs, and he preferred to turn his eyes away from "the obscene tableau."

John and Elaine instituted separate divorce suits in the autumn of 1940. He asked the judge for freedom from "harassment" by her. Elaine asked for a property settlement that was, according to the Los Angeles *Examiner*, "fairly lush in view of the beating the Barrymore bankroll has taken from creditors of late." Elaine was awarded the divorce, the house in Bel Air, $15,000 to clear the title to it of income tax liens, a lump sum of $8,500, but was enjoined from calling herself Mrs. John Barrymore any longer. She was allowed to call herself Elaine Barrymore if she wished to, and she told reporters that was what she intended to call herself.

"Do you intend to stay single?" John was asked by reporters. "One never knows what will happen tomorrow," John said. "That's a beautiful thought, isn't it?" John was allowed to remain in his Tower Road house, although certain of his creditors attempted to attach it. In an attempt to stave off these creditors, John continued working hard, although he had a recurrence of his gastric ulcer, collapsed several times, either of hemorrhages or of his continuing heart condition, and after one of his collapses required blood transfusions. Yet he made three more movies in 1941, and all that year and through part of the next appeared weekly on Rudy Vallee's variety radio program. At the time that his interlocutory divorce became final he attempted another reconciliation with Elaine—there is a difference of opinion as to which one of the pair initiated this *rapprochement,* but it seems likely that John pleaded with her to return and that this time she was the one who refused.

He was a desperately ill man, and yet at times he gave the illusion of health. It was now known that he had cirrhosis of the liver and a kidney disease. He suffered from a constant succession of colds. He played as a haggard old man in *The Invisible Woman* for Universal, in *World Premiere* for Paramount, and in *Playmates* for RKO. In these last films he mugged outrageously. His eyes could still light up when a comely woman crossed his path of vision. Harold Clurman was seated at the Paramount commissary at lunch with the heavy-lidded actor and noticed how his expression changed when he glanced at girls who passed by. "Mr. Barrymore," Clurman said, "it's amazing how differently you look every time a woman appears." Barrymore snapped, "Naturally!"

He was virtually an assistant to Rudy Vallee on his radio program through 1941 and on into 1942. "The comic basis of the program," wrote John K. Hutchens, "is the decline of the Barrymore greatness and the Barrymore fortunes. He is pictured as an aging ham, physically debilitated. Sometimes he derides himself with the preposterous snorts and inflections of an old-time ranting actor; more often he is the butt of jokes made by others."

These radio sketches were along the following lines:

Vallee: "Turn the motor off and come in."

Barrymore: "The motor is off."

Vallee: "Then what's the rattling?"

Joan Davis: "That's Barrymore."

During the last two years of his life John associated with an aging group of bohemians who affectionately called the once great actor "the monster." John Decker, a hard-drinking portrait painter, was one of these, and Barrymore was often to be found in his studio home on Bundy Drive. Gene Fowler kept a fond, anxious eye on his old friend. Diana Barrymore came west on a film contract in January of 1942, and for a time stayed with her father in the Tower Road establishment—but not for long. Their relationship became strained when John asked his daughter to call a certain telephone number and get a certain woman to come to see him.

On May 19, 1942, John attended a rehearsal for the Rudy Vallee radio program and collapsed in John Carradine's dressing room. He was taken to Hollywood Presbyterian Hospital, where it was found that he was suffering from bronchial pneumonia. He did not recover. He was actually suffering from several grave ailments. His kidneys were no longer functioning, and his circulation had begun to fail. Newspaper reporters collected in the hospital waiting room and set up a death watch. Ethel was notified of John's grave illness by Lionel and he conveyed to her John's expressed wish that she not come to his bedside. She was in Boston with *The Corn Is Green*.

Lionel remained in his failing brother's room during his last days. With him during the watch were Alan Mowbray, an actor friend of John's, and Gene Fowler, to whom Lionel was always in debt "for his staunch support of me during those hopeless days and nights." Toward the end Diana Barrymore paid several visits to John's hospital room. Elaine made several calls to the hospital but was not permitted to talk to John. Dolores (who had remarried) called several times, too, and did talk to her former husband, but she did not take her two children to see their father. John, during his periods of coma, would mumble "Mum Mum" from time to time. On the day of his death, a surprising telephone call to the hospital came from Evelyn Nesbit, whom John had once loved and gallantly proposed to, but he was beyond speaking to her or recalling her.

On May 29, in response to his request, the last rites of the Catholic faith were administered to John by the Reverend John O'Donnell, pastor of the Immaculate Heart Church. Late that evening John died.

That afternoon Lionel telephoned Ethel in Boston following her matinee performance. The call came to the theater's box-office telephone, and with a sense of foreboding Ethel rushed from her dressing room to the front of the theater. She fell, rose, and took the call, and was told that John would not last out the day. On her way back to the dressing room she found she could not walk, and only then became aware that she had broken a bone in her ankle. That evening, with her ankle taped tightly, she managed to play her performance. When she came on stage the audience gave her a stunning ovation for several minutes and through the tumult of sound that filled the theater she stood with head bowed. She knew who the ovation was for.

LIONEL
THE LIONHEARTED

chapter XXIII

ALMOST EVERY YEAR from 1933 on, Lionel spent much of Christmas day at the NBC radio studios in Hollywood. Dressed in appropriate costume, he would take his place before the microphone and become the voice that all America identified as that of Ebenezer Scrooge. These annual broadcasts of *A Christmas Carol* ran on for twenty years, with only two breaks for Lionel in the long routine. Hedda Hopper once asked him why he took such satisfaction in the role and, true to his reputation for crustiness, he answered: "It was the constant urge to dine. I like to eat and radio pays well." But it was customary for Lionel to mask the sentimental side of his nature. Not only did he like Dickens as a writer, but he harbored hopes that Scrooge's transformation might spark a few good or noble impulses among his hearers. One clear result was an increase in fondness for Lionel Barrymore, who made more progress toward becoming a national institution.

There was sad cause for the first interruption, in 1936, of his yearly series. The year before, his ailing wife, Irene, underwent a serious operation and did not rally to any appreciable extent. The already thin woman had what amounted to an obsession about the need to reduce, and so drastic were her methods (among them the Roman practice of regurgitation following meals)—that surgery was necessary. Lionel was beside himself the night of the operation, and

362

he could not be calmed. He kept crying out to Gene Fowler, who was present with him in the hospital, "I feel as if I've dived under a raft and can't come up."

He sent Irene to Phoenix, Arizona, in the hope she would regain her health, but, worried that she might become bored, he one day borrowed a projection machine and some reels of Walt Disney comedy cartoons and drove through the night so that she might have a bit of diversion the next day. He often sent her flowers when she was back home, and when teased about this practice demanded to know, "What's unnatural in a man sending flowers to his wife?" In Hollywood this almost unearthly devotion of Lionel's to Irene struck the film colony as strange. But Irene continued to fail, and she died the day of Christmas Eve, 1936. John went to comfort his distraught brother, stayed up most of the night with him, and the following morning went to the radio studio to perform Scrooge in Lionel's place. That same morning Lionel attended a Christmas Mass, collapsed afterward, went into a shell of isolation, and spent several weeks resting in a sanitarium.

He had already had sufferings enough during the year. Some months before, working in his home studio at some drawing on a heavy metal drafting board, he had an accident that broke his hip. He had leaned on the board, it had given way, and he fell. The accident was not only painful, it filled him with fear that his screen career was ended; and strapped up and put in traction at the hospital, he called for Louis B. Mayer to ask him what his future was going to be. Mayer, always a rock of strength for Lionel, assured him that something would be thought of, and later, when the New York office of MGM questioned Lionel's place on the payroll, Mayer threatened to quit if Lionel was fired. Lionel made a strong fight to recover and managed to get about with a limp. MGM's writers were instructed to invent scenes in which Lionel would not have to walk. He could sit, stand, lie in bed, hang from a ceiling, but no walking about. Studio writers adjusted their plot and character lines to keep Lionel at work.

The injury occurred at a time when Lionel had become one of Hollywood's biggest stars, and MGM was in the habit of casting him in the studio's more prestigious productions. He had appeared in a fine film version of *Captains Courageous*, with Spencer Tracy and Freddy Bartholomew as his co-stars. He had played the elder Monsieur Duval in Garbo's *Camille*, took the role of Billy Bones in *Treasure Island*, was the kindly Dan Peggotty in *David Copperfield* (still a high point among the many American attempts to screen Dickens), and had the plum role of the father in the excellent adaptation of O'Neill's *Ah, Wilderness!* These roles had had the desirable effect of sending his film stock upward. But it was in a low-budget horror film, *The Devil Doll*, that he demonstrated his chameleonic ability at characterization to the fullest. As an escaped convict from Devil's Island, he put to use a fellow convict's formula for reducing human beings to doll size, masquerading as a feeble old woman while doing so. Many in the audience noticed a resemblance to his sister in the disguise and make-up he used. If so, this was Lionel's strictly private joke.

His hip was mended enough for him to be able to travel to England in the late spring of 1937 to make *A Yank at Oxford*, with Robert Taylor as his co-star. When he returned on the *Queen Mary* it was noticed that he still leaned heavily on a cane. He was willing to discuss etchings with reporters (he had brought back two Rembrandt and three Whistler etchings, the Rembrandts in particular becoming his proudest possessions) but not acting. Would he ever return to the stage? "I'll never quit motion pictures as long as they'll have me," he said.

In Hollywood again, he immediately went to work with Clark Gable and Jean Harlow (her last picture) in *Saratoga*. With filming all but completed, Lionel tripped over a sound cable on the set, fell, and snapped his hip again. He spent more months in the hospital, but instead of emerging on his feet this time, he was wheeled out in a chair. The doctors did not encourage him to think that he would ever be able to walk unaided.

It took this second and more serious accident to reveal the greatness of spirit that lay beneath Lionel's gruff and reticent exterior. Out of screen action, and perhaps for good, he did not listen to L. B. Mayer's suggestion that the film version of *A Christmas Carol* that the studio had waiting for him be postponed until such time as he could act in it. He suggested instead that the production proceed as scheduled, with Reginald Owen in the role of Scrooge. Lionel watched the making of the movie on the sidelines, offering peppery coaching and advice. When Christmas of 1938 came around he insisted Reginald Owen take his place at the microphone. The following Christmas, by popular demand, Lionel was back on the radio as Scrooge and continued the series until the last year of his life.

Following Irene's death, Lionel refused to live in the house on North Roxbury Drive he had shared with his wife. He was taken in by the Wheeler family, made up of Mrs. Mary Ellen Wheeler and her three grown daughters, who lived in Chatsworth, in the San Fernando Valley. The Wheeler daughters were related to Irene on their late father's side, and one of them, Florence Wheeler, had acted as Lionel's secretary. All the Wheelers had become good friends of Lionel's and Irene's, and had been towers of strength during Irene's period of illness. They now devoted themselves to looking after Lionel. When he bought a rambling farm property in Chatsworth, the Wheelers moved in with him, and their presence became even more valuable after he was crippled.

It became known after a while that although Lionel refused to reside in the Roxbury Drive home, he kept it exactly as it had been. The garden was tended, the swimming pool filled with clear water. Inside the house Irene's clothes hung in the closets, cigarette boxes contained cigarettes, and perfume bottles were in their accustomed places on Irene's dressing table. A caretaker kept everything in order, and once every month or so Lionel would pay the house a visit, spending an hour or more in private reverie at his personal shrine.

Only once did he offer his house for someone's use; it was an offer that caused him much embarrassment and nearly cost him a lot more. He sent word to Richard Strauss, the composer, in Nazi Germany, that he was welcome to use his house if ever he saw fit to come to America. Strauss quickly accepted the offer, went so far as to make steamship reservations for himself and his wife, and asked Lionel to make out an affidavit, necessary before he could obtain an immigration visa. In complying with this request Lionel was astonished to learn that Strauss was regarded as a Nazi, that he had been seen in a photograph with Goebbels and Goering, and that Lionel might ruin himself by extending such great hospitality. All this was news to the innocent Lionel, who had enormous respect for the creator of such works as *Salome, Don Juan,* and *Til Eulenspiegel.* Sadly he wrote Strauss and withdrew his offer.

Eventually the house had to be sold, as tax difficulties mounted for Lionel. His shrine went to pay an income tax lien.

Lionel was loaned out by MGM to Columbia in 1938 for the Frank Capra production of *You Can't Take It With You,* the part of whacky Grandpa Vanderhof having been fortuitously written to be played in a wheelchair. On April 28 Lionel was notified that he was on call for a scene to be shot at the Columbia ranch. He arrived in make-up, cameras were lined up, and he was told to take his place at the head of a long table. What happened, however, turned out not to be in the script. A huge cake was brought in, and Capra led the cast and crew in a "Happy Birthday" rendition. Lionel had reached the age of sixty, and a celebration was in order.

Columbia's publicity department made Lionel less than happy when a story was put out to the effect that Lionel's fondness for his wheelchair was due to an injury he had suffered sliding down a bannister. Later the story was changed, and Lionel was portrayed as a sufferer from arthritis. He was very quickly inundated by a barrage of letters from arthritis sufferers all over the country, and he was never able to completely scotch the story. What he did suffer from more and more was an inflamed rheumatic condition that affected both his knee joints.

Full rescue for Lionel came about when MGM instituted the low budget *Dr. Kildare* series and found a role for him that he was able to repeat many times. In 1937, before his second hip injury, and while the studio scrounged for parts he could play, he had appeared in a low-budget film called *A Family Affair.* Lionel played a small town judge and the father of Mickey Rooney. Made for about $150,000, the movie was a box-office winner, and more pictures involving the same basic characters were planned. The second was put into production while Lionel was in London making *A Yank at Oxford,* and Lewis Stone took his place as Judge Hardy, becoming a Hardy perennial in that role. The same low budget unit looked around for another story that might be turned into a series, and came across two short stories by Max Brand that had appeared in a popular magazine and that involved an old experienced doctor and an enthusiastic young interne. Max Brand turned out to be the pseudonym of Henrik Faust, whose fertile mind was filled with innumerable Dr. Gillespie and Dr. Kildare stories. Lionel was thought of as the older doctor, but his wheelchair condition seemed to put an end to the idea until it was decided that Dr. Gillespie could function from a wheelchair in the stories.

Lionel saw the hand of L. B. Mayer behind the suggestion, although Mayer never owned up to it, and accepted the role with alacrity. It is doubtful if the Kildare series would have gotten under way if Mickey Rooney had not made such a success out of the Andy Hardy series, and Lionel certainly owed some gratitude to the energetic, pint-sized Rooney.

MGM, according to Bosley Crowther in *The Lion's Share*, "set things up so as to get quite a shock with the first entrance of the old doctor in his wheelchair, and then they hastily wrote a scene in which Dr. Kildare discovered that Doctor Gillespie suffered from cancer. This gave added courage and noble character to the philosophical old healer of others." Needless to say, Lionel suffered from "cancer" for many years thereafter, even though in one of the early films of the series it was revealed that his cancer was incurable. Through all of the films, which came to a total of fifteen, Lionel solved medical cases, and gave crusty advice first to Lew Ayres and then to Van Johnson. The films were made on almost absurdly low budgets, and earned MGM huge profits.

Lionel, in 1938, was probably the highest salaried of all wheelchair workers. When the *New York Times* listed the top salaries paid to Americans during the year, Lionel's name was on the list with a salary of more than $138,000. Where this money went no one seems to know, but it is safe to say that much went in taxes and interest on assessed and unpaid taxes. He never did get out of his tax bind, and he began to build an unwarranted reputation for stinginess. The truth of the matter is that the government left him just about enough to live on, and no more.

Very late in his life he was still dead-broke and in debt to the government for more than $100,000. Lionel never complained about this. But there was a point reached when he became terrified that the government might actually put him in jail for his debt. He made a pain-ridden trip to Washington, saw some officials of the Treasury Department, and agreed to turn his earnings over to the government, including his $1500 weekly MGM salary. He retained a small amount for his living expenses.

His payday was Thursday at the Culver City Studio, and on the afternoon of that day he would drive on the lot in his specially fitted car and get as close as he could to the accounting window. He would honk the horn of his car. Then came a familiar sight at MGM. A fishing pole with a small basket would emerge from the window. In the basket was a check for what remained of his salary. Lionel would take the check from the basket, endorse it, and put the check back. Again the pole came out, this time containing the cash he needed to live on for the week.

Asked how long he intended to play Dr. Gillespie, he replied, "I hope until hell freezes over." Hell froze over for the series in 1947, but it was by no means the end of his screen career.

Although his acting in the series could be considered of the bread-and-butter variety, Lionel gave of his best to the films. Otis Ferguson, the fine film critic for *The New Republic,* wrote about his Dr. Gillespie roles: "Poor Lionel Barrymore has played Mr. B. so long and successfully that he is under the handicap of having his considerable range of tricks known by heart; but he does a good and restrained piece of work here as the crusty old humanist. . . . I say 'poor' because if this had been his first part, those cocking eyebrows, snorts, chuckles, lip-smacking invective, and gnarled tenderness would be shouted up as an acting masterpiece."

At MGM during the forties Lionel became known as an encyclopedia of medicine because of the reading he did for the Kildare series, and he exhibited just as much lore on the subject of boxing. Most of the fight champions sooner or later took a tour through the studio, and they could virtually count on being entertained on the set or at lunch by Lionel. In 1940, on his sixty-second birthday, L. B. Mayer gave him a birthday party attended by a host of his friends, stars and notables among them, and the occasion was thought important enough to be broadcast nationwide and sent via short wave to Europe.

His wheelchair became identified with Lionel's acting, so much so that he was able to make canny use of it as a prop. No child actor, even so accomplished a one as Margaret O'Brien, was able to compete with Lionel in the art of scene stealing. The mature actors who worked with Lionel came to regard the wheelchair as the best scene-stealing vehicle since the chariot in *Ben Hur*.

"It certainly doesn't cramp my style," Lionel admitted to an interviewer, Hedda Hopper. (He was averse to doing interviews and the studio protected him from them, but he made an occasional exception for Miss Hopper and a few others.) "Its manipulation has become like second nature. Handling it is as automatic as driving my car."

He boomed the sales of wheelchairs for the manufacturer of the one he used. From all parts of the world came inquiries to Lionel as to the type of chair he used and where a similar one could be obtained. Many sufferers from infantile paralysis wrote, and one request came from an injured pilot in Manila who was impressed by the ease and abandon with which Lionel moved about during his scenes. The letters he received he sent on to the manufacturer, who supplied the information requested.

His dressing room at MGM had been set up for him as a combination studio and office, and was fitted out with the materials he needed for his copperplate etching and with a piano. Immobilized to a great degree and unable to climb the stairs to his dressing room, he moved the paraphernalia for etching and the piano to the Chatsworth house, setting them up in a room on the ground floor. After 1942 he devoted less time to etching and more to composing.

His composing was confined to not much more than the melodic line of a composition, but of these he turned out many, freely admitted that he borrowed from or was influenced by the composers he liked—Wagner, Brahms, and Mahler among them. When several of these pieces were played they were in the form of orchestrations by a musician friend of his, who would come out to the Chatsworth house, play Lionel's work a good deal better than Lionel was able to do, and help him with the arranging.

One of Lionel's compositions served as the musical motif for the background score of *Dr. Kildare's Strange Case*, which was filmed in 1940. In that same year Lionel dug up one of his old symphonic suites and donated it to a WPA-sponsored orchestra in Los Angeles. The composition was called *Tableau Russe*, and it resulted in Lionel's making his professional bow as a composer. A newspaper critic called the work "entertaining and exceptionally well orchestrated." After his brother's death Lionel worked on a tone poem called *In Memoriam*. One day Gene Fowler came to see him in Chatsworth, and Lionel brought out several sheets of music. His dream, he told Fowler, was to have the composition played some day by Eugene Ormandy and the Philadelphia Orchestra. This is precisely what happened. The score was brought to Ormandy's attention by James Fassett of CBS, and on April 22, 1944, *In Memoriam* was broadcast by Ormandy during a Sunday afternoon concert on the CBS network, and was presented as a tone poem dedicated to John Barrymore. Another of his pieces, *Partita*, was conducted by Fabien Sevitsky at New York's Lewisohn Stadium. Through these works and others he became an ASCAP member.

"It is not only amusing but pleasing to have all this happen at my age," he said. And although Fabien Sevitsky went on record that Lionel's *Partita* was melodically and rhythmically interesting and proved that he possessed as much musical as dramatic talent, Lionel himself was inclined to be more modest. "Some people play solitaire," he said. "I write music."

He had become more famous for his etchings, too. He was exhibited in several shows around the country. *Time* magazine, commenting on a show of art works by Hollywood stars, said that Lionel, represented by etchings, was by far the most craftsmanlike. (Some are still to be found as illustrations for Christmas cards.)

During the World War II years he did several months of radio work for the government on behalf of the war effort, and was frequently to be found at the Hollywood canteen. He was surprised, once, when the orchestra that entertained soldiers played three of his arrangements of MacDowell's piano music.

"That stuff's a little heavy for the boys," he growled.

He had his own weekly radio show, *Mayor of the Town,* on a national network in 1942 and continued in the highly popular role of the small town mayor for five years, being voted "best radio actor" for one of those years. In 1944 he campaigned actively on behalf of Governor Dewey during the Presidential race, and this activity was to cause him one of his great sorrows. Metro in 1946 cast him to portray Franklin Delano Roosevelt in *The Beginning of the End,* a film about the development of the atom bomb. It was soon made clear that Mrs. Eleanor Roosevelt objected very strongly to Lionel Barrymore portraying her dead husband because of some private statements purportedly made by Lionel during the previous Presidential campaign. The late President's son, James Roosevelt, was supposed to have conveyed his mother's objections to the studio, saying (according to a report in the *New York Times*) that "Mrs. Roosevelt felt that Barrymore should not have the honor of playing the President."

Lionel, upon hearing about the hubbub caused by his casting, wrote Mrs. Roosevelt a letter disclaiming any unrecorded verbal attacks by him on the President. The matter was important enough for Nicholas Schenck, president of Loew's Incorporated (the MGM parent firm), to deliver Lionel's letter personally to Mrs. Roosevelt, but she did not withdraw her objection to Lionel, and he was removed from the film.

Lionel, after bowing out of the movie, made a gallant public statement. He stated that he believed Mrs. Roosevelt to be "entirely justified in any such decisions that she makes." He added, however: "I could not have made the statements which someone has attributed to me since I know nothing but good things of the late President." Later, in *We Barrymores,* Lionel admitted that his dog, Johnnie, had written to Roosevelt's dog, Fala, but he was sure that if Roosevelt had ever read the letter he would have seen its intended humor and would certainly have collaborated with Fala on a reply.

Another Barrymore, Ethel, had contributed mightily to FDR's 1944 campaign when she made a remark (although it was attributed to Alice Longworth) about the likeness of Governor Dewey to the little man traditionally placed atop large wedding cakes, and any campaign work done by Lionel would have been nullified by the currency given to the remark, complete to a *New Yorker* cartoon showing Dewey on a cake.

By 1948 Lionel was a rotund 220 pounds due to his sedentary (injury enforced) habits, and his propensity for putting away large meals. Twentieth Century-Fox had been searching for an actor who could look, bellow, and act like Lionel Barrymore for its large-scale production of *Down to the Sea in Ships,* and after trying out various actors, decided to borrow the original from MGM. The picture's success was thought to depend upon the forcefulness with which an old whaling captain was played, and the studio's hesitance about Lionel had been caused by a prevalent theory that Lionel had been walking (or rather wheeling) through the Kildare pictures, and that he would not be up to the rigors of this sea-action movie.

Fox's hesitancy seemed justified during the first days of shooting. Henry Hathaway, the director, spent three days in an attempt to get a satisfactory first scene with Lionel. Lionel, with little time for preparation, either forgot his lines or blew up or stumbled in the midst of a line. On the third afternoon Hathaway carefully explained the scene to Lionel and discovered that the actor had fallen sound asleep and hadn't heard a word he'd said. Hathaway let loose. He charged Lionel with eating two complete orders of beef stew at lunch and a full loaf of bread. He went on to say that Lionel had made the rushes into a mess, and that Zanuck, if he saw them, was likely to fire everyone and start over from scratch with a new crew.

Lionel screwed up his face and thought for a minute. He then suggested a solution to Hathaway, that he allow him to go home for a week and think about the problem, meanwhile shooting around his scenes. "As for lunch," he said, "I'll eat cottage cheese for the whole week."

Lionel seemed like another man when he came back to the picture. He had dropped several pounds in weight and, more important, showed all his old acting authority. His stand-in of twenty years' experience, Frank Stevens, was being used for shots of Lionel walking. This was done by showing Lionel about to rise from his chair, and the camera would then take up Stevens, walking away. One day

Lionel roared at Stevens: "Frank, you old, idiot impostor, get out of the way and let an old man walk."

Lionel then amazed everyone by getting up and limping across the set, perfectly portraying the crippled seaman he was supposed to be. Nor would he use the platform rigged to hoist him from the stage to the mock-up of the ship. He dragged his way up the gangplank, and when told he didn't have to exert himself to that extent, answered disgustedly: "It has nothing to do with the damned show-must-go-on business. That's nonsense. This leg of mine has begun to show a little sense."

Later he said that when he had begun to follow his doctor's advice about dieting he had been told by the doctor that he might eventually be able to get around without the help of crutches, but that this wouldn't be possible without bringing his weight down. He habitually wore a support around his waist to prevent pain from the old hip fractures; when he became lighter in weight he found that the support also helped him in his efforts to walk.

It was generally agreed that Lionel had walked off with the picture, and again the critics used what had practically become a stock phrase in movie reviewing: "Lionel Barrymore gives one of the best performances of his long career."

Lionel, in addition to his other accomplishments, had always threatened to turn literary. He had written plays, among them a theater adaptation of several episodes from the long-running *Mayor of the Town*, and as far back as 1928 he had sent a play manuscript to Ned Sheldon by way of his brother John, but nothing was ever produced. In 1949 he decided to write his autobiography with the avowed purpose of having a best-seller and getting rid of his indebtedness to the government at one fell swoop. His collaborator in this enterprise was Cameron Shipp, well known and highly regarded as a journalist and co-author of the Billie Burke best-seller, *With a Feather on My Nose*.

Nearly every day during the summer of 1949 Lionel parked his car under a grapefruit tree in Shipp's patio, and Shipp would sit in the car with him and do the interviewing. In the back seat sat a young U.S.C. student, Maynard Smith, who took the conversations down in shorthand. Every now and then Smith would be sent to the kitchen to bring back beer and cheese.

Lionel's reminiscences (to Shipp) rambled, not always too coherently and sometimes unprintably. "You know," he said at one point, "Thalberg one day knew absolutely nothing about motion pictures and the next day knew everything." Shipp, anxious to build a complete story, discovered that Lionel remembered almost nothing of his marriage to Doris Rankin. It was as though he had erased it from his mind. To refresh his memory, Shipp offered Lionel some details of the marriage he himself had dug up. "Well, you don't say," Lionel said, but refused to go into the matter any further.

On Saturdays, interviewing was intermittent because Lionel liked to listen to the Metropolitan Opera broadcasts on his car radio. One of these Saturdays Shipp got into the car and asked Lionel to tell him about other members of the Barrymore family. Lionel turned on him, glared at Shipp over the top of his glasses, and said, "Oh, the hell with the Barrymores!" He then turned on the car radio and sat listening blissfully, refusing to touch the beer that Maynard Smith brought out to him. Smith sat in the back seat, listening to the opera, and slowly got tight on the forgotten beer. During the most magnificent moments of the opera, one of Verdi's, Lionel would weep copious tears. Once he crossed himself and said: "Jesus Christ, isn't that gorgeous?"

The writing of the book was interrupted several times by Lionel's absence on a film-making chore, but it was eventually completed, serialized in the *Saturday Evening Post,* and went through several printings upon publication in hard covers. But the total returns were still not enough to pay off Lionel's tax indebtedness.

With Maynard Smith aiding him as typist, Lionel next labored on a novel called *Mr. Cantonwine,* an odd tale about an "Uncle Sam" disguised as Martin J. Cantonwine who rambles through American history and who expresses the march of an emerging nation. Critics were puzzled by its almost surrealistic form, and couldn't quite understand why Cantonwine was always accompanied by a lady of questionable virtue. The *New York Times* critic wrote carefully: "How successful Mr. Barrymore has been in his over-all accomplishment is a matter that each reader must decide for himself."

While working for Lionel on *Mr. Cantonwine* Maynard Smith ran into difficulty about getting the fees due him, mainly because Lionel hardly ever had an extra dollar to his name. But one day Lionel handed Smith a check for ten dollars and said shyly, "Well, of course you can't do this on air." Maynard called up Cameron Shipp and wondered, in view of Lionel's financial condition, whether or not he ought to accept the check. "For God's sake, keep the damn thing," Shipp shouted at him. "It's priceless. No one else has ever seen a check from Lionel for ten dollars!" Smith never cashed it, but kept it as a curiosity.

Talking (in 1963) about his adventures with Lionel, Smith, now an administrative officer at the University of Southern California, remembered how impressed he was with the beauty of the furnishings of Lionel's house. "It was absolutely elegant," he said, "with furniture and possessions showing the most exquisite taste." Lionel had managed to keep the furnishings away from the tax collectors by putting them, along with the house, in the Wheelers' names. As far as anyone could recall, this act was the one instance of what might be termed "business sense" that Lionel ever exhibited.

If he privately damned the taxation system that kept him working until the end of his life, he had a deep-rooted faith in the strength of the American grain, and when asked to participate as narrator in a vast five-day pageant called "The California Story" held in Hollywood Bowl during September of 1950, he willingly donated his services. He went through the grueling rehearsals needed to synchronize his narration with the musical score by Meredith Willson. On the fifth and last night of the pageant, as twenty-five thousand spectators crowded the Bowl and overflowed onto the hillsides, Lionel's voice (emanating from the sound booth by which he was enclosed) rose with the crescendos of the music. "Through the land," he recited, "the grandsons and great-grandsons of the men of 1776 and 1850, those titans of independence and freedom . . . All the mighty chorus of the past . . ." His voice gained in strength, became Churchillian (said listeners later), and brought the huge crowd to its feet spontaneously. Applause burst out, more applause than Lionel had ever heard before. He sat in the sound booth, tired, wearing an old hat, as the applause changed into shouts for him.

He grinned, then struggled to his feet and was helped to his car. He drove home alone in the night.

Between 1949 and 1953 he appeared in five more films, one of them *Lone Star,* in which he played Andrew Jackson. His last appearance was in *Main Street to Broadway,* an all-star tribute to the theater, in which he played, for the first time, himself. He kept busy on the radio, as the host of the Hallmark Radio Playhouse, and never for a moment thought of retiring. In 1954 he spoke to Bob Thomas, an Associated Press correspondent, about his eagerness to get into television. "The only thing holding me back," he declared, "is the studio's hands-off policy toward television for its actors." He didn't want to jeopardize his life-term contract with MGM. He mentioned to Thomas that one of his heroes, Joe DiMaggio, was supposed to appear on his radio show and was late for a rehearsal.

Thomas mentioned that Marilyn Monroe, DiMaggio's wife, had a reputation for being even later.

"Is that true?" Lionel inquired.

Thomas said it was.

"Well, she can arrive late with me any time she wants," Lionel said.

The same year he was engaged on yet another literary work, a quasi-novel called *The Shakespeare Club.* It was evidently meant to be a fictional summation of such philosophical meanings as he had gathered throughout his life, but he didn't manage to achieve a sense of form with either his plot or characters, and the manuscript was never published. In fact it would have been entirely forgotten had not Maynard Smith kept a copy in memory of the old actor.

"Life itself is not an overly pretty thing," Lionel began, but whatever philosophical purpose he might have had in mind collapsed as he spotted his chance for a good line. "As capricious, frequently ironic, and occasionally downright hopeless as it can sometimes be, it is not as bad as it can be on television." He then went on to tell about an old actor friend of his, whose name was Mr. Montmorency. After two hundred and thirteen pages of meandering conversation and conversational asides, Mr. Montmorency died. Lionel wrote: "Montmorency was gone. Well, he had been very old. I was reminded of the words of Pope . . .

Thus let me live, unseen, unknown,
Thus unlamented let me die,
Steal from the world, and not a stone
Tell me where I lie."

Early in November, 1954, Lionel smashed up his vintage Oldsmobile against a wall, but was taken from the wreckage alive and relatively intact. But the stout old body was fading. He had a congestive heart condition complicated by the spreading of uremic poisoning. On November 15 he was on his terrace in the sunshine, reading a passage from *Macbeth* to Florence Wheeler. Suddenly struck by a heart attack, he pitched over into Miss Wheeler's arms. He remained in a coma while being rushed to the Valley Hospital in Van Nuys and died nineteen hours later without regaining consciousness.

The burial took place at Calvary Cemetery in a crypt beside that of his wife, Irene, and above that of his brother John, on which Lionel had had inscribed: GOOD NIGHT, SWEET PRINCE.

Some months later his personal effects were sold at auction. They included his books, his record albums, his original theater programs dating as far back as 1816, a marble head of John Barrymore done by Paul Manship, his Whistler and Rembrandt etchings, and six of his own etchings. Without knowing it, Lionel was still paying off his income taxes.

THE LAST OF
THE BARRYMORES

chapter XXIV

LATE IN 1945 Ethel Barrymore succumbed to the lure of the West and made her residence in California. Playing in New York in *Embezzled Heaven* through the winter of 1944–1945, she contracted pneumonia and was told by the doctors after her recovery that she had been near death. This news, plus several bad colds that followed the pneumonia, turned her thoughts more and more to the warm sun of Southern California. Following upon her winning of the Academy Award, offers to make movies came frequently. She accepted the role of a bedridden elderly woman in a murder mystery called *The Spiral Staircase*, hurried east once more after finishing it, took Philip Barry's *The Joyous Season* out on the road for Arthur Hopkins, and decided to close it down before risking what seemed sure to be the displeasure of the New York critics. The play was a revival of an earlier Broadway failure, and its reception by tryout audiences had not been encouraging.

So it was that Broadway audiences had seen the last of Ethel Barrymore in *Embezzled Heaven*. Of her performance Howard Barnes of the *Herald Tribune* had said: "The queen of the theater's royal family has imbued the play with simplicity, eloquence, and tremendous dramatic authority." (It was now customary to refer to Ethel not as the first lady but the queen.) More good reviews came her way for *The Spiral Staircase*. *Time* said about her: "She spends

378

most of this one propped up in bed, alternately purring and bellowing in a voice not unlike Brother Lionel's. She is superbly effective."

Ethel looked over the postwar Hollywood scene with a less clinical eye than formerly, and told a friend: "It's still a rather strange place. Clifford Odets doesn't rate out here at all, for some reason." But Ethel Barrymore did, and so did some of her old friends, like George Cukor, who saw to it that she received all the attention and homage she deserved when at last she made her home there. She first lived in a small house on Laurel Canyon Drive above Sunset Boulevard. Her son, Sammie, back from his Army service, joined her there, and she looked for a larger place.

She found one she was able to rent in Palos Verdes, on the coast south of Santa Monica, and fell in love with the large, rambling house that overlooked the blue of the Pacific. She naturally paid much too much rent, but movie work gave her an excellent income and she was able to afford it. The house in Mamaroneck was given over to Ethel Colt, who had recently married an Italian engineer, Romeo Miglietta, and was eventually put up for sale after Ethel decided she would never live in the East again. The Palos Verdes house she furnished simply but gave to it a smart, comfortable, and cheerful look, allowing little that would remind her of the past. One important exception to this rule was her placing of Sargent's portrait of her over the mantel in the living room.

She entertained frequently, gave dinners at which she sat at the head of a gleaming mahogany table. Her parties, Charles Brackett remembered, "were the best anyone gave. They were delightful, and you always met the most interesting people—Aldous Huxley, Gerald Heard, Gladys Cooper, Constance Collier, the Artur Rubensteins." She presided over these gatherings, Cornelia Otis Skinner said, "with the graceful grandeur of an Edith Wharton hostess."

When Ethel made a film at MGM, Katharine Hepburn, then the studio's number one star, turned her own dressing room over to her. During the making of *Night Song*, with Merle Oberon at RKO, Ethel and Miss Oberon were allotted the two biggest dressing rooms. A famous conductor, making his Hollywood debut in the film, was heard wondering why he deserved lesser treatment than the two ladies. "Shall we tell him?" Ethel whispered sweetly to Miss Oberon.

Ethel wasted little time between pictures in Hollywood. She made three and four each year during her first five-year period of residence in Hollywood, working for several noted directors. Alfred Hitchcock directed her in *The Paradine Case,* and noticing what he thought was a case of opening-scene jitters said to her, "Why are you nervous? It's only a movie." "Now suppose I said that to *you?*" Ethel flashed back. Hollywood loved her sense of humor, and many of her characteristic little *mots* were quoted with relish. "She was an old-fashioned star," Elia Kazan, who directed her in *Pinky,* said. "Old-fashioned in the sense that she knew what was due her. She was also a grand lady, who would give great nobility to any part she would play. 'That's wonderful,' I'd say to her after a take. 'Now let's do it once more.' 'What do you want another one for?' she asked me. 'Your collection?' "

Between takes Ethel would hurry to her dressing room, where she would listen to the ball games on her radio. She rooted less for single teams than for individual players, and when there was not a major league game to listen to would settle for the Coast League games. Tallulah Bankhead's addiction to baseball had become well known through the press agentry of Richard Maney, but Ethel did not regard her as a serious rooter. "She's a latecomer to baseball," Ethel said. "And she only likes one team—the Giants. I like all the teams." After a while, when interviewed about baseball, she would refuse to talk about the sport. "People are beginning to think I don't know about anything else," she explained. However, when asked why she insisted on freelancing instead of signing a term contract with a studio, she said, "The first thing I know they would be lending me out for a lot of money and a couple of outfielders."

She read avidly, gobbling up books at an incredible rate. Formerly, when out on tour, she had abandoned the books as she went from one place to another. Now she kept them, storing them in every closet of the house and finally in the garage. One day her son Sammie couldn't park his car in the garage because the books had taken up so much space. "Please give up reading, Mother," he told her, "or go on tour."

But touring was no longer for Ethel, although she sometimes said she missed the days when she played up to forty-three one-night stands in a row. Nor would she come back to the theater when pursued for the leading role in the Broadway production of *The Madwoman of Chaillot*. "Don't you think," she replied to a pleading wire sent her by the producer, "that after working for fifty years for cut flowers in my dressing room I should be permitted to sit in my garden for a while and watch them grow?"

Ethel did cultivate her garden, growing a profusion of flowers at the Palos Verdes place. She took an interest in Dee Dee and John, daughter and son of Dolores and John, who paid her frequent visits. Lionel came to see her less frequently, because Palos Verdes was a good distance from Chatsworth. Later she rented a house in the Pacific Palisades that was nearer to what passed as the center of things in Hollywood.

On her seventieth birthday Hollywood, the community she had formerly scorned, paid Ethel what was probably the biggest tribute ever given an actress. The occasion was sponsored by the Motion Picture Academy in cooperation with the NBC radio network. The half-hour show was carried worldwide, made possible by advance recording of the voices of the more than fifty participants, some living and some dead (and heard in recordings of their voices). Lionel spoke "live," but John's resonant voice came through in a recording made when she had been feted in 1941 on the radio. Among those of her living confreres who paid their respects to her were Alfred Lunt and Lynn Fontanne, Spencer Tracy, Cary Grant, Katharine Cornell. Herbert Hoover, Mrs. Eleanor Roosevelt, and President Harry S. Truman added their voices to the tributes.

Katharine Hepburn said on the program: "She has more friends than anyone I know, but she's not a dear, gentle soul. Barrymores don't come like that. She has a trenchant wit . . . She makes appallingly accurate observations. She doesn't know the meaning of fear or the meaning of caution. . . ."

At a little party George Cukor gave in her honor in his home that Sunday, August 15, 1949, Ethel sat very quietly listening with the others. "She looked so beautiful—" Zoë Akins said, "so young and strong and beautiful—that it seemed for the moment intolerable that she was not in her own theater in a play which made full demands on her beauty and her art." Ethel was thrilled by the program, with everything in it, even Elsie Janis's imitation of her voice, given for the last time. Delivered to her at Cukor's party was a cablegram, simply signed "Winston."

Charles Brackett, who had presided over the broadcast, was president of the Motion Picture Academy, and in March of the following year he asked Ethel to present the award for the best male acting performance at the annual Academy Award ceremony. Ethel came out on the stage when it was time to announce the winner, took the envelope handed her, and read out the name of Laurence Olivier, who won the award for his performance of Hamlet. There were some who thought they noticed a slight tone of incredulity in her voice. She came off and said to Brackett in the wings: "I didn't sound too Sonny Tufts, did I?" She was referring of course to one famous radio incident in which the master of ceremonies, handed the names of his guests for the program, said in disbelief: *"Sonny Tufts?"*

"Of course," Brackett recalled later, "Ethel thought Olivier's performance extremely inferior in what she regarded as a family property." He also remembered being present at a party given by Emlyn Williams and his wife while they were staying in Hollywood. Ethel remained seated in queenly dignity while the party swirled around her. At one point Mrs. Williams became engaged in a heated argument with two young men, and in her excitement knocked over Ethel's glass of water, which spilled on her dress. Servants ran in and tried to wipe away the damage, and in their eagerness another glass of water was tipped and spilled on Ethel. "My God," Mrs. Williams said in her agitation, "I'm glad it wasn't wine."

"Yes," said Ethel, "but it *is* rather cold."

Brackett often paid Ethel visits at her home, where he would have delightful chats with her that ranged over every conceivable subject. He, as well as George Cukor, commented on how Ethel's beauty stayed with her through the years. "She was the most beautiful older woman you ever saw in your life," Brackett said, and Cukor affirmed his judgment. When Ethel was ill and bedridden, she received Brackett in her bedroom one day. At the door he said: "May I see the most beautiful woman in California?"

Ethel's voice rolled out: "And *why* have I been demoted?"

After her daughter gave birth to a son in the late 1940s, Ethel made occasional trips to New York to see her grandson, of whom she was extremely fond, and who reciprocated her affection by calling her "Mum Mum." During one of these trips, in January of 1950, Ethel was asked to participate in the ANTA Album, the theater's annual benefit for itself. She agreed to do a scene from *The Twelve Pound Look,* her old favorite. The performance took place at the Ziegfeld Theatre on January 29, 1950, and was Ethel's last appearance before a theater audience. Bert Lahr took part in the same benefit, and was asked by another performer, "Bert, when does Ethel Barrymore go on?" At that moment came a great roar of welcome, followed by applause that carried to the sixth-floor dressing room. "She's on," Lahr told the other actor.

Ethel during the 1950s was seen less frequently on the screen, although she scoffed at the thought of retiring for good. Some of her better films were *Portrait of Jennie, Pinky* (the first Hollywood movie to deal forthrightly with the interracial problem), *Kind Lady,* and *Young at Heart.* But there were mediocre ones, too, about some of which the critics grumbled that the great lady's talents were being wasted. Her last movie was *Johnny Trouble,* made in 1956. Frank Sinatra, her co-star in *Young at Heart,* became one of the worshipers of the actress, and joined those who paid her visits.

Although she befriended John Barrymore, Jr., John's son, when he first began to make a try at a career on the stage and in films, she soured on him after he pulled out of the cast, which included Ethel Colt, of a summer theater production of *The Hasty Heart* in 1951, causing the producers to abandon the show. Ethel was outraged. "Never in three hundred years," she thundered, "has a Barrymore walked out of a contract. After all, we're professionals. We don't do things like that." When John Jr.'s erratic course continued, she shook her head unhappily over him. "He's so nervous, so jumpy," she said about him once. "And he doesn't read. I'm always suspicious of people who don't read."

Young John attended a military academy in the Los Angeles area when he was a child, then went to private and prep schools until he was seventeen, at which time he suddenly decided he would become an actor. Dolores Costello, his mother, was now married to her former obstetrician, Dr. John Vruwink, and she was not in the least interested in her son's taking up the life of an actor. John, Jr., was adamant, though, running away from home and hitchhiking to his stepfather's deserted ranch in Fallbrook, California, where he held out for two weeks without informing his mother of his whereabouts. She capitulated, and John, Jr., made the rounds. After initial resistance to someone who appeared to be trying to make use of his father's name, several producers gave him roles in B pictures. John gave an interview after seeing himself in one of these, a western called *The Sundowners,* and said: A couple of months ago I saw a revival of *The Great Profile.* I nearly jumped out of my skin seeing the similarity between some of my father's gestures and mine. It was pretty upsetting I should be so like him. I mean, a man I could hardly remember."

John, as time went on, seemed to have inherited less of his father's talent than his ability to get himself into temperamental and emotional scrapes. At twenty he married Cara Williams, an actress of twenty-seven. Divorce came six years later. His second wife was an Italian "starlet," Gabriella Palazzoli, with whom he was involved in some "wife-slapping" episodes, one of which resulted in an eight-month suspended sentence in Rome for insulting and resisting the police. He played several roles on television during the mid and late 1950s, then, after being fined by Actors' Equity for jumping a contract, went to Italy, where he worked in Italian pictures. By the time he was thirty his hair had turned prematurely gray, and while in Italy he took to wearing a beard which, with his bushy head of hair, gave him a vaguely biblical appearance. One newspaper termed him "the Beatnik Barrymore."

Ethel began writing her memoirs in 1953. She met Howard Thompson of the *New York Times* in April of that year and told him about her writing, disclosing that the book was taking shape by her own hand. "Every word, too," she said. "Lionel's were ghosted, of course. Right now I'm twelve years old."

Never having kept scrapbooks or more than a few mementos of her long career, she was somewhat at a loss as to the exact moment something important happened in her life. Then she announced proudly that she would do her memoirs "without dates and things like that." Once started, she was able to recall matters in sequence, and wrote the whole book in pencil on white paper. Lionel died shortly after the script was sent to the publishers, and Ethel, who had seen her brother only two days before his death, was too overwhelmed to attend his funeral. The *Ladies' Home Journal* decided to serialize her *Memories* (as she titled the book), and before going to press the editor called her up and asked her if she wanted to include something about Lionel.

Ethel thought for a moment and wrote on an empty envelope: "Since I have finished this book, Lionel has died. I would like to think he and Jack are together—and that they will be glad to see me. E. B."

She read this to the editor, Hugh Kahler, and heard no response from the other end. "What's wrong?" she asked.

"I'm crying," Kahler said.

"I am too," Ethel told him.

When the book came out in 1955 Ethel was flooded with congratulatory messages from her hosts of friends, who privately were disappointed that she chose to remain reticent about a good deal of her life. She, on the other hand, was delighted with the celebrity of being an author, and announced that she would probably start work on another book. (She didn't.)

She made several appearances on television from 1953 on, at first describing the new medium as "hell," but then willingly making guest appearances and for a short time acting as host on a series called *The Ethel Barrymore Theater*. When the scripts of that show struck her as weak, she withdrew from it. But at home she watched television frequently, finding it a particular comfort when bedridden. She had never gone to see her own movies, but now she saw herself occasionally on the small screen. When *Rasputin and the Empress* was shown on TV she watched the movie for the first time. "I thought I was pretty good," she confided to Leonard Lyons, "but what those two boys were up to I'll never know."

She was asked in 1955 if she now considered herself a permanent part of the film colony. "I came to the West Coast for my health," she answered proudly, "and I have worked in pictures to earn a living. But I have always belonged to the theater, and fundamentally I feel that there is as much difference between the stage and the films as between a piano and a violin. Normally you can't become a virtuoso in both."

Ethel's mind remained sharp and bright as she approached her eightieth birthday. Her son Sammie, established in public relations in California, remained with her. Her last public appearance was in a television program shown in November, 1957, and arranged as a recapitulation (not a good one) of her career; she would have appeared in a *Playhouse 90* drama in January, 1958, if a broken arm had not prevented her participation. She was saddened by the spectacular wreck her niece Diana was making of herself, and could not help but follow the process in the newspapers, which Diana "made" frequently. The last eighteen months of her life she spent confined to bed, the result of arthritic rheumatism and a heart condition. If she had been able to get up she would certainly have acted again, if only because she felt the need to earn money. The doctors' bills, the constant care of a nurse, now necessary, had again brought her to a precarious financial condition. An AFTRA pension and medical plan, for which Ethel became eligible, was of immense help to her during her last year.

George Cukor, infinitely faithful and kind, came to see her often. So did Katharine Hepburn, who revered her. "She was beautiful to look at," Miss Hepburn recalled of the times that Ethel greeted her as she lay regally in bed, "always very well groomed, and her dark hair well fixed. I would sit by her side and be thrilled by just the sight of her—that exquisite skin and those beautiful eyes. She always lay among silk bedsheets, and the bedcover was always filled with books. And around the bed were tables, all filled with books. . . . She always had several vases full of beautiful flowers which had been sent and which she seemed to like more than anything else. The ventilation in that room was wonderful; she sat in a violent breeze the entire time she was desperately ill. Anybody else in the room was apt to freeze to death, but not Ethel, no covers for her.

"I think she had a great faith in something, and she somehow gave me faith in something. It was a kind of faith in life, I think. I used to sit there and talk to her and then I would go away. But I'd always come back. People would say to me, 'You're so nice to go and call on Ethel,' and I would think to myself how very lucky I was to be able to see Ethel."

A week before her death, Elza Schallert of the Los Angeles *Times* came to see Ethel, and the aged actress talked of the theater she had known all her life, contrasting the past with the dizzy pace and the variety of the present. Her eyes gleamed for a moment when she was asked if she would like to continue acting. "It would have to be just the right part," she said judiciously, "in either a motion picture or a TV presentation. Just right . . ."

But there were to be no more parts for Ethel. On the evening of June 17, 1959, Ethel woke from a short nap, grasped her nurse's hand, and asked: "Is everybody happy? I want everybody to be happy. I know I'm happy." Then she fell asleep and did not wake.

Her death was recorded as having occurred on June 18, 1959. That night, at the Ethel Barrymore Theatre where *Raisin in the Sun* was being performed, the lights on the marquee and in the theater were dimmed for five minutes before the curtain rose. On June 22, a Requiem High Mass was given for Ethel at the Church of the Good Shepherd in Beverly Hills. Her casket was borne from the church by Joseph Cotten, Charles Brackett, Orry Kelly, and Philip Dunne. Through the heat of the day a small twelve-car cavalcade wound its way to Calvary Cemetery, where the casket was placed beside those of John and Lionel. "One could almost hear the whisper," wrote a reporter, *"That's all there is. There isn't any more."*

Not quite all. But it was clear that with Ethel's passing a dynasty was vanishing, and that the tradition that it represented was losing its force. "None of us," Helen Hayes said of Ethel, "can ever give the theater the luster she did." "A queen has died," said Clifton Webb. Offspring of the Barrymores were there to carry on, but they could not be considered crown princes or princesses. Dolores Mae Barrymore flirted briefly with acting in her late teens, but married, bore two children, and retreated into housewifely obscurity. "I want to forget all about the name of Barrymore," she said. Her brother, John Barrymore, Jr., changed his name to John Drew Barrymore when his own son was born in 1956, allowing him the honor of bearing the name of John Barrymore, Jr. "He hasn't the slightest interest in acting," Miss Williams (who divorced her husband in 1960) said about her child in 1962. "And I'm going to do my best to keep it that way."

Ethel's daughter, Ethel Colt Miglietta, had a larger consciousness of the tradition of her family, and although she never approached the stardom that had belonged to her mother, she maintained her devotion to the stage. As her fine singing voice developed, she appeared with several opera companies, gave many recitals, and developed a one-woman musical program with which she toured the country much as her mother had. The program, called *Curtains Up*, gave a singing and acting panorama of the American musical theater and was thought worthy enough to be sent by the State Department in 1963 on a tour of Europe.

John Drew Devereaux, a nephew of the Barrymores and grandson of John Drew, acted on the stage for many years, then took to stage managing on Broadway. He, too, was sturdily aware of the tradition of his family.

And there was Diana Barrymore, who seemed to vie with her half brother, John Drew Barrymore, in contributing sorry headlines to the newspapers. "Too much, too soon," was her verdict on herself; the "too much" referred to the amount of liquor she managed to consume, while the "too soon" had reference to her eager attempts to capitalize on the name of her father. Her mother, Michael Strange, had seen to it that she was raised to take a position in "society." To Diana, after being named "Personality Debutante of 1938," society meant café society. Soon she was acting on the stage with little training, went to Hollywood when she was twenty, appeared to little advantage in several films, and then proceeded to make her life into a trail of human wreckage, complicated by alcoholism, three marriages, innumerable affairs, and attempts at suicide.

Gerold Frank told Diana's story in *Too Much, Too Soon*, an autobiographical account that appeared in 1957. It quickly became a best-seller and was made into a film by Warner Brothers. Mr. Frank had searched her out in 1955, upon hearing she wished to tell her story, and found her living in a small, wretched hotel, adjacent to Madison Square Garden in New York City. "The door opened," Mr. Frank said in 1963, "and I saw what appeared to be an animated mop, a tall apparition with eyes glaring from under hair that was down all over her forehead. She was drunk, as was her third husband, who was then with her. I was so deeply moved, and I said to myself, 'Good Lord, this is the daugher of Michael Strange, one of the most magnetic women of her time, and of John Barrymore, the handsomest man and greatest actor of his time—the fruit of their love.'"

Invited inside, Gerold Frank sat down and saw Diana attempt to turn herself into a more "ladylike" condition. Patiently, over many months, he drew from her the story, and curiously, during that time, a kind of rehabilitation occurred in Diana. "She began to show some of the divine arrogance of the Barrymores," Frank said. The book took Diana out of her condition of poverty, brought her $150,000 all told, and although Frank tried to arrange it so that the money would be paid out to her as an annual income, she managed to dispose of it all by the time she died. As with all Barrymores at the times of their deaths, there was nothing left. The similarity ended there. She may have possessed the Barrymore pride, but little of the talent.

In her last year Diana developed an obsessive love for Tennessee Williams. She struggled to get off what a doctor had called "a dreadful merry-go-round of alcohol, barbiturates, stimulants." Meeting an acquaintance in Sardi's restaurant for lunch, she proudly held up what looked like a Bloody Mary and said, "Tomato juice." And it was, fixed by the bartender with a touch of tabasco, and swirled around in a shaker with cracked ice. But she couldn't hold out. On January 25, 1960, a maid found her lifeless body in bed one morning in her New York apartment. And there on the floor stood the evidence of the killer: three empty bottles.

The Barrymore curse . . . perhaps. But there were those who escaped it, and there may still be some strength in the line of Barrymores and Drews, for now the grandchildren are proliferating and one or another may hear the call of the stage. In fact, John Drew Miglietta, Ethel's grandson, was reported by his mother to have become suddenly stage-struck while a student at Portsmouth Priory in 1964. He made his first appearance, at age seventeen, in an all male version given by the school of *The Madwoman of Chaillot*. His mother attended a performance and said this young member of the proud Drew-Barrymore lineage was simply terrible as an actor. "The boys whose families had nothing to do with the theater were simply great," she added. But Lionel first time out was not great either, nor Ethel, nor John. It took some time before they were thought worthy of receiving their red apples. The tradition of the red apple is still there for any Barrymore descendant who wishes to claim it.

Index

A Note about the Author

Hollis Alpert is a leading film critic (for *The Saturday Review*) who also writes trenchant profiles of movie and theater people. In 1957 he received an award from the Screen Director's Guild for "Distinguished Contributions to Film Criticism." Six years ago he moved into novel writing and made an immediate success with *The Summer Lovers*, following it with *Some Other Time* and *For Immediate Release*. Hollis Alpert is also the author of a collection of essays, *The Dreams and the Dreamers: The Adventures of a Professional Movie Goer*. His fiction and non-fiction have appeared in such magazines as *The New Yorker, Esquire, Harper's Bazaar, Mademoiselle, The Saturday Review, Partisan Review* and *Theatre Arts*. Mr. Alpert is a New York resident.